City and Spectacle in Medieval Europe

Medieval Studies at Minnesota

Published in cooperation with the Center for Medieval
Studies, University of Minnesota

Volume 6. Edited by Barbara A. Hanawalt and Kathryn L. Reyerson
City and Spectacle in Medieval Europe

Volume 5. Edited by Calvin B. Kendall and Peter S. Wells
Voyage to the Other World: The Legacy of Sutton Hoo

Volume 4. Edited by Barbara A. Hanawalt
Chaucer's England: Literature in Historical Context

Volume 3. Edited by Marilyn J. Chiat and Kathryn L. Reyerson
The Medieval Mediterranean: Cross-Cultural Contacts

Volume 2. Edited by Andrew MacLeish
The Medieval Monastery

Volume 1. Edited by Kathryn Reyerson and Faye Powe
The Medieval Castle

City and Spectacle in Medieval Europe

Barbara A. Hanawalt and Kathryn L. Reyerson, editors

Medieval Studies at Minnesota, Volume 6

University of Minnesota Press

Minneapolis

London

The University of Minnesota Press gratefully acknowledges
assistance provided for publication of this book by the Carl D.
Sheppard Fund.

Published by the University Minnesota Press
111 Third Avenue South, Suite 290
Minneapolis, MN 55401-2520

http://www.upress.umn.edu

Second Printing 1999

Printed in the United States of America on acid-free paper

Library of Congress Cataloging-in-Publication Data
City and spectacle in medieval Europe / Barbara A. Hanawalt and
　　Kathryn L. Reyerson, editors.
　　　　p.　　　cm. — (Medieval studies at Minnesota ; v. 6)
　　Papers from a conference at the University of Minnesota, 1991.
　　Includes bibliographical references (p.　　) and index.
　　ISBN 0-8166-2359-7 (alk. paper)
　　ISBN 0-8166-2360-0 (pbk. : alk. paper)
　　　1. Festivals — Europe — History.　　2. Rites and ceremonies —
Europe — History.　　3. Cities and towns, Medieval.　　4. Civilization,
　　Medieval.　　I. Hanawalt, Barbara.　　II. Reyerson, Kathryn.
　　III. Series.
　　GT4842.C58　　1994　　　　　　　　　　　　　　　　93-30869
　　394.2'694'0902—dc20

Contents

Contents

Acknowledgments

In producing *City and Spectacle in Medieval Europe,* the editors extend their thanks to a number of people and agencies that made both the initial conference possible and the subsequent volume a reality. The original idea for the focus of the conference came from a suggestion of Professor Joseph Alchermes of the University of Minnesota. The topic generated considerable enthusiasm among the scholars we identified as having contributed to the ongoing discussion of civic ceremonial. The conference participants made the whole intellectual endeavor a great success.

Major funding for the conference came from a grant from the National Endowment of the Humanities Scholarly Conferences division. The College of Liberal Arts contributed from its conference fund and provided us with matching funds from the University of Minnesota Foundation. Further financial support came from the University of Minnesota Professional Development and Conference Service. We would like to acknowledge the private donation of Mr. and Mrs. R. James Gesell facilitating the conference. Contributors to the Carl D. Sheppard Publication Fund helped make this book possible.

The Center for Medieval Studies relies upon its research assistants for editorial work on our series volumes. Eleanor Congdon, Alice Klingener, Edward Schoenfeld, and Gregory Waltigney assisted on this volume and on earlier ones.

Our relationship with the University of Minnesota Press in publishing the series, Medieval Studies at Minnesota, has been a very fruitful one, and we are grateful for the collaboration.

Introduction

Barbara A. Hanawalt and Kathryn L. Reyerson

U rban ceremonial in the Middle Ages took various forms and served a number of different ends—private, collegial, political, and religious. Broadly construed, urban ceremonial included public functions of multiple sorts. From private, but public, celebrations of births, marriages, and deaths to the grand entries of rulers into cities, the spectacles were designed to impress events on collective memory. Medieval celebrants had a variety of rituals that made their public messages memorable. The simplest was the visual witnessing of a written charter so that in the future those present could say that they had seen the writing. The most complex were ducal or royal entries in which tableaux, replete with allegorical meanings, were displayed to the ruler. The spectacle might have been meant to overawe the population and reinforce hierarchical order, or its aim might have been to bring a sense of community among the celebrants and the watching population. Some of the spectacles were, of course, designed for a higher audience—to win divine beneficence for a city. The essays in this volume reflect a wide range of spectacles, both in their form and in their function.

The study of medieval spectacle is not new, but the time has come to move beyond simple descriptions of them and simplistic explanations about the functions they served in their communities. The essays collected here were an outgrowth of a conference held at the Center for Medieval Studies at the University of Minnesota in 1991, with the express purpose of moving toward a more synthetic understanding of medieval urban spectacles. Scholars in art history, history, and literature have focused on the entertainments, plays, liturgical celebrations, tournaments, processions, royal visits, knightings and coronations, funerals, marriages, and many other public ceremonies that defined urban relationships, glorified cities, and attracted visitors and their money into the urban marketplace. This volume brings together specialists in these fields for an interdisciplinary discourse to determine the points of conjuncture and to encourage the further pursuit of this rich, multi-faceted topic. The resulting essays dovetail at many places and have led to new insights regarding the quality of medieval urban life, the shared values of medieval urban culture across Europe, and the relationship between urban ceremonial and various art, literary, and liturgical forms. In the process of exploring urban ceremonies, the essays raise numerous theoretical issues, which this introduction highlights. They also demonstrate common concerns across disciplines and point to areas that would present fruitful directions for new research.

The essays cover the period of the twelfth to the early sixteenth centuries, but most of them are located in the late medieval period. At first glance, the late chronology would suggest that the ceremonies were a new occurrence for medieval Europe, but discussion at the conference clearly indicated that laconic entries in accounts and chronicles allude to urban spectacles at an earlier date. It was the taste for elaborate description that was new. The account from the early fourteenth century that Elizabeth A. R. Brown and Nancy Freeman Regalado have used is an early instance. Most of the examples in the volume, from Spain, England, France, Italy, and the Netherlands, come from the fifteenth century. The essays show not only an increased interest in detailed descriptions, but also a transformation of the forms of the ceremonies themselves. The tableaux with standing allegorical figures who remained silent began to change into representations with words and action. The royal entries began to be forms of advertisement for the power of towns or their guilds. In the Netherlands, the private ceremonies of marriage, baptism, or burial among the ducal families became public occasions. The taste, style, and cost of city spectacle expanded with the opulence of the fifteenth century.

If the written descriptions are limited to the later period, the numerous urban ceremonies have left their mark on the artistic and architectural remains of the High and Late Middle Ages. Art historians give us information about the representation of ceremonial in sculpture, monuments, fresco, and manuscript illuminations.[1] Architectural and archaeological specialists reveal the buildings, sites, and frameworks for urban ceremonial.[2] Bram Kempers's chapter, for example, discusses the role that icons of the Virgin played in the processions that marked the wars Siena fought for its survival and describes the pictorial representations of these processions through the city.

The ceremonies, although newly elaborated in the late Middle Ages, also presented strong conservative traits. A certain atavism evident in the respect for tradition emerges in the papers of Sheila Lindenbaum, James Murray, Ben McRee, and Kempers. Murray compared a chronicle account of the entry of the counts of Flanders in the twelfth century with a fourteenth-century account of the entry of the dukes of Burgundy. Concern for a careful observation of tradition is prominent, as one would expect in a society in which correct performance of ritual was necessary for its efficacy. Care for the storage of costumes and habits signals a concrete preoccupation with the repetition of ceremony according to specific norms in the chapters by Lindenbaum and McRee on the London watch and the entry of local lords into English towns. Brown and Regalado argue for the influence of Ramon Llull's Order of Knighthood in the traditional form of the ceremonies surrounding the knighting of the sons of Philip the Fair. Kempers also documents the concern for tradition in his examination of contemporary chronicle commentaries about liturgy in Siena Cathedral. The town's aspiration for confirmation of privileges echoes in the study of Brigitte Bedos-Rezak on the symbolic, ritualistic character of the written charter, sealed with the *échevins'* seal, for which reissuance was sought in order to have another icon within the urban archives. Lorraine Attreed describes the city officials of York consulting records to determine what earlier relations had existed between the town and the Clifford family.

Recent studies have shown that some civic ceremonies had a specifically political focus—to signal the installation of a new regime of urban government or to welcome royalty.[3] The rituals attached to coronations, funerals, marriages, and entries reinforced the power of the monarchy, with the accompanying reassurance of the privileges of the townspeople. The tension underlying political ceremony was noted by Hugo Soly and appears in varying contexts in several chapters.[4] The dilemma, from the standpoint of the ruler, was how to encourage citizen loyalty while enhancing the ruler's power. Brown and Regalado reveal in minute detail the carefully crafted political statement of Philip the Fair at the knighting of his sons, evocative as it was of royal grandeur and the subtle diplomacy of the crusading vow. Also in evidence at the festivities, which lasted nine days, were satirical and critical commentaries by the Parisians, contained within the scenes or *faëries* that they presented for the pleasure of the onlookers.

The chapters by Lindenbaum, McRee, Murray, Kempers, Teofilo Ruiz, and Gerard Nijsten provide new subtleties of interpretation to the political arguments of commonality and social harmony advanced in earlier work by Charles Phythian-Adams and Merwyn James.[5] Miri Rubin had earlier alluded to a different interpretation of the significance of late medieval ceremony.[6] The exclusiveness of the participants and their emphasis on separateness, not wholeness; hierarchy, not collegiality; emerges in studies of the English watch and English guilds by Lindenbaum and McRee, respectively. In his examination of the Saint George Guild of Norwich, McRee discovered that ceremonial proceedings were rife with the factional struggles of the city in the 1430s and 1440s. When the guild marched with dragon, saint, and hapless maiden, the underlying text was one of specific political and partisan orientation. In the early sixteenth-century watch of the lord mayor of London, Lindenbaum found a celebration of oligarchy, devoid of democratic tendencies and without any intention to promote urban cohesion. Consolidation of power was at issue with the specific exclusion of women and artisans, laborers and servants, with the aristocratic overtones of the watch, couched as it was in imitation of noble customs. Challenges to this power echoed in efforts to preserve property, whereas "ritualized violence" in the form of the pageant "Soldan" was carefully orchestrated to preserve order and thus stave off any royal pretext for intervention in city matters. In the end, however, Henry VIII was able to co-opt the powerful political capital inherent in the watch.

In many an urban ceremony, the perspective of the ruler was placed against that of the town. Good lordship was the aim sought by English towns, as Lorraine Attreed has demonstrated in her examination of the four English towns of York, Norwich, Exeter, and Nottingham. Medieval English towns undertook pageantry and expense with the hope of benefits, in the form of charters, reductions in fiscal obligations, and new privileges. In the case of York, appropriate spectacle and welcome for Richard, when duke of Gloucester, resulted in useful patronage from him as King Richard III. Attreed discerned a give-and-take in relations between town and political authority, with the maintenance of urban social unity and autonomy balanced against the dependence of the monarch on loyal support from towns.

Murray, Nijsten, and Lawrence Bryant deal with the ruler's entry, with Murray evoking as models the earlier entry analogy with the Bible and Christ, made by Ernst Kantorowicz, and the analogy with the Advent liturgy, as noted by Johan Huizinga.[7] Kantorowicz discerned two forms of advent, Christ's entry into Jerusalem and that of John the Baptist as precursor of Christ. Bruges favored the latter interpretation. The articles of Kempers and Ruiz also reveal the liturgical emphasis in urban ceremonials. The orchestration of the liturgical ceremonies by the ruler and the active participation of ruler and family are borne out by Ruiz in his study of fifteenth-century Jaén in Castile. The enactment of biblical stories, which involved the constable Don Miguel de Lucas de Iranzo, formed part of the ritual of Jaén. Kempers provides a rich description of the major processional icons of the Cathedral of Siena and their role in urban ceremony. Significant civic moments in Siena, such as the battle of Montaperti in 1260, were commemorated in ceremonies in the cathedral. The extreme participatory suffering of the flagellants of late medieval Spain, in imitation of the Passion and Crucifixion, represents another dimension of liturgy, explored in depth by Maureen Flynn. For Bedos-Rezak, new charters sought by medieval towns became "sacred texts and icons, for the rituals of a civic liturgy."

Civic ceremonials had military, triumphal purposes to announce and commemorate the successful defense of the town or to celebrate the victorious entry of a conqueror. Nijsten notes the triumphal entries of the duke of Guelders into towns of his principality. The duke's spending on ceremonies enhanced his power and legitimized it. While some of the quasi-military celebrations had entertainment overtones, such as the *palio* that is still held annually in Siena or the tournaments held in city streets, others provided an opportunity publicly to display and reward military skills, as did the archery contest in medieval England or in

Guelders. Tournaments and archery contests characterized interactions of duke and towns in the Low Countries and as far away as Castile.

Well-organized ceremonial could represent considerable political capital in the interplay of power and propaganda. Ruiz reminds readers that ceremonies were representations of power from ruler to ruled. The ability of the ruler to manipulate symbols and capitalize on aspects of popular culture led Ruiz to argue for a skillful control of resistance, the very appropriation of popular language and festive forms for the purposes of hegemony. Urban ceremonies offer a unique laboratory for observing the interaction of elite and popular culture in medieval towns.[8] For Castile in general, but particularly for Jaén, the festivals sponsored by Constable Don Miguel de Lucas de Iranzo "blurred the distinctions between the private and the public and between high and low culture. This they did by integrating into public ritual and civic festivals elements of courtly and popular culture."

Flynn addresses the dichotomy of elite and popular attitudes in examination of public flagellations. In this unique late medieval spectacle, the *disciplinantes*, belonging to the confraternities of the Vera Cruz of late medieval Spain, told the story of the last agony of Christ by expiation of their own sins in self-scourging. There was a definite popular-versus-elite split in ideas over flagellation and corporal suffering. Elite intellectuals privileged the approach of contrition, given the higher position of the intellect in the "natural" scheme of things. Popular reactions favored physical pain in echoes of the Passion and the Crucifixion. Mortification of the flesh brought sanctification, and in a burst of psychic energy participants and observers recalled that the suffering of Christ secured the salvation of mankind.

As was characteristic of medieval culture, the secular and the religious combined closely in urban rituals. The doorway to the church was not a barrier, and religious festival spilled out into the street. Statues of patron saints, reliquaries, the host for Corpus Christi Day played as important a part in civic as in church ceremony. When plague or drought threatened Paris, Saint Catherine was carried in solemn procession through the streets. Kempers discusses the processions of the icons of Siena Cathedral in civic and religious ceremonial. The space before and in the church was the locale for all public activity, be it of a judicial, political, economic, or religious nature. Church liturgies such as drama moved from the sanctuary to the narthex to the porch in front of the church and became public performance. In the process the focus of the drama became more secularized.[9] Brown and Regalado signal an early instance of the development of dramatization of secular and religious themes offered at the 1303 knighting entertainments. The Parisian crafts sponsored this theatricality.

Corporate groups such as craft and parish guilds and colleges and universities held their processions, feasts, and entertainments in public. McRee, Nijsten, and David Nicholas provide much concrete information about the ceremonial display and expense. McRee sees a move toward differentiation and establishment of collective identity as characteristic of the medieval ceremonies of guilds. On the one hand, guilds sought to foster unity among their members while, on the other hand, projecting unity to the larger community. This was accomplished with feasts, processions, livery, candles, and charitable giving. The public dramas performed by craft guilds have received much attention from literary scholars, such as those involved in the Records of Early English Drama project at Toronto. The civic processions of liveried guilds offered an opportunity to display and reinforce the public hierarchy of occupation. University students celebrated their academic progress in streets and taverns. Much of medieval charitable activity took place in the context of the guilds. And even charity occasioned a ritualized response.[10] As Bedos-Rezak has noted, writing itself was a spectacle in northern France when, for example, the whole town of Abbeville witnessed the grant of the city charter.

Other civic ceremonies of a rowdier sort permitted the acting out of aggressions. Mardi Gras offered simply one possibility, through disguise and anonymity, of role reversal. Role reversal formed part of the ceremonies of Jaén, as it did in towns of Guelders or at Ghent during Shrovetide rituals.[11] Urban ceremonial could offer a brief and necessary release through role reversal, playacting, and disguise, providing a form of limited liberation from the moral, sexual, and hierarchical constraints of urban society. By the same token, the reversals culminated in a confirmation of the traditional order.

Since medieval urban centers provided cramped living conditions for the majority of their inhabitants, much of life was lived in the public sphere. Indeed, the dimensions of the public and private spheres were different in the Middle Ages than they are today. Life was lived very much in community, and many aspects of domestic family life had a public focus. Baptism started with carrying the infant to the church; marriage contracts were made at the church door. Bedos-Rezak has observed that in Arras, "in order for spouses to obtain a written deed of donations between them, both had to appear in the presence of the *échevins* and, in order to demonstrate their marital love, the wife had to kiss her husband." In the case of rulers, these ceremonies in the towns of the duchy of Guelders or at Jaén were enacted on a grand scale that involved the urban inhabitants intimately in the life of the ruler's family. Death was accompanied by crowded deathbed scenes, elaborate funeral processions, public mourning, and public alms-giving.[12]

The sensory impact of medieval urban ceremonial was significant. Through the chronicle accounts of van Eyck, Murray evokes its soundscape, landscape, colors, and sights. Lindenbaum does the same for the performance of the Night Watch in London. And in a very graphic way, so does Nicholas, through a study of the expense accounts for ceremonials, although Ghent appears to be an exception among medieval towns in its relative lack of ceremony. Most impressive of all is the incredible texture of ceremony that Brown and Regalado can trace through the commentary of eyewitnesses at the elaborate festivities surrounding the 1303 knighting. Three kings were present in Paris—Philip the Fair himself, his son and heir Louis, king of Navarre, and his son-in-law, Edward II of England, husband of his daughter Isabelle, along with many nobles and a papal emissary. Pomp and pageantry reached new heights in the nine-day celebration.

The ceremonies of medieval towns, whether in reception of some outside political authority or in observance of specifically urban customs, were complex collective gestures, which must be decoded through their signs and symbols and which are capable of encompassing, communicating, transmitting, defining, transforming, and even transcending normal, everyday life for the period of the celebration. Contemporary accounts and the remaining artifacts and paraphernalia of ceremonies provide scholars with a vivid slice of medieval urban life, full of color, sound, and texture.

In the analysis of ceremony and spectacle, the authors have drawn on a number of theoretical models. Present in the minds of all the writers is the influential work of Johan Huizinga, *The Waning of the Middle Ages*. In his investigation of the writings, paintings, and ceremonies of the fourteenth and fifteenth centuries in the Low Countries and in France, he persistently employed the image of decay. The period was one in which old forms were used and expanded so that they became analogous to overripe fruit. He even pointed to a self-mockery among noble practitioners about their exaggerated forms of behavior and ceremonies. For northern Europe, he observed, the transition to the Renaissance was made with less of a break than in Italy, and older ideas and practices became amalgamated with the newer humanistic forms.

The urban ceremonies documented in these essays speak less to decay and decline and more to an expansion of public interest and participation in urban events. If parade and pageant seemed overdone to the nobility, even though they did not abandon them, their imitators among the bourgeoisie were not yet jaded. The latter found their own purposes served in creating ceremonies that established their own hegemony along with that of their rulers. For northern Europe, the advent of a "renaissance" has always been more problematic than it was for Italy. But even in Venice, as Edward Muir points out, humanistic traditions and the move to modernity did not bring about a decline of ritual; indeed, ritual peaked in the sixteenth century. Venetian civic ceremonies brought stability to politics and helped to preserve and further the republic. While humanism influenced some of the forms of ritual, the basic celebratory occasions did not change from the Middle Ages.[13]

For the northern European urban centers, complete independence from a king or a duke was not possible, so that ceremonies had to reflect a defining of boundaries between ruler and ruled as well as establish internal pictures of order. With so many messages to convey, the themes of the tableaux, the social classes who participated and what they wore, and the gifts presented to the monarch take on interpretive significance. To a certain extent, the symbols were at the center of the struggle, with cities appropriating some royal symbols or creating those that royalty would use to its own advantage.

The expression of a variety of new voices in the Lancastrian ceremonies has led Bryant to explore Claude Lévi-Strauss's idea that ceremonies are a "bricolage," a pastiche of symbols brought together in a game of which the final outcome is a differentiation of power among the participants.[14] While it is true that the late medieval period experimented with ceremonies and symbols, the basic power relations were already drawn, or they were being played out in other contexts than in the actual ceremonies. But the suggestion that ceremonies are put together of various pieces and are not fully formed or constant is very valuable. Bryant's use of Clifford Geertz's idea of "blurred genres" is most helpful not only for the Lancastrian entries but also for the other civic ceremonials portrayed in these essays.[15] The very fluidity of the ceremonies means that Geertz's description of court and state ritual in *Negara: The Theatre State in Nineteenth-Century Bali* is not useful for analyzing these late medieval city spectacles. The forms are by no means so standard that any deviation from them would mean a flaw in ritual. While older forms are revived and even revered as giving legitimacy, they are not held as religious practices, a deviation from which would bring divine retribution. Nicholas's use of the term "theater state" in the title of his essay underscores the lack of concern among the citizens of Ghent for maintenance of ritual in relation to their princes.

Flynn's essay speaks most directly to a binding nature of ritual. Her study explores participants who are engaged in a form of religious worship. She has found Mircea Eliade's observation that ritual is a means of spanning the chronological distance between present and past a helpful framework for looking at the penitential reenactment of Christ's passion.[16] Broad community participation was a way of perpetuating community memories of its supernatural origins, thereby binding its members with its past and with its religious heritage. The observation of neighbors enduring the physical suffering of Christ on Holy Thursday and spattering the pavement with their blood was a graphic reminder of religious origins.

The records provide rich descriptions of events, and Nijsten has employed the anthropological technique of "thick description" to recreate the atmosphere at the Guelders celebrations. But the information that survives does not speak to emotions of either the performers or of the spectators. What were the motives of the performers as they dressed for their parts in the street theater? Did they think of the importance of their city's position, of their guild's strength and prestige vis-à-vis other guilds? Did they imagine class solidarity? Did they even, perhaps, really honor the entering monarch? It is even more difficult to get at the emotions of the spectators watching the pomp and circumstances. Because of our inability to extract information on the psychological state of the participants, Victor Turner's hypotheses on "consensus in the *communitas*" that is performing the rituals are difficult to observe.[17]

We might have more of a sense of individual motivations if we were dealing with the world of carnival, but this particular celebration of the world turned upside down did not play a major role in the papers. The carnivalesque celebrations that the early modernists have described and that Mikhail Bakhtin has theorized in *Rabelais and His World* played less of a role in medieval chronicles and records.[18] To be sure, the boy bishops were a part of the Christmas ritual as was mumming, and carnival was celebrated in northern Europe as well as in southern, but we know less about these inversions.

The theoretical models for periodization of spectacle and even description of them will be an ongoing subject of discussion. In a recent lecture, Margaret Knapp, a theater historian, suggested a framework of narrative paradigms that would introduce more flexibility into our discussion of theater and other types of performance. In the past, texts or political events have acted as the dividers between the medieval and renaissance periodization. She suggests, instead, that several narratives may be present. The performance mode might describe such disparate types of public performances as drama, acrobats, dances, performing animals, parades, minstrels, hangings, tournaments, and self-display. Any single performance, such as city spectacles, could contain any of these elements or a combination of them. The performance narrative can be distinguished from the style narrative, which may be public or private, indoors or outdoors, on a stage, in a hall, in city streets, in a court, in a theater. Finally, the means narrative speaks to economic issues of performance and to costumes, actors, citizens, guild members, rulers, and so on. This use of different narratives permits us to look at a range of types of performance narratives, from simple, public events such as a marriage to city spectacle to Shakespearean theater.[19]

As rich as the offerings in this volume are, the essays by no means exhaust the field of urban spectacle. The omissions are both matters of subject and of analysis. For instance, the essays speak a great deal about dress (and even undress), about shared meals and drinking, and about gift exchanges. All of these elements in the ceremonies had significance for medieval spectators and participants that has not been analyzed in the essays. The space in which the ceremonies occurred also receives little attention, but to medieval urban inhabitants, space was not neutral. Selection of particular spaces for events speaks to exclusion of some urban inhabitants as well as inclusion of others. Space creates social as well as literal boundaries. There is also the question of appropriate spaces for particular functions. Why are some spaces preferred for public execution and others for parades? What is significant about meeting on the turf of the prince as opposed to the city?

Of the many subjects still to be investigated in urban spectacle, the more private ones are the most obvious omission in this volume. Baptisms, reading of the banns at the church door, marriages, and burials were all performed in public and with as much spectacle as the families could afford. Had these smaller, private rituals been included, we would have seen more of women and children in ceremonial. The parish, the parish guild, the city quarter, rather than the major streets, were the arenas for women's and children's rituals. The more ordinary festivals such as saints' days, as well as rituals marking life passages, brought out a different sort of urban inhabitant.

The ceremonies surrounding the poor receive only fleeting mention. One wonders what the twenty-nine poor people who had their feet washed by the monarch thought of the ritual. What does it say about a society's attitude toward the handicapped that they had an event for the blind to catch a pig? Charitable giving also does not appear in this volume, although medieval benefactors took great pains to provide a complete description in their wills about how their pennies for the poor should be publicly distributed. Although Huizinga dwelt on the horrendous public spectacle of judicial punishment, the essays do not cover this aspect of medieval public drama.

We have said that urban spectacle was not new in the late Middle Ages, but that it was evolving and that we know much more about it because it was written down. One question that arose in our discussions at the conference was the significance of writing down ceremonies. With a written record, the ceremonial process can become more fixed, less spontaneous. But also with the written account, the possibility of moving on to a theatrical form, such as the masque, becomes a possibility, as does the entry of the elements of these spectacles into literary works.

One volume of essays does not exhaust the possibilities of future work. In referring to ceremonies as spectacles, we imposed an unconscious limit on the essays in the volume. The conception became one of large public shows with political overtones. But the areas of religious rituals, carnivals, liturgy, domestic customs, and observances are as much a part of the medieval ceremonial life as the urban spectacle.

Notes

1. For example, W. Tronzo, "Moral Hieroglyphs: Chess and Dice at San Sovino in Piacenza," *Gesta*, 2d ser. 16 (1977): 15–25; Patricia Fortini Brown, "Painting and History in Renaissance Venice," *Art History*, 3rd ser. 7 (1984): 263–94.

2. See Ingo Herklotz, *"Sepulcra" et "monumenta" del Medioevo: Studi sull'arte sepocrale in Italia* (Rome: Edizioni Ruri Nantes, 1985; 2nd ed., 1990).

3. Pathbreaking in this regard is the work of Lawrence M. Bryant, *The King and the City in the Parisian Royal Entry Ceremony* (Geneva: Droz, 1986) and "The Medieval Royal Ceremony of Entrance into Paris," *Annales: Economies, Sociétés, Civilisations* 41, no. 3 (1986): 513–42 [hereafter *Annales: ESC*]. From another time period and geographic focus comes J. L. Nelson's *Politics and Ritual in Early Medieval European History* (London: Ronceverte, W.Va.: Hambledon Press, 1986) and "Symbols in Context: Rulers' Inauguration Rituals in Byzantium and the West in the Early Middle Ages," *Studies in Church History* 13 (1977): 97–119. Further treatment of nonreligious ceremony is offered by S. F. Moore and B. G. Meyerhoff, eds., *Secular Ritual* (Assen: Van Gorcum, 1977); and Teofilo F. Ruiz, "Monarchy without Religious Rite: Kingship in Late Medieval Castille," *Annales: ESC* 39, no. 3 (1984): 429–53. A further perspective is offered by Noël Coulet in "From Integration to Exclusion: The Place of the Jews in Medieval Solemn Entrance Ceremonies," *Annales: ESC* 34, no. 4 (1979): 672–83.

4. Hugo Soly, "Plechtige intochten in de steden van de Zuidelijke Nederlanden tijdens de overgang van Middeleeuwen naar Nieuwe Tijd: Communicatie, propaganda, spektakel," *Tijdschrift voor Geschiedenis* 97 (1984): 343.

5. Charles Phythian-Adams, "Ceremony and the Citizen: The Communal Year at Coventry, 1450–1550," in *Crisis and Order in English Towns, 1500–1700*, ed. Peter Clark and Paul Slack (London: Routledge and Kegan Paul, 1972); and Mervyn James, "Ritual, Drama and Social Body in the Late Medieval English Town," *Past and Present* 98 (1983): 3–29.

6. Miri Rubin, "Corpus Christi: Fraternities and Late Medieval Piety," *Studies in Church History* 23 (1986): 97–109.

7. Ernst Kantorowicz, "The King's Advent and the Enigmatic Panels in the Doors of Santa Sabina," *Selected Studies* (Locust Valley, N.Y.: Augustin, 1965); and Johan Huizinga, *The Waning of the Middle Ages*, trans. F. Hopman (New York: Doubleday Anchor Books, 1955; originally published as *Herfsttij der Middeleeuwen* in 1919 and first translated into English in 1924 [London: Arnold]).

8. See also A. McKay, "Ritual and Propaganda in Fifteenth-Century Castille," *Past and Present* 107 (1985): 3–43. The broader theoretical context for political ceremonial appears for more recent eras in works such as S. Wilentz, *Rites of Power: Symbolism, Ritual and Politics since the Middle Ages* (Philadelphia: University of Pennsylvania Press, 1985).

9. In the process the focus of the drama became more secularized. Significant work on these phenomena has been done by scholars such as David Brett-Evans, *Von Hrotsvit bis Folz und Gegenbach: Eine Geschichte mittelalterlichen deutschen Dramas. I, Von der liturgischen Feier zum volkssprachlichen Spiel. II, Religiöse und weltlische Spiele des Spätmittelalters* (Berlin: Erich Schmidt Verlag, 1975); C. Gauvin, "Rite and Game in Medieval English Religious Drama," *Revue d'histoire du théâtre* 1977(2): 128–40; and James, "Ritual, Drama and Social Body in the Late Medieval English Town."

10. See F. M. Flynn, "Charitable Ritual in Late Medieval and Early Modern Spain," *Sixteenth Century Journal* 16, no. 3 (1985): 335–48; Rubin, "Corpus Christi"; and R. F. E. Weissman, *Ritual Brotherhood in Renaissance Florence* (New York: Academic Press, 1982.)

11. See D. Fabre, "Le monde du carnaval," *Annales: ESC* 31 (1976): 389–406. Bronislav Geremek, *The Margins of Society in Late Medieval Paris*, trans. Jean Birrell (Cambridge: Cambridge University Press, 1987), has shown that the mendicant, vagabond elements in

Paris celebrated a *roi des fous* or a *roi des voleurs* in a day of mockery of kingship and public order.

12. See Philippe Ariès, *Western Attitudes toward Death* (Baltimore: Johns Hopkins University Press, 1974), and *The Hour of Our Death* (New York: Knopf, 1981).

13. Edward Muir, *Civic Ritual in Renaissance Venice* (Princeton, N.J.: Princeton University Press, 1981).

14. Claude Lévi-Strauss, *The Savage Mind* (Chicago: University of Chicago Press, 1970).

15. Clifford Geertz, "Blurred Genres: The Refiguration of Social Thought," in *Local Knowledge: Further Essays in Interpretive Anthropology* (New York: Harper Torchbooks, 1983), pp. 19–35.

16. Mircea Eliade, *The Sacred and the Profane* (New York: Harcourt, Brace and World, 1959).

17. Victor Turner, *Dramas, Fields, and Metaphors: Symbolic Action in Human Society* (Ithaca, N.Y.: Cornell University Press, 1974).

18. Trans. Helene Iswolsky (Bloomington: Indiana University Press, 1984).

19. Margaret Knapp, "Medieval/Tudor/Elizabethan: Periodization and Narrative Paradigms in English Theater History" (Lecture delivered 22 October 1992 at the Center for Medieval Studies, University of Minnesota, Minneapolis).

PART I

Ritual Significance in
Municipal and Royal Politics

CHAPTER 1

Configurations of the Community in Late Medieval Spectacles
Paris and London during the Dual Monarchy

Lawrence M. Bryant

This article views London and Parisian royal spectacles during the Lancastrian ascendancy of the 1420s and 1430s as sources for late medieval public history and as contrivances for political control. In the past, historical taxonomies put these spectacles among royal entry ceremonies or medieval plays. Local urban political considerations and the institutions that initially shaped them have received almost no attention. This article does not, therefore, survey the more familiar solemn and decorous forms that make medieval public life appear to us like a "perpetual *morale en action*," in Huizinga's words. Rather, it points out the stimulus that the Lancastrian period gave to the transforming of public symbolism from representations of "simple and fixed figures" of popular culture and liturgy into more complex images of the "mechanism of government."[1] I will analyze here several highly promoted spectacles as privileged places for political inventiveness.[2] Lancastrian spectacles, I demonstrate, opened new spaces for political expression and thought at a time when the customary political vocabulary was in disarray and incapable of addressing the malaise and near anarchy of existential conditions.[3] I readily concede that Huizinga remains unsurpassable in illustrating how processions, religious and guild dramas, grand gestures, and popular festive practices "veiled cruel reality" and made public "life an art."[4] However, I seek to show that the spectacles of the Lancastrian period were so rich that many voices are yet to be heard and their effects to be considered.

The article is organized in terms of four distinct "problems" or categories that I find common to the study of medieval spectacles: the problem of approaching spectacles as an object of study; medieval distinctions between licit and illicit forms of representation and ritual; medieval inventiveness in joining a variety of spectacles into a single ceremony (such as the king's entry or progress); and the problem of representing authority and highlighting privileged places in the community's ceremonial configurations.[5]

Most historians are familiar with responses to crisis as cultural shaping moments. For instance, Hans Baron's *The Crisis of the Early Italian Renaissance: Civic Humanism and Republican Liberty in an Age of*

Classicism and Tyranny presents a much debated thesis, in which various streams come together to form a new and enduring "pattern of conduct and thought" in public life.[6] Although the politicosocial events were different in Northern Europe from those of Italy, and it would be more difficult to establish cultural productions of the order of the Florentine Humanists, the sense of urgency and even despair experienced by communities, leaders, and political moralists in the face of profound political changes can be translated across the Alps. As a Parisian bourgeois lamented, "Since the days of Clovis ... [never] has France been so desolated and divided."[7] I call attention to Baron's thesis in order to note that the northern fifteenth-century crises of authority provoked different responses. In spectacles London merchants and Parisian officials discovered ways of articulating their identity and sense of place in a new and unfamiliar political terrain. In doing so, they shaped other patterns for conduct and thought that became fixed parts of English and French political traditions.

While humanism was not a major cultural force under the Lancastrians, the sixteenth-century humanists' enthusiasm for reexamining political practices seems to be anticipated in the new configurations for spectacles that London guilds and Parisian officials devised. Rather than the classical texts that inspire Italians, the sources for the urban restaging and rethinking of political ideas were the traditions of kingship and of the community.[8] Perhaps, when we have more evidence, we shall know the ways in which communities constructed their own identity in their spectacles with kings, and we shall have a better sense of the role the Lancastrian dual monarchy played in the closure of certain sets of attitudes and forms about politics that we usually call "medieval" and the opening to new ways of organizing the world that we variously label "Renaissance," "Reformation," or "Early Modern."[9]

Medieval Spectacles as Objects of Historical Study

As objects of historical study, medieval spectacles present problems of sources and their interpretation. I draw eclectically from a wide range of approaches and scholars. For those who are interested, I offer this short detour as a prelude to the specific discussion of late medieval spectacles.

The many spectacles surrounding medieval kings tangled, blended, and "blurred" a variety of theories and practices into the appearance of a style and vocabulary for governing and managing life.[10] Late medieval people treated such spectacles as fashions (according to Huizinga) and, thus, they left no monuments. The London and Parisian spectacles, however, were offered as visible proof that the Lancastrian kings truly were heads of the "whole civic or mystical body of the realm."[11] Rather than one grand spectacle of a mystical union, these urban/royal encounters consisted of a series of minispectacles, each of which was produced by miscellaneous groups from town prostitutes to highest officials. The king alone, like the thread in a necklace of many stones, connected spectacles that had foundations in different traditions and social groups. Each participating group decided the appropriate gestures, oaths, costumes, plays, symbols, and processions for its public image. Until late in the fourteenth century, no overriding perspective or shared idea other than being seen with the king gave form to all the miniparts of the spectacle. Even the meaning of kingship varied according to the context and the actors, or, to be more exact, there were as many images of kingship as there were groups performing spectacles. The medieval participants' concoctions to celebrate their kings' visits were more demonstrations of the variety and dynamics of urban life than signs of communal submission to monarchical authority. At the same time, the performance of spectacles around the king tended in appearances to blend a multifarious social world into a political ideal.[12] Only gradually over the centuries were royal officials, court poets, and monarchical clients capable of transforming communal spectacles into an ideology: of focusing spectacles into choreographed ceremonies and celebrations of the political theory of unified monarchical hierarchies.

The towns and communities that staged, designed, and framed medieval spectacles have received far less attention than the kings who happened to take part in them. Among the reasons for this lack of attention is the difficulty of interpreting diversity and decentering celebrations. However, to understand medieval urban spectacles, we must acknowledge their assertions of the power of community practices and the relative weakness of monarchical ones. In many spectacles, rulers necessarily had to take care not to lose control of their symbolism and imagery as they were absorbed into the shows and populations of powerful towns. Historians assume, but cannot always document, the impact made on "popular sentiment" by these transitory gatherings around kings.[13] Even Marc Bloch found it difficult to find "exact information" on the royal miracle in the crises of the fifteenth century.[14] In the unstable and volatile urban spectacles of the 1420s, each participating group left an uneven trail of records that, taken together, reveal their sense of urgency.

To adapt a concept from Claude Lévi-Strauss, the urban spectacles brought together preexisting elements that amalgamated over time to form something distinct from the parts, or a *bricolage*. Lévi-Strauss has argued for the playfulness of *bricolage* among tribal societies and for its two directions: as a "game" that begins with the presumption of equality among participants and ends by differentiating among participants, such as winner and loser, or as a "ritual" that starts with divisions or asymmetry and seeks to unite through "making all participants pass to

5

the winning side by means of events, the nature and ordering of which is genuinely structural."[15] What can we say of *bricolage* as an aid to understanding late medieval spectacles?

First, Lancastrian spectacles never seemed to be "genuinely structural" and complete as a ritual form—never fully capable of ordering events and focusing memory. Their message was ambiguous, carrying more societal consequences than games but less cultural weight than rituals. Even their most serious parts seemed to have "gamelike" improvisations that called attention to a lack of consensus. The myths and sentiments expressed were those that served the moment when two configurations met: an urban community whose parts represented themselves in temporary ritualized interactions and a princely authority that compelled the community to act as a whole to acknowledge the fixity of a historical royal event. When the urban and royal spectacle forms were mixed, they resulted in play and rivalry rather than high ritual. Other rival forms, practices, and groups always found ways to counter and undo any claims advanced by particular ritual "players" about the symbolism's greater meaning. For example, a letter to the king on privileges that predated the spectacle could later be used to counter the acting out of relations in the spectacle. It is precisely the lack of fixity or essential structure that prompts my using "spectacles with kings" and "entry" as terms for the Parisian and London performances of this time rather than "ceremony" or "ritual."[16] It is also this lack of fixity that the Lancastrian rulers most sought to mitigate in their public performances.

Secondly, Lancastrian spectacle lacked the "reiterated form, staged and acted by its own audience ... [that] makes (to a degree, for no theater ever wholly works) theory fact," that Clifford Geertz sees in cultural performances.[17] Rather, the form of each spectacle varied according to the relative weight and influence of other groups and their cultural practices such as literacy, record keeping, law, and the complex of cultural artifacts known as "medieval civilization." The spectacles were never solely in the service of one idea, myth, or sentiment.[18] To understand them historically, we must avoid a Lancastrian-king-centered reading of them and treat imagery and symbols as products of the "playfulness" of the moment. The king and other performers drew from a diversified cultural reservoir for the gestures, rites, and lore of their public roles. Theories and practices of kingship and urban religious rites were ephemeral and incapable of the reiterations that could turn occasional performances into ritual form. Only at a later period, when all the social and cultural parts outside spectacles were brought under the control of a centralizing idea, did "reiterated form" develop. (Centralizing ideas after a century of conflicts in France and England took the guises of national and political myths such as ancient constitutions, dynasticism, and absolute monarchy.) Lancastrian spectacles with kings were more important as an interlude in which major political figures and besieged

6

communities sought to influence and control events, albeit only as a temporary political experiment. Their failure to be fully ritual or ceremonial in the sense of Lévi-Strauss meant that spectacles were not images of consensus within a community; rather they represented urban groups' successful preservation of arenas for self-identification and assertion of rights.

Cultural anthropologists have struggled far more than historians with the problem of how persons and objects represent ideas in spectacles.[19] Victor Turner has forcefully argued that cultural performance "is constitutive of social experience and not something merely additive or instrumental." In seeking to understand conflict as a dynamic between "events in process" (temporal structures) and ideas and images (atemporal structures), however, Turner tends to reify stability and a high degree of consensus among the performing community, which he defined as *communitas*. He takes the position that the *communitas* is "social anti-structure," citing Znaniecki's definition of "a bonding uniting people over and above any formal social bonds."[20] It is easy enough to see Lancastrian London and Paris defining themselves as communities through their representations of themselves in spectacles with kings and to see the king lending a temporary structure to the less formalized community.[21] It is more difficult to see the towns as *communitas* when the issues of Lancastrian legitimacy prompted powerful urban groups (London merchants and Parisian *parlementaires*) self-consciously to shape the symbolism of spectacles to their particular political advantage. Rather than attempt to resolve this tension between performance and intentions of performers, we should remember that medieval political ideas were, as Ernst Kantorowicz has described them, "a tangle of intersecting, overlapping, and contradictory strands of political thought all of which somehow converge in the notion of the Crown" and which had "too many layers of life effective at the same time and actively concatenated as to permit any straightforward explanation."[22] The fifteenth-century bewilderment over ways of conducting relations between the king and community presented new opportunities to tangle the strands of political ideas, thereby adding new metaphors and images to late medieval political thought.[23] In this sense, spectacles with kings were the experimental arenas (to somewhat reverse Geertz's view) for making practice into theory.

Because of this confusion, communities substituted the interplay of symbols and gestures for theory and consensus. During the Lancastrian ascendancy, we only become hopelessly confused if we seek a single "root metaphor," explanation, theory, theme, or "strategy" (to use Michel Foucault's term) that informed the staging of spectacles.[24] On the other hand, through historical hindsight we find that those taking part in spectacles for kings laid foundations for future theory and strategies. In lieu of an established theory for order, a collective performance of order temporarily amalgamated symbols and people (who were themselves personifications with symbolic value) around the person of the king. This temporary dramatization of the notion of the "Crown" momentarily stabilized the polysemy of gestures, images, and symbols through which medieval social and political relations were conducted.[25] We can apply to each specific urban reception of kings Jacques Le Goff's imperative "that we consider a symbol in its context or, preferably, in the system to which, in general, it belongs."[26] Since the political symbolism of the 1420s resulted from amalgamations, no specific symbolic system prevailed. Such was the paradox of medieval spectacles that if any of the several systems that claimed dominance over spectacles (including royal and religious systems) should have succeeded in defining them, it would at the same time have destroyed their distinct characteristic. In the Renaissance, programs became carefully scripted syntheses with little of the tangle of ideas that vitalized their late medieval predecessors.

My understanding of the Lancastrian spectacles benefits from the efforts of contemporary theorists to consider how an aesthetic and a text carry authority and are understood. In looking at the role of analysis of textuality in reconstructing historical events, Gabrielle M. Spiegel rightly points out that "the object of historical study must be constructed by the historian long before its meanings can be disengaged." "The notion of play, inconsistency, and difference" all contribute to establishing the object of study.[27] As historical object, a spectacle must be twice constructed: first as a series of performances, and then as a historical event. We cannot disassociate the performances from the "historical event" of which they are a component part; spectacles cannot be taken as transparent and unproblematic descriptions of historical events.

The beginning point for studying medieval spectacles, as with other objects of history, is to separate them from the systems and theories that lead to their preservation and classification.[28] The historian might turn with benefit to Jacques Derrida's notion of the decentering of structure in his critique of Lévi-Strauss. Rather than attempting to understand phenomena in terms of a center that establishes a "structure on the basis of a full presence beyond play," we should be willing to see the full operations of play in a temporary structure whose center floats within the structure and valorizes now one element, now another.[29] To apply this abstraction to the concerns of this discussion, we can look at the king in spectacles as a floating center that is reshaped with every change of position or association in the frame of each spectacle: reshaped with every representation that future spectacles adapt for their productions and with the selections and clusters from spectacles that narrative-makers and system-builders put together to form texts and archives.[30]

This lengthy introduction attempts to illustrate some of the problems involved in interpreting spectacles. Lancastrian spectacles, for instance, were two things at the same time: an interplay between the king and each group he encountered during his visit and the composite of all the encounters. Such spectacles resemble what Don Handelman has labeled a "proto-event": an event prior to the time when "the structure of performance tends to give way to the performance of structure."[31] The notion of "proto-event" keeps before us the indeterminacy of performances staged between two worlds: one local and disassociated from a history of events and the other seeking to wield ideas into a symbolic system. One of the things that spectacles as objects of historical study can help us understand is how powerful groups who were concerned with articulating their identity and sense of place in an uncertain world discovered ways for transforming rituals into actual power. By the late sixteenth century, a genealogy of the spectacles with kings was constructed that gave weight to the newly invented French and English states. The task here is to recover the historical spectacles of the Lancastrian period prior to their classification as events in other histories, whether cultural, social, or political ones.

Spectacles and Forms of Representation

The beginnings of medieval spectacles have most commonly been seen in the disappearance of ancient forms of spectacles and the reemergence of their redeemable aspects in Christian rituals. Glynne Wickham's *The Medieval Theatre* describes the process as one of displacement: the dual forces of late antique Christianity and Germanic conquest succeeded in bringing to an end "the old theatrical world of Greece and Rome ... as an organized institution," and pagan *panis et spectacula* and *ludi scenici* were overpowered by Christian solemnity and liturgy.[32] However, cultural historians also see in a thousand years of clerical and chronicler diatribes widespread survivals of non-Christian spectacles. According to Robert Muchembled, pagan contributions were perpetuated within medieval rural culture and readily spilled over into the more instituted *fêtes* of the towns: "Popular culture ... found expression in rural society in a vision of the world that was superficially Christianized but fundamentally magical."[33] Muchembled persuasively argues that only after 1400 was the power of Crown and church capable of penetrating general lay culture. It took several more centuries for this alliance to break the hold of magical associations over communal consciousness. From the point of view of urban spectacles, institutional Christianity appears as a legitimizing veil over the forms and images of spectacle.[34] The church subverted events with potential for *spectacula* and *ludi scenici* (such as coronations, receptions, and assemblies) with the solemnity and *gravitas* of Christian ritual. As Edward Peters aptly notes, "Many basic political ideas were expressed rather through ceremony and pictorial representation of ceremony than through explicit texts."[35]

Urban spectacles took shape in the interplay between solemn performances and communal perceptions. Participants and audiences filtered rituals and ceremonies through their own ways of comprehending and dealing with the world. When sources reveal it, the element of participants' comprehensions of an activity gives us a guide to the emergence of distinct communal spectacles. While the clergy aimed to make earthly representations imitations of eternal truths and order, townsmen, on the other hand, sought less hierarchical ways of describing the world. Community representations were augmented or changed according to circumstances. Ecclesiastical ceremonies were anchored in their mimesis of eternity. They accommodated slowly to changes in form and in circumstances. In seeking to preserve the illusion of unchanging ceremonies, a place was left open for the mimesis of worldly and communal experience to take shape.[36] The rise of medieval urban spectacles cannot be indexed in a "history of events" that considers spectacles as successions of dates, places, and prominent persons. Rather, as Clifford Geertz put it, the metahistorical characteristic of ceremonies makes it impossible "to put one's finger exactly on the point at which things stopped being what they were and became instead something else."[37] However, performed ceremonies are not metahistorical, and a society's pretension that they are enables us to establish a trail of changes from one thing to another in images and sociocultural groups' performances. Townsmen devised ways to act out their political identities by attaching themselves to ceremonial traditions long before they thought of writing themselves into politics and history. Many medieval urban "events" came to be remembered and recorded in ecclesiastical and royal ceremonies, and from these records emerged the townsmen's political identity and decorum. Spectacles changed just as other aspects of society did, but the significance of their alterations is in the ways that the society came to remember and to interpret them.

From the twelfth century the common practice throughout Europe was to deliver sermons or, in Italy, orations in a classical civic style on the occasion of royal entries.[38] Only in the late fourteenth century did the composite of medieval urban corporations and groups join together to make a frame for royal visits. In escorting their ruler into their sphere, urban groups entered a variety of celebratory practices that included roles for the monarch as honored and sacred object, audience, and willing actor. Youths greeted kings with mock battles and morality plays, sometimes bringing them into the action, while officials came to give reverence and to seek favors. Some guilds marched in uniforms and carried a canopy over the ruler while others performed in *tableaux vivants*. At various stages of the route the clergy took over the king, then his judges accompanied him and finally returned to his courtiers. The king's role was passive; he was like an object that was moved by others from place to place and group to group.[39] The urban groups, through their welcoming rituals, constructed the foundations for a symbolic system that was distinct from those of church and court, but they left it up to kings and lawyers to interpret them. Only in the crisis of the early fifteenth century did communities such as Paris seek to transform kings from a passive symbol to an active, renovating agent. London, on the other hand, tended to enforce the notion of royal passivity.

Gordon Kipling forcefully argues that the pageantry of entry celebrations was a coherent, unified, and evolving spectacle where "medieval kings expected edifying moral instruction in their civic triumphs, the better to emphasize the Christ-like humility of their coming to rule."[40] He finds in the structural and formal aspects of the liturgy of Advent the impulse for the form and themes for spectacle. Because the church favored the observance of "God's wrathful Second Coming more than his merciful First," entry programs universally took on a funereal and penitential tone. The predominant medieval theme among spectacle devisers, however, was taken from the popular notion of a "Third Advent" when Christ comes to receive the Saints into the celestial Jerusalem. In this form, the king's ritual progress was marked by his movement from the state of sinner to saint to being Christ-like, and the city's image was to move from human artifact to an angelic one to heaven. The movement from human mortality to eternity gave townsmen ample opportunity for instructing rulers on the dangers of abusing the high office that God had placed upon them. At the same time as the king moved toward eternity (and physically into the heart of the city), he became more blessed and more suited to mediate between heaven and earth. Over time literary forms tended to supplant liturgical ones, but differences in civic entry spectacles, according to Kipling, were only variations on the liturgy from which their form and message were derived.

While Kipling's richly textured and well-researched work presents the most persuasive case that can be made for the derivation of the form of entry spectacles from Christian liturgy and urban piety, I have found a multiplicity of messages. Most important, "the impulse for staging medieval entries and giving structure to their drama was constitutional as well as social."[41] J. W. McKenna makes a strong case that "the royal shows and pageants in this decade indicate the extent to which certain pervasive political conceits, deliberately fostered and disseminated, permeated the trappings which surrounded the public life of Henry VI."[42] All three of us agree that the period had a proclivity toward experimentation with ideas and imagery of community. We differ on the impulse behind it: Kipling finds a liturgical one; McKenna, one in which ruling elites deliberately propagated a program of political motifs; and I, a constitutional (that is, customary), social, and processual one. If we take the point of view of the king as a "floating center" of the spectacle, it becomes an artificial quarrel. There were powerful groups acting within liturgical forms in Lancastrian spectacles, but there were also groups "imagining" or seeing themselves in feudal and urban forms, as well as court poets seeking to propagate the experiments with royal images to a larger public. This propagation of new images was not only in spectacles but even extended to the royal seals, in what has been called a "nationalisation du ciel," and to many other forms and objects, as Collette Beaune has shown us.[43] As previously observed, spectacles were the products of the tangle of groups and ideas who deemed it necessary to participate in a king's visit.[44]

Lancastrian spectacles with kings, particularly in France, had little of the attitude that Robert Muchembled asserted was typical of communal *fêtes*, a "consciousness of belonging."[45] Rather, they represented an uncertainty about belonging and are better understood as describing what John Bossy calls "the social miracle"; that is, the desire for union of the social universe in charity and peace, not the consciousness or reality of it.[46] The Lancastrian political intrusions prompted a shift from spectacles as occasional communal expressions of belonging to a sacred union to spectacles as precise images of the urban place in the existing political order. Bossy has detected "migrations of the holy" in post–Hundred Years' War France in such examples as the appropriation of Corpus Christi imagery into the political cult of the king, as seen in Charles VIII's Rouen entry in 1485. He correctly sees such transpositions as a part of a secularization process resulting in sixteenth-century humanists' celebrations of sacred royal majesty.[47] However, the process had been going on for at least a half century and as a consequence of communal, and particularly Parisian, reconciliation to the Lancastrian monarchy. Parisians took the lead in defining the fundamental and unchanging aspects of monarchy. They defined the true form of urban government and then fashioned a proper king for it. Their efforts in the 1420s can be seen as a French version of what Marvin Becker has described as "the tilt toward civility."[48]

The new forms of spectacle not only identified towns as sacred communities, but also as part of a quasi-sacred, juridical sphere associated with the king. By 1440 the French *bonnes villes* had experienced "un changement complet d'attitude s'opère à l'égard de la royauté" and had moved from uncertainty to a consciousness of belonging. These towns entered into an "entente cordiale" with the kings that remained firm for over a century against the attacks of great lords, rival princes, and factions.[49] On the other shore, London merchants were struggling to find ways to express loyalty to Henry VI and opposition to the court aristocracy who kept alive an unpopular war.[50]

Community Spectacles and Civic Ceremonies: Paris

While John Bossy explored the waning of sacred society, Bernard Chevalier looked to the waxing of political society. He sees the emerging sense of urban identity in the *bonnes villes* as inexorably bound to their celebrations and public displays: "c'est de la ville et de la fête qu'il jaillit telles que le XIVe siècle les invente l'une et l'autre."[51] Unlike Huizinga, who described the milieu as mired in "bizarre pomp, cumbrous forms of expression, a worn out fancy and an atmosphere of melancholy gravity," Chevalier found expressions of a self-confident and innovative new culture and society.[52] His sense of the festive world accords more with Bakhtin's notion that "the exterior freedom of popular festive forms was inseparable from their inner freedom, and from their positive outlook on the world. Together with this new positive outlook, they brought the right to express it with impunity."[53] Chevalier's notion of the new urbanity steers his *bonnes villes* into a middle, accommodating position instead of toward one of the shores of Bakhtin's dialectic: either "the prism of medieval ideology" or the "carnivalization of human consciousness, philosophy, and literacy."[54] The leaders of the *bonne villes*, according to Chevalier, came to act in "perfect accord" with the monarchy and social order while slowly breaking away from the forms and attitudes of an older culture.[55]

The Parisians sought to formalize accord with their Lancastrian rulers by turning to contractual and admonitory symbolism for their spectacles.[56] Nudged by their rulers, they turned from the vagaries of "sentiments" and local autonomy to a prescribed form with a legal, cultural, and "national" meaning.[57] Henry V and even more so Henry VI, who was the progeny of both royal lines, "clearly utilized public appearances and state ceremonies to impress the populace and to create a particular impression or image of themselves."[58] The Lancastrians acted not only to display symbols but to assert the historical legitimacy of their political claims through their performances.[59] They carried the Parisians with them. Using urban shows as an advertisement and endorsement of a historical event has a general correspondence with the larger (and primarily Italian) movement of the time that has been called "the new European ceremonialism" of the fifteenth century.[60]

The Treaty of Troyes (21 May 1420) declared the Valois successor to the French throne illegitimate and supplanted him with the progeny of Henry V and Catherine of Valois. Henry V had, therefore, to turn from defeating the French population to winning them over by persuasion. In a variety of forums, Frenchmen acknowledged the new royal heir. Before Henry V's 1420 Parisian entry, the people of the city joined the university and magistrates in swearing to preserve the Treaty of Troyes, thereby recognizing the Lancastrian claim. Only after the oath did the citizens— dressed in uniform red robes and joined by the other corporations— march outside the city to greet Henry V and their old king, Charles VI. In the wake of the entry, the Anglo-Burgundian party took over the government of the city and much of the kingdom. After Henry V's death, a chronicler noted that in 1424 "all Parisians took an oath [to the regent, the Duke of Bedford]—citizens, householders, carters, shepherds, cowmen, abbey pigkeepers, chambermaids, and the very monks." Oaths were given in public assemblies and blurred the corporate nature of French privileges. The English constrained rich and poor, crown officials and guilds, lay and secular to act in unity. Oath-taking days were declared feast days and street spectacles were produced. Making and breaking oaths carried serious consequences because the Valois and Lancastrian kings could confiscate property and privileges for the crime of *lèse-majesté*. Thus, a large number of Parisian inhabitants were compelled to participate in politics.[61]

Following their native mode, the English sought to interject central kingship into a French political world that had a long tradition of regional princes and politics.[62] Apologists not only propagated Henry VI's lineage from St. Louis as "true heir" to France, but they also intensified crown imagery to call attention to the distinctions between Henry's English and French crowns. The Parisian bourgeois did their part to strengthen the alliance and in a letter to the officials and people of London acknowledged Henry VI "by grace of God, King of France and of England." They promised to obey all his commands and pleasures with "firm hope" that their London "brothers" would do the same.[63] At the time, the English rulers set new standards for splendor and social inclusiveness in French urban assemblies and ceremonies. (In this period, and until the sixteenth century, no clear distinctions can be made between assemblies and ceremonies as ways of conducting politics.) This escalation of public rituals under monarchic auspices, however, paralleled a general weakening of English military and political power. A flurry of ceremonial activities and public events between 1429 and 1432 in Paris and London formed part of "a gigantic propaganda exercise" to reverse the government's bad fortune.[64]

On 6 November 1429 the eight-year-old Henry VI was crowned king of England, a premature coronation in response to the 17 July 1429 coronation of the Dauphin Charles at Rheims. This *coup de théâtre* gave the Valois claimant an opportunity to appropriate French royal symbols and hope for a political restoration. Because the unexpected coronation and the role of the warrior maid, Joan of Arc, threatened to undermine the dual monarchy, plans were made for Henry VI to travel to France in order to restore the aura of majesty and legitimacy to his French crown. Since it was inappropriate for his first crown to be the French one, a coronation was hastily arranged at Westminster. In England Henry VI had long been a powerful political symbol around whom and in whose presence the Lords of the Council maintained an uneasy political peace. Polydore Vergil, who had an acute eye for ceremonial politics, wrote that the English sent Henry VI into France with a new army, "partly to comfort his owne people, partly to keepe under and in obedience the cankred courage of Frenche men, eyther for feare, eyther els for favor, seeing the yonge king was so amiable and lovely countenaunce."[65] As in the deposition of Richard II and bastardization of Dauphin Charles, the Lancastrians devised an instant tradition; in this case a Parisian coronation.

The lack of enthusiasm for Henry VI on the part of the French towns and Paris resulted from his promoters' failure to meet the traditional obligations of the French monarchy more than from any clearly discernible pro-Valois sentiments. Most notably, the regency was criticized for not paying the salaries of royal officials, not protecting offices and liberties, not maintaining peace, and not ensuring abundance of food and goods. In general, the problems of bad times were placed at the Lancastrian door and contrasted with the imaginary virtues of former kings as put forth by such capable publicists as Christine de Pisan. A change of policy, however, may have been all that was looked for, and the coronation held hopes for such a change. The Parisians exhibited no signs of disloyalty when they wrote to encourage London's officials to support the war effort and to relieve Paris.

After months of careful planning, Henry VI entered Paris on the first Sunday of Advent (2 December 1431), eleven years to the day after his grandfather, King Charles VI, and his father, Henry V, had entered the city to celebrate Henry V's status as regent and heir of the French throne. The English controlled the ceremonial symbolism around the king's person, and probably anticipated activities that imitated the London progress to Westminster. Henry VI inserted some symbolism of his own into the Parisian progress. He followed his father's practice of having a crowned helmet carried before him to announce his right to rule both by conquest and by inheritance (an addition that the Valois monarchy would keep in the form of a closed French imperial crown).[66] Bedford counted on the real, physical presence of Henry VI to have an effect similar to that of the Host in Corpus Christi celebrations and to overawe reluctant Frenchmen. Pointing to the enthroned Henry VI, he reportedly gave an oration to nobles and officials in Paris where the "holy" was clearly transferred to the person of king: "Hither is he brought for that cause, that he may be proclaymed your King, and that both he may knowe his French people, and they likewise him, who are wont principally among all other nations to esteeme, honor, and both faithfully and also carefully obey their King (if I may say so) in the very steede and place of God."[67]

By 1431 Parisian corporations knew from experience how the English (like the church) staged rituals and knew that they interpreted participation in them as political obligations upon each individual. Parisian corporations, however, had their own arsenal of official symbols and traditional gestures to dramatize corporate liberties and protections. Thus they seized this public occasion to devise an alternative spectacle-strategy, and coincidentally began to introduce civic notions into French public law. A rhymed "Complaint of the ville of Paris" circulated with the warning that the English should remedy the city's ills "or you will lose Paris and all France."[68]

Until the 1420s the Parisian *prévôt des marchands* had served as an intermediary between the crown and the guilds; he and the *Hôtel de Ville* had dominated civic ceremonies. The turbulence of the times and the English policy of general oaths had weakened Parisian corporate authority and the power of the guilds. The English had compelled Parisians belonging to corporations—the university, the clergy, the magistrate, and the guilds—to act in unison. While the policy strengthened the regency by forcing the city to speak with one voice, the community presented an unprecedented unified front and thereby diminished the regency's sources of information. Moreover, by uniting the corporate bodies, the various parts of the body politic lacked a loyal intermediary voice to represent their particular interests. The English established the foundation for such a voice by giving the Parlement of Paris the political role of registering and sanctioning the general oaths to the Lancastrian succession. The Anglo-French assemblies and legal maneuvering were to establish the Frenchness of the dual monarchy by countering the Dauphin's Parlement of Portier, which upheld Salic Law. Once brought into politics, however, the Parlement of Paris sought to preserve its privileged place as intermediary between the Lancastrian king and the community. Indeed, as its private advice and requests to the king were ignored, it moved out of the *palais de justice* and became increasingly public and political in profile and voice.[69] The English dual monarchy had created the means for a venerable French institution to redefine its role in the political community and in its relationship to the monarchy.

The Parlement of Paris declared its high status as a French public institution by overseeing the ordinance for the 1431 processions marking Henry VI's coronation entry. In joining the entry ceremony, it began to appropriate to its legal position the communal symbolism of the *Hôtel de Ville* and the solemn display of ecclesiastical/royal processions.[70] As in Charles VI's 1422 funeral nine years earlier, the Parlement wore the most valued color in costume symbolism, the bright red robes with fur hoods that symbolized the right of sovereign justice.[71] In 1431 the robe of the First President of the Parlement was characterized as "habit royal." Much as Henry VI had his appurtenances and helmet conveyed before him, the First President had his fur cap carried before him by an usher.[72] The *parlementaire* ceremonial planners placed their institution in the most honored position at the end of the urban processional that went from the city to greet Henry VI. In the symbolism of costume and rank, Parlement claimed the place of highest French institution after the king and claimed the status of a French vox populi.[73] The Parisians "made" history to prove to the English their "possession" of rights and status. Their performance fulfilled legal expectations. In France, the prerogative acted out in the 1431 performance became memorialized as a constitutional moment. Its claims were placed at the center of *parlementaire* political discourse and descriptions of the French political community until 1789.[74]

Street pageantry underscored the new costume symbolism. At the Gate of St. Denis, a pageant with a ship (Paris) held personifications of those who greeted the king—the clergy, the university, and the bourgeois—each of whom handed the king a symbolic, heart-shaped bouquet. A placard (and probably a speaker as well) said that the city's three estates greeted him with loyalty, humility, and common consent. The display featured the political notion of "common consent" among more traditional courtier or liturgical greetings of "love," "courtesy," or "obedience." Much of the imagery called attention to French and crown symbolism. A fountain of the lily was surrounded by savages (probably sponsored by the Parisian Watch). The Confraternity of the Passion depicted the Passion of Jesus on a two-hundred-foot stage. A pantomime of the life of the Parisian martyr-bishop Saint Denis instructed the king that all French kings have been styled "Very Christian." An actor disguised as a deer sought Henry VI's protection from a pack of dogs. The deer (*cerf*) was an image associated with royal magnanimity, justice, and the Parlement of Paris.

The *tableau* that most dramatized the dual monarchy's political program was before the Châtelet and included among the actors Parisians of the best families.[75] They showed the young king surrounded by his French and English counselors, who supported the two crowns. They told the king that "his true French subjects" guarded his crowns and carried out his justice and that he should protect the judges, because through justice kingdoms endure and "the people in all their power" would be kept in obedience to him. The pageant was called a "lit de justice," with the implication that Paris was the particular place where French justice was carried out. This pointedly political spectacle all but explicitly said that the king needed to be personally present when he was to conduct French justice and, when absent, needed to substitute the Parlement as his representative. The 1431 street pageants and processions barely disguised their subversive politics. Polydore Vergil's judgment eighty years later that among those many "signs and shewes of joy and gladness, . . . of most excellent towardness and disposition, . . . many perchaunce there were, who did all that honor with holowe heartes."[76] But the pageant also suggested a practical solution for managing the two kingdoms by honoring the laws and institutions of each. Such a program might have strengthened the dual monarchy, and the Parisians may have supported it more than the Londoners. When Henry VI returned to London, the Parisians wrote to ask "votre très hauste mageste roial" to pity and to aid the "roial peuple de votre dicte ville."[77]

Charles VII was making history of his own during Henry VI's "coronation march" through France. In a series of ceremonial entries into towns, Charles VII simultaneously acknowledged the liberties of the *ville* and received gestures of obeisance. These spectacles were as certain a way of claiming territory as were military victories. But the towns also manipulated the spectacles by putting into the legal and historical record political arrangements and privileges that had been negotiated in advance. When Charles VII became king of Paris, his 1437 entry at the Châtelet emphasized justice and judgment. Kipling sees the program as having its source in the liturgical formula for Advent and being devised "to provoke kingly meditation upon the severe and wrathful God who will judge his reign according to Divine Law, not the law of men.... Charles VII comes to his kingdom more to be judged than to do justice himself."[78] But this theme of exaltation and humility in the civic triumph seems to declare the autonomous and quasi-sacred quality of earthly justice as a divine gift to humankind and the primary obligation of kings. The king had forgiven Paris for the Lancastrian years, preserved its Parlement, and restored its liberties. His entry date (November 12) was planned to coincide with Parlement's first session following the city's return to the Valois monarchy, and the Parlement marched with the same symbolism before this new king as it had before Henry VI.[79] Rather than "wrathful God," the theme of law and judgment probably represented Charles VII's exalted acts of forgiving Paris, preserving its institutions, and thus recognizing Parlement's authority. He was a secular savior; justice his theology; the Parlement his church.

The 1431 and 1437 Parisian ceremonial performances were not isolated occurrences; rather, they only represented the forging throughout France of an autonomous urban form of spectacle. It flourished as a ritual for the continuous celebration of this political union and of its overseers in the Parlements and the royal chancery. Some of the ways in which spectacle and ceremonies were configurations of the community have already been seen in watching the Parlement of Paris symbolize its status in the body politic to the Anglo-French king. Charles VII acknowledged this status and preserved the consolidation of urban authority that the Lancastrians had put in place. We turn now more specifically to the problem of how London configured itself in spectacles.

Privileged Places and Configurations of the Community: London

In going about "the unpacking of performed meaning" in London's celebrations for Henry VI's return, we should remember that the staging was in part a response to the French configuring of themselves and kingship in their spectacles.[80] While Parisian processions and street plays in December 1431 designed an image of government in the king's absence, London's spectacles in February 1432 emphasized the king's presence.[81]

London street images, at first view, appear to be silent about the specific shape of English institutions other than that of the mayor of London.

The struggle to maintain the dual monarchy had fortified English national sentiments. Englishmen resented the financial drain to maintain the French crown. As far as English national feelings can be gauged, they were overwhelmingly against Henry VI's French wars. Parliament refused direct taxes to Henry V in December 1420, and in debates members expressed anxiety about the impact on the English constitution of joining the English and French crowns when Charles VI died.[82] London officials in their letters to Henry V between 1418 and 1422 consistently sent a double message—one of gladness: London is glad when the king is well, victorious, and happy; one of sadness: London is sad when the king is absent.[83] By the late 1420s the "politically leading class" had little inclination for the war and "the persistent interest of the *court aristocracy* was all that kept the English [war] effort alive."[84]

The coronations of Henry VI put stress on government by consensus in England, because the king (as young as he was) became another uncertain factor in his council. Since Henry V's death, a narrow urban oligarchy in London had stripped the lesser guilds of influence and easy access to offices. The coronation march into France concerned the London leaders because it suggested a renewal of the war effort and greater demands on London's oligarchy, whose privileges were justified by their ability to maintain peace and carry out the king's will. The London spectacles for Henry VI's return from France praised both the blessings of London and the virtues of its ruling oligarchy. Most notable in 1432 was the costume symbolism. For the first time in a London reception, the mayor (John Welles) set himself apart in "in rede crymsyn velwett, a grete velwet hatte furred royally, a girdell of gold aboute his mydell, and a bawdrike of gold aboute his neck, trillyng down behynde hym."[85] To those who knew the Parisian entry processions, Welles's costume would have recalled the spectacular insinuation of the First President of the Parlement of Paris into urban spectacles two months earlier. The London mayor in his furred hat may have been imitating the First President just as other London communal officials may have been imitating the procession of the Parlement and the *Hôtel de Ville*. The sheriffs and aldermen wore scarlet with fur collars, while the guilds appeared more modestly, looking like a lord's retinue in uniformed white robes with embroidered devices indicating their craft. Foreigners dressed in the manner of their homelands.

The costuming of 1432 delineated differences in politicosocial status in the urban hierarchy. The mayor elevated himself above all the citizenry. Previous civic costume symbolism had varied in London, but the mayors and guilds had processed before kings dressed alike, usually in red.[86] In the 1432 costuming the mayor was posing as an earl to symbolize the city's power and honored place near the king. One suspects that the city staged this spectacle primarily to represent the privileged status of the mayor of London. John Carpenter claimed this status had a long tradition:

> Hence it is, that ever since England was a kingdom, the honor due to an Earl, as well in the King's presence as elsewhere, has belonged to the chief officer of London, who is styled "Mayor," so long as he continues in the office of the Mayoralty: hence it is too that the sword is born before him, as before an Earl, and not behind him.[87]

The sword and costume were, in fact, newly invented civic symbolism, probably to build up London's importance in its competition with Paris's political pretensions. The spectacle gave reminders of the special status of the mayor of London in the coronation banquet, where he served as the royal butler, and of London, which served as the king's chamber.[88]

For centuries, London had staged a precoronation progress from the Tower of London, where kings stayed immediately before their coronation, to Westminster.[89] The spectacle space of 1432 was different, since the costumed officials, citizens, and foreigners greeted the king at Blackheath en route from the coast. The mayor in crimson welcomed Henry VI "out of his realm of France" and back "into your blessed Realm of England, and especially into your most notable City of London, otherwise called your chamber."[90] The Latin account of the spectacle gives a slightly different version of the English speech, which characterized England as "noble roialme of Englond," seemingly more in keeping with the rich display of the greeting.[91] London had by far much greater weight in the procession than the king's traveling retinue, which was remarkably small in terms of the Lords who had joined Henry VI in Paris.

The mayor of London joined the royal party on the march into the city while the guilds lined the welcoming route in what appeared to be as much a tribute to the mayor as to the king: "A strete bitwene eche partue lyke a wall, Alle cladde in white, and the moste princypall Afforn in Reede with theire Meire Rydyng."[92] The king was not haloed by a canopy since courtiers, not townsmen, had the privilege to carry it. In Paris and much of France it was different; the guilds both marched in procession and had the honor of conveying the king through towns under the canopy. The mayor appears to have been positioned as London's only token of honor and mediation between the community and the king in the procession.

The contrast between the Parisian and the London manner of welcoming Henry VI deserves attention because it represents national differences in ways of symbolizing the relations between king and community. In Paris Henry VI had a huge noble retinue, royal symbols before him, and canopy over him representing the "national" union around the French crown.[93] At the same time the king and city remained two parties with spectacles calling attention to the king's office and to French institutions. Henry VI was presented as an incomplete embodiment of French kingship until other legal parts of the body politic joined with him. All major guilds had their turn at being near the king in carrying the canopy. The spectacles described the "tangle" of the king with his new institutions; a pattern of government including the "consent" of the three estates, duty to the church, authority of the dual councils, maintaining of French laws, a French anointing and coronation, and a communal sharing of the king by the town fathers.

The London spectacles, on the other hand, had the mark of the court and treated the king intimately and personally. Allegorical plays made particular use of metaphors of clothing and appurtenances. The metaphors enabled the Londoners to cast an English interpretation on the nature of rulership as a sort of corrective to the Parisian images. Seven street theaters were constructed for the occasion. Like the procession, they called attention to the readiness of London through the mayor to serve and to protect the person of Henry VI. In the relative weight of imagery, we find in London that the mayor stands out over national offices; personal service, over institutions; patronage and lordship, over contractual notions.

As at Paris, the king's procession gives us a better understanding of the street dramas. The king entered at London Bridge, where a tableau showed a giant champion of London holding an upright sword and guarding two antelopes who supported the arms of France and of England. The arms and giant represented Henry VI's "title by just inheritance to reign in peace, plenty, and happiness [plesaunce]." The giant threatened to "clothe with confusion" the king's enemies.[94] The sword of the champion seems likely to represent the mayor's sword, which was not, contrary to Carpenter's prescription, carried before him. The mayor was probably reluctant to assert this claim because the king had no regalia carried before him. It looks as if the king and his party were either taken by surprise at the reception or did not desire a welcome with spectacles from the city. Clearly, London was claiming the king as its and England's own when Henry VI's policy was to show impartiality. The king's costume and retinue (or lack thereof) seemed to indicate a desire for a low-keyed return from France—a return that would not have called attention to the differences between the realms. London pointedly noted the differences between the two crowns.

After leaving the "champion" and crossing the bridge, Henry VI encountered three beautiful female figures representing Nature, Grace, and Fortune. Grace was described as the source of gladness in towns and cities, while Fortune, "apperying to hym with many noble sygne," showed the two crowns that Henry was divinely ordained to wear.[95]

These three figures gave the king the gifts of nature (strength and fierceness), grace (science and cunning), and fortune (prosperity and richesse). They presented Seven Virtues, who certainly metaphorically (but perhaps actually) dressed Henry VI with crown, scepter, sword, mantle shield, helmet, and girdle while they sang a rondel of welcome to his "Ryall mageste," which had the stanza:

> London your Chambre for to se,
> To worship your London in degre,
> The piler of worship at thye be,
> Wherfor nowe synge and saye wt me ..."[96]

Part of the program's conceit depended on the king not being in ceremonial costume, but it also suggests that London was taking a free hand in morally and materially fashioning the king as they served him. From the bridge, Henry VI, "richely arrayed with ryall apparayle," made his way to a Cornhill pageant entitled the Tabernacle of Wisdom, where he received the gifts of learning, the seven sciences, and "Sapience" to embellish his crown. Sapience held a placard with the verse from Proverbs 8:15, which admonished the king to learn from the wise since kings are judges of the earth.[97] (It is not clear whether the verse was in English or Latin, but the courtier priest and poet John Lydgate composed a rhyme account to ensure that the spectacle's message reached an English reading audience.) The Cornhill pageant put the king's cortege on the traditional route for precoronation progresses and led him past four more street pageants. One had a child in the middle of a throne "rayed like a kyng" with allegorical figures for Mercy, Truth, and Clemency and with personifications of two judges and eight sergeants. It reminded the king to draw about him men expert in the law. Unlike the Châtelet program in Paris, this one did not identify the members of his royal council. Rather the idea of learning, good counsel, and maintaining law was continued in the abstract and allegorical mode with images based on scripture.

On Henry VI's approach to Saint Paul's Church, a procession replete with the most distinguished members of the government—including the chancellor and most of the high clergy—exited from the church to greet him. Henry's only reported act while at the church was to give an offering. Up to this point the city alone had served and escorted the king. From Saint Paul's, Henry was conveyed to Westminster Abbey by the principal officials of the kingdom who completed dressing the young king by giving him the scepter of Saint Edward during the singing of a Te Deum. According to the poet of the occasion, the people took cheer in seeing "their king with two crowns shine / from two Trees truly formed [ffette] the line." In England, Henry VI's dual lineage from Saint Edward and Saint Louis had been the Lancastrian justification of the dual monarchy and had figured in both the London and Parisian pageants.[98] The finale came several days later, when the mayor and aldermen of London went to Henry VI with a gift of a thousand marks of gold—a gift that, since 1392 and Richard II's restoration of the city's liberties, had been the entry gift to new rulers.[99] The mayor delivered his speech while kneeling and again reminded the king that London was "otherwise called your chamber." Lydgate ended his poem on the same note: "The kyngis chambre off custume men the [London] calle."[100]

The insistence on being the king's chamber probably referred to London's desire for ready access to the king and the city's service in provisioning the court as well as the armies in France. For over a century, however, "chamber" had been a central metaphor in the political discourse and struggle among great lords and princes, the chancellery, and the king's household over institutional relations and the right administration of the kingdom.[101] By Henry VII's reign the outer chambers were "places of ceremony, and magnificence, where meals were served with pomp, entertainments offered, and public business transacted."[102] Sources are not available on London's contribution to the king's maintenance in the 1430s, but clearly the city as *royal chamber* was not asking for a role in determining law as did Paris in the name of a *lit de justice*.[103] In the London spectacles, the elite represented the city's place in relationship to the king and not to the national political order. "Chamber" represented an established and intimate relationship between king and community. The "community" was personified in the mayor as earl and butler, but also in allegories that showed how London prepared and dressed the king to live and rule.

After 1431 in Paris and 1432 in London civic spectacles became fixed in their different ways of representing national political life. In France, citizens turned spectacles into instruments for establishing *bon accord* between the ruler and the towns of "le bon peuple qui s'organise," as Chevalier put it.[104] In London, allegory remained the major mode for spectacles during the rest of Henry VI's reign, probably because it served a political world whose monarch had more power in symbolism than in obedient subjects, resources, or troops. English political relations were worked out in allegories in a way that they could not be in political practices. London operated within a politics of uneasy truce among volatile lords and nobles. The city shaped ceremonials for the king in order to accentuate the personal and symbolic ties between them. The mayor's role emphasized a mutual benefit of city and crown in his status as earl and butler and in his promotion of the city as a royal chamber, presenter of a pageantry that turned the city into the royal court. All together these parts dramatized a feudal and courtier configuration of London.

London's presentation of itself in procession and drama emphasized personal service to the king and the abstract virtues of "ryall mageste" embodied in Henry VI. Royal majesty was a quality that limited the king's ability to act by emphasizing his importance as a person and a symbol. In his presence all was service and honor; in his absence, conflict and contest. The spectacle avoided political representations by giving a weak king transcendent qualities associated with the sacred. London was thus able to exclude from the spectacles a discourse about institutional relations and the jockeying for power among the princes. The merchant class, by centering their community in the mayor, privileged courtier discourse and silenced lesser guilds. In comparison with the Parisian *parlementaires,* they impoverished civic symbolism and discourse. On the other hand, London had no institutions comparable to those of Paris. Rather than personifying a university, Londoners showed an allegorical tabernacle of wisdom with Aristotle. In place of the prestigious Parlement of Paris, justice was represented in London as coming from a child enthroned and surrounded by the allegories—Truth, Mercy, and Clemency. Allegory substituted for the famous institutions that London lacked. London did have the king, and, in the play of imagery but not in political practices, it centered all these qualities in him. Celebration of royal majesty had the aspect of a game between a city who served and a ruler who passively received the service. There was king worship but no unified body politic in the imagery of the spectacles.

Across the Channel, Paris mixed the gamelike aspects into civic discourse by favoring personifications, reciprocity, and legal understandings. Unlike the case in London, the king paraded with the panoply of royalty, but his subjects implied in this ceremony that the Parlement, the advisers in the *lit de justice,* and urban corporations each helped to define kingship. Their ceremonies decentered the king from royal entries and joined him to all parts of the ceremonial community. Parisians (as experience and their reactions to Lancastrian programs had taught them) modeled in their spectacles a decentered body politic that acknowledged the king but preferred his absence in the normal workings of the community, even as Claude de Seyssel depicted it eighty-five years later in describing the bridle of the "polity."[105]

The Parisian entry of 1431 began when a personification of *Fama* told Henry VI that Paris deserved to be well governed, and the processions of Paris literally duplicated the community before the king: the university, the cathedral clergy, the officials of the *Hôtel de Ville,* and the Courts of Paris, including the Parlement of Paris. All the institutions personified in the entry, other than the king, resided in the city. They made a nearly complete and ideal community. The university personified Wisdom; the Parlement of Paris was Justice; the *Hôtel de Ville* was Prosperity. This ideal undercut any notion of a king ruling without these well-established institutions. The correspondence between political realities and the symbolism of the spectacles enhanced their ritual and unifying function. Henry VI had little choice but to confirm this body politic because the Parisians represented him within it. The traditions that the spectacles appeared to reinforce (but were actually inventing) insisted that Henry VI act through these groups and in his absence trust in the Parlement to guard French laws. London preferred to deal with the king in his chamber rather than his law court. London spectacles disguised rather than reflected political practices.

After the return of the Valois in 1435, the Parisians and other French towns developed spectacles that configured clearly recognizable institutions and estates. Their ceremony was a *theatrum urbis et orbis* of the concrete administrative offices of the monarchy and the institutional mediators for the community. When Parisian imagery drifted toward allegory, the allegories still represented recognizable institutions. The symbolism of urban spectacles struck the right balance as a representation of social and political realities between the monarchy and the *bonnes villes*. Only in the sixteenth century, with a failure of *bon accord* and impending civil war, would French civic spectacle drift to the discourse of "royal majesty" and the English court styles. Parisian unifying configurations were then refashioned into a preponderance of allegories rather than political institutions, and Parisian spectacles, too, defined relationships in terms of courtier submission and duty rather than law and reciprocity. Although urban political spectacles, by the seventeenth century, came to symbolize the universal principle of submission to kings, their Lancastrian beginnings as Parisian and London ways of representing particular communities and governmental forms should not be forgotten.

Notes

The writing of this article was made possible in part by the School of Historical Studies, Institute for Advanced Study, Princeton, N.J., where I spent the academic year 1989–90, and by a summer research grant from the Graduate College, California State University, Chico. Special thanks go to Gordon Kipling for sharing his ideas and studies with me and to Murray Markland and Barbara A. Hanawalt for their careful readings and suggestions.

    1. Johan Huizinga, *The Waning of the Middle Ages: A Study of the Forms of Life, Thought and Art in France and the Netherlands in the 14th and 15th Centuries* (Garden City, N.Y.: Doubleday Anchor Books, 1954), p. 54. "Although in reality the mechanism of government had already assumed rather complicated forms, the popular mind pictures it in simple and fixed figures." The figures are enumerated, and Huizinga gives a telling example of Philip the Good's knowledge of "the political language which the people understands" by displaying in a festival his precious plate: "The demonstration of the solvency of the state took the form of an entertainment at a fair" (ibid., pp. 16–17).

    2. Eric Hobsbawm has launched the term "invented tradition" as "a set of practices, normally governed by overtly or tacitly accepted rules and of a ritual or symbolic nature, which seek to inculcate certain values and norms of behaviour by repetition, which automatically implies continuity with the past" ("Introduction: Inventing Traditions," in *The Invention of Tradition*, ed. by Eric Hobsbawn and Terence Ranger [Cambridge: Cambridge

University Press, 1985], p. 1). However, Hobsbawm's concerns are primarily with the last two hundred years when political institutions had secure "traditions" and "customs" from which to claim space and "to invent tradition." In the late Middle Ages, as I shall show, those secure places and customs—as some sort of well-stocked laboratories for invention—were fragile, and "rules" of social interactions were in disarray.

3. How late medieval use of spectacles unwittingly supplies later ages with a political vocabulary is explored by Sarah Hanley, *The "Lit de Justice" of the Kings of France: Constitutional Ideology in Legend, Ritual, and Discourse* (Princeton, N.J.: Princeton University Press, 1983). For formation of political practices and vocabularies in spectacles, see particularly chapters 1 and 2.

4. Huizinga, *Waning of the Middle Ages*, p. 55.

5. I have considered these problems in a more general way in my article "The Medieval Entry Ceremony at Paris," in *Coronations: Medieval and Early Modern Monarchic Ritual*, ed. Janos M. Bak (Berkeley and Los Angeles: University of California Press, 1990), pp. 88–118, and in an earlier version, "L'Entrée royale à Paris au Moyen Age," *Annales: Economie, Société, Culture* 41, no. 3 (May–June 1986): 513–43.

6. Hans Baron, *The Crisis of the Early Italian Renaissance* (Princeton, N.J.: Princeton University Press, 1966), p. 410.

7. *A Parisian Journal: 1405-1449*, trans. Janet Shirley (Oxford: Clarendon Press, 1968), p. 147 (for the year 1419). For an excellent short survey of the period, which also cites this passage, see Jacques Le Goff, "Le Moyen Age," in *L'État et les pouvoirs*, in the series *L'Histoire de la France* (Paris: Seuil, 1989), pp. 127–80. The significance of the Anglo-French wars in the development of national consciousness has long been recognized, as Jacob Burckhardt noted: "France owes the consciousness of its national unity mainly to its conflict with the English": *The Civilization of the Renaissance in Italy*, trans. S. G. C. Middlemore (New York: Harper Colophon Books, 1958), vol. 1, p. 142.

8. See Jean Jacquot, "Presentation," and Elie Konigson, "La Cité et le Prince: Première entrées de Charles VIII," in *Les Fêtes de la Renaissance, III*, ed. Jean Jacquot and Elie Konigson (Paris: Editions du Centre National de la Recherche Scientifique, 1975), pp. 7–32, 55–70. For a later period, Russell Major calls attention to such sources of political ideas as "popular political thought" (Russell Major, *Representative Government in Early Modern France* [New Haven, Conn.: Yale University Press, 1980], p. 171).

9. I am not interested in the problem of periodization; I agree with Jean Delumeau that it muddles our understanding ("Si l'on supprimait des livres d'histoire les deux termes solidaires—et solidairement inexact—de 'Moyen Age' et de 'Renaissance,' notre compréhension de la période qui s'étend de Philippe le Bel à Henri IV s'en trouverait facilitée." Jean Delumeau, *La Civilisation de la Renaissance* [Paris: Les Editions Arthaud, 1984], p. 7). However, as his book shows in chapter after chapter, we are bound to interpret the period in terms of the tension between these sets of attitudes.

10. I have profited greatly from Clifford Geertz's articles "Blurred Genres: The Refiguration of Social Thought" and "Centers, Kings, and Charisma: Symbols of Power," in *Local Knowledge: Further Essays in Interpretative Anthropology* (New York: Harper Torchbooks, 1983), pp. 19–35, 120–46. Clifford Geertz uses the notion of "blurred," both in the sense of "genre mixing" among current scholars and of cultural formations, particularly as seen in performances.

11. For a sense of forces working to define the nature of the political community and of kingship, but not specifically related to these events, see Ralph E. Giesey, "The French Estates and the Corpus Mysticum Regni," in *Album Helen Maud Cam* (Louvain: Publications universitaires de Louvain, 1960), pp. 151–71; Ralph Giesey, *The Royal Funeral Ceremony in Renaissance France* (Geneva: Libraire Droz, 1960), pp. 51–135; and Ernst H. Kantorowicz, *The King's Two Bodies* (Princeton, N.J.: Princeton University Press, 1957), chap. 5, particularly pp. 218–23.

12. As Huizinga put it, "The Middle Ages never forgot that all things would be absurd, if their meaning were exhausted in their function and their place in the phenome-

nal world, if by their essence they did not reach into a world beyond this" (Huizinga, *Waning of the Middle Ages*, p. 201).

13. As discussed by Bernard Guenée in his introduction to *Les Entrées royales françaises de 1328 à 1515*, ed. Bernard Guenée and Françoise Lehoux (Paris: Èditions du Centre National de la Recherche Scientifique, 1968); and Konigson, "Entrées de Charles VIII," pp. 66–69.

14. Marc Bloch, *The Royal Touch: Sacred Monarchy and Scrofula in England and France*, trans. J. E. Anderson (London: Routledge and Kegan Paul, 1973), p. 64.

15. The notion as a way of understanding symbolic forms is associated with Claude Lévi-Strauss, *The Savage Mind* (Chicago: University of Chicago Press, 1970), pp. 16–33.

16. Like the idea of symbolism, ceremonial was not a concept as much as a practice until the ceremonial compilations of the sixteenth century. In regard to ecclesiastical distinctions, Aimé-Georges Martimort points out that a ceremonial was a book that gave some precision to the places, dress, and gestures of ritual actors but was vague on the actual order of readings and rites (Martimort, "Qu'est-ce qu'un cérémonial," in "Les 'Ordines,' les 'Ordinaries,' et les 'Cérémoniaux,'" *Typologie des Sources du Moyen Âge Occidental*, fasc. 56 [1991]: 90).

17. Geertz, "Blurred Genres," p. 30. In *The Interpretations of Culture* (New York: Harper Torchbooks, 1973), Geertz cautions against fixed models or forms: "Human behavior is inherently extremely plastic," and man is the "self-completing" animal; "the agent of his own realization, he creates out of his general capabilities that define him. Or ... it is through the construction of ideologies, schematic images of social order, that man makes himself for better or worse a political animal" (p. 218).

18. Ralph Giesey, "Models of Rulership," in *Rites of Power: Symbolism, Ritual, and Politics since the Middle Ages*, ed. Sean Wilentz (Philadelphia: University of Pennsylvania Press, 1985), p. 42. Giesey identifies the problem for "ceremonial studies" as one of maintaining "a congruence between long-established constitutional history (wherein ... [he includes] not only legal and political but also theological and philosophical aspects) and the kind of affective comprehension of kingship that anthropologists apply so well when studying societies that have no thick transcription of their 'constitution.'" He points out, "If new methods are to add to traditional understanding, let them not at the same time subtract from it."

19. This description is based on John J. MacAloon's excellent introduction to *Rite, Drama, Festival, Spectacles: Rehearsals toward a Theory of Cultural Performance* (Philadelphia: Institute for the Study of Human Issues, 1984), p. 2.

20. Victor Turner, *Dramas, Fields, and Metaphors: Symbolic Action in Human Society* (Ithaca, N.Y., and London: Cornell University Press, 1974), chap. 1, "Social Dramas and Ritual Metaphor," and p. 45. At the same time Turner cautioned against thinking of "community" or "society" as "static concepts" and noted that "such a view violates the actual flux and changefulness of the human scene" (p. 24).

21. Bryant, "The Medieval Entry Ceremony at Paris," pp. 88–118.

22. Kantorowicz, *The King's Two Bodies*, pp. 381, 447.

23. Turner's metaphor for his development of theory seems also to stand as a "root metaphor" for his view of the movement of ideas from social life to conceptualization: "Randomly distributed through some monstrous logical system, they [scattered ideas] resemble nourishing raisins in a cellular mass of inedible dough" (Turner, *Dramas, Fields, and Metaphors*, pp. 23–35).

24. Michel Foucault, "The Formation of Strategies," in *The Archaeology of Knowledge and the Discourse on Language* (New York: Harper Torchbooks, 1972), pp. 64–70. Sarah Hanley has forcefully made this point in regard to the relationship between sixteenth-century political and ceremonial formation: "There was no archaeology of knowledge discernible during this period; there were different modes of perception competing for place" (Hanley, *Lit de Justice*, p. 143).

25. It is frequently pointed out that symbols are difficult to contain or define, that

their service is to reconcile in ambiguities rather than definitions (Huizinga's "Symbolism in Decline," in *Waning of the Middle Ages*, pp. 200–225). More recently, Clifford Geertz, in *Negara: The Theatre State in Nineteenth-Century Bali* (Princeton, N.J.: Princeton University Press, 1980), p. 105, writes, "Like dream symbols, religious symbols are richly polysemic (that is have multiple senses), their significance spreading out profusely in an embarrassment of directions." Jacques Le Goff notes among "the pitfalls in the history of symbols" that there is the "polysemy of symbols, which frequently makes their interpretation uncertain: which of possible meanings is the correct one?" (Le Goff, "The Symbolic Ritual of Vassalage," in *Time, Work, and Culture in the Middle Ages*, trans. Arthur Goldhammer [Chicago: University of Chicago Press, 1982], p. 269).

26. Le Goff, "Symbolic Ritual of Vassalage," p. 269.

27. Gabrielle M. Spiegel, "History, Historicism, and the Discourse of the Medieval Text," *Speculum* 65 (1990): 75.

28. Seventy years ago, Lucien Febvre made this very clear as a matter of historical method: "It would, generally speaking, be a big step forward if we could be given a genealogical dossier for every historical question of any importance. For the time being, we can say that we are never supplied with impartially classified facts that we are free to combine as we please. We come up against more or less arbitrary selections of events and interpretations made long ago, and clusters of ideas and documents which have become classic; in short, what we always find are those 'major problems' posed sometimes centuries before under the sway of habits, ideas, and needs which are no longer ours" (Lucien Febvre, "The Origins of the French Reformation: A Question Badly Put," in *A New Kind of History*, ed. Peter Burke and trans. K. Folca [New York: Harper Torchbooks, 1973], p. 46).

29. Jacques Derrida, "Structure, Sign, and Play in the Discourse of the Human Sciences," in *Writing and Difference*, trans. Alan Bass (Chicago: University of Chicago Press, 1978), p. 279.

30. Such a historical approach is brilliantly discussed in Roger Chartier's *Cultural History*, trans. Lydia G. Cochrane (Ithaca, N.Y.: Cornell University Press, 1988). Citing the work of Marcel Mauss and Emile Durkheim, Chartier emphasizes that images and symbols are fashioned according to the divisions of the social world and are objects for "a cultural history of the social realm that has as its goal the comprehension of configurations and motifs—of representations of the social sphere—that give unconscious expression to the positions and the interests of social agents as they interact, and that serve to describe society as those social agents thought it was or wished it to be" (p. 6).

31. Don Handelman, *Models and Mirrors: Towards an Anthropology of Public Events* (Cambridge: Cambridge University Press, 1990), p. 21. Handelman distinguishes between "performance" (doing) and "logic of forms through which doing is done." He takes the position that "all types of public events are open to fluctuation and change through their enactment. But that this is so in differing degrees, and these variations in flexibility and openness are related to the logics of design of public events" (ibid., p. 19).

32. Glynne Wickham, *The Medieval Theatre* (Cambridge: Cambridge University Press, 1987), p. 22.

33. Robert Muchembled, *Popular Culture and Elite Culture in France: 1400–1750*, trans. Lydia Cochrane (Baton Rouge, La., and London: Louisiana State University Press, 1985), p. 92.

34. For early examples, see Peter Brown, *The Cult of the Saints: Its Rise and Function in Late Antiquity* (Chicago: University of Chicago Press, 1981). For Paris, see Bronislaw Geremek, *The Margins of Society in Late Medieval Paris*, trans. Jean Birrell (Cambridge: Cambridge University Press, 1987), pp. 159–66, and Bryant, "The Medieval Entry Ceremony at Paris," pp. 88–90.

35. Edward Peters, *Europe and the Middle Ages*, 2nd ed. (Englewood Cliffs, N.J.: Prentice-Hall, 1989), pp. 122–23.

36. In dealing with human actors, even in solemn ceremonies, we encounter the sorts

of problems of response that David Freedberg has analyzed for images; indeed, a king in a royal ceremony was more image than person (Freedberg, *The Power of Images: Studies in the History and Theory of Response* [Chicago: University of Chicago Press, 1989]). In the realm of ideas this shift has been analyzed as part of "the strategic reorientation [of mimetic tradition] that began in the twelfth century" when "the transcendent hierarchy of life was flattened into an organic unity, and the principle of change itself became, in some sense, subject to change" (Karl F. Morrison, *The Mimetic Tradition of Reform in the West* [Princeton, N.J.: Princeton University Press, 1982], pp. 175–76).

37. Geertz, *Negara*, p. 5. I draw from Clifford Geertz's distinctions, but the problems of dealing with the metahistorical character of rituals and the dynamics of social life were raised in the works of Marc Bloch and Lucien Febvre and continue to be of concern to historians of medieval and early modern Europe, particularly in the scholars associated with *Annales: Economie, Société, Culture* and a number of more recent journals.

38. A good example of classical oration and the hostility to it by those in the ruler's service is Otto of Freising's account of the efforts of Roman citizens to control the coronation entry of Frederick I in *Gesta Frederici*, lib. 2, cap. 29, ed. G. Waitz (*Monumenta Germanicae Historica, rerum germanica* [Hannover: Hahnsche Buchhandlung, 1912], pp. 148ff.).

39. The best single document on a French town's organization for the visit of the king has townsmen and guilds performing offices in the form of the Court. Jehan Foulquart's 1478 memorandum is in the B.N., mss. supplement français 1515–2, v. 1, and is reproduced in part in *Archives adminstratives de la ville de Reims*, ed. Pierre Varin (Paris, 1843), vol. 2, part 1, pp. 559–81.

40. For this paragraph I take freely from chapter 3 of Gordon Kipling's manuscript for his forthcoming book on liturgy, drama, and the civic triumph entitled "Third Advent: Grace in This Life and Afterwards Glory." He has graciously let me read parts of his study in advance of publication. I heartily thank him. Of interest on this topic are his articles "Richard II's 'Sumptuous Pageants' and the Idea of the Civic Triumph," in *Pageantry in the Shakespearean Theatre*, ed. David M. Bergeron (Athens: University of Georgia Press, 1985), pp. 83–103, and "Triumphal Drama: Form in English Civic Pageantry," *Renaissance Drama* 8 (1977): 41–45.

41. Bryant, "Medieval Entry," p. 90.

42. J. W. McKenna, "Henry VI of England and the Dual Monarchy: Aspects of Royal Political Propaganda, 1422–1432," *Journal of the Warburg and Courtauld Institutes* 28 (1965): 145–62.

43. Brigitte Bedos-Rezak, "Idéologie royale, ambitions princières et rivalités politique d'après le témoignage des sceaux (France 1380–1461)," in *La "France Anglaise" au Moyen Age, Actes du 111e Congrès National des Sociétés Savantes* (Paris, 1988), vol. 1, p. 507. She notes Henry VI's "avide appropriation des formules iconographiques en usage sur les sceaux des rois Valois." Professor Bedos-Rezak kindly called my attention to the essential study of French medieval imagery by Collette Beaune, *Naissance de la Nation France* (Paris: Editions Gallimard, 1985), published in English as *The Birth of an Ideology: Myths and Symbols of Nation in Late Medieval France*, trans. Susan Ross Huston, ed. Fredic L. Cheyette (Berkeley and Los Angeles: University of California Press, 1991. Beaune traces the models for a "kingdom-wide festival that the king [Charles VII] ordered in 1450 to celebrate the monarchy's victory in Normandy" (p. 127) to nearly half a century of Valois appropriation of local festivals to serve their cause against the English (chap. 4, "Sanctuaries and Festivals of the Kingdom of Bourges," pp. 126–51).

44. Jesse D. Hurlbut has made the point that the "possibilities of signification" and understanding of any connoted message in entry programs depended on the presence of the prince (Hurlbut, "Propaganda and Connotation in the Fifteenth-Century Burgundian Ducal Entries" (paper given at the 23rd International Congress on Medieval Studies at Kalamazoo, Mich., 5–8 May 1988).

45. Muchembled, *Popular Culture and Elite Culture in France*, pp. 126–53.

46. John Bossy, *Christianity in the West: 1400–1700* (Oxford: Oxford University Press, 1985), chap. 4, "The Social Miracle," pp. 57–74.

47. Ibid., chap. 8, "Migrations of the Holy," pp. 152–61. This chapter would have greatly benefited from consideration of Kantorowicz's *The King's Two Bodies*.

48. See Marvin B. Becker, *Civility and Society in Western Europe, 1300–1600* (Bloomington and Indianapolis: Indiana University Press, 1988), pp. 54–59, for a critique of Bossy's neglect of social theories. Unfortunately, this article was written before I knew of Becker's stimulating synthesis on the receding of "archaic and feudal practices" before professional and civic ones (ibid., p. xvii).

49. Bernard Chevalier, *Les Bonnes Villes de France* (Paris: Aubier Montaigne, 1982), pp. 100–106.

50. M. R. Powicke chronicles the growing discontent with the English occupation of France after Agincourt (Powicke, "Lancastrian Captains," in *Essays in Medieval History Presented to Bertie Wilkinson*, ed. T. A. Sandquist and M. R. Powicke [Toronto: University of Toronto Press, 1969], pp. 371–82). J. R. Lander follows the continuing problem of the French conquest in "The Hundred Years War and Edward IV's 1475 Campaign in France," in *Tudor Men and Institutions: Studies in English Law and Government*, ed. Arthur J. Slavin (Baton Rouge: Louisiana State University Press, 1972), pp. 70–100.

51. Chevalier, *Les Bonnes Villes de France*, p. 274. This thesis is the subject of a chapter that serves as an excellent introduction to late medieval spectacle, "La ville en fête: Le consensus cultural" (ibid., pp. 263–86).

52. Huizinga, *The Waning of the Middle Ages*, p. 324. Huizinga's view results in part from his defining the age in terms of feudal and ecclesiastical "forms" and "impulses."

53. M. M. Bakhtin, *The World of Rabelais*, trans. Helene Iswolsky (Cambridge: Massachusetts Institute of Technology Press, 1968), p. 271. Bakhtin recognized this vision of freedom in the Renaissance uses of carnival, but his point is very general and overemphasized for the early fifteenth century and probably later. He writes that popular festive forms take literary and philosophical shape in the search for new values. Rabelais gave these forms "special functions [that] become even more obvious in the light of the problem that all Renaissance literature was trying to solve, namely, to find forms that would make possible and would justify the most extreme freedom and frankness of thought and speech. The exterior, so to say, censored right and the interior right were undivided."

54. Ibid., *World of Rabelais*, pp. 273–74.

55. Bernard Chevalier, "L'Etat et les bonnes villes en France au temps de leur accord parfait," in *La Ville, la bourgeoisie et les genèses de l'état moderne (XIIe–XVIIIe siècles)*, ed. Neithard et J.-Ph. Genet (Paris: Editions du Centre National de la Recherche Scientifique, 1988). Huizinga, too, noted the emerging of an independent urban festive form "toward the fifteenth century" in chap. 19, "Art and Life" (*Waning of the Middle Ages*, pp. 242–64), but it was stifled in his view between the artifices of the Court and the ambitions and pride of the rich middle class: channels of patronage led to the failure of a new style and art.

56. Geertz looks at three types of ruler-centered ceremonies in his "Centers, Kings, and Charisma," in *Local Knowledge*, pp. 120–46: admonitory and convenantal, exemplary and mimetic, and "explosions of divine energy." I see a mix of these in Lancastrian spectacles, but the direction of development seems to be toward admonitory and legal or contractual symbolism.

57. I think that the effort was not so much for implanting "sentiments," although the language and acts use highly sentimental appeals, but for making models and imposing them in law. I make the distinction because of Bernard Guenée's excellent essay on the place of "national sentiment" in late medieval state building: "Ideas and sentiments manifest themselves in beliefs or have to reckon with images which, established in the very depths of the soul, weigh more upon the life of a nation than many material forces and many wise reasonings." He cites some of the myths that "influenced the political life of

France" in the period and notes that studies of them "are far from complete" (Guenée, "The History of the State in France at the End of the Middle Ages as Seen by French Historians in the Last Hundred Years," reprinted in *The Recovery of France in the Fifteenth Century,* ed. P. S. Lewis, trans. G. F. Martin [New York: Harper and Row, 1971], pp. 325–52).

58. McKenna, "Henry VI of England and the Dual Monarchy," p. 156.

59. A few years later Lorenzo Valla challenged the papacy's territorial claims by asserting that valid documents generated historical events: "Let us suppose that you may be able to adduce even genuine documents ...; even so, were the grants actually made which are found in the documents? Where is any taking possession, any delivery?" (Valla, *The Treatise on the Donation of Constantine,* ed. and trans. Christopher B. Coleman [1922; reprint, New York: Russell and Russell, 1971], p. 63).

60. Richard C. Trexler, in his introduction to *The "Libro Cerimoniale" of the Florentine Republic* (Geneva: Librairie Droz, 1978), p. 10.

61. André Bossuat, "The Re-Establishment of Peace in Society during the Reign of Charles VII," in *The Recovery of France,* ed. Lewis, pp. 61–81.

62. "La période qui va de 1360 à 1415, caractérisée par la disparition des grandes assemblées royales, est bien au contraire celle des états régionaux princiers qui jaillissent partout" (Chevalier, *Bonnes Villes,* p. 46).

63. *Collection générale des documents français qui se trouvent en Angleterre,* ed. Jules Delpit (Geneva: Slatkine Reprints, 1971), p. 234.

64. Ralph A. Griffiths, *The Reign of Henry VI* (Berkeley and Los Angeles: University of California Press, 1981), p. 220; McKenna, "Henry VI of England and the Dual Monarchy," passim.

65. Polydore Vergil, *Three Books of Polydore Vergil's English History ... from an Early Translation,* ed. Henry Ellkis, Camden Society, no. 29 (London, 1844), p. 39.

66. Lawrence M. Bryant, *The King and the City in the Parisian Royal Entry Ceremony: Politics, Ritual, and Art in the Renaissance,* Travaux d'Humanisme et Renaissance, no. 216 (Geneva: Droz, 1986), pp. 107–10.

67. Polydore Vergil, *English History,* p. 40. I have not found any contemporary reference to this speech, and it may well be a humanist rhetorical addition reflecting the idea that meaning in history was in capturing the correct sense of an occasion. I use it because it is a case of a later writer seeing a particular attitude and ritual taking shape in the English occupation. Obviously, more research is required. *The Parisian Journal,* trans. Janet Shirley (Oxford: Clarendon Press, 1968), pp. 268–74, which reported ceremonial events with care, makes no mention of the speech.

68. *Documents français ... en Angleterre,* p. 238.

69. "Relation de l'entrée solennelle de Henri VI a Paris," *Documents français ... en Angleterre,* pp. 239–44; and Bryant, *King and City,* pp. 84–92.

70. Bryant, "Medieval Entry Ceremony at Paris," pp. 102–3. For a century of entry ceremonies, the urban processions exited some distance from the city to greet the king; the Parisian aldermen and masters of the major guilds conveyed the king through the city under a canopy; street *tableaux* and choirs entertained and instructed him; and the king was received by the clergy in procession at Notre Dame Cathedral.

71. Giesey, *The Royal Funeral Ceremony,* p. 59. There was the ritual precedent in the royal funeral ceremony for Charles VI in 1422, where the red robes were worn in the funeral cortege. As Ralph Giesey has noted, "The symbolical act of not showing mourning at the royal funeral was paralleled by self-perpetuation in office until the funeral was completed."

72. Bryant, *King and City,* p. 86. In the sixteenth century, this hat symbolism was greatly elaborated as a mark of Parlement's status in the kingdom by writers such as Jean Bodin.

73. Ibid., pp. 80–81. In part, the judges might have looked back to the hopeful moment in 1389 when a coup by the *parlementaires* and royal counselors, called the Mar-

mosets, succeeded in breaking the power of Charles VI's uncles on the monarchy. The coup was celebrated in the 1389 entry and coronation of Isabella of Bavaria, the first in Paris for which we have accounts of extensive street theaters.

74. Lawrence Bryant, "*Parlementaire* Political Theory in the Parisian Royal Entry Ceremony," *Sixteenth Century Journal 7*, no. 1 (April 1976): 15–24.

75. *The Parisian Journal* described the program and noted with some surprise, "These were very good people, doing this" (p. 270). This "acting" can be contrasted with the usual entertainers in Paris who "had the permanent mistrust of the Church" and remained "on the margins of society," according to Geremek, *The Margins of Society,* p. 162.

76. Polydore Vergil, *English History,* p. 40.

77. *Documents français ... en Angleterre,* p. 250.

78. Kipling, "Third Advent," chap. 3 (see note 40 above); see also Bryant, *King and City,* pp. 181–82.

79. Bryant, *King and City,* pp. 87–88; see also n. 43 above.

80. See Geertz, "Blurred Genres," p. 29, for the phrase that entails a method of approach.

81. The exact date of the "welcoming" spectacles is not certain.

82. Lander, "The Hundred Years War," pp. 74–77.

83. *Documents français ... en Angleterre,* pp. 219–34.

84. Powicke, "Lancastrian Captains," p. 373.

85. John Stow, *The Survey of London* (1603; London: Dent and Sons, 1929), p. 479; and Sylvia L. Thrupp, *The Merchant Class of Medieval London* (Ann Arbor: University of Michigan Press, 1968), p. 149.

86. In special circumstances, as in 1392 before the liberties of London were restored, the guilds had appeared in "splendidly distinctive liveries" (Kipling, "Richard II," p. 87).

87. John Carpenter on the government of London (extracts from the *Liber Albus,* as printed in *Munimenta Gildhallae Londonensis,* ed. H. T. Riley (London, 1861), pp. 13–15.

88. *Munimenta Gildhallae Londonensis,* "Iber Custumarum," pp. 427–68; and Thrupp, *The Merchant Class of Medieval London,* pp. 259–60.

89. In Henry IV's 1399 precoronation progress, care seemed to have been taken to preserve the appearance of tradition amid unusual circumstances. The mayor and a group of citizens uniformly dressed in red, great lords, and about fifty new Knights of the Bath formed a cavalcade of over eight hundred to escort the king from the Tower of London to Westminster and the coronation. Perhaps even then guildsmen in livery lined the route through the city. This progress anticipated the crowning and the meeting of a new Parliament (Charles Lethbridge Kingsford, ed., *Chronicles of London* [London: Alan Sutton, 1977], p. 48 and notes).

90. John Lydgate's "Ordenaunces for the kyng," as printed in *Chronicles of London,* ed. Kingsford, p. 99. The status of London as the king's chamber had been traditional for at least the previous hundred years.

91. "Soveraigne lord as wel come be ye to your noble roialme of Englond and in especial unto your notable cite London other wise called your chambre as en (ever) was cristen prince to place or people and of the good and gracioux achevying of your coronne of Ffrance, we thanke hertlich our lord almighty which of his enles mercy send you grace in joye and prosperite on us and all your other people long for to regne" ("Relation de l'entrée de Henri VI à Londres," in *Documents français ... en Angleterre,* pp. 244–48).

92. Kingsford, ed., *Chronicles of London,* p. 99.

93. Bryant, *King and City,* p. 230, table 7, and chap. 4.

94. Kingsford, ed., *Chronicles of London,* is my source for this discussion (pp. 96–116, and 301–3 nn., which is the long rhymed poem — "one of the best descriptions of a mediaeval civic pageant [p. 301 n. 28]" — most probably written by John Lydgate).

95. Ibid., pp. 96–116. Lydgate's "two crowns" could have several layers of meaning: in particular, the earthly and heavenly crowns that had figured in London pageants of Richard II and Henry V, and the French and English crowns. I do not desire to get caught

up in medieval exegesis, but the English occasion was so arranged that one can see the suggestion that the French crown had more of the earthly aspect (being won in war) and the English a more divine one (being inherited and freely given).

96. Lydgate (in *Chronicles of London*, ed. Kingsford, p. 104) gave a version with the stanza praising "ryall mageste" where the "Relation de l'entrée ... à Londres" only referred to "Souveraigne lord" (p. 246), which is John Carpenter's version.

97. "Understondith and lernyth off the wyse, / On riht Remembrying the hyh lorde to queme, / Syth ye be Juges other ffolke to deme" (Kingsford, ed., *Chronicles of London*, p. 106).

98. Ibid., pp. 112–14; on the Jesse Tree symbolism, see Griffiths, *Reign of Henry VI*, pp. 218–22; and, most important on this image, Richard Osburg, "The Jesse Tree in the 1432 London Entry of Henry VI: Messianic Kingship and the Rule of Justice," *Journal of Medieval and Renaissance Studies* 16 (1986): 213–22.

99. John Stow, *Annals of England*, as cited in *Alliterative Poem on the Deposition of King Richard II*, ed. Thomas Wright, Camden Society, old series no. 3 (London, 1838): 58.

100. Kingsford, ed., *Chronicles of London*, p. 114. The organization of Henry VI's household is beyond the scope of this article, but by the end of the fifteenth century, the various "chambers," such as grand and inner, established the degrees of intimacy and access one had to the king. David Loades writes, "So the king's Chamber servants patrolled a sizeable territory, and meticulous attention had to be paid to everything that happened within it. There was constant tension between the king's honour, which required him to be accessible to his subjects (particularly the nobility), and common prudence and convenience, which dictated the tightest possible control of access" (Loades, "The Institutions," in *The Tudor Court* [Totowa, N.J.: Barnes and Noble, 1987], pp. 44–58 ["The Domus Regie Magnificencie"], at p. 44). I thank my student Matthew McIntire for calling this passage to my attention.

101. The discourse was in place at least since Edward II's reign (1307–27), when Hugh le Despenser used the office of Chamberlain "to undermine all other influences" and make the Chamber "another instrument of the king's personal action" (C. W. Previte-Orton, *The Shorter Cambridge Medieval History* [Cambridge: Cambridge University Press, 1971], 2: 889–90).

102. Loades, *Tudor Court*, p. 46.

103. This image of London as the king's chamber seems to look back to Richard II's temporary dissolution of the liberties of London and removal of the monarchy's residence to York. The form of reconciliation was in a London entry of 1392. "Chambers" also suggests the courtier aspect of the relationship between London and the king. The expression of the notion was common in London royal progresses through that of James I.

104. Chevalier, *Les Bonnes Villes*, p. 76.

105. Claude de Seyssel, *The Monarchy of France*, trans J. H. Hexter, ed. with introduction by Donald R. Kelley (New Haven, Conn., and London: Yale University Press, 1981), particularly where the preservation of the monarchy and "mystical body" is seen in "maintain[ing] each estate in its liberties, privileges, and praiseworthy customs, and so to superintend all of them that one cannot lord it over the others excessively nor all three join against the head and monarch" (p. 94).

CHAPTER 2

Civic Liturgies and Urban Records in Northern France, 1100–1400

Brigitte Bedos-Rezak

T he medieval city is daughter to the written word in the genealogical scheme of Paul Zumthor.[1] The much-discussed genesis of the
medieval town has called for many parents, but this addition of
literacy to the list of proposed geographic, economic, demographic, social,
political, and military procreators is not meant to define the moment of
conception of the medieval urban revival.[2] Rather, an examination of
northern France's medieval towns as textual communities[3] allows
insights independent of the issue of origins.[4] As literate modes developed within towns,[5] involving specific interrelationships with orality,
ritual, and ceremonial,[6] urban documentary practices came to form a
physical and visual testimony that at once marked the city as different
from, although still continuous with, the rest of society. Such practices
within the city were collective activities that took their form and meaning from contemporary medieval perceptions of these very activities. In
this sense, documentary modes must also be considered symbolic acts,
the forms of which brought together processes formerly separate. As such
they fostered a symbiosis between townspeople's personal experience of
urban identity and the city's role both as a site of ceremony and political prestige and as a crucible of communal values. Among those trappings necessary to legitimate the urban state and its ruling elite, to govern the social order, and to keep alive the consciousness of community
were urban records that, quite apart from their more obvious functions,
elicited attachment, involvement, and commitment on the part of
townspeople. The manipulation of the written word, in its interaction
with orality, played a critical role in marking the city as an authoritative
center of credibility, as a *locus credibilis*.[7]

The earliest form of documentary activity in northern French medieval towns dates from the eleventh century, when urban-based
échevins are recorded as witnesses to written transactions between lay
lords and churchmen.[8] Such transactions occurred in the context of a literate monopoly that, since the dissolution of the Carolingian order, had
been in the hands of clerics and monks. There is little extant evidence
that laymen in northern France in this period engaged in literate communication. Rather, the ties that gave fundamental structure to social

order, such as marriage, vassalage, and lordship, were created through rituals and ceremonies. Legal procedures also involved oaths, symbolic uses, or ordeals, and quite typically disputes were settled by means of feuds and armed force. Secular administrative procedure and the management of property seem simply not to have been documented. No records of land transfers between laymen are available, no economic contracts are known. For transactions between laymen, oral exchanges and symbolic objects, not written charters, were required. Even the royal chancery's documentary output (which clerics executed) remained small and limited in scope. At this time only churchmen were both capable and desirous of executing legal transactions by written means.

The process and control of written records, therefore, remained the monopoly of religious establishments that drafted and preserved documents recording deeds of land endowments made to them and acts settling disputes over land ownership in their favor. The sacred authority of the clergy, who identified themselves with the written and sacred word that they alone might interpret, supported these charters. A sense of divine accountability permeated these documents, a situation further stressed by their exclusive concern with land donated to monasteries and their patron saints by secular nobles seeking salvation of their souls. For the laity, therefore, the primary context for a sustained development of written documents begins in the twelfth century as a complex set of ideas concerned with earthly and otherworldly transactions. In their effort to stabilize their own gifts to saints, thus strengthening their control over the supernatural world, secular nobles gradually complemented the highly ritualized traditional ceremony of alienation through recourse to written deeds. By the twelfth century, clerics wrote lay charters in secular chanceries. Thus the format of lay aristocratic charters evolved in the specific historical and ideological context of the church's need and preference for writing.[9]

Twelfth-century urban documentary practice stemmed from a very different tradition, even though the earliest written notations of *échevins* as witnesses are to be found in charters involving churchmen. The *échevins'* authority as preferred witnesses derived specifically from their legal capacities. Since Carolingian times their qualifications lay in being men of local standing by virtue of property ownership who were also of good character and had legal competence. They served as lawmen and professional judges in the local court (the *mallus*) of a count and acted as signatories to private deeds recording transactions performed in their presence; and their presence (*in mallo publico, coram scabinis*) endowed any agreement with publicity, solemnity, and authenticity. The tribunal of *échevins* as an institution survived the collapse of other Carolingian administrative structures and evolved into those lordly courts based in cities, which ultimately came to stand near the very origin of urban government, whether by direct continuity, or by serving as models for later imitation.[10] Thus *échevins*, as urban officials, first appeared in eleventh- and twelfth-century documents because of their testimonial capability, a quality that they shared with other powerful members of the urban community referred to as *legitimi homines, primores urbis, viri authentici, honesti viri*.[11]

The town itself became an object of documentation as lords granted urban franchises and privileges. From the beginning, these concessions included, if only sporadically, the notion that contracts and agreements made in the *échevins'* presence had a particular strength and authenticity.[12] In relying on the special qualifications of the *échevins*, however, lords were not creating a new custom. Rather, the novelty was the formal, written records of customs previously bestowed orally, which now enshrined the modalities of traditional collective practices.[13] In reporting the presence of *échevins* during the making of contracts, charters of liberties were fostering the validatory role of oral proofs produced by the specific individuals' testimonials. A rather exceptional clause, the charter that John, count of Ponthieu, granted to the city of Abbeville in 1184, recognized writings emanating from the urban governing group as equally valid with oral testimonials. According to article 31 of this charter, the transaction made in the *échevins'* presence was to remain valid, despite the later absence of the transacting parties, provided that an authentic and public charter issued by the mayor and the *échevins* could be produced.[14] The charter of Abbeville was subsequently granted to several other towns in Picardy,[15] thus recognizing as normative the authority of documents that urban administrators issued. Such urban documentary competence does not seem to have required a systematic promulgation to develop extensively. Towns soon became the producers of a wide variety of written documents, but their documentary practices were self-generated rather than deriving from constitutional authorization.

Medieval towns issued deeds as a collective entity for matters involving their own political decisions, foreign policy, and property rights. Such charters were issued in the name of the whole urban community and sealed with the great seal of the town.[16]

Another category of town writings was administrative documents regulating urban management, social order, jurisdiction, and customs. Such documents included ordinances that governed urban guilds, fiscal accounts, lists of bourgeois who had sworn themselves to the commune and who, possibly, had received certificates as bourgeois, and the texts of oaths *échevins* swore when entering upon their functions.[17] Customals containing codifications of urban collective practices are compiled in a seemingly haphazard way that does not project a sense of consistent policy development.[18] This textual organization embodies the particularistic nature of the statutes, suggesting that they arose as responses or adaptations to specific circumstances. Such statutes emphasize individual identity: a person of wealth, status (whether a member of the commune or a foreigner), or family (parent, spouse) and his or her social actions, which are represented not as abstract categories, such as murder, theft, or violence, but as actual events embedded in, and expressive of, the urban social network. The referents of social acts and their legal treatments were actual circumstances that are to be remembered in the form of particular, lived experiences. Written urban ordinances of the late fourteenth century still articulated and gave meaning to a specific social structure. They had not yet evolved into trans-temporal abstractions functioning as their own referents in the practice of law and civic liturgy. At this point and in this respect, northern French medieval towns cannot be said to have developed a fully literate structure of collective organization. Rather, the modalities of its collective identity were constantly reinforced by townspeople daily reenacting, through the very form of their relationships with one another, the articulating principles of their community.

The reciprocity of this dialectic between group identity and individual experience significantly shaped the forms and modes of issuance of documents, which urban governments produced in ever greater numbers for citizens who wished to endow their contracts with a maximum of authenticity and legal effectiveness. Within the context of thirteenth-century documentary practice, all individuals could, and most did, commit themselves by affixing their seals to charters recording their transactions.[19] The intensity of this phenomenon was greatest in northern France, since in the south the notariate provided an effective alternative method of documentary validation. In northern French towns, however, individuals turned to their *échevins* for the issuance and execution of documents recording their personal contracts in familial (donations between spouses), private (wills), and economic (donations, sales) matters. Townspeople thereby allowed intervention of the group in their personal affairs, seeming to place greater trust in urban representatives than in their individual selves. This behavior brings into focus the urban document's specificity, the nature of its authority, and the elements that rendered this authority effective. Urban documentation involved the evolution of an innovative definition of authenticity, a gradual accretion of several differentiated layers of authority (public and official, personal and private), and a specific and competitive manifestation of power. Ultimately urban documentary practices manifest the town's symbolic significance as a source for and a locus of trust.

In the course of the twelfth century, *échevins* came to record in writing those private transactions made in their presence. The earliest documents present evidence of experimentation in the variety of their internal and external features. Such documents might be sealed with the town's great seal, or not; they might have many witnesses, including the *échevins* alone or with others; they might be issued in the name of various urban officials, including the mayor;[20] and they might be written either in Latin or the vernacular. But irrespective of all other variables, the presence of the *échevins* remained a constant element. As already mentioned, the legal strength long attached to these officials' oral testimony was transferred to their written one.[21] It remained characteristic that urban documentary practices were executed within a judicial context. Such a genesis, secular and mundane, stood in contrast to the clerical ascriptive origins of contemporary lay noble charters. The urban document, therefore, presented a problem of authoritative validation. The earliest urban records functioned simply as memoranda by means of which the appropriate *échevins* could record, so as to remember, transactions made in their presence and through which they could be summoned should their testimony be needed. The usefulness of such records might thus lapse with the death or disappearance of those witnesses whose names they recorded. Gradually, the testimonial capacity of the individuals came to inhere in the document, no longer merely a memorandum, but now itself an adequate testimony of the transaction it recorded.[22] Such documents, however, continued to be made in the presence of individual *échevins* even after experience and practice assured that the document's force would survive the demise of these persons. Medieval vocabulary registers this concept, a documentary record being in several instances referred to as a "force."[23] As with urban customals, force emanated from historically situated persons, not from the trans-temporal and abstract office of *échevin.* Yet the deeds which the *échevins* produced were described in contemporary urban statutes as "public" and "authentic," indicating that in medieval semantics, to be public was to be authentic, and that the quality of authenticity resulted specifically from being well known.[24] All of these notions, far from carrying abstract rule-referent meaning, were largely interpretive of and semantically dependent upon local social systems.

What made an urban record renowned, authentic, and thus trustworthy? This question underlies consideration of the form into which urban records finally settled during the thirteenth century. This format, known as the chirograph, consisted of several copies of a vernacular text recording the making of a covenant in the presence of specifically named *échevins,* each copy being separated by a word written in especially large letters, for example, CHIROGRAPHUM.[25] The identical texts were then cut apart by an incision of the parchment through the word so that parties to the conveyances could each receive an identical version of the text. Authenticity could be proven by matching the copies' cut edges with a reference copy deposited in the city archive. This copy served as the matrix from which the other versions derived their authenticity. Ecclesiastical institutions and the nobility used chirographs to some extent, but not in the systematic way that came to characterize the documentary practice of northern French towns. In these towns there was a veritable equation of chirographs with urban records.[26]

Perhaps the most significant outcome of the documentary format and practice towns adopted is the fact that it led to the need for urban archives. These archives, stored in the town hall, compelled a definition of this most urban of spaces as the very source for documentary authenticity.[27] Even when seals came into use they did not displace the chirographic format, and were, according to some customals, affixed to prove the presence of the version in the urban archive, the *locus credibilis*.[28] Thus, even though urban chirographs were not issued specifically in the town's name,[29] they drew their effectiveness from it as an aggregative space, as a symbolic form that transformed the stressful potential for, and process of resolving, conflict and dissension into a vision of successful and stable settlements. I will return later to the manifold significance of the interaction between documentary practices and urban space. Here, though, it is perhaps useful to emphasize that the referent for the concepts of public and authentic, formerly a human being, had been replaced, not by an abstract office, but by a tangible space endowed by contemporaries with the magical quality of producing credibility. This process of reification appears to indicate that medieval culture dealt with such concepts as the official, the public, or the community through symbolization and emblematization, rather than abstraction.

Control over the written word in the Middle Ages was always a manifestation of power. Urban documentary practices seem to have competed successfully with those of local bishops, lords, royal officials, or abbeys in the issuance of authentic deeds.[30] Yet the matter was never definitively resolved and, by the middle of the fourteenth century, lords reasserted their control by requiring that the use of urban seals of jurisdiction be contingent upon current lordly authorization.[31] That documentary production both in text and in practice continued to formulate a discourse on power, indeed had become a defining part of the pattern of public power, is demonstrated by the royal ordinance of Moulins (1566) that deprived towns of their capacity to issue deeds.[32]

At once sign, memory, and symbolic activity, writing within towns underwent those various kinds of manipulations characteristic of signs that transcend their message and their function. Towns produced writing; they also consumed it. A recurrent goal of city officials was to preserve as many versions as possible of their charters of privileges, placing them for security in a special chest in the town archives. One method was to have the charter copied with superb calligraphy and illumination, as was done in a thirteenth-century urban cartulary of Amiens, for instance.[33] Most desirable were documents issued by the granting lord and his or her heirs. These latter were repeatedly asked to issue charters of confirmation that enshrined liberties already inscribed in earlier documents. The issue was not simply documentary preservation, since that was accomplished through copies made by town clerks. Indeed, even when their charters were destroyed by fire or war and town officials gave these reasons in asking for a newly written document, the granting lord made it clear that the freshly written text merely reproduced the content of the one previously conceded. No, there were other purposes. Town officials of Aire-sur-La-Lys asserted in 1374 that their charter had been destroyed by fire and requested a new one from Marguerite, countess of Flanders. Yet, thanks to the preservation of the archives of this town it is clear that the charter alleged to have been destroyed had not been; it is still extant. The townspeople were therefore not trying to coax new privileges from the countess, since both she and they had retained copies of the initial document, which was necessarily the basis for her "new" charter.[34] The allegation of destruction appears to have been simply a ploy to obtain yet another icon representative of the town's chartered status. It was not a restatement of the privileges themselves that was so critical to the process since, as already discussed, the formal documentary grant merely confirmed, rather than created, them.[35]

The crucial element was the form these privileges received: written, sealed, objectified, and thus available as sacred texts and icons for the rituals of a civic liturgy. Mayors and other town officials, upon entering their tenure, swore to "keep the charter,"[36] a term of significant ambivalence that alluded to both the physical preservation of the document and obedience to its content. The charter's symbolic function, subsuming both text and its medium, reified the concept of collective rule and thereby substantiated that rule's power to act in history.

It is revealing that the town charter was usually referred to simply as "the charter," a generic term conveying at once absolute self-reference and the discursive specificity of its articles. Charters once issued were rarely, if ever, adjusted to reflect further evolution in urban privilege or practice. Yet their textual immutability appears not to have prevented change, since many urban activities developed that were neither originally nor later included in the charter's wording. Significantly, when a town wished to enunciate more precise regulations, it produced a customal rather than tampering with the original charter.[37] When a charter originally granted to a specific town was thereafter conceded virtually verbatim to other towns, what was propagated was the concept of the charter rather than its particular contents.[38] It was the idea of the charter rather than a document specifically related to the local customs of the recipients. The charter, encoding aspiration rather than codifying legal process, functioned as a textual object in which the text itself was both enshrined and a shrine for the performance of a liturgy of urban ceremonials. This attitude toward written statutes was widespread among urban populations. For example, guilds asked to have their own ordinances committed to writing, and these were later read to newly selected heads of the guild during the ceremony of their installment.[39] Such postures cannot be dissociated from broader trends toward legal exactitude that also involved a growing acceptance of the strength of written proofs and codifications. This in turn implied that a charter's particular content be specifically accessible so it could be consulted in legal and administrative matters or quoted in support of a claim. To this specific end, charters of privileges were transcribed and translated from Latin into French.[40]

The use of the vernacular is eminently characteristic of all types of records towns produced; the earliest extant document in Old French is a 1204 chirograph from the northern French city of Douai.[41] Extensive use of the vernacular suggests that town officials, and possibly other burgesses, could, indeed had to be able to, read.[42] For example, chirographs had to be identified for retrieval from the bags in which they were kept; burgesses received certificates of their bourgeoisie; officials took their oaths in French according to a written formula; statutes had to be read and heard.[43]

The use of the written word in medieval towns left much room for the retention of oral modes, suggesting that much of what was set down in writing was still meant to be received by the ear, to be invoked visually as an icon, or to be supplemented by ritual gestures.[44] A sensitive index of this interplay between the oral and the written is provided by their respective roles in urban legal, administrative, and economic systems. Procedures involving debt payments required that the creditor bring his title to the *échevins* who would have it read aloud and thereafter declare that the creditor must be paid.[45] When a debtor's possessions were sold to satisfy his obligations, the creditors' names had first to be put into writing, and then shouted at various urban locations so that they might make good their claims. The claim was then to be presented in writing to the *échevins*. If a creditor had lost his written claim, he could still prove his right by swearing on the saints (*fianchier et jurer sour sains*) in the presence of the *échevins* that he had lost it. After he was reimbursed, the creditor was required to return the written deed, which indicated the debt owed to him, and the debtor received a written receipt of his payment.[46]

In fiscal matters the towns of Amiens, Senlis, and Douai proclaimed orally the amount of the annual tax to be paid, while in Arras and Saint-Quentin a written brief was issued. In juridical matters, written testimony on the witnesses' part was not mandatory, nor were complainants even allowed to provide the *échevins* with written exposition of their grievances, but whoever denied a chirograph brought against him was fined if the counterpart of the chirograph could be found in the archives. Furthermore, the judgments of *échevins* had to be put in writing so as to avoid falling into oblivion.[47] Administrative matters, surviving ordinances, customals, accounts, list of burgesses, registrations of contracts, judgments, and archival techniques all point to a literate management system.

In economic matters an evolution occurred that transferred the strength of town officials' oral testimony to documents made in their presence and thereafter kept in the town archive. A concern developed for documentary authentication, testifying to a growing reliance upon written proofs. The functions of contracting, agreeing, selling, and buying, all previously performed orally, lent themselves readily to documentary forms. Yet one may wonder how the gradual penetration of documentary modes affected these functions when in fact the memory and the word of a town official (even of a dead one who could be consulted in his tomb), or a verbal oath sworn in his presence, could still compensate for the absence of written deeds, even after these came to be conceived as a record and memory of the actual transfer.[48] Charters of privileges themselves were confirmations of customary practices, immemorial in origin.[49] The social value of memory remained important, and the ritual performances and gestures that had long created memory were transferred to those "obstacles to oblivion," the written words, also conceived as memory. The equation of writing and memory, asserted within medieval documents themselves,[50] may go far to explain why, throughout the Middle Ages, written documents continued to be the focus of rituals that have heretofore been too often and too exclusively associated with oral culture. In urban theater, writing and the written occupied a singular place.

The act of writing itself was performed as a spectacle in medieval towns. Up to the thirteenth century, parties who desired an urban chirograph were responsible for its generation and would appear before the *échevins*, the prepared text of their conveyance in hand, already written out but for blank spaces to be filled in with the names of those officials then in session.[51] Scribes who kept shop in front of the town hall offered their services in preparing such texts.[52] The town, however, eventually monopolized scribal activity and with its own clerical staff reestablished complete control over those deeds upon which it conferred validity.[53] It is, therefore, puzzling that no surviving urban account displays an entry for the acquisition of scribal materials such as parchment. It is conceivable that even after the parties were required to have a town clerk write their deed, they nevertheless continued to provide him with parchment. In any case individuals certainly experienced the writing process, which involved various gestures on their part. Here again, memory, ritual, and writing went hand in hand well into the fourteenth century. In a contract between two spouses, for instance, the husband promised to respect the contract's tenets by placing his hands within those of the *échevins*.[54] In Arras, in order for spouses to obtain a written deed of donations between them both had to appear in the presence of the *échevins* and, in order to demonstrate their marital love, the wife had to kiss her husband.[55] A purchaser of real estate not only recorded his transaction in writing, but also performed the seisin of the property by coming to the city hall where he placed his hand upon the rod of justice.[56]

Townspeople desired the document; purchased its support; enacted ritually the covenant it recorded; witnessed its writing, sealing, or division and distribution into several parts; received it; paid for it; ritually touched it; and brought it back home, there to be kept for possible later use. In late-thirteenth-century Saint-Omer where burgesses were offered the possibility of having their chirographs sealed, they had to bring them to two *échevins* who sat daily in the city hall to supervise such sealing.[57] Where a dispute arose, the parties would retrieve their chirographs, carry them to the court, and exhibit them.[58] Could they read the document or quote from it? I have found no evidence. Assuming that they owned several of these deeds, may we not expect that they would have been able to distinguish between them so as to resort to the appropriate one? Apart from legal considerations, and given the fact that oral testimony clearly remained valid, were there other reasons why urban people had recourse to the written word, and specifically to a type of document involving a public institution, the town court, rather than to a personal document issued under one's private seal? Within the towns, no doubt, institutionalized exchanges in courts quickly became broadly acceptable, and the evolution from written beneficiary-produced to court-produced deeds was also rapidly accepted. Going to the city hall for such transactions, to the pulsating center of urban life, may have added significance, especially since the document thereafter remained symbolically present in the hall. For in essence when a portion of the chirograph bearing the names of all the parties was placed in the urban archive, the parties were inscribed within the ongoing narrative of the city's history, making them part of the very substance of the collective identity from which they as individuals derived the means, and meaning, of their social behavior.

Townspeople both as individuals and as community members were involved in the liturgy surrounding state documentation. When the city of Abbeville was granted its charter of privileges, its *memoriale cirographum*, the final clause states that the entire city of Abbeville was witness since the document had been made within its sight and hearing.[59] When a town produced its own solemn documents, the city hall took on an enhanced theatrical aspect in which the tolling of a bell, display of the scriptural object of the gathering, the liveries of the town officials, the sealing of the document, and the presence of the crowd all constituted dramatic and interpretive acts of the very life of the city.[60] Likewise, ordinances, treaties, and agreements with kings, princes, and churchmen were not solely created by abstract wording. They were also enacted through the forms of scribal actions in which either the community as a whole or particular groups of persons, such as the town's officials or the members of a guild, participated. The written deed was thus a center-piece of a ceremony meant to foster memory, consensus, loyalty, and shared experience. Similarly, when new town officials were inducted, they were read the texts of charters and ordinances. In Saint-Valéry-sur-Somme, the newly elected mayor carried the city's seal at his belt throughout his installation.[61]

The seal was an iconic personification of the urban collectivity; it received respectful treatment and was kept with great care in a chest, the keys of which were distributed to the *échevins* and to town representatives.[62] Worn-out seals were not destroyed but preserved as relics in the sanctuary of the archives.[63] The introduction of a new seal required a special entry in the town's register. In Douai the great seal could not be affixed without the consent of the whole community. A special bell called the townspeople together for this purpose.[64] To the extent that they rooted urban literate codification in living experience, such ceremonies were ritualistic, with the document functioning as a ritual object. The ceremonies were also symbolic in that they offered urban society a form of behavior by which to place itself within a context of rules. The document operated as a symbolic form to which the citizens adhered and which they assimilated to their individual experience. The documentary process enabled the town to serve as a space of communication, information, and connection. Furthermore, through its manipulation of the written word in association with rites and ceremonies, the town generated an urban calendar and mapped out a sacred geography.

Just as a special bell called the community to documentary witness,[65] so too did the cities set aside specific days for issuing chirographs. Documentary practices thus contributed to shaping the town's time frame and drew citizens into collective rhythms. While a document sealed with the town's great seal represented the community as an integrated group, it evidently did not abolish all divisions within the group. Social complexity created spatial forms of symbolic significance within the context of these literate modes.

From the earliest appearance of urban government in the the twelfth century, *échevins* witnessed and wrote deeds in cemeteries, in front of churches, or at crossroads, that is, at those sites consecrated by layers of religious traditions—Celtic, Roman, Christian.[66] The public and sacred nature of these sites, as well as the presence of the *échevins*, endowed the documents with effectiveness and special significance. The central squares of medieval towns, containing the town hall—with its law court, belfry, and archives—as well as the cathedral, were often established on a place imbued with older sacrality. In Lille, the fountain Au

Cange, near which the city hall was built and where all declarations were made, was presumed to be miraculous. Even as city halls became sites uniquely sought after for judicial and documentary purposes, they appropriated those sacral powers that had emanated from the sites' older usage.[67] Written charters came to reify and symbolize the sacrality of the locus of their emission and conservation: the town hall and, by extension, the town itself. From such a locus, records derived and transmitted, if not sacrality, an absolute authenticity. This logic of legal and administrative practice enabled the city hall to acquire near-consecrated status. Writing, in imposing on its users constraints of time and place, rooted the town hall's central role within the mysteries of a state liturgy that involved the sacraments of authentication. As a *locus credibilis*, the town hall required special protection. Between 1150 and 1300 monsters and animals, functioning as protective spirits, appeared as weathervanes perched upon the tower of the building containing the commune's treasure and its archives.[68]

City archives present themselves as an element crucial to the medieval urban experience, contributing as they did to the stabilization of legal, social, and economic processes and serving to mark the city as an ideological and political entity. A stipulation in a 1266 charter between Abbeville and John, count of Ponthieu, provides an insight into the role urban records played in defining urban space. The count agreed that, should he need to consult Abbeville's charters, he must consult them within the city and may not ask that they be removed.[69] As guardians and repositories of civic traditions, the archives defined the city's geographic boundaries and historical dimensions with a spatiotemporal representation that was perceived as an essential principle of its order. In 1346 the English burnt the archives of the little town of Le Crotoy in Picardy. Its inhabitants begged the king of France to search in his registers for Ponthieu for copies of their urban charters and privileges so that they could reconstitute their archives and, therefore, the essence of their identity. The king obliged them.[70]

Archives and documentary practices were vital elements in the medieval urban experience. Townspeople appear to have been attached and committed to them, resorting to town clerks and *échevins* for recording private transactions. In doing so they recognized the existence of urban power as potentially coercive but, nevertheless, endowed with a set of responsibilities that were separate from, yet related to, their own private interests and activities. The town hall and its writing bureaus drew into its purview the infinite variety of daily experience. The symbiosis achieved in urban organization between documentary production and the necessity for archives endowed urban administration with a cultural and ideological role. Urban records helped to establish the medieval city as a quasi-sacred center of ceremony and political prestige, while documentary rituals and obligations reinforced urban social cohesion. This role enabled towns to make an impact on their inhabitants, whose membership was diverse and riven by factional and social antagonisms and by competing loyalties toward parishes or lordships. Urban society as a whole developed a large measure of self-awareness through its practice of documentation, which gave it a historical perspective on its past. The production and manipulation of documents, including the recording and archiving of private transactions, offered a communality of forms that evolved from and fostered the townspeople's adherence to common principles, shared definitions of collective identity, and participation in the same rituals. In this respect, the medieval urban identity may be said to be largely a matter of symbolic practices, many of which related to writing. It is no mere coincidence that when urban theories were developed in the thirteenth century, seals and archives ranked among the constitutive, and still later the constitutional, elements of township.[71] In the course of an evolution from ritual to symbolism in its documentary practices, the medieval city derived an official form. By embellishing the routines and techniques of their documentary writing through ceremony, medieval towns marked the essence of their society with an authentic identity and with credibility.

Notes

1. Paul Zumthor, *La lettre et la voix de la "littérature" médiévale* (Paris: Editions du Seuil, 1987), p. 102: "Les villes sont filles de l'écrit."
2. See examples of suggestive syntheses in Robert S. Lopez, "The Crossroads within the Wall," in *The Historian and the City*, ed. Oscar Handlin and J. Burchard (Cambridge: MIT Press and Harvard University Press, 1963), pp. 27–43; Jacques Le Goff, ed., *La ville médiévale* (Paris: Editions du Seuil, 1980); Le Goff, "The Town as an Agent of Civilization," in *The Fontana Economic History of Europe: The Middle Ages*, ed. Carlo M. Cipolla (London: Collins/Fontana Books, 1972), pp. 71–106; Susan Reynolds, *Kingdoms and Communities in Western Europe, 900–1300* (Oxford: Clarendon, 1984), passim; Fritz Rörig, *The Medieval Town* (Berkeley and Los Angeles: University of California Press, 1969), passim; and Yves Barel, *La ville médiévale* (Grenoble: Presses universitaires de Grenoble, 1977), passim.
3. I borrow here the expression felicitously coined by Brian Stock in *The Implications of Literacy* (Princeton, N.J.: Princeton University Press, 1983).
4. For the formulation of these questions, I am especially indebted to Sylvia Thrupp, "The Creativity of Cities: A Review Article," *Comparative Studies in Society and History* 4 (1961–62): 54–64; Richard Fox, *Urban Anthropology: Cities in Their Cultural Setting* (Englewood Cliffs, N.J.: Prentice-Hall, 1977); Susan Reynolds, *Kingdoms and Communities*; Anthony Cohen, *The Symbolic Construction of Community* (London: Tavistock Publications, 1985); Frederic Cheyette, "The Invention of the State," in *The Walter Prescott Webb Memorial Lectures: Essays on Medieval Civilization*, ed. Bede Lackner and Kenneth Philp (Austin and London: University of Texas Press, 1979), pp. 143–78; Pierre Bourdieu, *Outline of a Theory of Practice* (Cambridge: Cambridge University Press, 1977); and Robert Redfield and Milton Singer, "The Cultural Role of Cities," in *Classic Essays on the Culture of Cities*, ed. Richard Sennett (New York: Meredith, 1969), pp. 206–33.
5. Historians tend to attribute high rates of literacy to towns; see, for example, Stock, *Implications of Literacy*, p. 17; Jean Dunbabin, *France in the Making, 843–1180* (Oxford:

Oxford University Press, 1985), pp. 272–73; John Gilissen and Ivan Roggen, "Le problème du droit privé urbain en Belgique," in *Recueil de la Société Jean Bodin. Tome VIII: La ville* (Brussels: Imprimerie des Travaux Publics, 1957), pp. 221–84, at p. 275; Robert Lopez, "The Culture of the Medieval Merchant," *Medieval and Renaissance Studies* 8 (1979): 54–62, at 54–57; Lopez, "The Crossroads," p. 37; and "Histoire et Urbanisation" (anonymous), *Annales: Economies, Sociétés, Civilisations* 25 (1970): 829.

6. The ceremonials and rituals surrounding documentary writing have been noted by historians working on or publishing urban records, but have been dismissed as picturesque and of little interest. See, for instance, the remarks by Henri Sellier in his otherwise important and comprehensive work, *L'authentification des actes par l'échevinage* (Lille: Raoust, 1934): "La réception des actes était accompagnée et suivie de diverses formalités. Car dans bien des pays, les usages locaux pouvaient avoir établi des formes, au demeurant fort pittoresques, mais dont la connaissance est peu utile.... L'écrit étant obligatoire par lui-même, les formes extérieures sont en général de peu d'importance et sans intérêt" (p. 115). As a result, new work needs to be done on urban documentary practices based on the direct consultation of city archives.

7. See below, pp. 44–45.

8. Arthur Giry, *Manuel de diplomatique* (Paris: Imprimerie Lahure, 1893), p. 852; Paul Bonenfant, *Cours de diplomatique. II: Diplomatique spéciale* (Liège: Editions Desoer, 1948), p. 106; Georges Espinas, *La vie urbaine de Douai au moyen âge*, 4 vols. (Paris: Picard, 1913), 1:206, 522; and Sellier, *L'authentification des actes*, p. 18. The term *échevins* will be preferred throughout this chapter over the synonymous terms *scabini* and aldermen.

9. The processes of acculturation that account for the promotion of written documents by the northern French aristocracy are an object of my ongoing research; see Brigitte Bedos-Rezak, "The Confrontation of Orality and Textuality: Jewish and Christian Literacy in Eleventh- and Twelfth-Century Northern France," in *Congrès international Rashi: Actes*, ed. Gabrielle Sed-Rajna (Paris: Editions du Cerf, forthcoming), and "Diplomatic Sources and Medieval Documentary Practices: An Essay in Interpretive Methodology," *The Past and Future of Medieval Studies*, ed. John Van Engen (Notre Dame, Ind.: University of Notre Dame Press, forthcoming).

10. The presumption of continuity between Carolingian and municipal *échevins* is a very complex subject, demonstrated for several northern French cities: Cambrai, Noyon, Laon, Lille, Saint-Omer, Bergues, Saint-Quentin, Arques, and so on. It seems that these urban *échevins* remained, perhaps for a while, perhaps permanently, lordly agents, responsible for civil law (and documentary procedures) and operating in coexistence with another, distinct, administrative body, that of the *jurés* who were responsible for breaches of the laws of the city, and thus for the settlement of criminal affairs. In some towns, *échevins* and *jurés* fused into one administrative body, in others the local lord was asked to select the *échevins* from the *jurés*, in yet others the *échevins* simply replaced the *jurés*. On these issues, the most thorough and recent study, with additional bibliography, is that of Robert-Henri Bautier, "Du scabinat carolingien à l'échevinage communal: Le problème de l'origine des échevinages médiévaux," in *Les chartes et le mouvement communal* (Saint-Quentin: Société académique de Saint-Quentin, 1982), pp. 59–81. See also Alain de Boüard, *Manuel de diplomatique française et pontificale. II: L'acte privé* (Paris: Editions Picard, 1948), pp. 229–30.

11. Augustin Thierry, *Recueil des monuments inédits de l'histoire du Tiers Etat. Tome premier: Pièces relatives à l'histoire de la ville d'Amiens depuis l'an 1057, date de la plus ancienne de ces pièces, jusqu'au XVe siècle* (Paris: Didot Frères, 1850), p. 22; Sellier, *L'authentification des actes*, pp. 17–18; Boüard, *Manuel de diplomatique*, pp. 229–31; and R.-H. Bautier, "L'authentification des actes privés dans la France médiévale: Notariat public et juridiction graçieuse," *Notariado pùblico y documento privado: De los origenes al siglo XIV. Actas del VII Congreso Internacional de Diplomatica* (Valencia: Conselleria de Cultura, Educacio i Ciència, 1986), pp. 701–72, at 737–39. For a similar situation in Bel-

gian Flanders, see James M. Murray, "Failure of Corporation: Notaries Public in Medieval Bruges," *Journal of Medieval History* 12 (1986): 155–66, at 162–63.

12. Few charters of customs actually referred to the testimonial competence of any urban group in contractual matters (Sellier, *L'authentification des actes*, pp. 19–20). In the charter of *commune* granted to Amiens (ca. 1117, according to A. Thierry), article 44 reads: "[S]i conventio aliqua facta fuerit ante duos vel plures scabinos, de conventione illa amplius non surget campus vel duellum, si scabini qui conventioni interfuerint, hoc testificati fuerint" (Thierry, *Recueil des monuments*, 1:42, 50, 113, in Philip Augustus's confirmation of the *commune*, in 1190). In the thirteenth-century customal of Amiens, article 74 reads: "[C]hi parole de tesmoingnage d'eskievins de le chité d'Amiens. Derechief, tout quanque doi eskievin tesmoignent et recordent, est ferme et estable, et passe sans che que nus puist dire ne faire riens encontre, ne à loi de bataille venir" (ibid., p. 146). In the charter granted to Arras by Philip Augustus in 1194, article 35 reads: "[N]ullum donum, nulla venditio, nulla concessio, nulla investitura tenebit, nisi facta fuerit coram scabinis" (G. Espinas, *Recueil des documents relatifs à l'histoire du droit municipal en France des origines à la Révolution: Artois*, 3 vols. [Paris: Recueil Sirey, 1934–1943], 1:277). See further instances in Bautier, "Authentification des actes privés," p. 739 (Saint-Omer in 1127, Cambrai in 1184).

13. On charters of liberties as confirming earlier oral grants, and as determined by already extant communal practice rather than being their constitutive and constitutional elements, see the remarks of Reynolds, *Kingdoms and Communities*, pp. 34–35, 161, 163; of Bautier, "Du scabinat carolingien," p. 65; and of John Gilissen, "Les villes en Belgique: Histoire des institutions administratives et judiciaires des villes Belges," *Recueil de la Société Jean Bodin. Tome VI: La ville* (Brussels: Imprimerie des Travaux Publics, 1954), p. 547.

14. A. Thierry, *Recueil des monuments inédits de l'histoire du Tiers Etat. Tome quatrième: pièces relatives à l'histoire municipale d'Abbeville et à celle des villes, bourgs et villages de la Basse Picardie* (Paris: Imprimerie impériale, 1870), pp. 9–14. The charter of Abbeville evidences much interest for urban documentary practice; article 19 reads: "[S]i aliqua nova questio et a retro temporibus non judicata, inter juratos aut intrinsecus aut extrinsecus orta fuerit, judicio scabinorum terminabitur, et ne quod judicatum oblivioni tradatur, autentice scripture commendabitur" (ibid., p. 11). While article 30 establishes the traditional authenticity of the *échevins'* testimony in contractual matters, "preterea statutum est quod, si in presencia duorum vel trium scabinorum contractus emptionis, venditionis, permutationis, pignoris, vel alius contractus initus fuerit, eorum testimonio causa disrationabitur, salvo jure meo in eo qui convictus fuerit" (ibid., p. 13), article 31 asserts the testimonial value of the written proof issued in the name of the *échevins*: "Hoc idem erit, si carta publica et autentica a majore et scabinis tradita, dictis scabinis non apparentibus, fuerit producta" (ibid., p. 13).

15. The charter of Abbeville was granted to Noyelles-sur-Mer in 1194 (Thierry, *Recueil des monuments* 4:600), to Hiermont in 1192 (ibid., p. 603), to Crécy in 1194 (ibid., p. 606), to Waben in 1199 (ibid., p. 611), to Marquenterre in 1199 (ibid., p. 613), to Ponthoiles in 1201 (ibid., p. 617), to Doullens in 1202 (ibid., p. 621), to Saint-Josse-sur-Mer in 1203 (ibid., p. 633), to Port-le-Grand in 1218 (ibid., p. 687), and to Vismes in 1212 (ibid., p. 689).

16. Brigitte Bedos [Rezak], *Corpus des sceaux français du Moyen Age. Tome Ier: Les sceaux des villes* (Paris: Imprimerie nationale, 1980). In each entry for a given great seal, a short analysis of the document to which it is appended presents the nature of the issues about which the town was collectively concerned.

17. A 1242 urban ordinance for the butchers of Amiens, in Thierry, *Recueil des monuments* 1:242; 1286 urban ordinance for the guild of the coopers of Amiens, ibid. 1:253; 1311 urban ordinance for the furriers of Amiens, ibid. 1:348; 1387 fiscal account of the city of Amiens, ibid., 1:757–83; and 1365 fiscal account of the city of Abbeville, ibid. 4:151–61. On bourgeois receiving deeds confirming their status, and being "mis en l'escrit

de le ville," see Espinas, *Vie urbaine de Douai* 1:393. See the mention of a 1228 list of those who swore the *commune* in Amiens, *isty juraverunt communiam anno Domini millesimo CCo vicesimo octavo*, in Thierry, *Recueil des monuments* 1:202. See for instance the oath to be sworn by the *échevins* of Hénin-Liétard in Espinas, *Recueil des documents* 2:565–73, no. 489 (second part of the thirteenth century): special recommendations are made for the use of writing in special circumstances, in article 19 (p. 569), "Et si vous dit on ke tout cil ki refuseront la loi de le vile par devant vous, ke vous le metes en escrit, et les faites crier en vo eskievinages ke il ont refusé le loi de le vile, et k'il ne sunt mie bourgois ne en puent jamais estre"; also in article 32 (p. 571): "Et si faites mettre en escrit toutes les trives, et aussi queres les dettes de le vile à vos pooirs. Ce vous me on en vos sairement."

18. On the *Livres urbains* (documents containing urban ordinances and customs), see Gilissen and Roggen, "Le problème du droit privé urbain," pp. 244–45. The customal of Lille, called *Livre Roisin*, was composed by Jean Roisin, town clerk of Lille sometime after 1280. This customal has been edited by Raymond Monier, *Le livre Roisin* (Paris: Les Editions Domat-Montchrestien, Loviton et Cie, 1932). On the customal of Saint-Omer (thirteenth century), see Gilissen, "Les villes en Belgique," pp. 577–78. See the thirteenth-century texts of the customs of Amiens in Thierry, *Recueil des monuments* 1:121–76.

19. On seals, see the following works by Brigitte Bedos-Rezak: "Les sceaux juifs français," in *Art et archéologie des Juifs en France médiévale*, ed. Bernhard Blumenkranz (Toulouse: Privat, 1980), pp. 207–28, reprinted in *Form and Order in Medieval France: Studies in Social and Quantitative Sigillography* (London: Variorum, 1993), no. 11; "Les sceaux au temps de Philippe Auguste," in *Colloques Internationaux CNRS n. 602. La France de Philippe Auguste. Le temps des mutations. Actes*, ed. R.-H. Bautier (Paris: Editions du CNRS, 1982), pp. 721–36; reprinted in *Form and Order*, no. 2; "Signes et insignes du pouvoir au Moyen Age: Le témoignage des sceaux," *Comité des Travaux historiques et scientifiques. Section de philologie et d'histoire jusqu'en 1610. Actes du Cent Cinquième Congrès national des Sociétés Savantes* [Caen, 1980] (Paris: Editions du Comité des Travaux historiques et scientifiques, 1984), pp. 47–62; reprinted in *Form and Order*, no 1; "The Social Implications of the Art of Chivalry: The Sigillographic Evidence (France, 1050–1250)," *The Medieval Court in Europe*, ed. E. Haymes, *Houston German Studies* 6 (1986): 142–75, reprinted with revisions in *Form and Order*, no. 6; "Women, Seals and Power in Medieval France, 1150–1350," in *Women and Power in Medieval and Early Modern Europe*, ed. M. Erler and M. Kowaleski (Athens, Ga., and London: University of Georgia Press, 1988), pp. 61–82, reprinted in *Form and Order*, no. 9; "Seals and Sigillography, Western European," in *Dictionary of the Middle Ages*, vol. 11, ed. J. Strayer (New York: Scribner, 1988), pp. 123–31; "Medieval Seals and the Structure of Chivalric Society," in *The Study of Chivalry*, ed. Howell Chickering and T. Seiler (Kalamazoo, Mich.: TEAMS, Medieval Institute Publications, 1988), pp. 313–72; "Medieval Women in French Sigillographic Sources," in *Women and the Sources of Medieval History*, ed. Joel T. Rosenthal (Athens, Ga., and London: University of Georgia Press, 1990), pp. 1–36, reprinted in *Form and Order*, no. 10.

20. See Thierry, *Recueil des monuments* 4:28, on a sale made in 1250 in the presence of the *échevins* of Abbeville: "Ego Gauffridus Piffes, major, et scabini Abbatisville, notum facimus universis, quod constita in nostra presentia Emelardis Le Coutillière recognovit se vendidisse.... In cujus rei testimonium, presentibus litteris sigillum nostrum apposuimus."

21. See pp. 35–36 and note 48. Giry, *Manuel de diplomatique*, p. 852, quotes urban charters of customs as declaring explicitly that the testimonies of *échevins* were worth double those of ordinary witnesses.

22. In Cambrai, article 5 of the ordinance of 5 June 1382 reads: "[D]ésormais les lettres en ferme [ie. in city archives] vaillent à tous jours, comme recordées, soient li esquevin vivant ou non" (Sellier, *L'authentification des actes*, pp. 147–48). See an overview of the evolution of the urban record in Boüard, *Manuel de diplomatique*, pp. 233–36.

23. Monier, *Le livre Roisin,* p. 45 n. 62: [when the creditor has had his debt reimbursed, he] "doit rendre tantot l'aiuwe et la force d'esquevinage à chelui qui le debte li a paié" (Espinas, *La vie urbaine de Douai au moyen âge* 1:556–57).

24. See note 14 above; article 31 of the charter of Abbeville for "public" and "authentic." On the semantic blur surrounding the word *authenticus* in the Middle Ages, see Auguste Dumas, "Etudes sur le classement des formes des actes," *Le Moyen Age* 43 (1933): 81–97, 145–82, 251–64; *Le Moyen Age* 44 (1934): 17–41; see especially 43: 150–61 and 156 on the medieval association between authentic and public.

25. See diplomatic descriptions of chirographs in Giry, *Manuel de diplomatique,* pp. 851–52; Sellier, *L'authentification des actes,* pp. 63–70; Boüard, *Manuel de diplomatique,* pp. 236–41; Bautier, "L'authentification des actes privés," 743–44.

26. On the use of chirographs by churchmen and nobles, see Michel Parisse, "Remarques sur les chirographes et les chartes-parties antérieures à 1120 et conservées en France," *Archiv für Diplomatik* 32 (1986): 546–67. Fifty thousand urban chirographs from the thirteenth century onward are still extant in the city archives of Douai, as well as several thousands each in the city archives of Valenciennes and Abbeville (Bautier, "L'authentification des actes," p. 744). Article 4 of the 1352 charter of the town of Saint-Josse reads: "[E]t porra on par devant eulx [the *échevins*] passer et faire toutes obligations, acors, recognoissanches faites entre parties; et de ychelles feront chartres ou chirograffes, dont il tenront une des parties, et en bailleront à cascune partie autant se elles le requierent" (Thierry, *Recueil des monuments* 4:638). The urban chirograph remained in use through the second half of the fourteenth century. The later-developed system of registering deeds of title from which were issued as many originals as needed also involved the maintenance of these registers in urban archives. See mention of registers in the 1343 statute for the administration of Rue, article 3: "Item, que les escriptures des chartes de le dite ville et des autres coses seront faites à l'anchien usage, et y ara caier propres pour les chartes, et seront passées en plain eskevinage, et les chirographes recordées, et les chartes seelées; et y ara propre caier as causes, as mises et as recheptes, chascun a l'ordenanche, et un pour les plais, prochiés et arrés" (Thierry, *Recueil des monuments* 4:672).

27. Boüard, *Manuel de diplomatique,* pp. 238–41; Bautier, "L'authentification des actes privés," p. 739; Espinas, *La vie urbaine de Douai au moyen âge* 1:536; and Sellier, *L'authentification des actes,* p. 144, quoting an article from the customal of Cambrai: "Lettres en ferme [i.e., in city archives] sont mères en elles, faisantes plainte foy de ce qu'elles contiennent."

28. Giry, *Manuel de diplomatique,* p. 853; and Sellier, *L'authentification des actes,* pp. 74–75, 142–43. See note 31 below for further mentions of the use by towns of seals of jurisdiction (*sigilla ad causas, ad contractus, ad recognitiones*). Contracts were delivered by towns under their own seals of jurisdiction from the late thirteenth century onward (Bautier, "L'authentification des actes," pp. 745–47); such seals are described and discussed in Bedos [Rezak], *Sceaux de villes,* pp. 32–33, 40–41, 49–57, 69–72 ff. Although the urban seal of jurisdiction conferred full authenticity upon the act to which it was affixed, thus rendering obsolete the need for keeping a copy of the document for authentication, medieval towns maintained registers in which were entered the texts of the deeds they issued, and from which could be dispensed as many originals (*authentica*) as needed (Sellier, *L'authentification des actes,* pp. 76–78; and Giry, *Manuel de diplomatique,* p. 854).

According to the Customal of Mons: "Et sy est ordonné que toutes loix ayant ferme aueront ung seel en leur ferme ... pour seeler les chirograffes qu'ils recepvront, pour démonstration que la contre-partie soit en ferme" (quoted by Boüard, *Manuel de diplomatique,* p. 243 n. 2). The Customal of Mons (Belgium) was followed by French towns in Hainaut: Maubeuge, Avesnes, and Bavay. See Gilissen and Roggen, "Le problème du droit privé urbain," p. 234.

29. On this aspect of the urban chirograph, see the remarks by Sellier in *L'authentification des actes,* pp. 196–97.

30. Bautier, "L'authentification des actes," pp. 748–72, and "Origine et diffusion du

sceau de juridiction," *Comptes-rendus de l'Académie des inscriptions et belles-lettres,* 1971, pp. 304–21; and Sellier, *L'authentification des actes,* pp. 170–73, 178. Churchmen, still perceiving as a unity the control over divine scripture and bureaucratic writing, tried to maintain their scribal monopoly and to staff writing bureaus with clerics from their ranks. When, in the twelfth century, Flemish burghers attempted to organize their own schools, churchmen protested vigorously to the pope, requesting that he stop the classes that "laymen, prompted by their insolence, had dared to organize" (Henri Pirenne, "L'instruction des marchands au Moyen Age," *Annales: Economie, Société, Culture* 1[1929]: 13–28, at 24).

31. See cases of lordly permission granted to Saint-Omer and Saint-Quentin in Giry, *Manuel de diplomatique,* pp. 652, 853.

32. Boüard, *Manuel de diplomatique,* p. 244.

33. In Douai, the chest for privileges (*huge as privileges*) was distinguished from that of the chirographs (*sacs as eschievinages, liquelz sas reposera dans le haulte huge*) (Espinas, *La vie urbaine de Douai* 1:556). On the "religious" care that surrounded the preservation of the charter of Amiens, see Thierry, *Recueil des monuments* 1:180, 831–32.

34. "Marguerite, fille de roy de France ... scavoir faisons à tous, presens et avenir, que, comme les maieur et eschevins de nostre ville d'Aire se soient trais par devant nous et nous aient monstré comment leurs chartres, franchises et privileges ont esté arses et pillées par feu de fortune et de meschief, qui est avenu en la dite ville, et sur ce, nous aient supplié eulx pourveoir de remede convenable; et nous aions commis aucuns de nostre conseil pour veoir et pour soy informer de et sur les dites chartres et privileges et de l'usage accoustumé comment il en avoient usé paravant la fortune dudit feu ... nous de notre grace especiale, en consideration a ce que dit est, avons ottroié et ottroions aux dis maieur, et eschevins et communauté de nostre dite ville que, nonobstant qu'ils ne facent foy de leurs dites chartres et privileges perdues par le dit feu, comme dit est, il aient et avoir puissent, jouir et user à plein, sans aucun contredit, des usages, privileges ... ci apres déclairiés" (Espinas, *Recueil des documents* 1, no. 44:90–92, 1374).

In 1253–54, Mahaut of Artois, countess of Boulogne, issued a charter confirming the privileges of the city of Marck, which had lost its charter during the war: "Desqueles loi et desqueles coustumes il perdirent leur chartre par l'ost de Flandres." (On the survival of the allegedly destroyed charter, see Espinas, *Recueil des documents* 1:90 n. 1.) On the back of the newly delivered charter, there is the following note: "[V]enredi devant la Magdalaine, baillierent li eschevin de Merc cest escrit et reconnurent par devant les hommes Mgr d'Artois que c'estoit li transcris de leur chartre mot à mot, ensi comme il est contenu en leur chartre scelée." So the townspeople of Marck had a copy of the original charter that had been destroyed, against which they could check the new charter, and yet desired the issue of a physically, not textually, new charter (Espinas, *Recueil des documents* 3:138–48).

35. Thierry, *Recueil des monuments* 1:37–38: the burgesses of Abbeville had bought the right to become a commune from a count of Ponthieu, for which they had no charter. A successor to this count, John, count of Ponthieu, granted them permission in writing to have their commune. Espinas, *Recueil des documents* 2:252 (ca. 1275): the *échevins* of Beuvry got a written confirmation of their liberties from the count of Artois, on the basis of the immemorial standing of these liberties: "Ce sont les coustumes et li usage de le vile de Buevry de si lonc k'il puet souvenir."

36. Oath sworn by the échevins of Béthune (between 1325 and 1350): "S'enssieut le serment que les eschevins font chacun an à l'église à leur creacion: Vous jures à warder les drois de Dieu et de sainte Eglise, les drois de Mgr., vesves femmes, orphelines, chartres, previlleges, us et coutumes de la ville de Bethune" (Espinas, *Recueil des documents* 2:105–6 n. 302).

37. See note 40 below. One of these customs is the use of the great seal, which belatedly became a constitutional element of the commune, although its use was never spelled out in charters of privileges. On this point see the following articles by Bedos [Rezak]: *Les Sceaux des villes,* p. 15; "The Town on French Medieval Seals: Representation and Signifi-

cation," in *Town Life and Culture in the Middle Ages and Renaissance: Essays in Memory of J. K. Hyde,* ed. Brian Pullan and Susan Reynolds, *Bulletin of the John Rylands Library of Manchester* 72 (1990): 35–48, reprinted in *Form and Order,* no. 12; and "Les types des plus anciens sceaux des communautés urbaines du Nord," in *Les chartes et le mouvement communal* (Saint-Quentin: Société académique de Saint-Quentin, 1982), pp. 39–50, at pp. 41–42. On urban customals, see Gilissen, "Les villes en Belgique," p. 578; and Monier, *Le livre Roisin,* passim. The town of Amiens, in 1317, asked the king of France to clarify some points in its charter, adding some and suppressing others. Yet when comparing the new charter to the old one, the changes are trivial and formulaic rather than affecting content. See text of the 1317 charter in Thierry, *Recueil des monuments* 1:375–77.

38. For instance, the charter of Abbeville was granted to many towns in Ponthieu; see note 15 above. The charter of Saint-Quentin was granted to Gamaches, Airaines, Domart, and Bernaville (Thierry, *Recueil des monuments* 4:695, 730, 733, 736).

39. An express request that guild ordinances be put in writing is not found in every written ordinance, and therefore may not have been a formulaic preamble. For instance, in Amiens, the coopers (in 1286: "et ce sont ces coses faictes et ordonnées à la requeste des cuveliers d'Amiens, en le voulenté et ou rappel des maieur et eschevins d'Amiens"), the weavers (in 1308), the furriers (in 1348), and so on, requested their ordinances (Thierry, *Recueil des monuments* 1:253, 338, 348), while the butchers in 1282 (ibid. 1:242) received their statutes from the mayor and *échevins* of Amiens.

The reading of ordinances to new guild leaders is explicit in this text: "Et que li maieur que on establira de le bannière devantdicte [the guild of the furriers] doivent oyr lire cest escript [the ordinance] chacun an à l'entrée de leur mairie, en le présence de leurs compagnons, pour ce que chacun soit introduit de mener et soustenir à droit le mestier de le banière devantdicte" (ibid. 1:349).

40. Monier, *Le livre Roisin,* p. 84: In the customal of Lille, article no. 127 makes provision for the case where the count of Flanders would not be in Lille at the required time to renew the body of *échevins* according to the terms of the charter, "si que li cartre parolle." In article 57 of the charter of Marck, town officials are allowed, when rendering judgment, to delay their decision for up to two weeks in order to consult the charter: "[E]t de toutes ches causes kin sunt escrites en cheste chartre, li esquevin et li korman, quant il doivent faire jugement, se il ne sunt bien conceillié, il doivent avoir terme, s'il voellent, de conseillier soi desi qu'à quinse jors dusc'à tant qu'il aient veu cheste chartre" (Espinas, *Recueil des documents* 3:148). In 1225, the conditions for a peace treaty between the bishop and the city of Cambrai included that each party would bring its charters to court: "Dendroit le conte de que li vesques Godefrois et si ancisseur ki devant lui ont este ont qui cartres et privileges des rois et de empereurs d'Alemaigne et dendroit les cartres et les privileges anchiens ke li vile a des empereurs et des rois d'Alemaigne, est tele li concenance kon les portera et les uns et les autres u les transscris saieles ... en le cort d'Alemaigne et ce que li cors dira par jugement li queil doivent valoir et estre estaule" (M. Gysseling, "Les plus anciens textes français non littéraires en Belgique et dans le nord de la France," *Scriptorium* 3 (1949): 190–210, at 208). Thierry, *Recueil des monuments* 1:259: In 1288, the *échevins* of Amiens defended their rights in Parlement against the usurpations of royal officials with reference to the tenets of their charter: "[C]um major et scabini ville Ambianensis dicerent in nostra curia quod ad eos pertinebat cognicio assecuramentorum ... per quedam puncta carte sue." See other examples of references to *lettres anchiennes* in ibid. 1:351–52; 4:75.

On the translation of charters from Latin into French, see Thierry, *Recueil des monuments* 1:181. The communal charter of Amiens, granted in confirmation of earlier urban customs by King Philip Augustus in 1190 (ibid. 1:104–14), was translated as early as 1209. Several such medieval translations are still extant in the city registers that were kept in the archives at the town hall. Ibid. 1:71: in the fourteenth century the town of Amiens had a translation made of a twelfth-century charter to make it intelligible to all. This charter (ibid. 1:74–86) enunciated the rights of the count of Flanders and of three other lords of Amiens over the city. These rights came to be exercised by the town in the thirteenth century and were considered as part of its customs, important enough to be made available in the vernacular. Yet the communal charter was not altered to include them.

41. On the early appearance of the vernacular in urban deeds, see Bautier, "L'authentification des actes privés," p. 747; Giry, *Manuel de diplomatique,* pp. 467–68, 851; Gysseling, "Les plus anciens textes français," pp. 195 (text of the Douai chirograph), 196–97, 199, 201, 204, 206–7; and Jacques Monfrin, "L'emploi de la langue vulgaire dans les actes diplomatiques du temps de Philippe Auguste," in *La France de Philippe Auguste,* ed. Bautier, pp. 785–90, at pp. 787–88. See note 40 above, on the translations into the vernacular of urban charters of privileges.

42. See note 40 above, article 57 of the charter of Marck, in which the *échevins* are expected to consult the terms of the charter before rendering judgment. A 1349 ordinance of Amiens about the wages of the tanners concludes: "Qui icelle ordenance accordèrent et conseillèrent à estre publiée devant Saint-Martin-aux-Waides et ou marquié, lequelle ordenance fu publiée le [xx]ii jour de septembre an ccc xlil" (Thierry, *Recueil des monuments* 1:547). Article 17 of a 1343 ordinance regulating the administration of Rue reads: "[E]t seront les lettres du corps de le ville coppiées en un livre bien appareillés, qui sera wardés du maieur et des eskevins, et par quoy ils les verront toutes fois que il leur plaira et sans dangier de clerc" (Thierry, *Recueil des monuments* 4:674). Among the accounts of Abbeville are expenses for the wages of minstrels who sang and read their *roumans* and who went to school in Soissons (ibid. 4:228–29).

43. On notes written on the back of chirographs to enable their consultation, see Sellier, *L'authentification des actes,* p. 69. On the certificates of bourgeoisie, see Espinas, *La vie urbaine de Douai* 1:393. See French texts for the oaths of *échevins* in Espinas, *Recueil des documents* 2:565–73. The *échevins* of Arras, upon undertaking their new functions, had first to swear an oath in the church of the "Magdelaine," and then go to the town hall where they would have the statutes read and shown to them, and after hearing them, they would swear to keep their tenets: "[S]itost que esquevin seront revenu en hale dudit serment de le Magdelaine, premiers et avant toute oevre, ces presentes lettres soyent lieutes et exposées ... presens les dis esquevins et les vint quatre, qui pour le tamps seront. Et ycelles lieutes et par euls oyes, seront tenu li dit esquevin, et cascuns par lui, de jurer et promettre à tenir et à warder" (ibid. 1:363).

44. In late thirteenth-century Hénin-Liétard, the *échevins* swore that the names of those who went against the laws of the city would be put in writing, and then declaimed out loud, "[E]t si vous dit on ke tout cil ki refuseront le loi de le vile par devant vous, ke vous les mets en escrit, et les faites crier en vo eskievinage ke il ont refusé le loi de le vile, et k'il ne sunt mie bourgois ne puent jamais estre" (Espinas, *Recueil des documents* 2:569).

45. "Quiconques voelt avoir record [de] debte dont il a aiiuwe d'eschevins, il doit s'aiuwe faire lire devant eschevins, et quant liute sera, li siergeans qui presens sera, doit dire à eschevins: 'a il bien s'aiuwe?' Et eschevin diront: 'Oil, il a bien s'aiuwe ... Faites li le sien avoir, si avant que se chirographe ou ceste lettre parole'" (Monier, *Le livre Roisin,* art. no. 63, p. 46).

46. See an extensive description of this procedure, such as it was followed in Lille, in Monier, *Le livre Roisin,* pp. 44–45, 55.

47. For fiscal matters, see Jean Lestocquoi, *Les villes de Flandre et d'Italie sous le gouvernement des patriciens, XIe–XVe siècles* (Paris: Presses universitaires de France, 1952), p. 191.

In juridical matters, see Thierry, *Recueil des monuments* 4:112. A mayor of Abbeville (in 1315 and 1319) had to justify his financial management of the town, and could do it either by letters or witnesses (*par lettres ou par témoins*). The 1343 ordinance of Lille that stipulates that the *échevins* may not receive a written procedural document bearing the parties' grievances starts with these words: "Comme de tamps passé, on ait accoustumé à plaidier en le halle de Lille, de bouche et non par escript, et non obstant che, aucunes parties qui y ont plaidiet, se sont efforchiet de aporter une escripture de leur plaidoierie qu'il apiellent intendit." (Monier, *Le livre Roisin,* p. 48). See Thierry, *Recueil des monuments* 1:447, 452, 799–800, on late fourteenth-century urban ordinances of Amiens on the validity of the chirographs. The writing of judgments to prevent their lapse into oblivion was prescribed in article 19 of the 1184 charter of Abbeville (ibid. 4:11: "[E]t ne quod judicatum oblivioni tradatur, autentice scripture commendabitur").

48. See pp. 36–38. Thierry, *Recueil des monuments* 4:27: In a 1237 agreement between Simon, count of Ponthieu and the town of Abbeville, the testimony of the *échevins,* verbal or written (*ore vel litteris*), is deemed sufficient to assure the validity of the transactions made or renewed in their presence. In Colmar, if one of the two *échevins* who had witnessed a transaction was dead, and if the surviving one was called to testify, he would do so on the tomb of his dead colleague, under oath (Sellier, *L'authentification des actes,* p. 148). The testimony of the *échevins* was enough to entail the writing of a transaction long after it had been accomplished; see examples of such documents in Gysseling, "Les plus anciens textes français," pp. 201, 207. In some cases the *échevins* could issue the written transaction of a dead party, as long as they had witnessed it (Sellier, *L'authentification des actes,* p. 62).

49. See notes 17 and 36 above. See the remarks of Paul Ourliac, "Coutume et mémoire: Les coutumes françaises au XIIIe siècle," in *Jeux de mémoire: aspects de la mnémotechnie médiévale,* ed. Bruno Roy and Paul Zumthor (Montreal: Presses de l'Université de Montréal, 1985), pp. 111–22, at p. 118, on the fact that to invoke memory for what is immemorial is not illogical.

50. See notes 14 and 47 above. On memory as the basis for customs, see Ourliac, "Coutume et mémoire," pp. 111–22.

51. The names of the *échevins* were usually in a different handwriting: see Monique Mestayer, "Les contrats de mariage à Douai du XIIIe au XVe siècle," *Revue du Nord* 61 (1979): 353–80, at 375, who deduced from this that initially the interested parties took charge of the writing of their deeds. See same conclusions in Espinas, *La vie urbaine de Douai* 1: 535; Gilissen, "Les villes en Belgique," p. 592; and Sellier, *L'authentification des actes,* p. 39.

52. Boüard, *Manuel de diplomatique,* p. 235.

53. On town clerks, see Espinas, *La vie urbaine de Douai* 1:857, and Boüard, *Manuel de diplomatique,* p. 235, with additional bibliography. Little is known about town clerks, about their origins and education. They produced documents that, unlike those of ecclesiastics, were unaffected by classical law (see Gilissen and Roggen, "Le problème du droit privé urbain," p. 276).

54. "Jehans de Hollaing du tout a tenir et a remplir bien et loyalment et par le foy de sen corps ad ce mise et fianche corporelment es mains des eschievins chi desous nommés de non aller ou faire venir contre les coses et convenences desseured" (Mestayer, "Les contrats de mariage à Douai," p. 371).

55. The two spouses "comparent devant deux échevins et recognoissent l'amour de mariage qu'ils ont l'un pour l'autre, et en iceluy demonstrant, la femme va baiser son mary en la présence desdits échevins" (Sellier, *L'authentification des actes,* p. 115).

56. Sellier, *L'authentification des actes,* p. 121.

57. Those who want to have their deeds sealed must come to "le hale pardevant ii eskevins ki i seront chascun jour, et aporchent leur chirographes de leur connissanches escrites et endentées si ke li partie deseure demoura a le hale, et l'autre partie ara une keuwe ki sera seelée du seel des counissanches ki fait est propre a che hues" (Giry, *Manuel de diplomatique,* p. 853).

58. See an example of such an instance in Espinas, *La vie urbaine de Douai* 3, art. no. 295, p. 242 (ca. 1250): "Sacent tout que Engherrans Brussamons aporta en le hale un cyrographe qui parloit...."

59. "Tota eciam testis est Abbatisvilla, quia factum est in conspectu et populi tocius audientia" (Thierry, *Recueil des monuments* 4: 14).

60. On the fact that the urban world put a premium on visual recognition, see Louis Wirth, "Urbanism as a Way of Life," in *Classic Essays on the Culture of Cities*, ed. Sennett, pp. 143–64, at p. 155. In 1350, Lille issued an ordinance forbidding any burgess bearing the livery of a lord to become an *échevin* while in the lord's livery (Monier, *Le livre Roisin*, p. 124). Expenses for the liveries and banners of the city of Amiens are reported in a 1389 account (Thierry, *Recueil des monuments* 1:775); for the liveries of Abbeville, see the 1365 account in ibid. 4:158.

61. Thierry, *Recueil des monuments* 4:705.

62. On this point, see Bedos-Rezak, *Sceaux des villes*, pp. 13–20; "Les types les plus anciens," pp. 41–42; and "Town on French Medieval Seals," passim. For rules governing the use of urban seals, see Espinas, *Recueil des documents* 3:149–50; Monier, *Le livre Roisin*, art. no. 57, p. 43; and Sellier, *L'authentification des actes*, pp. 86–87.

63. A. Guesnon, *Sigillographie de la ville d'Arras et de la cité* (Arras: Topino, Libraire, et Paris: Durand, Libraire, 1865), p. 35 n. 6.

64. See seal entry in urban registers in Thierry, *Recueil des monuments* 1:509; and Espinas, *La vie urbaine de Douai* 1:915, 926; see 3:17 no. 23 (1225) and 3:20 no. 27 (ca. 1225), the texts of documents sealed with the great seal of the city and given in the name of *nos scabini totaque communitas ville Douaci*. In Arras, too, the affixing of the great seal required the assembly of the town (Guesnon, *Sigillographie de la ville d'Arras*, p. 36). In Amiens, also, the city charters sealed with the great seal were given in the name of *scabini et tota communitas civitatis Ambianensis* (Thierry, *Recueil des monuments* 1:302–3, 316–17, 396–404).

65. See mention of bells with reference to urban audiences in Thierry, *Recueil des monuments* 1:445, 448, 456.

66. Sellier, *L'authentification des actes*, pp. 51–55; Anne Lombard-Jourdan, "Du problème de la continuité: Y-a-t-il eu une protohistoire urbaine en France," *Annales: Economies, Sociétés, Civilisations* 25 (1970): 1121–42, at 1134; Louis Carolus-Barré, *Les plus anciennes chartes en langue française, t. I: Problèmes généraux et recueil des pièces originales conservées aux Archives de l'Oise* (Paris: Librairie Klincksieck, 1964), p.71 and charter no. 61, p. 69; and Espinas, *La vie urbaine de Douai* 3, no. 22: 17.

67. Lombard-Jourdan, "Du problème de la continuité," p. 1136; M. J. Thiebaut, "Beffrois, halles et hôtels de ville dans de nord de la France et l'actuelle Belgique, au Moyen Age," *Les chartes et le mouvement communal*, pp. 51–57, at pp. 51–52. On the fountain Au Cange in Lille, see Monier, *Le livre Roisin*, pp. 156–57 and passim; and Arnold van Gennep, *Le folklore de la Flandre et de Hainault, département du Nord*, 2 vols. (Paris: Maisonneuve, 1935–36), 2:446–47. By the thirteenth century, judgments and writings must be made "en pleine halle."

68. Le Goff, "The Town as Agent of Civilization," p. 80. Some city seals show a banner with an animal floating atop the city hall (see Bedos [Rezak], *Sceaux des villes*, index *sub* "bannière," p. 539). No substantial work is available on medieval urban banners and bestiary; see, however, the suggestive remarks of Michel Pastoureau, "Du vague des drapeaux," *Le genre humain* 20 (1989): 119–34.

69. Thierry, *Recueil des monuments* 4:33: [The charter is given in the name of the count of Ponthieu:] "et se il convenoit ke aucune de leurs chartres fust monstrée dedens les murs d'Abevile, les devons aler veir sans hors porter."

70. Thierry, *Recueil des monuments* 4:679.

71. In late Rome, the archives, *gesta municipalia*, had also characterized the city, which may partially explain why the medieval jurists, newly acquainted with Roman law and struck by this analogy between medieval and imperial cities, associated urban status with the maintenance of archives (Sellier, *L'authentification des actes*, p. 197).

CHAPTER 3

La grant feste
Philip the Fair's Celebration of the Knighting of His Sons in Paris at Pentecost of 1313

Elizabeth A. R. Brown and Nancy Freeman Regalado

One of the most striking medieval urban celebrations was held in Paris at Pentecost 1313 to celebrate the knighting of Philip the Fair's three sons on 3 June 1313 and the assumption of the Cross three days later.[1] Never, the chroniclers proclaimed, had such a *feste* been seen in France; it rivaled the fabled feast of Ahasuerus.[2] Yet, although this *feste* is one of the most splendid, most fully developed, and best described of any held in the Middle Ages, it has not received the scrutiny it merits.

The *feste* was an extended spectacle where great crowds of spectators saw large-scale public performances in which participants staged grandly impressive acts: the crusading ceremonies and public processions of royalty, nobles, and city dwellers.[3] Within this spectacle were festivities where participation was restricted and selective: the knighting ceremony, princely banquets, and craft feasts. It also contained musical performances and theatrical entertainments that everyone could see and hear in the streets of Paris; these included dramatic tableaux where actors represented scenes from the Bible and popular tales. Taken all together, the festivity, performances, and dramatic scenes constituted a celebration that engaged every level of the Parisian population, at times as actors, at others as spectators. Music, costumes, decorations, lights, feasting, processions, and ceremonial gestures and words exalted the participants and made them impressive to spectators. These elements dramatized the values that underlay the royal, aristocratic, or bourgeois ceremonies and festivities. Organized by the king, the celebration of knighting and crusading vows may be read as an elaborate spectacle whose purposes were political and personal and whose lavishness displayed kingly largesse and royal power. On the other hand, the costly grandeur of street decorations, costumes, and entertainments provided by the Parisians staged their independent role within the body politic. The display of urban wealth and splendor dramatized the aspirations and power of the bourgeois while the tableaux they sponsored offered counsel intended to maintain the political and spiritual health of Philip's reign. Spectacle thus joined king and city in a festive experience of *communitas*.

Before 1313 numerous splendid festivities had celebrated knightings and other solemn occasions. The knighting of Frederick Barbarossa's sons at Mainz on Pentecost in 1184 was a wondrous ceremony that inspired chroniclers and poets[4]—and perhaps Philip Augustus, whose son Louis (VIII) was splendidly knighted at Compiègne on Pentecost in 1209.[5] Lavish display marked similar ceremonies for Louis IX's brothers, Robert of Artois at Compiègne on the octaves of Pentecost in 1237 and Alfonse of Poitiers at Saumur on the Feast of Saint John the Baptist in 1241. When Louis IX knighted his eldest son Philip (Philip the Fair's father), his nephew Robert of Artois, and sixty-seven other young men on Pentecost in 1267, prelates and barons from most of France gathered in Paris, which was marvelously decorated with multicolored hangings and precious ornaments. The celebration lasted for more than a week and was marked by a royal pilgrimage to Saint-Denis and the preaching of the Cross on the Ile-Notre-Dame.[6] This *feste* resembled in many ways the jubilee that accompanied the coronation of Marie of Brabant, second wife of Philip III, on the Feast of Saint John the Baptist in 1275.[7] Again the congregation of magnates, again the splendid display of garments and jewels, again week-long rejoicing in Paris, where, a chronicler says, the bourgeois "firent feste grant et sollempnel." In the spring of 1301, when Philip the Fair made a grand tour of Flanders, the people of Ghent marched forth to meet him, dressed in new clothes, the most important people in different costumes that reflected their hostile division; they presented the king with rich gifts and, most important, performed various entertainments (*ludos diversos*) and jousts (*hastiludia*), on which 27,000 *l.* were spent. Similar festivities greeted the king in the different places that he visited, and the Annals of Ghent report the dissension that arose in Bruges over payment for expenses.[8] Just seven years before Philip the Fair's *feste*, Edward I of England held the fabulous Feast of the Swans at Westminster to honor the knighting of his son and namesake, Edward (II). At Pentecost of 1306 some three hundred men, including the mayor of London, were knighted with Edward and feasted at a great banquet attended by the Patriarch of Jerusalem. There oaths were taken on swans to conquer Scotland, and the king is said to have pledged never thereafter to bear arms against Christians, but to depart forever for the Holy Land.[9]

The *grant feste* of 1313 was thus hardly the first of its kind. Nor was this the first time an observer had termed such a celebration the greatest ever held in France or elsewhere; similar observations had been made of the festivities of 1184, 1267, and 1275—and indeed of a reception that Robert of Artois gave for Philip III at Arras in 1271.[10] What distinguishes the Parisian *feste* of 1313 most sharply from earlier occasions is the richness and variety of the documentation that survives, particularly concerning the urban festivities.

In almost every case the records for 1313 are fuller and more abundant than those available for the earlier celebrations. Most extraordinary are two unusual eyewitness sources. Five illuminations and six informative captions depict and comment on the week's events. These appear as the preamble to a Latin translation of a Spanish collection of animal fables called *Dimna et Kalila,* which the physician Raymond of Béziers began for Philip the Fair's wife Jeanne, completed on Pentecost in 1313, dedicated to Philip the Fair, and presented to the king later in the year.[11] These illuminations and captions represent the perspective of privileged insiders who witnessed the knighting and crusading ceremonies. Even more unusual is a long, detailed account of the festivities that was included in an anonymous metrical chronicle written by a Parisian clerk. The chronicle commences in 1300, although the author seems to have written it between 1313 and early 1317; the single copy that survives in Paris, Bibliothèque nationale, Ms. fr. 146, stops abruptly in the autumn of 1316, and the manuscript that contains the work was created shortly thereafter, probably in 1317.[12] Those involved in the production of the manuscript knew the king and his court; its format bespeaks its origin in the royal chancery. This makes the chronicle's treatment of Philip the Fair's *feste* particularly valuable. The chronicler was a cleric linked to the royal chancery and sympathetic to the bourgeois of Paris. He had seen the events he reports; events he did not witness find no place in his account. His perspective is that of a spectator in the streets: he offers no descriptions of indoor ceremonies or banquets except a peek through the flaps of the tents sheltering Edward II's feast at Saint-Germain-des-Prés. What he relates is recorded in unprecedentedly rich detail in a passage of 429 lines, more than a third of which (166 lines) describe the festive contributions made by the Parisians. Beside this account those in other chronicles, contemporary and later, pale in importance, although they provide details that the metrical chronicle does not mention.[13] Many years would pass before other chroniclers would record in equal detail the civic celebrations that accompanied solemn royal ceremonies.

The Pentecost *feste* of 1313 marked the brilliant zenith of Philip the Fair's reign (1285–1314). The rapid succession of unhappy events that preceded Philip's death a year and a half later, on 29 November 1314, stand out against the great celebration in somber relief: the execution of Jacques de Molay, Grand Master of the Templars, and the Templar Master of Normandy on the small island in the Seine near the royal palace on 18 March 1314; the revelation of the adultery scandal that led to the imprisonment of the king's three daughters-in-law in April 1314; the death of Pope Clement V on 20 April; the conclusion of inglorious truces with the Flemings in July 1313 and September 1314; the formation of noble alliances to protest royal policies in November 1314.[14] Fortune's wheel turned as surely toward misfortune for the king of France as it did for his powerful minister, Enguerran de Marigny, who was widely credited with the construction of the king's great palace on the

Ile-de-la-Cité and who helped prepare the *feste* that glorified it, but who was disgraced and hanged, decried as a crafty Renart, on 30 April 1315, just five months after his master's death.[15] These sad events lay in the future, however, when a host of people gathered in Paris in June 1313 to participate in Philip the Fair's festivities, presided over by a trio of kings (Philip himself; his son and twenty-three-year-old heir Louis, king of Navarre since his mother's death in 1305; and Philip's son-in-law, twenty-nine-year-old Edward II of England) and by Pope Clement V's emissary, Cardinal Nicolas de Fréauville, cousin of Enguerran de Marigny and Philip the Fair's former confessor.[16]

The *feste* lasted a full eight days (see Table 3.1). It was solemnly inaugurated at the cathedral of Notre-Dame on Pentecost, 3 June, a feast day traditionally considered particularly appropriate for knighting.[17] The celebrations had begun the day before, however, when Philip the Fair's daughter Isabelle and her husband Edward II entered Paris. Philip the Fair had long pressed the couple to attend the festivities, offering Edward the prospect of grace and favor regarding the duchy of Guyenne, which the English king held of Philip.[18] The couple had left Dover at sunrise on 23 May, accompanied by a host of English nobles and ecclesiastics,[19] and leaving behind them a realm torn by strife between the nobles and the king and threatened by the Scots.[20]

Doubtless progressing along the *grant rue de Paris* that led from Saint-Denis to Paris, Edward and Isabelle entered the city on 2 June, the vigil of Pentecost.[21] There, as one chronicler reports, they were received with solemnity and joy as "the whole city rose up and went forth to meet them."[22] Later in the day they surely dined at a banquet given by Philip the Fair.[23] Philip showered them with bounty—more (perhaps considerably more) than 2000 *l. par.* worth of supplies for their stay and for the feast that Edward was to provide the next week. The French king gave them 94 oxen, 189 pigs, 380 rams, 200 pike, 40 quarrels, 160 carp, and 80 barrels of wine; nothing was stinted.[24] And when Edward required money, he found it easily available. Enguerran de Marigny lent him 15,000 *l. st.* sometime during his stay in France, and Philip the Fair lent 33,000 *l.* more in June. This brought relief to a needy monarch, who had had to borrow heavily at home to cover the expenses of the trip.[25] Repayment would prove burdensome, but for the moment he was able to comport himself as befitted a king of England.

After Philip the Fair's banquet, the young men who were to be knighted doubtless gathered at Notre-Dame to confess and spend the night fasting and praying. The evidence that survives suggests that the ceremonies at the cathedral followed the traditional form outlined some forty years earlier in Ramon Llull's *Order of Knighthood*.[26] Thus on Sunday, before the ceremony, they would have heard mass and then a sermon setting forth the twelve articles of faith, the ten commandments, and the seven sacraments. Before being knighted they would have knelt

TABLE 3.1. *La grant feste* of 1313 (events and activities recorded in the metrical chronicle of BN, Ms. fr. 146, with additions, in italics, from other sources)

Saturday, 2 June	*Parisians march out to meet Edward II of England and Isabelle* (SCR) Banquet offered by Philip the Fair
Sunday, 3 June (Pentecost)	Ceremony of knighting Banquet given by Philip the Fair
Monday, 4 June	Banquet offered by Louis, king of Navarre Construction of bridge from the Ile-de-la-Cité to the Ile-Notre-Dame
Tuesday, 5 June	Midday banquet in tents given by Edward II at *Saint-Germain-des-Prés* (JSV) Feast offered to the ladies at the Louvre by Philip the Fair Construction of bridge completed
Wednesday, 6 June	Rain and wind in the morning Processions across the bridge to the Ile-Notre-Dame Assumption of the Cross after noon by nobles, religious, and others on the Ile-Notre-Dame (CGN, RB) Banquet offered by Louis of Evreux, half-brother of Philip the Fair
Thursday, 7 June	Edward II and Isabelle oversleep *Nobles ladies take the Cross* (JSV) *Edward II makes an offering in the Sainte-Chapelle* (PRO, fol. 3v) Crafts, bourgeois, *and all the people of Paris* (RB) parade *from the Ile-Notre-Dame through the cloister of Notre-Dame to the palace to be viewed by the three kings* (JSV, RB) Banquet offered by Charles of Valois, brother of Philip the Fair Crafts and bourgeois parade *in the evening* (JSV) after dinner to the *Pré-aux-Clercs* (GC) and Saint-Germain-des-Prés Crafts feast individually Street festivities through the night
Friday–Sunday, 8–10 June	Parisian "luminaire" begins on Friday and continues for three nights
Saturday, 9 June	*Queen Isabelle takes the Cross* (PRP)
Duration unspecified (includes Wednesday and Thursday)	"mainte faërie" (dramatic tableaux and entertainments)

Date unspecified	March of the Great Watch, 800 men clad in livery
Date unspecified (three days)	Fountain with wine and "maintes fictions" (imaginary scenes and figures)
Continuously, by day and night	Music, food, and drink; streets crowded with richly clad nobles and bourgeois, and crafts in livery; streets hung with brightly colored drapery

Related Events

After Trinity Sunday, 10 June	Royal entertainment at Pontoise; *minstrel Bernard le Fol and 54 naked dancers perform on 19 June* (PRO, fol. 30r)
	Fire in the quarters of Edward and Isabelle at Pontoise, forcing the couple to flee in their nightclothes
Friday, 15 June	*Possible tournament held at Compiègne* (CR)

Key to Additional Sources
CGN: Continuation of the Universal Chronicle of Guillaume de Nangis, ed. Géraud 1:396
CR: *Comptes royaux,*ed. Fawtier and Maillard, no. 27687
GC: *Grandes Chroniques,* ed. Viard, 9:287–90
JSV: Chronicle of Jean of Saint-Victor, in *Recueil des historiens* 21:656–57
PRO: PRO, E 101/375/8
PRP: PRO, E 30/1422
RB: Raymond of Béziers, *Dimna et Kalila* (BN, Ms. lat. 8504, fols. Bv–1r)
SCR: Chronicle of Saint-Catherine-du-Mont of Rouen, in *Recueil des historiens* 23:408–9

before the altar. A miniature in *Dimna et Kalila* shows Louis, the first to be knighted, with hands lifted to heaven, being belted by Edward of England in the rite described by Llull. It also shows Philip the Fair giving his son the ceremonial slap that Llull says followed a ritual kiss; the blow, according to Llull, ensured that the young knight would remember the signal honor he had received. After he had been belted, another illustration demonstrates, Louis of Navarre joined Edward II and Philip the Fair in belting other aspirants, who numbered almost two hundred. They included Louis's brothers Philip and Charles; their cousin Philip (the future Philip VI), son of Philip the Fair's brother Charles of Valois; Robert of Artois, whose lawful heritage, the county of Burgundy, had passed to France as the dowry of his sister Jeanne, married to Prince Philip; and the half-brother and son of Enguerran de Marigny.

All who were knighted received splendid testimony of Philip the Fair's largesse.[27] The gifts traditionally bestowed by the lord who knighted[28] were exceedingly lavish in 1313; the king spent more than 32,000 *l. par.* on horses for the new knights. Most were given a horse and a palfrey, some a single mount, a few money with which steeds could be purchased. Gilded reins went to fifty knights; white reins were distributed to others. Token stipends (*vadia*) were disbursed, 10 *l. par.* to the king's sons and 5 *l. par.* to the others. Although full records of other special expenses have not survived, the king in all likelihood gave the new knights robes and perhaps ceremonial beds for their vigil, gifts that his forebears had bestowed at earlier royal knightings.

After the ceremony, Llull said, the new *chevaliers* should ride through the city and display themselves, to impress upon them the shame they would attract if they failed to keep their vows. So too Llull thought that the occasion should be celebrated with great feasts and dinners, and with jousting and sports.[29] Philip the Fair perhaps deemed tourneying, long decried by the church, incompatible with the ceremony he had ordained; on 28 December 1312 he had reiterated an earlier prohibition against jousts, tournaments, and other passages of arms, outlawed until the Feast of Saint Remi because of the rites that he intended for Pentecost.[30] Yet a fifteenth-century chronicler recorded that in 1313 the king "held jousts and tournaments to make his *feste* more excellent."[31] The author probably invented this detail, for aside from the tournament of children depicted in one of the tableaux mounted by the Parisians for the *feste*, no feats of arms were celebrated in or near the city during Pentecost week, although a tournament was perhaps planned for Compiègne in mid-June.[32]

There may have been no tournaments or jousting, but the new knights were royally feasted, and on many occasions during the week they displayed themselves, magnificently attired in garb that they often changed. A grand company of French magnates was present; their names form a litany in the metrical chronicle, which includes not only those who attended the ceremonies but also some of the most important young men who were knighted. Of the assemblage the chronicler wrote, "Even if one counted in French and in Latin, from night to day, one could not give the sum of all the nobles."[33] Robert of Béthune, count of Flanders, and his son Louis, count of Nevers and Rethel, were conspicuous by their absence, understandable in view of the conflict between Flanders and France that would shortly erupt; the metrical chronicle says that the count of Flanders did not dare to come because of the power of the king of France.[34]

On Sunday after the ceremony at Notre-Dame, Philip the Fair entertained his guests, perhaps, as a late chronicler said, presiding at table wearing the royal diadem.[35] On Monday Louis of Navarre gave a banquet, thus assuming precedence over his brother-in-law Edward of England, whose feast took place the next day.[36]

The lavish banquet that Edward offered was held at high noon at Saint-Germain-des-Prés, where he and Isabelle were lodged.[37] It was a stunning occasion. Tents hung with rich cloths were open for all to view. Even in broad daylight, lights and torches burned in abundance, a grand display of regal wealth.[38] The guests were served by attendants on horseback, and other amusement was provided. The reward of 20 *s.* that

William Craddock, crowder and singer, received on 6 June for making minstrelsy before Edward II was surely given to him for his performance the day before at Edward's feast.[39] A castle of love (*castrum amorosum*), constructed by the armorer of Louis of Navarre for 100 *s.*, was a chief attraction, perhaps used to provide entertainment between the courses of the meal.[40] Philip the Fair gave a feast for his daughter Isabelle and his daughter-in-law Marguerite, queen of Navarre, both splendid in their crowns, and the other ladies at the Louvre.[41]

On Wednesday morning Paris was struck by rains and wind; the prescient might have seen in this a sign of divine skepticism regarding the ceremony that was soon to occur, the second capstone of the week's festivities. But the storm moved on, and the ritual assumption of the Cross took place as planned. On Monday and Tuesday the Parisians had constructed a huge bridge of planks, balanced on boats, 160 feet long and 40 feet wide, to link the Ile-de-la-Cité and the Ile-Notre-Dame, a marshy expanse that belonged to the cathedral chapter of Paris and that was under the bishop's jurisdiction.[42] On Wednesday afternoon, royalty, new knights, nobles, and bourgeois thronged the bridge as they assembled on the Ile-Notre-Dame.[43]

Cardinal Nicolas of Fréauville and other prelates, mounted on a dais, met the multitude.[44] Sermons were preached, and then, beginning with the kings of France, Navarre, and England, a crowd of the faithful—commoners as well as nobles—received the crosses that bound them to free the Holy Land. Thus Philip the Fair fulfilled the solemn vow that he had made on 3 April 1312 at the Council of Vienne: that he, his children, his brothers, and "a copious multitude of nobles of his kingdom and other realms" would within the year assume the Cross and within six years set forth to succor the Holy Land, whether or not France was at war, and that if he were prevented by death or any other impediment his eldest son would act in his place.[45] At the ceremony in 1313 the cardinal doubtless announced the grand indulgence issued by Clement V on 10 February, which promised full remission of their sins to all who embarked for the Holy Land on crusade or, according to their rank and means, sent others to fight in their places.[46] The willingness of so many clerics and lay people to assume the Cross in Paris was doubtless promoted by guarantees that Philip the Fair issued on that Wednesday. The king, clearly anxious to see a spectacular number enlist with him, made pledges to all who took the Cross that if they were kept by death, illness, or any other personal impediment from fulfilling their vows, no one could require anything more of them or their heirs; it would be their decision whether to offer or leave anything to aid the Holy Land, and if anyone constrained them to do so, the king promised personally to see that they were protected from harm.[47] After the solemn rite, the noble entourage returned to the Ile-de-la-Cité, where the kings and their guests were feasted by Philip the Fair's half-brother Louis of Evreux, who had long been close to Edward of England and had helped persuade him and Isabelle to come to France.[48]

The wives of those who had taken the Cross on Wednesday, inspired by their husbands, made similar undertakings on Thursday, although their vows were contingent on their husbands' departing for the Holy Land.[49] Some of them felt pressed to follow their husbands' lead. Jeanne of Burgundy, wife of Philip of Poitiers, later said that Philip had "made her assume the Cross" and that she herself had taken no vow to make any compensation for failing to implement her pledge.[50] Queen Isabelle, more cautious than the other ladies, deferred until Saturday her assumption of the Cross, and she obtained from Cardinal Nicolas a formal certificate of his agreement that she would set forth only with her husband and that she would be bound to furnish only such support for the Holy Land as her devotion moved her to offer.[51]

Isabelle's failure to take the Cross with the other ladies may or may not have been deliberate. She and Edward had overslept on Thursday morning, to the amusement of the metrical chronicler.[52] Thus Edward failed to attend a conference scheduled with Philip the Fair, and Isabelle may have missed the ladies' crusading ceremony. But Edward reached the palace later and made amends for his earlier absence by offering 24 florins for the mendicants of Paris and 20 *s.* at the shrine of the Crown of Thorns in the Sainte-Chapelle,[53] where the ladies may have taken the Cross, as Isabelle would do on Saturday. He, and perhaps Isabelle as well, then joined Philip the Fair and his sons to view the grand assemblage of all the people of Paris that trooped from the Ile-Notre-Dame through the cloister of Notre-Dame to Philip the Fair's new palace.

Jean of Paris, cleric and canon of Saint-Victor, used the term *processionaliter* (which had imperial as well as ecclesiastical connotations) to describe the march of the Parisians.[54] Processional movements are powerful representations of social structure: their movement, orientation, and composition reflect personal and institutional roles and relationships; their progress enables all to see and be seen within a dynamic ensemble that exhibits principles of ideological order and social structure.[55] Given the immense crowds and obstacles such as bridges, gates, and narrow streets that impeded forward motion through the city, it may well be asked in what sense Thursday's assembly may be compared to a procession in which a well-defined body of participants moves past spectators along a path in whose trajectory and fixed temporal and spatial limits symbolic meaning can be found. The vast, animated throng of Parisians does not resemble the elite cortege of dignitaries that paraded with their retinue in royal and ecclesiastical processions: its mass is greater; the focus falls on groups rather than individuals; the king gazes from a fixed position at his people, who view the splendor of three monarchs as they pass before the palace. Yet the gathering of the Parisians is defined by processional features: it marks a special occasion; it has a

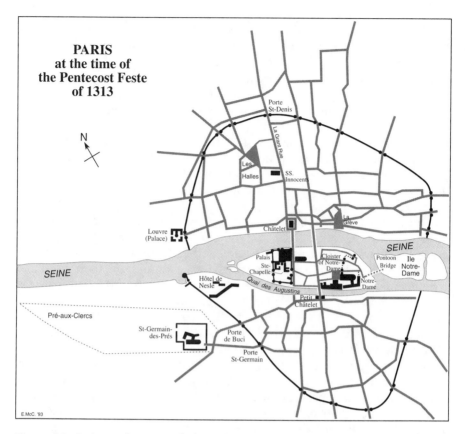

Figure 3.1. Paris at the time of the Pentecost *feste* of 1313. (Illustration by Eliza McClennen.)

beginning and end in time; it moves through city spaces along a specific trajectory articulated by significant monuments and structures (the church of Notre-Dame, the royal palace, the city wall); its participants are identified by their costumes, movements, and order of march.

Three locations where large crowds could gather—the Ile-Notre-Dame, the royal palace, and the Pré-aux-Clercs near Saint-Germain—marked out a route from east to west and punctuated a movement that began in the morning and lasted into the evening (see Figure 3.1). The parade of Parisians commenced with an assembly on the marshy meadows of the Ile-Notre-Dame, whose ecclesiastical connections had been underscored by Wednesday's crusading congregation. Mounted trumpeters preceded the line of march. They led twenty thousand on horseback and thirty thousand on foot, the metrical chronicle says, seeking to impress with numbers that, if accurate, would have been equivalent to a quarter of the city's population.[56] The Parisians passed over the grand bridge that now, thanks to their efforts, joined the Ile-Notre-Dame and the Ile-de-la-Cité. Then they progressed through the cloister of Notre-Dame and the narrow streets of the Cité before marshaling before the king's splendid new palace. The three kings reviewed the host—from the windows of the king's apartments, according to one source, or at the entry to the palace, according to another.[57] Drums beat, horns and trumpets sounded, and the royal entourage watched as the Parisians passed, two by two, each craft garbed in special livery. The costumes, order, and music of the procession made visible the affluence and social organization of the city while its unified motion reflected an ideal of the community's solidarity.[58] Never since Paris was built, the metrical chronicle declares, had there been such a noble display, which signaled the true worth of the Parisians.[59]

The massive parade continued on in the evening, after dinner. The Parisians crossed to the left bank and out beyond the city's walls to the great meadows that stretched between the Seine and Saint-Germain-des-Prés. There Edward and Isabelle were staying, and their presence transformed the space of the abbey of Saint-Germain into a site that was both royal and ecclesiastical. The Parisians must have squeezed over the Petit-Pont and moved west through the narrow Porte de Buci and Porte de Saint-Germain that breached Philip Augustus's wall; some may have crossed by ferry to the Left Bank.[60] At last they fanned out over the meadows of the Pré-aux-Clercs between Saint-Germain and the river. For the second time the throng assumed an impressive, orderly line of march as the Parisians showed themselves to Edward and Isabelle, who had returned to their lodging at Saint-Germain after attending the feast offered by Charles of Valois. From a little tower, surrounded by a host of ladies and damsels, the royal couple gazed in amazement, the chronicles report. Never would the English and their king have believed, the metrical chronicler proudly comments, "that so many wealthy and such noble persons could come forth from a single city."[61]

The *feste* of 1313 was both theatrical and political. Aristocratic responsibilities, wealth, and power (reiterated privately by the noble banquets and knighting ceremonies) were affirmed publicly when they were displayed to the people of Paris at the crusading ceremonies and through the magnates' ostentatious exhibition of splendor. In return, the power of the Parisians was confirmed when their wealth and numbers were shown to royal spectators. Spectacle thus gave weight to the importance of each group within the city.

The Parisian bourgeois and crafts, who had constructed the bridge between the Ile-de-la-Cité and the Ile-Notre-Dame and had organized and financed the preparation, had assessed the princely offering of 10,000 *l. par.* that Paris gave the king for his son's knighting.[62] The bourgeois, many of whom had profited handsomely from preparations for the *feste*,[63] rivaled the kings, princes, and nobles in their expenditures. The metrical chronicler's verses introducing the bourgeois's celebration, contrast *borjois* and *borjoisie* with the nobility, while emphasizing the noble magnificence of the festivities that the bourgeois presented. As odious as comparisons might be, the chronicler says, this celebration was distinguished by five marks of lordliness: the illuminations that the bourgeois provided, beginning on Friday and continuing to Sunday; the sumptuous garb they wore; their well-furnished numbers night and day; the variety of musical instruments; and the richly adorned crafts.[64]

The Parisians' wealth, which had been used prodigally to decorate and illumine the streets of Paris and to provide the liveries and costumes, transformed the city and joined its inhabitants in common rejoicing. All Paris was decked in hangings—white, black, yellow, red, blue, and green. For three days the bourgeois provided a fountain of wine, ornamented with "mermaids, civet-cats, lions, leopards, and many fabulous inventions."[65] "For the *feste* that the bourgeois mounted," the metrical chronicle says, "the royalty thanked them."[66]

Throughout the week, for the nobles and themselves, the bourgeois staged theatrical *tableaux vivants* and entertainments in the city's streets—*faërie* or enchantments, as the metrical chronicle terms them (see Table 3.2).[67] The poet describes more than two dozen tableaux and entertainments, devoting eighty-three lines to them. His is the earliest record of street tableaux staged for a Parisian royal festival,[68] providing the first evidence of dramatic staging in Paris and its environs,[69] and the sponsorship of Parisian theater by the municipal crafts.[70] The tableaux presented episodes both secular and religious. In the curious order in which the metrical chronicle lists them, biblical tableaux appear next to scenes from popular tales. Jesus laughs with his mother and eats an apple, cheek by jowl with Renart the Fox costumed as a doctor. The Blessed Virgin and the Magi are listed next to a Paradise and a Hell scene; then comes the Last Judgment, then the Resurrection, then a children's tournament, Christ and the Apostles praying, the slaughter of the Innocents, the martyrdom of John the Baptist, and Herod and Caiaphas in a miter. Next the chronicle describes two scenes from the tales of Renart—the fox chanting an epistle and the Gospels, then Hersent the she-wolf spinning. Next Adam and Eve, and Pilate washing his hands; then merry "bean kings" and wild men. Then the whole life of Renart: eating chickens and hens; disguised as bishop, pope, and archbishop; and finally borne in his funeral cortege.

The author enumerates the scenes, pointing here and there and punctuating his account with "la," "la," "vit on la." His account suggests throngs of spectators successively viewing an ensemble of scenes staged simultaneously. Whether the strange order in which he enumerated them reflects their actual locations cannot be known. Only one site is named: les Halles, the covered market located just west of the Church of the Innocents, which housed an enclosed, rabbit-filled wood where tame animals were chased.[71] By the early fifteenth century, various locations

TABLE 3.2. The *Faërie* of 1313: Street tableaux staged and entertainment presented during the *Feste* listed in the order given in BN, Ms. fr. 146 (*Chronique métrique*, lines 4953–5048)

Christ Child laughing with his mother
Renart the Fox as a doctor
Christ Child eating apples
The Virgin with the Magi
Paradise with ninety angels and souls singing "inside"
Hell with more than a hundred devils tormenting groaning souls
The Last Judgment
The Resurrection

A children's tournament
Christ and the Apostles praying
The slaughter of the Innocents
Martyrdom and beheading of John the Baptist
Herod and Caiaphas in a miter
"Fire, gold, silver flying up"
Renart the Fox singing an Epistle and the Gospels
"Crosses and feather plumes"
Hersent the she-wolf spinning
Adam and Eve
Pilate washing his hands

Bean kings and wild men
"All this was done by the weavers; the beltmakers also staged the life of Renart"
The whole life of Renart, eating chickens and hens
Renart disguised as a bishop, pope, and archbishop
"Renart was there in every possible disguise"
Funeral procession of Renart

Lads dancing in white shirts
Nightingales and parrots singing
An enclosed wood with rabbits in the Halles
Tame game animals "beaten on the back"
Pennants, flags, banners
Music
Castles and towers
Ladies dancing and caroling
Luminaire of wax candles
Decorated fountain of wine, "a joyful gift of the bourgeois"
Well-dressed bourgeois ladies dancing

Key: religious scenes, *Renart material*, **festive entertainments**, "descriptive comments" along the royal entry route into Paris were associated with different crafts; some of the same scenes (such as the Magi and the slaughter of the Innocents) were represented in 1313.[72] But les Halles was not a site of later entry pageantry, nor is there evidence that in 1313 the scenes were associated with the entry of Edward and Isabelle into Paris on the day before Pentecost.

As the chronicle's account shows, the tableaux depicting Hell and Paradise were staged within large-scale constructions intended to last for more than a single day and perhaps for the entire week of the *feste.* Framing the Hell were curtains that were blown down by Wednesday's storm but were quickly restored.[73] Black, reeking smoke poured from its inner area; into it souls were cast, and there they howled in torment; from it more than a hundred devils could emerge simultaneously.[74] The Paradise held ninety angels and likewise had an inner space, within which souls sang.[75] If these tableaux were staged on the fixed, raised platforms typical of later medieval French street theater,[76] they would have been impressively large[77] but easily constructed by the affluent and well-organized Parisians who had set up the pontoon bridge to the Ile-Notre-Dame in just two days.

Some *faërie* may have been mounted on wagons or wheels; the metrical chronicle mentions "castles and towers," which, like ships, were popular sets that could be mobile.[78] Some revelers may have been costumed, since the metrical chronicle makes a tantalizing reference to people strutting over the pontoon bridge and wearing "maintes riches desguiseüres," a term that can mean costumes or disguises as well as finery.[79] A later account in the *Grandes Chroniques,* which compresses the information in the metrical chronicle and contains no reference to the subjects of the tableaux, mentions *jeux* accompanying the Parisians' assemblage on the Ile-Notre-Dame.[80]

Unlike the mute, immobile tableaux of some early-fifteenth-century entries,[81] the tableaux of 1313 were lively and filled with movement; figures sang, spoke, groaned, spun, and jumped about. But the scenes do not seem to have been full dramas. For ten of them the chronicler uses a single verb suggesting a simple action without any dramatic development: the Christ Child laughs, Renart intones the Gospels. In the case of nine tableaux, only the subject is indicated, but three scenes involved sustained and repeated actions: the souls singing in Paradise;[82] the devils "throwing and casting souls about," emerging "side by side to lure toward them souls, which they treated very harshly";[83] the wild men prancing about "with great merriment."[84] In every case the *faërie* of 1313 presented familiar scenes, not complex allegories, that could be understood without dialogue, extended dramatic action, or additional commentary.

The *faërie's* varied themes playfully reiterated the central elements of the aristocratic *feste*: the articles of faith, youthful knights, kings, processions. Taken together the biblical tableaux constitute an ensemble of scenes[85] presenting the central episodes of Christian belief and illustrating the lessons that the new knights had heard expounded at Notre-Dame. The scene of the Magi recalled the three kings of France, England, and Navarre, whose presence dignified the *feste*. The children's tournament, "where none was more than ten years old," evoked the knighting of Philip the Fair's sons while it underscored the absence of tourneying at the *feste*.[86] The fox in clerical garb caricatured the splendid ecclesiastical ceremonies, as Renart's funeral cortege echoed the *feste*'s different ceremonial processions.[87]

The scenes from the stories of Renart, the only known medieval staging of the tales, had political overtones that would not have been lost on spectators familiar with the popular satire. The tableau showing Renart as a doctor presented the episode in which the fox heals the ailing King Noble with a remedy concocted from the skins of his courtiers.[88] This scene, like the one showing the greedy fox eating chickens and hens (in Latin *galli*, which also signifies "the French"), would surely have recalled Philip the Fair's red-headed minister, Enguerran de Marigny, who was at the apogee of his power in 1313. As the metrical chronicle reports, when Enguerran was taken to trial in the spring of 1315, the Parisians taunted him with cries of "Begone, Renart! Your scheming and trickery have killed us. You've stolen the kingdom's wealth."[89] Other tableaux also had moral and political implications. Figuring the evil ruler who sheds the blood of the righteous, King Herod orders the slaying of the Innocents, and Herod Antipas receives the head of John the Baptist and appears with the chief priest Caiaphas, both guilty of Jesus' death. Their images contrasted starkly with that of the good kings, the Magi. Even the comic "bean kings" carried a moral message, representing as they did the ephemeral kings-for-a-day of Epiphany, and suggested the transitory nature of royal power.[90] Provocatively intermingled, the religious and satirical scenes constituted a discourse of festive counsel that celebrated knighting and crusading ceremonies while reminding the king of his duty to protect the kingdom from evil and from over-mighty councillors. Celebration and admonition were complementary, for the king's subjects thought themselves bound not only to glorify but also to advise their ruler.[91] The bourgeois thus presented diversions for themselves and lessons for their betters. Their festive participation asserted the worth of an educated urban elite as they gave their commentary on the issues of the day and the responsibilities of their king.

Who were the Parisians who planned, mounted, and participated in the celebration? Focusing on the bourgeois, the metrical chronicle points to Parisians of varied status, identified by occupation, dress, sex, and festive activity. The proud elite of the Parisian bourgeoisie with its "rights, customs, practices, and privileges" financed and dominated the festivities.[92] At different points in the celebration, the individual Parisian crafts were identified by their insignia, processional order, and separate banquets. In Thursday's parade they marched two by two, each craft wearing distinctive livery and feasting at subsequent banquets that were, extraordinarily, permitted them on this occasion, in addition to those held at their annual assemblies.[93] Members of the Great Watch (which included representatives of every craft except the richest, who were exempt) marched through the swirling throngs, eight hundred strong, identified by their special garb.[94] The chronicle specifically mentions just two crafts, the "tisseranz" and the "corroier" as sponsors of dramatic tableaux.[95] The "tisseranz" included many groups in the important Parisian cloth industry, from "le commun des menuz mestres tesseranz" to the women who wove fine silk, to the "drapiers que Dieu gart," the "mestier hautain," the "granz mestres tesseranz," who sold cloth made by the lesser masters.[96] The "corroier," men and women, belonged to a specialized craft that made belts of silk or leather studded with metal nails, luxury items for a Parisian clientele of nobles and rich bourgeois.[97] The bourgeois sponsors also paid the minstrels who played the instruments that the metrical chronicle mentions.[98] At the opposite end of the social scale were the merry *ribaus* or rabble, whose white shirts and dancing distinguished them from the crafts parading in livery.[99] Dancing is the only festive activity assigned to women, whether noble or bourgeois: "*dames* danced carols with lovely turns"; "*bourgeoises* dressed in finery danced and pranced for all to see."[100] Although the metrical chronicler singles out different groups of Parisians, for him they were most impressive as a mass, "an enormous throng, well decked out by night and day."[101]

The week-long celebration ended on Trinity Sunday. This brought to a close the rejoicing and expenses of the Parisian bourgeois, but the king's outlay continued after he, Edward, and Isabelle retired from Paris to Pontoise to deal with affairs of state.[102] Philip left the city on 9 June, passing through Poissy on his way to Pontoise;[103] Edward and Isabelle remained in Paris on Trinity Sunday, when Edward awarded ten marks to a friar, John de Dunkhull, who was setting forth for the Holy Land in Christ's service.[104]

The royal company remained at Pontoise for the rest of the month; their stay was dramatically interrupted by a fire that broke out in Edward's wardrobe, destroying many of the couple's belongings and causing the English king and his queen to flee in their nightdress into the street.[105] This incident apart, life seems to have continued at Pontoise much as it had at Paris. Alms were offered to mendicants and poor on 18 June, and the prior of the church of Saint-Pierre of Pontoise received 30 *s.* for the damage done to his meadows by Edward's oxen, pastured there for four days.[106] Feasting and celebration doubtless continued, but the pace was far less hectic than before. Nonetheless wine flowed, and on 11 June Edward offered 20 *s.* to a particularly outstanding minstrel; later the minstrel Bernard Le Fol and fifty-four companions distracted Edward by dancing nude before him—on 19 June, the anniversary of the murder of Piers Gaveston, Edward's favorite—and received 40 s. from Edward for their show.[107]

The week in Paris had not been devoted solely to festivity,[108] and it was probably before leaving Paris that, at Philip the Fair's request, Edward renewed for a year his truce with the Scots, which expired on Trinity Sunday, 10 June.[109] At Pontoise, business took precedence over pleasure. Edward received numerous deputations of his Gascon subjects,[110] and he and his father-in-law treated matters of mutual concern. For his part, buoyed by the support he had received in Paris and doubtless on the counsel of the magnates who had gathered there, King Philip summoned the Flemings to answer for their failure to carry out the harsh treaty imposed on them in 1306. Sure that these negotiations would fail, and perhaps (as the metrical chronicle says) pressed by his sons and the other new knights, he summoned his subjects to appear at Arras on 5 August, ready to force the Flemings to obey.[111] Philip also seized the occasion to institute reform of the realm's coinage, thus following in the footsteps of his grandfather Saint Louis, whose coins remained the standard by which all others were judged.[112]

In gratitude for the attendance of Edward and Isabelle at the *feste*, Philip issued numerous privileges in Edward's favor.[113] They were granted not at Pontoise but rather at Poissy, the site of Saint Louis's birth and baptism, where Philip had established a Dominican nunnery in his grandfather's honor and where the two kings passed the last days of Edward's visit, from 2 to 6 July.[114] There the two kings received William of Villanova, the bishop whom the pope was sending to convert the Tartars; both kings gave him handsome presents.[115] Before Edward and Isabelle left Poissy gifts were exchanged; the king of England received from Philip the Fair four horses and armor; Edward presented 40 s. to Hurell, Philip's minstrel.[116] While Edward and Isabelle were en route to England, Philip issued additional privileges in their favor. These were granted at Paris on 12 and 13 July, just before Edward and Isabelle sailed for Dover.[117]

The departure of Edward and Isabelle brought to an end the great festivities and extraordinary largesse that, since the beginning of June, had reigned at Philip the Fair's court. For him and for the kingdom of France the Pentecost *feste* had served many purposes, fiscal, political, and emotional, which suggest why he held the extraordinary celebration.

Expensive as it was, the *feste* brought Philip promise of financial gain, since the knighting of Louis, his eldest son, enabled him to impose a customary aid on his lay subjects.[118] Further, the assumption of the Cross gave the French king access to the clerical tenths destined for the Crusade that Clement V had awarded him on 6 June 1312.[119] Equally important was the tactical advantage that Philip gained, since all who opposed him could now be decried as enemies of the Holy Land.[120]

The grand crusading ceremony on the Ile-Notre-Dame also demonstrated that Philip the Fair had replaced his cousin and rival, Edward I of England, as the hope of the Holy Land. While he lived, Edward was the premier crusader of Christendom; he remained dedicated to the Holy Land until he died. After Edward's death in 1307, and doubtless before, Philip the Fair was blamed for preventing Edward from embarking on the crusade he planned in 1287 by provoking war between England and France.[121] In 1313 Philip assumed the position that Edward had held, and it was under his aegis that Edward's son and heir took the Cross. The pope himself called Philip "most eager champion of the Crucifix." He declared the warriors of France "best trained for combat" (*ad bella doctissimi*), saying they were considered more glorious in battle than others because of their tested virtue. Victory over Christ's enemies, the pope proclaimed, was promised to the king and "the lofty house of France."[122]

Finally, the magnificence of the *feste* of 1313 witnessed Philip's grandeur and authority, eclipsing as it did earlier celebrations. It outshone the Feast of the Swans of 1306 at which Edward I had knighted his heir; it surpassed the festivities of 1267 that had accompanied the preaching of Louis IX's last crusade and the king's knighting of Philip the Fair's father, a man toward whom Philip harbored deep animosities.[123] Through the celebrations Philip also compensated for the bleakness of his own knighting at age sixteen on the Feast of the Assumption in 1284, held just before the French army departed on a so-called Crusade against Aragon, an expedition that the young Philip opposed and that brought shame and defeat to France.[124] In 1313 it was Philip who presided as a Louis *redivivus* over the splendid knighting of three sons, one of them a king, at a ceremony linked with genuine crusading in defense of the Holy Land.

The *grant feste* of 1313 manifested Philip the Fair's power and the glory and wealth of the royal family; it provided a fit setting for the assembled nobles and princes to display their finery and to take their solemn vows to aid the Holy Land; it elevated and ennobled Paris and all the city's inhabitants. The procession of the Parisians and the theatricalization of the streets in the spectacle of the *grant feste* conferred symbolic value upon the king and city. The celebrations of this Pentecost week realized the expressive word-play Parisius-Paradisus:[125] the elements of the *feste* suggest the transformation of Paris into Paradise. The *tableau vivant* of Paradise was echoed by the bourgeois's rich hangings, music, and illumination by day and night, which changed the urban space for eight full days into an emblem of the celestial. Getting was turned toward spending as festive largesse replaced the harsh economy of daily life with a heavenly state of outpouring riches. Throughout the celebration, everyone could drink and eat, night and day, in every part of Paris, "with no restriction";[126] the lavish banquets and continuous feasting call to mind the eschatological parable of the wedding banquet. These symbolic overtones explain the hyperbole the metrical chronicler uses to describe the *feste* of 1313 and contrast markedly with his sober, cautious reporting of other events. "The joy, the pleasure, the *feste* ... These are marvels without equals," he wrote, communicating the state of rejoicing that can be seen as the essence of Paradise and of festive celebration.[127] The chivalric, religious, and urban celebrations in Paris thus witnessed the moral and political well-being of the realm of France, as they glorified its king.

NOTES

1. We should like to express our gratitude to Barbara Hanawalt, Kathryn Reyerson, and all those at the University of Minnesota who made possible the conference where this essay was first presented. The invitation to give the paper has led us to plan a book on the *feste* of 1313. In it we shall deal in greater detail with the material surveyed here and treat a number of themes that constraints of space do not permit us to consider in this essay. Here we focus on the celebration itself and the role of Paris in the festivities; in the book we shall consider the larger historical context and the political significance of the *feste*; we shall also publish illustrations and a selection of texts (with translations) that relate to the celebration, with full documentation for the statements that appear here. We profited greatly from suggestions that we received at the conference and would especially like to thank Lawrence M. Bryant and Edward R. Haymes. In revising the paper we have received generous help from Michael T. Davis, Richard C. Famiglietti, Samuel Kinser, Alan E. Knight, John C. Parsons, Dana L. Sample, and Kenneth Varty. Special thanks to Eliza McClennen, who prepared the map. We wish to express our gratitude to the staffs of the Archives nationales and the Bibliothèque nationale in Paris, the Public Record Office in London, the Library of Congress, the libraries of Columbia University and New York University, and the New York Public Library. Elizabeth Brown's research was made possible by grants from the American Council of Learned Societies, the National Endowment for the Humanities, and the PSC-CUNY Research Award Program. Nancy Regalado is grateful for the hospitality of the Centre d'Etudes Supérieures de Civilisation Médiévale at Poitiers, where she presented material concerning the *feste* in July 1990, and for a fellowship from the National Endowment for the Humanities (1992) that provided support during the period when this article was completed. The following abbreviations are used: AN—Paris, Archives nationales; BM—Bibliothèque municipale; BN—Paris, Bibliothèque nationale; *d.—denier(s); l. (par.)/(t.)—livre(s) (parisis)/(tournois); l.st.*—pound(s) sterling; MGH—Monumenta Germaniae Historica; PRO—London, Public Record Office; *s.—sou(s)*/shilling(s).

2. *La chronique métrique attribuée à Geffroy de Paris: texte publié avec introduction et glossaire,* ed. Armel Diverrès, Publications de la Faculté des lettres de l'Université de Strasbourg, no. 129 (Paris: "Les Belles Lettres," 1956), line 4921; see Esther 1.5–9. The only surviving copy of the chronicle is reproduced in facsimile in *Le Roman de Fauvel in the Edition of Mesire Chaillou de Pesstain: A Reproduction in Facsimile of the Complete Manuscript Paris, Bibliothèque Nationale, Fonds Français 146. Introduction by Edward H. Roesner, François Avril, and Nancy Freeman Regalado* (New York: Broude Brothers, 1990), fols. 63r–88r.

3. John J. MacAloon states that spectacle is an "irreducibly visual" performative genre that gives "primacy to visual sensory and symbolic codes" ("Olympic Games and

the Theory of Spectacle in Modern Societies," in *Rite, Drama, Festival, Spectacle: Rehearsals Toward a Theory of Cultural Performance,* ed. John J. MacAloon [Philadelphia: Institute for the Study of Human Issues, 1984], pp. 245, 243].

4. Josef Fleckenstein, "Friedrich Barbarossa und das Rittertum: Zur Bedeutung der grossen Mainzer Hoftage von 1184 und 1188," orig. pub. 1971, reprinted in *Das Rittertum im Mittelalter,* ed. Arno Borst, *Wege der Forschung* 349 [1976]: 392–418, esp. 392–96; and Heinz Weber, "Der Mainzer Hoftag von 1184 als politisches Fest," in *Feste und Feiern im Mittelalter: Paderborner Symposion des Mediävistenverbandes,* ed. Detlef Altenburg, Jörg Jarnut, and Hans-Hugo Steinhoff [Sigmaringen: Jan Thorbecke, 1991], pp. 181–92.

5. Charles Petit-Dutaillis, *Etude sur la vie et le règne de Louis VIII (1187–1226),* Bibliothèque de l'Ecole des Hautes Études, Sciences philologiques et historiques, no. 101 [Paris: Emile Bouillon, 1894], pp. 10–11; and *Œuvres de Rigord et de Guillaume le Breton, historiens de Philippe-Auguste,* ed. H.-François Delaborde, 2 vols., Publications de la Société de l'Histoire de France, nos. 210, 224 [Paris: Renouard, H. Loones, 1882–85], 1:226 [Guillaume le Breton].

6. See Louis Le Nain de Tillemont, *La vie de saint Louis,* ed. Jules de Gaulle, 6 vols., Publications de la Société de l'Histoire de France, nos. 47, 50, 53, 55, 57, 66 [Paris: Jules Renouard, 1847–51], 2:300–302, 424, 428; 5:13–14, 34–37.

7. See Guillaume de Nangis, *Gesta Philippi Tertii Francorum Regis,* in *Recueil des historiens des Gaules et de la France,* ed. Martin Bouquet et al., 24 vols. [Paris: Palmé et al., 1738–1904], 20:496–97; and *Les Grandes Chroniques de France,* ed. Jules Viard, 10 vols., Publications de la Société de l'Histoire de France, nos. 395, 401, 404, 415, 418, 423, 425, 429, 438, 457 [Paris: Champion and C. Klincksieck, 1920–53], 8:52–53. On this celebration and on the festivities at Arras in 1271 [for which see below], see Noël Coulet, "Les entrées solennelles en Provence au XIVe siècle: aperçus nouveaux sur les entrées royales françaises au bas Moyen Age," *Ethnologie française* 7 (1977]: 63–82, at 69. Coulet suggests that the two festivals were connected with entries, but the surviving sources do not specifically discuss any such ceremonies.

8. *Annales Gandenses, Annals of Ghent,* trans. Hilda Johnstone [London: Nelson, 1951], pp. 12–13. See n. 92 below.

9. See Constance Bullock-Davies, *Menestrellorum multitudo: Minstrels at a Royal Feast* [Cardiff: University of Wales Press, 1978], pp. xxi–xxxi. We should like to thank Douglas Jansen, who first called our attention to the parallels between the Feast of the Swans and the *grant feste* of 1313.

10. See *Recueil des historiens* 20:488–89 [Nangis, *Gesta Philippi Tertii*]; and *Grandes Chroniques* 8:40.

11. BN, lat. 8504, fols. Bv–1r. On the work, see Silvestre de Sacy, "Notice de l'ouvrage intitulé Liber de Dina et Kalila, Manuscrits Latins de la Bibliothèque du Roi, nos. 8504 et 8505," *Notices et extraits des manuscrits de la Bibliothèque du Roi, et autres bibliothèques* 10, no. 2 (1818]: 3–65; Auguste-Léopold Hervieux, *Les fabulistes latins depuis le siècle d'Auguste jusqu'à la fin du Moyen Age,* 2nd ed., 5 vols. [Paris: Firmin-Didot, 1893–99], 5:39–79, 380–85 [*Jean de Capoue et ses dérivés*]; and the review of Hervieux's study by Charles-Victor Langlois, in *Journal des savants* [March 1898]: 158–73.

12. Diverrès, in *Chronique métrique,* pp. 9–21. On the manuscript, see Roesner, Avril, and Regalado, "Introduction," in *Le Roman de Fauvel,* pp. 4–7; and Elizabeth A. R. Brown, *Adultery, Charivari, and Political Criticism in Early-Fourteenth-Century France: Les Livres de Fauvel,* forthcoming.

13. See esp. the *Memoriale historiarum* of Jean of Paris, canon of Saint-Victor, in *Recueil des historiens* 21:630–89, at 656–57, whose account is based on the metrical chronicle but who presents details absent from the single surviving manuscript of this chronicle; on the relationship between the metrical chronicle and Jean's work, see Diverrès, in *Chronique métrique,* p. 16; and n. 61 below. Independent testimony is given by the chronicle of Sainte-Catherine-du-Mont of Rouen: *Recueil des historiens* 21:397–410, at 408–9. The chronicle may well have been written contemporaneously; it was begun in the

early thirteenth century and was extended by different writers to 1345 (*Recueil des historiens* 23:397).

14. *Chronique latine de Guillaume de Nangis de 1113 à 1300 avec les continuations de cette chronique de 1300 à 1368,* ed. Hercule Géraud, 2 vols., Publications de la Société de l'Histoire de France, nos. 33, 35 (Paris: Jules Renouard, 1843), 1:400–405. For the truces, see Frantz Funck-Brentano, *Les origines de la guerre de Cent ans: Philippe le Bel en Flandre* (Paris: Champion, 1897), pp. 639–40, 660–64; for the leagues, see Elizabeth A. R. Brown, "Reform and Resistance to Royal Authority in Fourteenth-Century France: The Leagues of 1314–1315" (1981), in her *Politics and Institutions in Capetian France* (Aldershot: Variorum, 1991), no. 5.

15. Jean Favier, *Un conseiller de Philippe le Bel: Enguerran de Marigny,* Mémoires et documents publiés par l'Ecole des Chartes, no. 15 (Paris: Presses universitaires de France, 1963), pp. 215–17; Raymond Cazelles, *Nouvelle histoire de Paris, de la fin du règne de Philippe Auguste à la mort de Charles V, 1223–1380* (Paris: Association pour la publication d'une Histoire de Paris, 1972), p. 165; and André Du Chesne, *Les Antiqvitez et Recherches des villes, chasteaux, et places plvs remarquables de toute la France. Divisees en hvict Livres. Selon l'ordre et ressort des huict Parlemens ...* (Paris: Jean Petit-Pas, 1609), pp. 181–82. For Enguerran as Renart, see Favier, *Un conseiller,* p. 215; *Chronique métrique,* lines 6987–88; and p. 70 and n. 89, this volume. On Philip's palace, see Jean Guerout, "Le Palais de la Cité à Paris des origines à 1417: essai topographique et archéologique," *Paris et Ile-de-France: Mémoires de la Fédération des Sociétés Historiques et Archéologiques de Paris et de l'Ile-de-France* 1 (1949): 57–212; 2 (1950): 21–204; 3 (1951): 7–101; and esp. 2:44, for the Pentecost celebration.

16. Georges Lizerand, *Clément V et Philippe IV le Bel* (Paris: Hachette, 1910), p. 53; Favier, *Un conseiller,* p. 14. Clement V named Nicolas a cardinal on 12 December 1305. The pope dispatched him to France in March 1313 to further plans for the Crusade (*Regestum Clementis Papae V ...,* ed. L. Tosti et al., 10 vols. [Rome and Paris: Typographia Vaticana and E. de Bocard, 1885–97], 8:287, nos. 9649–50; see also 399–403, no. 9941; and 403–4, nos. 9942–63).

17. Edmond Faral, *Les jongleurs en France au Moyen Age,* 2nd ed. (Paris: Champion, 1964), pp. 97–98; and Michel Stanesco, *Jeux d'errance du chevalier médiéval: aspects ludiques de la fonction guerrière dans la littérature du moyen âge flamboyant,* Brill's Studies in Intellectual History, no. 9 (Leiden: Brill, 1988), p. 64.

18. Louis of Evreux was in England in the fall of 1312, helping Edward negotiate with his barons and the Scots, and it seems clear that he extended Philip's invitation to Edward and Isabelle; *Chronique métrique,* lines 4654–88, exaggerates his accomplishments in England. Louis was accompanied by Enguerran de Marigny and the marshal of France, as well as by French lawyers (Favier, *Un conseiller,* pp. 121, 123–24, esp. p. 124 n. 1; and *Annales Londonienses,* in *Chronicles of the Reigns of Edward I. and Edward II.,* ed. William Stubbs, 2 vols., Rolls Series, no. 76 [London: Her Majesty's Stationery Office, 1882–83], 1:210–11, 215, 225–29).

19. For Edward's itinerary between his departure from Dover on 23 May and his return there on 15 July, see Elizabeth M. Hallam, *The Itinerary of Edward II and his Household, 1307–1328,* Publications of the List and Index Society, no. 211 (London: Swift, 1984), pp. 98–102.

20. For background, see May McKisack, *The Fourteenth Century, 1307–1399,* vol. 5 of *The Oxford History of England,* ed. George Clark (Oxford: Clarendon Press, 1959), pp. 21–31; particularly useful is Jeffrey S. Hamilton, *Piers Gaveston, Earl of Cornwall, 1307–1312: Politics and Patronage in the Reign of Edward II* (Detroit: Wayne State University Press, 1988), pp. 98–107.

21. PRO, E 101/375/8, fol. 19r–v.

22. "Chronicle of Sainte-Catherine-du-Mont of Rouen," in *Recueil des historiens* 23: 408–9.

23. *Chronique métrique,* lines 4839–40.

24. *Comptes royaux (1285–1314)*, ed. Robert Fawtier and François Maillard, 3 vols., Recueil des historiens de la France, Documents financiers, no. 3 (Paris: Imprimerie nationale, 1953–56), nos. 27701, 27760–64, corrected from Rouen, BM, MS 3401 (Leber 5870, Menant 4), fols. 61r, 65r–v. On 14 June Edward paid the Parisian citizen Falu 60 *s.* for the grass eaten by the oxen that Philip the Fair had given to him (PRO, E/101/375/8, fol. 32r). Compare the 400 oxen, 800 sheep, 400 pigs, and 40 boars requisitioned for Edward I's Pentecost celebration in 1305 (Bullock-Davies, *Menestrellorum multitudo*, p. xvii).

25. Favier, *Un conseiller*, pp. 46, 125–26; and Natalie Fryde, "Antonio Pessagno of Genoa, King's Merchant of Edward II of England," in *Studi in memoria di Federigo Melis*, vol. 2 (Naples: Giannini, 1978), pp. 157–78, at 168–70. On 1 May 1313 Pope Clement V granted Edward 74,000 *fl.*, but the English king did not actually receive the money for some time (Lizerand, *Clément V*, p. 367). On 4 May Edward ordered Antonio Pessagno, his chief financial agent, to contract loans up to 20,000 *l. st.* (*Foedera ...*, ed. Thomas Rymer et al., 4 vols. in 7 [London: Record Commission, 1816–69], 2, no. 1: 214). Pessagno was in France with Edward, as the account for payments that he made at Pontoise between 1 and 7 July 1313 demonstrates (PRO, E 101/375/7). On 16 May the king received a loan of 2000 marks (1,333 *l.* 6 *s.* 6 *d. st.*) from William Testa, Cardinal Priest of Saint Ciriac, which was to be repaid in Paris on 10 June (*Calendar of Close Rolls, 1307–1313*, pp. 572–73, and see also pp. 586–88). This loan had not been repaid on 13 October 1313 (*Foedera* 2, no. 1: 229–30).

26. For the Catalan text and a discussion of the text's transmission, see Ramon Llull, *Llibre de l'orde de cavalleria*, ed. Albert Soler i Nopart, Els nostres clàssics, Textes en llengua catalana dels origens al 1800, Collecció A, Volums en octau, no. 127 (Barcelona: Barcino, 1988), pp. 9–12, 61–68; for the French version, Llull's *Livre de l'ordre de cheva-lerie*, ed. Vincenzo Minervini, Biblioteca di Filologia Romanza, no. 21 (Bari: Adriatica, 1972), pp. 11–69. See Jocelyn N. Hillgarth, *Ramon Lull and Lullism in Fourteenth-Century France* (Oxford: Oxford University Press, 1971), p. 154 n. 21, 339 n. 56. Particularly relevant to the knighting ceremony is Llull, *Llibre*, pp. 197–200, 219 (*Livre*, pp. 136–43, 174). The *Ordene de chevalerie*, written in the first half of the thirteenth century and conceived in a crusading spirit, also contains a detailed description of the knighting ceremony with moral allegorical interpretations of each act; it circulated widely in France and England (Raoul de Hodenc, *Le Roman des eles*; the anonymous *Ordene de chevalerie*, ed. Keith Busby, Utrecht Publications in General and Comparative Literature, no. 17 [Amsterdam-Philadelphia: Benjamins, 1983], pp. 71–119; discussion in Stanesco, "Le Rituel symbolique de l'adoubement," in *Jeux d'errance*, pp. 45–70, at 52–56).

27. Partial copies of the list of knights and the horses they received are found in Rouen, BM, MS 3401 (Leber 5870, Menant IV), fols. 584–59r [ed. with some errors in *Comptes royaux (1285–1314)*, nos. 27622–646]; BN, Clairambault 832, pp. 269–92; BN, fr. 7855, pp. 104–13; and *Reliquiae manuscriptorum ...*, ed. Johannes Petrus von Ludewig, 12 vols. (Frankfurt and Leipzig: Halae salicae impensis Orphanotrophei, 1720–41), 12:48–60. The copies were made from the original royal household account, which was destroyed in 1737; they contain a total of 197 names of new knights. In collaboration with Richard C. Famiglietti, we shall publish a composite list in our book.

28. See Llull, *Llibre*, p. 200 (*Livre*, p. 143).

29. Ibid.

30. For Philip's ordonnance, *Ordonnances des roys de France de la troisième race ...*, ed. Eusèbe-Jacob de Laurière et al., 22 vols. and *Supplément* (Paris: Imprimerie royale et al., 1723–1849), 1:509–10.

31. BN, fr. 23018 (*Chronique des Cordeliers*), fol. 207v ("fist Joustes et tournoyes pour plus sa feste exauchier").

32. An entry in the king's household account shows that the furrier of Philip of Poitiers received 5 *l. par.*, warranted by the chamberlain Pierre de Chambly, for going from Maubuisson to Compiègne on 15 June 1313 "to arrange lodgings for Philip for tourna-ments" ("ad capiendum hospicia pro dicto domino Philippo pro torneamentis"; *Comptes*

royaux (1285–1314), no. 27687). Note, however, that on 17 and 18 June, royal messengers were dispatched to forbid jousting (ibid., nos. 27688, 27690, 27705). Frustrated by the prohibition against tourneying that Pope Clement V would issue on 14 September 1313 and that Cardinal Nicolas de Fréauville would proclaim in France ca. 9 October, the king's sons and other young knights successfully petitioned the pope to moderate his stance, and Clement consequently authorized tournaments for three days before Lent (20 February) in 1314 (Lizerand, *Clément V*, pp. 363–64).

33. "Si di qu'en françois n'en latin, / Ne del vespre ne dou matin, / De la noblece n'est il somme" (*Chronique métrique*, lines 4875–78). For the names of magnates, see ibid., lines 4773–92.

34. Ibid., lines 4793–4796; and see Funck-Brentano, *Philippe le Bel en Flandre*, pp. 621–54. The *Chronographia*, written between 1415 and 1422 at Saint-Denis and probably relying on the metrical chronicle or on a source influenced by it, is confused on this point. Without mentioning Louis of Nevers, the chronicle states that the duke of Brittany (whom the metrical chronicle mentions twice as present at the *feste*) and the count of Flanders did not attend the *feste* because "they said they did not want to take the Cross until they saw that preparations had been made for the expedition" ("qui dicebant se nolle crucesignari donec viderent paratam dispositionem pro viagio transmarino"; *Chronographia regum Francorum*, ed. Henri Moranvillé, 3 vols., Publications de la Société de l'Histoire de France, nos. 252, 262, 284 [Paris: Renouard, 1891–97], 1:211). The closely related *Anciennes chroniques de Flandre* (*Recueil des historiens* 22: 399) gives a similar account, adding that Clement V suspected that the count did not want to attend the *feste* because he was angry over the French seizure of Flemish lands; according to the chronicle, the pope feared that the count would make trouble while the king was on crusade and thus used his influence to press for peace. On these chronicles, see Auguste Molinier and Louis Polain, *Les sources de l'histoire de France des origines aux guerres d'Italie (1494)*, 6 vols. (Paris: Picard, 1901–6), no. 3103. The *Chronique normande* (written between 1369 and 1372) mentions only the absence of the count of Flanders (*Chronique normande du XIVe siècle*, ed. Auguste and Emile Molinier, Publications de la Société de l'Histoire de France, no. 205 [Paris: Renouard, 1882], 29). This chronicler says that Charles, the second son of Charles of Valois, as well as the count's first son Philip, born in 1293, was knighted in 1313.

35. "Rex autem illa die resedit in mensa, regio diademate coronatus" (*Chronographia* 1:211; *Anciennes chroniques de Flandre*, in *Recueil des historiens* 22:399; and see note 41). On the wearing of crowns at royal festivities (and particularly the crown that Philip VI wore for the knighting of his eldest son), see Charles du Fresne, sieur du Cange, *Histoire de S. Lovys* ... (Paris: Mabre-Cramoisy, 1668), part 2, "Dissertation V. Des Cours et des festes solennelles des Roys de France," pp. 159–63; also published at the end of vol. 7 of Du Cange, *Glossarium mediae et infimae latinitatis*, ed. Léopold Favre, 7 vols. (Paris: Firmin-Didot, 1840–50), 7:19–23. On Pentecost of 1184, before his son's knighting festivities, Frederick Barbarossa and his wife wore "imperiales coronas," their son King Henry "regalem coronam" (MGH SS 21:538 [Gislebert of Mons, *Chronicon Hanoniense*]). Introducing his tally of the "mainte haute personne" who attended the *feste*, the metrical chronicle lists first "Roy et roynë en couronne"; he also says that when Philip the Fair entertained the ladies at the Louvre on Tuesday, "Double royne i ot couronnee," which indicates that Isabelle of England and Marguerite of Burgundy, wife of Louis of Navarre, wore crowns on this occasion (*Chronique métrique*, lines 4771–72, 4862).

36. For the different noble banquets given during the week, see *Chronique métrique*, lines 4839–72.

37. Ibid., lines 4845–58; Jean of Saint-Victor, in *Recueil des historiens* 21:657; and PRO, E 101/375/8, fols. 3v, 32r. The author of the *Chronique métrique* seems clearly to have been an eyewitness to this banquet, the only one that he describes in detail.

38. "Si n'i avoit n'amont n'aval / Ou il n'i eüst parement / Et luminaire grandement /

Qui chierement fu achaté, / Mes c'estoit fet par nobleté, / Grans torches ardre en plain mydi; / Por ce que le vi, je le di" (*Chronique métrique,* lines 4852–57).

39. PRO, E 101/375/8, fol. 30v; and Constance Bullock-Davies, *Register of Royal and Baronial Domestic Minstrels, 1272–1327* (Woodbridge: Boydell Press, 1986), p. 34.

40. PRO, E/101/375/8, fol. 30. For a *castello* filled with cooked animals that looked alive, brought in between courses at a banquet given for Pope Clement V in 1308, see Enid Welsford, *The Court Masque: A Study in the Relationship between Poetry and the Revels* (Cambridge: Cambridge University Press, 1927), p. 45 n. 1.

41. "Et cel jor nostre roy de France / Moustra au Louvre sa vaillance, / Car aus dames fist la disnee. / Double royne i ot couronnee" (*Chronique métrique,* lines 4859–62). See ibid., line 5067, for the chronicle's description of the Parisians' march "aprés disner" to Saint-Germain-des-Prés on Thursday. The chronicle does not make clear whether this banquet was held at the same time as Edward's feast at Saint-Germain-des-Prés, although it would have been curious for Philip the Fair to miss his son-in-law's entertainment. In his account, Jean of Saint-Victor says only that Edward offered "prandium solempnissimum" and that Philip "omnes dominas habuit illa die in Lupara" (*Recueil des historiens* 21:657).

42. *Chronique métrique,* lines 4913–15. See Louis Halphen, *Paris sous les premiers Capétiens (987–1223): étude de topographie historique,* 2 vols. (Paris: Leroux, 1909), 1:51–54, 98; and Cazelles, *Nouvelle histoire,* p. 229.

43. *Chronique métrique,* lines 4885–4918.

44. BN, lat. 8504, fols. Bv–1r. The miniature showing the taking of the Cross is now mounted beside the fifth caption, which describes the parade of Parisians; it was intended for the third caption, which describes the reception of the "uexillum angeli celestis .a. reuerendo patri in christo domino nicholao .diuina prouidencia .tituli. sancti eusebii presbitero cardinalis [*sic*]." Sylvia Schein, *Fideles Crucis: The Papacy, the West, and the Recovery of the Holy Land, 1274–1314* (Oxford: Clarendon Press, 1991), p. 255, dates the ceremony 5 June.

45. Nangis, *Chronique* 1:391–92. The bull of 10 Feburary 1313 empowering Nicolas de Fréauville to preach the Crusade mentions the French and also "ad illud venient[es] undecunque signum recipere volent[es] supradictum" (*Regestum Clementis V* 8:401, no. 9941, 10 February 1313). The bull that Philip the Fair obtained from Clement V on 29 December 1305, which absolved him in advance from crusading vows that he judged it impossible to keep, mentioned as legitimate excuses not only physical illness but also wars (Lizerand, *Clément V,* pp. 424–25). On 21 December 1312 Clement V had given Philip permission to defer the ceremony until Pentecost because of his intention to knight his sons and "[alia] adhibere solempnia, que circa festum pentecostes proximo futurum poterunt comodius ordinari" (*Registrum Clementis V* 8:25–26, no. 8964). On 30 December 1312 Philip the Fair summoned a council of prelates and barons of France to discuss crusading plans (*Lettres de Philippe le Bel relatives au pays de Gévaudan,* ed. Jean Roucaute and Marc Saché [Mende: Privat, 1896], p. 141, no. 74; and Constantin Fasolt, *Council and Hierarchy: The Political Thought of William Durant the Younger,* Cambridge Studies in Medieval Life and Thought, 4th ser., no. 16 [Cambridge: Cambridge University Press, 1991], pp. 305–6). See also Ewald Müller, *Das Konzil von Vienne, 1311–1312: Seine Quellen und seine Geschichte,* Vorreformationsgeschichtliche Forschungen, no. 12 (Münster in Westfalen, 1934), pp. 107–74. The comment of the continuator of Nangis's chronicle, "sed nihil fecit," tersely characterizes the outcome of these proceedings (Christopher J. Tyerman, "Sed Nihil Fecit? The Last Capetians and the Recovery of the Holy Land," in *War and Government in the Middle Ages: Essays in Honour of J. O. Prestwich,* ed. John Gillingham and J. C. Holt [Cambridge, Eng.: Boydell Press, 1984], pp. 170–81).

46. *Registrum Clementis V* 8:401–2, which gives other details of the indulgence. See also the supplementary bull concerning the indulgence that the pope dispatched to Cardi-

nal Nicolas on 21 May 1313, in BN, Doat 16, fols. 127r–29v, included in a letter of Nicolas dated 17 January 1314 at Paris, itself contained in an act of 4 April 1314.

47. Arthur Bertrand de Broussillon and Eugène Vallée, *La maison de Craon, 1050–1480: étude historique accompagnée du Cartulaire de Craon,* 2 vols. (Paris: Picard, 1893), 1:329–30, no. 411.

48. See n. 18 above. On Edward's relations with Louis, see Hilda Johnstone, *Letters of Edward, Prince of Wales, 1304–1305,* Publications of the Roxburghe Club, no. 194 (Cambridge, Eng.: Roxburghe Club, 1931), pp. xix, xxxvii, 4, 11, 78; and Roland Delachenal, "Trois lettres d'Edouard premier prince de Galles, fils d'Edouard Ier, roi d'Angleterre," *Annuaire-Bulletin de la Société de l'Histoire de France* 59 (1922): 175–80, at 177–78.

49. Jean of Saint-Victor, in *Recueil des historiens* 21:656–57.

50. In her will of 27 August 1319 Jeanne left the Hospitalers 500 *l.* for crusading, "ia soit ce que nous ny aions point de veu. Mes pour la volunte que nous y eusmes quant nostresires li Roys qui estoit lors Quens de poitiers nous fist prendre la Croiz" (AN, J 404A, no. 23). The testament stated that Philip V had given her 30,000 *l. par.* for her bequests, and her legacies were probably understood to be specified in this currency. In the codicil that she drew up in May 1325 Jeanne reiterated this statement ("Item combien que nous naiens mie veu / au Passage doutremer / pour tant seulement que nostre bon seigneur / que dieux abssoile / nous fist prandre la croiz"), there ordaining that when the common passage was undertaken by those of royal blood (*Royaux*), her executors should spend 500 *l.* on a fitting knight to make the passage for her (ibid., no. 30); in this act the first bequest was made in *l. t.*

51. PRO, E 30/1422.

52. *Chronique métrique,* lines 5057–65.

53. PRO, E 101/375/8, fol. 3v ("in oblatione Regis ad coronam Spineam Christi in Capella Regis ffrancie Parisius per manus Johannis Merlyn liberatis denariis eidem Regi qui denarii allocantur eidem Johanni inter alias particulas suas ad compotum factum apud Pontisare" on 23 June following).

54. "Omnes artifices processionaliter incedebant"; "Quinta feria omnes artifices et burgenses se in equis et pedites ostenderunt processionaliter" (*Recueil des historiens* 21:656–57). See Du Cange, *Glossarium,* s.v. "processio."

55. Alan E. Knight discusses the processional context of medieval drama in *Aspects of Genre in Late Medieval French Drama* (Manchester: Manchester University Press, 1983), pp. 117–40; Louis Marin, "Notes on a Semiotic Approach to *Parade, Cortege,* and *Procession,*" in *Time Out of Time: Essays on the Festival,* ed. Alessandro Falassi (Albuquerque: University of New Mexico Press, 1987), pp. 220–28; Barbara Kirschenblatt-Gimblett and Brooks McNamara, "Processional Performance," *Drama Review* 29:3 (Fall 1985): 2–3; and Susan Davis, *Parades and Power: Street Theater in Nineteenth-Century Philadelphia* (Philadelphia: Temple University Press, 1986), pp. 159–66.

56. For the population of Paris, see Cazelles, *Nouvelle histoire,* pp. 131–40. One manuscript of the chronicle of Jean of Saint-Victor changes "equites viginti millia" to "equites quindecim millia" (*Recueil des historiens* 21:657).

57. Jean of Saint-Victor, in *Recueil des historiens* 21:657 ("ita quod rex cum multis nobilibus eos vidit per fenestras"); a caption in Raymond of Béziers states that the three kings viewed the parade from the entry to the palace (*ad hostium*) (BN, Ms. lat. 8504, fol. 1r).

58. Davis, *Parades and Power,* p. 159.

59. *Chronique métrique,* lines 5089–92.

60. Perhaps some landed at the quay that Philip IV ordered built at the Port Saint-Germain next to the Hôtel de Nesle and that was completed in 1313 (Cazelles, *Nouvelle histoire,* p. 212).

61. *Chronique métrique,* lines 4868–70 (Charles's feast), and 5070–80, esp. lines 5070–74 ("Dont esbahi si grandement / Furent Anglois, plus c'onques mes, / Car il ne

cuidassent jamés / Que tant de gent riche et nobile / Pouïst saillir de une ville"). Jean of Saint-Victor renders this, "Quos videns rex Angliae obstupuit, et omnes sui. Vix enim credere valeret quod de una sola civitate tanta et tam nobiliter parata potuerit exire multitudo" (*Recueil des historiens* 21:657).

62. The *Livre des sentences du parloir aux bourgeois* (1268–1325) records the names of the assessors chosen in December 1313. The men represented the drapers, the changers, the goldsmiths, the second-hand-clothes dealers (*frepiers*), the merchants, the mercers, the spice merchants, the furriers (*peletiers*), the sea-fishmongers, the weavers, the middlemen (*corratiers*), the bakers (*talmeliers*), and the butchers; the *Chronique métrique* mentions (lines 4996–97) the weavers (*tisseranz*) and belt-makers (*corroier*). See Antoine-Jean-Victor Le Roux de Lincy, *Histoire de l'Hôtel de Ville de Paris* ... (Paris: Dumoulin, 1846), pt. 2, Appendix 2, p. 173; and Alfred-Louis-Auguste Franklin, *Dictionnaire historique des arts et métiers et professions exercés dans Paris depuis le treizième siècle* ... (Paris: Welter, 1906). For the variety of crafts in Paris in the mid-thirteenth century, see *Les métiers et corporations de la ville de Paris, XIIIe siècle: Le livre des métiers d'Etienne Boileau*, ed. René de Lespinasse and François Bonnardot, Histoire générale de Paris, no. 5 (Paris: Imprimerie nationale, 1879). For the record of collection of the *taille* for the knighting aid, see Karl Michaëlsson, *Le livre de la taille de Paris l'an de grace 1313*, Acta Universitatis Gotoburgensis, Göteborgs Högskolas Årsskrift, no. 57(3) (Gothenburg: Wettergren & Kerbers, 1951), pp. ix–xxvi, 1–2. The imposition and levy of the knighting aid was accomplished with dispatch in Paris but opposed in other parts of the realm (Elizabeth A. R. Brown, *Customary Aids and Royal Finance in Capetian France: The Marriage Aid of Philip the Fair* [Cambridge, Mass.: Medieval Academy of America, 1992] pp. 188–207).

63. *Chronique métrique*, lines 4704–5.

64. Ibid., lines 4942–52. On the Parisians' admiration for knightly and noble ideals and practices, see Cazelles, *Nouvelle histoire*, pp. 110, 118, 395.

65. *Chronique métrique*, lines 4811–14, 5081–82 (street decorations); 5039–43 (fountain).

66. "Borjois tel feste demenerent / Que les royaus les mercïerent" (*Chronique métrique*, lines 4939–40).

67. "Et d'autre mainte faërie / Est il bien droit que je vous die" (*Chronique métrique*, lines 4953–54).

68. The next such reference to street tableaux is Jean Juvenal des Ursins's report of the entry of Charles VI to Paris in 1380, in which he wrote that the streets were "tendues et parées bien et notablement, et divers personnages, et plusieurs hystoires, et cryoit on Nouel" (Bernard Guenée and Françoise Lehoux, *Les entrées royales françaises de 1328 à 1515*, Sources d'histoire médiévale publiées par l'Institut de Recherche et d'Histoire des Textes, no. 5 (Paris: Editions du Centre National de la Recherche Scientifique, 1968), p. 58 (*Histoire de Charles VI*).

69. In a letter of remission of 1380 issued in Paris, Charles V refers to "jeux qui furent faiz et ordenez en l'onneur et remembrance de la Passion nostre Seigneur Jhesu Crit [sic] en nostre bonne ville de Paris par aucuns des bourgois et autres bonnes genz d'icelle" (Antoine Thomas, "Le théâtre à Paris et aux environs à la fin du quatorzième siècle," *Romania* 21 (1892): 606–11, at 610. For a mystery play staged for Charles V in Rouen in 1367, see Victor Le Clerc, "XIVe siècle: Discours sur l'état des lettres, lère partie," in *Histoire littéraire de la France*, vol. 24 (Paris: Welter, 1896), pp. 3–334, at 187.

70. For the next evidence known to us—forty plays produced by the Parisian goldsmiths between 1339 and 1382—see *Miracles de Nostre Dame par personnages*, ed. Gaston Paris and Ulysse Robert, 8 vols., Publications de la Société des Anciens Textes Français, no. 4 (Paris: Firmin Didot, 1876–93). See also Dorothy Penn, *The Staging of the "Miracles de Nostre Dame par personnages" of Ms. Cangé*, Publications of the Institute of French Studies (New York: Columbia University Press, 1933); and Graham A. Runnalls, "Mediæval Trade Guilds and the *Miracles de Nostre Dame par personnages*. Part I:

Guilds, *Confréries,* and the theater in Mediæval France; Part II: The Parisian Goldsmiths and the *Miracles de Nostre Dame par personnages," Medium Aevum* 39 (1970): 157–76, 277–87.

71. *Chronique métrique,* lines 5011–14.

72. Lawrence M. Bryant, *The King and the City in the Parisian Royal Entry Ceremony: Politics, Ritual, and Art in the Renaissance,* Travaux d'Humanisme et Renaissance, no. 216 (Geneva: Droz, 1986), pp. 169–70. See also Guenée and Lehoux, *Entrées,* pp. 25–26, who suggest that the development of the religious and allegorical *tableaux vivants* staged along the route is a fifteenth-century phenomenon; see, however, Jean Froissart's account of the Parisian entry of Isabeau de Bavière in 1389, in idem, *Œuvres,* ed. Joseph-Marie-Bruno-Constantin, baron Kervyn de Lettenhove, 25 vols. (Brussels: Académie royale de Belgique, 1867–77), 14:10–11; Bryant, *King and City,* pp. 28–29; and Bernard Ribemont, "L'entrée d'Isabeau de Bavière à Paris: une fête textuelle pour Froissart," in *Feste und Feiern* (see n. 4), pp. 515–24.

73. "Le mescredi un vent venta, / Qui les cortines adenta / Et derompi, mes redreciees / Furent tost et apareillees" (*Chronique métrique,* lines 4973–76).

74. "[E]nfer i fu noir et puant: / Les ames getant et ruant, / Dyables i ot plus de cent, / Qui tuit sailloient adjecent / Por les ames a elz atrere, / A cui faisoient maint contraire. / La les creüt on tormenter / Et les veoit on dementer" (*Chronique métrique,* lines 4965–72). For sets contructed of scaffolding covered with painted cloths and tapestry, see Gustave Cohen, *Histoire de la mise en scène dans le théâtre religieux français du Moyen Age,* 2nd ed. (Paris: Champion, 1951), p. 90. For the use of smoke, Cohen, *Mise en scène,* pp. 54, 92–99; and esp., in the earliest vernacular mystery, *Le mystère d'Adam (Ordo representacionis Ade),* ed. Paul Aebischer, Textes littéraires français (Geneva and Paris: Droz and Minard, 1964), p. 70.

75. "... Et les anges en paradis / Bien encor quatre vints et dis, / Et les ames dedenz chanter" (*Chronique métrique,* lines 4961–63).

76. See Cohen, *Mise en scène,* pp. 53, 67–71, 87–90.

77. Elie Konigson describes a platform for a Paradise measuring eight by twelve feet and accommodating thirty-two persons, which was built at Bourges in 1536 (*L'espace théâtral médiéval* [Paris: Editions du Centre National de la Recherche Scientifique, 1975], p. 243). These dimensions suggest that the Paradise of 1313 would have had to measure eight by thirty-five feet simply to hold ninety angels. A platform nearly two hundred feet long was constructed for a mystery in 1431 (Bryant, *King and City,* p. 151).

78. "Vit on la, et chastiax et tours" (*Chronique métrique,* line 5017). *Annales Londonienses* 1:220 gives a contemporary description of the procession of the fishmongers of London in 1312, "coram quibus praeibat quaedam navis, quodam mirabili ingenio operata, cum malo et velo erectis, et depictis de [armis regum Angliae et Franciae] et varietate plurima." See also Robert Withington, *English Pageantry: An Historical Outline,* 2 vols. (Cambridge, Mass.: Harvard University Press, 1918–26; reprint, New York and London: Benjamin Blom, 1963), 1:126.

79. "La vit on maintes armeüres, / Maintes riches desguiseüres, / Qui Nostre Dame en l'Isle aloient" (*Chronique métrique,* lines 5053–55). Cf. the line, "Desguisez sont de grant maniere," which accompanies the miniatures in the *Roman de Fauvel* of BN, fr. 146, fols. 34r, 34v, 36v that represent Parisians clad in costumes and masks, holding a charivari (*Le Roman de Fauvel par Gervais du Bus ...,* ed. Arthur Långfors, Publications de la Société des Anciens Textes Français, no. 64 (Paris: Firmin Didot, 1914–19), p. 165, line 697). See Nancy Freeman Regalado, "Masques réels dans le monde de l'imaginaire: le rite et l'écrit dans le charivari du *Roman de Fauvel,* MS BN fr. 146," in *Masques et déguisements dans la littérature médiévale,* ed. Marie-Louise Ollier (Montreal and Paris: Presses de l'Université de Montréal and Vrin, 1988), pp. 111–26; and Roesner, Avril, and Regalado, "Introduction," in *Roman de Fauvel,* pp. 10–12.

80. "[T]ouz les bourgois et maistres de Paris ... vindrent ... ou dessus dit ille de Nos-

tre Dame, ... a grant joie et a grant noise demenant et de tres biaus jeux jouant" (*Grandes Chroniques* 8:288–89).

81. See, for example, Guenée and Lehoux, *Entrées*, p. 69 (1431).

82. See n. 75 above.

83. See n. 74 above.

84. "... homes sauvages / Qui menoient granz rigola[ge]s" (*Chronique métrique,* lines 4993–94).

85. See Frank's discussion of the development of the Passion Play, in *Drama*, pp. 125–35.

86. "La fu le tornai des enfanz, / Dont chascun n'ot plus de dis anz" (*Chronique métrique,* lines 4979–80).

87. This story, found in Branch XVII of the *Roman de Renart* (ca. 1205), was often represented in miniatures; it also appeared on a sculptured frieze of 1298 in the Cathedral of Strasbourg. See Robert Bossuat, *Le Roman de Renard*, 2nd ed. (Paris: Hatier, 1967), pp. 58–62, 169, 191; and Kenneth Varty, "The Death and Resurrection of Reynard in Mediaeval Literature and Art," *Nottingham Medieval Studies* 8 (1964): 70–93.

88. This story is found in the late-twelfth-century Branch X of the *Roman de Renart*.

89. "Touz celz qui après lui venoient / Que plus que mains le maudisoient / Et disoient: 'Avant, Renart, / Honte te doint saint Lïenart! / Ton barat et ta tricherie / A touz nous a tolu la vie. / L'avoir du rëaume as emblé'" (*Chronique métrique,* lines 6985–91; see n. 16 above. For Enguerran's red hair, see Jean Favier, "Les portraits d'Enguerran de Marigny," *Annales de Normandie* 15 (1965): 517–24, at 520. Because the metrical chronicle calls Boniface VIII a "renart" (line 2162) and presents Renart dressed as a pope, John Flinn concludes that the scenes of Renart shown in 1313 expressed Gallican hostility to the temporal authority of the papacy (*Le Roman de Renart dans la littérature française et dans les littératures étrangères au Moyen Age* [Toronto: University of Toronto Press, 1963], pp. 147–55). See Nancy Freeman Regalado, "Medieval Drama and the Construction of Popular Political Culture: Stagings of the *Roman de Renart* at the Parisian Pentecost Feast of 1313," *Medievalia*, special number, ed. Millia C. Riggio and Martin Stevens (forthcoming).

90. In *Un songe*, a poem included in BN, fr. 146, Geffroi de Paris uses the image of the bean king to represent the baby king Jean I, who was born in November 1315 and lived for only a few days (*Six Historical Poems of Geffroi de Paris ...*, ed. Walter H. Storer and Charles A. Rochedieu, University of North Carolina Studies in the Romance Languages and Literatures, no. 16 [Chapel Hill: University of North Carolina Press, 1950], pp. 64 [lines 109–19], 68 [lines 247–60]). See Elizabeth A. R. Brown, "The Ceremonial of Royal Succession in Capetian France: The Double Funeral of Louis X" (1978), in her *The Monarchy of Capetian France and Royal Ceremonial* (Aldershot: Variorum, 1991), no. 7, pp. 227–71, at 264–66.

91. Roesner, Avril, and Regalado, "Introduction," in *Roman de Fauvel*, p. 8; and Brown, *Adultery, Charivari.*

92. "... leur franchises, leur coustumes, leur usages, leur privilèges": a petition presented by the bourgeois of Paris to Philip the Fair in 1298, in *Réglemens sur les arts et métiers de Paris rédigés au XIIIe siècle, et connus sous le nom du Livre des métiers d'Etienne Boileau*, ed. G.-B. Depping, Collection de documents inédits sur l'histoire de France, 1st. ser., Histoire politique (Paris: Crapelet, 1837), pp. 452–53; on the source, ibid., p. xvi. For the privileges, ambitions, and status of the bourgeois of Paris, see Cazelles, *Nouvelle histoire*, pp. 42–43, 96–97, 109–11, 424–25. Dissension over payment for the gifts presented to Philip the Fair and the garments that were worn for the royal entry to Bruges in 1301 led to the arrest of a weaver and his associates, who protested against the plans of the municipal magistrates to use common funds for these expenses (*Annales Gandenses*, p. 13).

93. Runnalls, "Mediæval Trade Guilds," 268.

94. "La fu le grant gait, l'en le vit: / Huit cens touz vestuz d'un abit" (*Chronique métrique*, lines 5051–52). On the *guet*, see *Métiers et corporations*, ed. Lespinasse and Bonnardot, pp. cxli–liv; Franklin, *Dictionnaire historique*, pp. 375–76; and Cazelles, *Nouvelle histoire*, pp. 186–91.

95. "Tout ce firent les tisseranz. / Corroier aussi contrefirent / . . . La vie de Renart" (*Chronique métrique*, lines 4996–99).

96. Franklin, *Dictionnaire historique*, pp. 270–74, 693–95, and his *Les corporations ouvrières de Paris du XIIe au XVIIIe siècle: Histoire, statuts, armoiries d'après les documents originaux ou inédits* (Paris: Firmin-Didot, 1884), "Drapiers: tisseurs et marchands," pp. 1–5, esp. p. 2; cf. the terminology of the regulations issued in April 1270 by Renaut Barbou, *prévôt des marchands* from 1269 to 1275, and reissued on 24 December 1285 by Oudart de la Neuville, *prévôt* from 1285 to 1287 (*Réglemens*, ed. Depping, pp. 392–96). Franklin (*Corporations ouvrières*, p. 3) notes that the merchants who made the largest contributions to the *taille* of 1313 were three drapers who paid, respectively, 150, 135, and 127 *l.*

97. Franklin, *Dictionnaire historique*, pp. 294–95.

98. "Estrumenz de maintes manieres" (*Chronique métrique*, line 5016).

99. "Et en maintes guises dancier / En blanches chemises ribaus / I vit on, liez et gais et baus" (*Chronique métrique*, lines 5006–9). The *ribaut* or roustabout of the Place de Grève was a stock figure for the urban poor of Paris (Rutebeuf, "Dit des ribauds de Grève," in *Oeuvres complètes*, ed. Edmond Faral and Julia Bastin, 2 vols. [Paris: A. et J. Picard, 1959–60], 1:531). In Jean de Meun's *Roman de la Rose*, Lady Reason describes the carefree life of the *ribaut*, who spends the meager sums earned by carrying sacks of coal in the Place de Grève on drinking and dancing before a company of thieves (Guillaume de Lorris and Jean de Meun, *Le Roman de la Rose*, ed. Félix Lecoy, 3 vols., Classiques français du Moyen Age, nos. 92, 95, 98 [Paris: Champion, 1965–70], lines 5015–36, 5250–54, 5267–70).

100. "Dames caroler de biax tours"; "Par Paris toute la semainne, / La furent borgoises parees, / Balans et dansans regardees, / En cui avoit toute richece / Et fete aussi toute largece" (*Chronique métrique*, lines 5018, 5044–48). The metrical chronicler expatiates on the beauty of Queen Isabelle (ibid., lines 4745–54), but he does not report her assumption of the Cross nor that of the ladies who made their vows on Thursday. He mentions the banquet that Philip the Fair gave for Isabelle, Marguerite of Navarre, and other *dames* in recounting the various royal feasts that were offered during the week (ibid., lines 4745–54, 4859–62, 5059–65, 5117–28).

101. "[T]res grant compaingnie / Par nuit et par jor bien garnie" (*Chronique métrique*, lines 4949–50).

102. *Chronique métrique*, lines 5099–5132.

103. *Comptes royaux (1285–1314)*, nos. 27773, 27775, entries showing that Philip the Fair left Paris on the vigil of Trinity Sunday and spent the next day in or near Poissy.

104. PRO, E 101/375/8, fol. 32r.

105. *Chronique métrique*, lines 5105–28.

106. PRO, E 101/375/8, fols. 4r, 31v.

107. PRO, E 101/375/8, fol. 32r. See Bullock-Davies, *Register*, pp. xii, 9, 120. The prudish Henry VI of England was said to have fled when naked dancers appeared at a Christmas celebration (John W. McKenna, "Piety and Propaganda: The Cult of Henry VI," in *Chaucer and Middle English Studies in Honour of Rossell Hope Robbins*, ed. Beryl Rowland [London: Allen and Unwin, 1974], pp. 72–88, at 78; and John Blacman, *Henry the Sixth: Collectarium mansuetudinum et bonorum morum Regis Henrici VI*, ed. Montague Rhodes James [Cambridge: Cambridge University Press, 1919], p. 8).

108. Thomas N. Bisson mentions but does not explore the political purposes served by the *feste*, in "The General Assemblies of Philip the Fair: Their Character Reconsidered" (1972), in his *Medieval France and Her Pyrenean Neighbours: Studies in Early Institutional History*, Studies Presented to the International Commission for the History of Repre-

sentative and Parliamentary Institutions, no. 70 (London: Hambledon Press, 1989), pp. 97–122, at 100.

109. PRO, C47/29/8/2, a protest, badly damaged, drafted by the Commons in Parliament later in the summer of 1313.

110. *Rôles gascons*, vol. 4: *1307–1317*, ed. Yves Renouard (Paris: Imprimerie nationale, 1962), pp. 268–93, esp. 268 n. 1.

111. Funck-Brentano, Philippe le Bel en Flandre, pp. 632–33; *Chronique métrique*, lines 5133–48; Claude de Vic and Jean-Joseph Vaissete, *Histoire générale de Langue-doc . . .*, ed. Auguste Molinier, 15 vols. (Toulouse: Privat, 1873–93), 9:339–40; and Léon Ménard, *Histoire civile, ecclésiastique et littéraire de la Ville de Nismes . . .*, 7 vols. (Paris: Chaubert, 1750–58), 2:11 n. 3.

112. *Ordonnances* 1:519–31, for the ordonnance of 15 June and later modifications.

113. For the privileges, see Elizabeth A. R. Brown, "Diplomacy, Adultery, and Domestic Politics at the Court of Philip the Fair: Queen Isabelle's Mission to France in 1314," in *Documenting the Past: Essays in Medieval History Presented to George Peddy Cuttino*, ed. J. S. Hamilton and Patricia J. Bradley (Woodbridge: Boydell Press, 1989), pp. 53–83, at 56–62. For Philip's explanation of his beneficence, repeated in a number of the graces, see *The Register of Walter de Stapeldon, Bishop of Exeter (A.D. 1302–1326)*, ed. Francis Charles Hingeston-Randolph (London: Bell, 1892), p. 161; see also Brown, "Diplomacy, Adultery," 37–38 n. 36.

114. Hallam, *Itinerary*, p. 100.

115. PRO, E 101/375/8, fol. 30r (Edward's gift of 10 *l.* 2 *s.* 1 *d. ob. st.*, made on 4 July at Poissy); and *Comptes royaux (1285–1314)*, no. 27745 (Philip the Fair's gift of 40 *l.*, undated, but presumably made at the same time as Edward's).

116. PRO, E 101/375/8, fol. 30r; Bullock-Davies, *Register*, p. 72.

117. Brown, "Diplomacy, Adultery," pp. 61–62.

118. Brown, *Customary Aids*, pp. 188–207.

119. Elizabeth A. R. Brown, "Royal Salvation and Needs of State in Early-Fourteenth-Century France," in her *Monarchy of Capetian France*, no. 4, pp. 1–56, at 19–20.

120. See the letter of Clement V of 20 June 1313, in Etienne Baluze, *Vitae paparum Avenionensium*, ed. Guillaume Mollat, 4 vols. (Paris: Letouzet et Ané, 1914–27), 3:122–23; and Bernard Barbiche, *Les actes pontificaux originaux des Archives nationales de Paris*, 3 vols., Index actorum Romanorum Pontificum ab Innocentio III ad Martinum V electum; C.I.S.H. Commission internationale de diplomatique (Vatican City: Biblioteca Apostolica Vaticana), vol. 3, no. 2466.

121. See esp. Simon D. Lloyd, *English Society and the Crusade, 1216–1307* (Oxford: Clarendon Press, 1988), pp. 30, 34, 113–53, 231–39; and Michael Prestwich, *Edward I* (Berkeley: University of California Press, 1988), p. 557; cf. Schein, *Fideles Crucis*, p. 86. A contemporary lament on Edward's death declared, "Le rei de Fraunce grant pecché fist, / Le passage à desturber / Qe rei Edward pur Dieu emprist, / Sur Sarazins l'ewe passer" (*The Political Songs of England, From the Reign of John to That of Edward II*, ed. Thomas Wright, Publications of the Camden Society, o.s., no. 6 (London: Camden Society, 1839), p. 241, cf. p. 247.

122. *Regestum Clementis V* 8:400–401 ("carissimus in Christo filius noster Philippus rex Francorum illustris christianissimus princeps," "viri ad bella doctissimi predicti regni Francie bellatores ac regem ipsum preliatorem promptissimum Crucifixi," "dicti regni viri fortes et strenui . . . qui solent gloriosiores in preliis probate virtutis exercitio reputari"; "[e]idem quoque regi et inclite domui Francie, cui Dominus benedixit, huiusmodi felix victoria belli promittitur, hec illis paratur ad gloriam et eis, sicut speratur, ad meritum reservatur").

123. For Philip and his father, see Elizabeth A. R. Brown, "The Prince Is Father of the King: The Character and Childhood of Philip the Fair of France" (1987), in her *Monarchy of Capetian France*, no. 2, pp. 299–300, 320–26, 331–32; for Philip's attitude to Saint Louis, ibid., pp. 310–12, 326–28, 332–34.

124. For the Aragonese enterprise, and for Philip's feelings about Aragon and his ties to Aragon through his mother, see Brown, "Prince Is Father," pp. 293–94, 312, 314, 323–24, 330, 331. The chronicles give at best passing notice to Philip's knighting in 1284 (*Recueil des historiens*, 20:528–29 [Nangis, *Gesta Philippi Tertii*]; Nangis, *Chronique* 1:262; and *Grandes Chroniques* 8:101, esp. n. 2).

125. Charlotte Lacaze, "Parisius-Paradisus, an Aspect of the Vie de St. Denis Manuscript of 1317," *Marsyas: Studies in the History of Art* 16 (1972–73): 60–66. See also Konigson, *L'espace théâtral*, pp. 77–94; and Coulet, "Entrées solennelles," p. 77.

126. "Et de jor et de nuit, sen ni, / La pooit on boivre et mangier / Par tout Paris, sanz nul dangier" (*Chronique métrique*, lines 5032–34).

127. "La joie, le deduit, la feste, / ... / Ce sont merveilles sanz pareilles" (*Chronique métrique*, lines 4805 and 4825). MacAloon sees joy as a mood that distinguishes the genre of festive celebration, ("Olympic Games," pp. 246–50).

PART II

Public and Private Religious Expression in the Urban Context

CHAPTER 4

Icons, Altarpieces, and Civic Ritual in Siena Cathedral, 1100–1530

Bram Kempers

Introduction

"Centuries of confusion and oceans of ink might have been saved had historians in treating of the two early Madonna paintings that ostensibly followed one another upon the high altar of the Cathedral of Siena, the one still in the Cappella del Voto in the Cathedral, the other now in the Museo dell'Opera (No. 22), turned to a systematic study of the surviving documents. That they never did appears surprising when it is realized that many documents lay always easily accessible to them." Thus ran the opening sentences of the standard book published by Garrison in 1960 on the two oldest paintings of the Virgin in Siena Cathedral.[1]

Siena Cathedral is interesting not only to specialists in the field of early Italian icons and altarpieces, but also to sociologists, anthropologists, and historians. Its interest lies in the unusual situation that arose between 1250 and 1350 whereby the civic authorities of Siena, headed by an elite composed of merchants and bankers, assumed a dominant role previously enjoyed by the bishop and canons and by the feudal nobility. Using as a basis the chapter's liturgy and processions of nobles, the city authorities succeeded in creating a new form of civic ceremony in the cathedral, resulting in some unique developments in art and architecture.[2] The duomo's ritual and imagery were modified to demonstrate continuity and change in communal authority. The cathedral acquired a crucial role in the new civic order through a wide range of ceremonial displays and more permanent memorials.

The notable role of Siena's citizens with regard to the cathedral is apparent from the illustration on the cover of the annual report of the Gabella—one of the Sienese tax authorities—for 1483 (see Figure 4.1).[3] It depicts citizens and members of the clergy standing before a chapel, looking at the figure of the Virgin Mary. She is emerging from her pictorial frame to receive the keys offered her by a citizen who is standing on a small dais in front of the altar. The inscription indicates that this portrays the bestowal upon the Virgin of the keys of the city and shows the

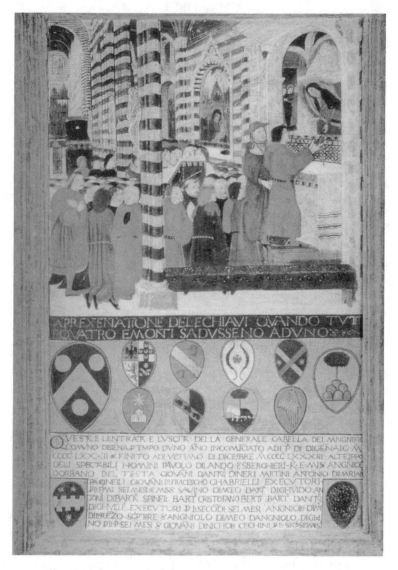

Figure 4.1. "The Second Bestowal of the Keys to the Virgin in the Cathedral," Gabella panel 1483, Siena, Archivio di Stato. (Photo, Grassi.)

union of all four of Siena's political parties, which were linked to the major social groups or classes.[4]

Behind representatives of the four classes, singers can be seen standing next to a lectern with a gradual. Two altars in alcoves are depicted in the right-hand aisle, one with an altarpiece. The "Cappella delle Grazie" in the foreground has a marble canopy decorated with sculptures and civic coats of arms.

The prevailing opinion is that both the panels to which Garrison referred originally stood in turn on the high altar before Duccio's Maestà
was placed there in 1311. The oldest panel is usually known as the
"Madonna degli occhi grossi," the Madonna with the bulging eyes. It
survives in a truncated form and is kept in the Cathedral Museum. The
panel depicts a seated Virgin with a blessing Christ on her lap and two
angels in the background. It is thought that this panel painting was originally executed as an antependium and that it was later placed on the
high altar as an altarpiece around 1240. As such it would have played a
major role in the history of the altarpiece as a new genre within the context of the liturgy at the high altar.[5]

The second panel is known as the "Madonna delle Grazie" or
"Madonna del Voto" and is ascribed to Guido da Siena. The half-length
Madonna has Christ on her arm and they make a gesture to one another.
The painting is dated 1261 or later, but not after 1280. This panel, which
has also been cut down from its former size, was placed in the Cappella
del Voto in 1662, where it still is today. It is generally assumed that the
second panel painting was commissioned as an altarpiece for the high
altar of the cathedral after the battle of Montaperti in 1260.[6] Both these
representations of the Virgin are accordingly seen as the precursors of
Duccio's Maestà, which is also among the collection of the Cathedral
Museum.[7] Yet there are no contemporary sources with regard to the two
early Madonna paintings; the earliest written evidence dates from the
late fourteenth century, after a thorough renovation of the cathedral. As
there is a lot of confusion, not the least in nomenclature, I propose the
following designations: the first will be christened the Madonna-in-
relief; the second, the Madonna delle Grazie.

Therefore, more ink must flow in the battle against intellectual confusion, not just in the interests of art-historical research, but also in
order to achieve a sociological and historical interpretation that does
justice to the function of devotional images for the people who revered
them, who carried them in processions, who derived their standards and
values from them, and who subsequently moved them and sawed pieces
off them, to the annoyance of later generations of scholars.

Sociological and anthropological research traditionally focuses on the
function of ritual, the lines that divide the sacred and the profane, the
invention of collective symbols, and the effect of gift relationships within the development of individual societies. The French tradition of
Emile Durkheim and Marcel Mauss stresses the question of how such
concepts contribute to the suppression of conflict and the achievement
of consensus. In the German tradition of Karl Marx, Max Weber, and
Norbert Elias, emphasis is placed instead on changes and conflicts that
are at least as important as continuity and consensus.[8] These approaches
have been applied to the culture of the late Middle Ages and the Renaissance.[9] Sociological and anthropological concepts in fact deal with

themes traditional to art historians: liturgy, processions and public spectacle, *Kleinarchitektur* (like choir walls and pulpits), iconography, and ecclesiastical donations. Therefore, I should like to explore this same sort of approach with regard to the public use of painted images in Siena Cathedral, posing seven questions, each of which forms the subject of a separate section:

1. How was the space of Siena Cathedral arranged from the profane to the sacred?
2. Did the customary use of icons of the Virgin in processions also extend to Siena?
3. What was the function of the new "Cappella delle Grazie" and of the first altarpiece depicting the Madonna?
4. What were the functions of Duccio's Maestà in relation to the two earlier Madonnas?
5. How did alterations lead to confusion as of the fifteenth century?
6. Which Madonnas and saints did the artist of the Gabella panel in fact see in 1483?
7. What was the political significance of the church ritual that he depicted?

1. Context: Architecture and Ritual

In about 1658 a ground plan was made of the cathedral, which shows the situation as it was then and incorporates a draft for a new side entrance, side wall, and chapel—the present Cappella del Voto (see Figure 4.2).[10] A large chapel is drawn on a level with the third bay, with the inscription "Cappella della Madonna." The "Cappella delle Grazie," as it is more commonly known, is situated in the Casa del Arcivescovo, which directly adjoins the southern wall of the cathedral. Two more bays follow, the second next to the tower opposite the Cappella di San Giovanni Baptista. Where the transept widens for the second time there is a door that makes the cathedral directly accessible from the city center: the Porta del Perdono. To the north side of the church a door in the nave leads to the Canonica, which at the front of the cathedral becomes the "house of the master of the *opera,* or cathedral works."[11] Opposite the duomo is the hospital, and behind the episcopal palace the remains of the Duomo Nuovo, which was never completed, are shown.

The Gabella panel artist stood to the left of the second column on the right-hand side of the nave and recorded in the background a large pulpit and part of an iron gate within a marble wall, which are all missing from the 1658 plan. The presbytery (or chancel, as the sacred space is sometimes called) has been sketched in so summarily that the drawing is not useful as the basis for a reconstruction. In 1506, writes Sigismondo Tizio in his chronicle of Siena, the altarpiece was removed, as were some

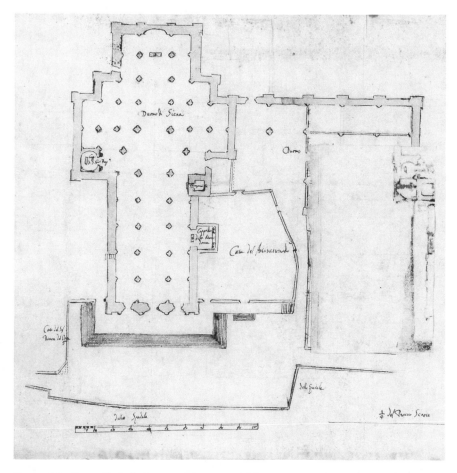

Figure 4.2. Siena Cathedral, ca. 1658, Roma Biblioteca Apostolica Vaticana (BAV), Archivio Chigi P. VII 11, fols. 38v–39r. (Photo, BAV.)

statues on the altar, the choir, and the pulpit. He describes in so many words how the choir was removed "from the middle of the church" and records that this was done against the canons' will.[12] Preliminary discussion of this decision by the civic authorities had taken place on 19 and 23 June 1506 at the instigation of the ruler at the time, Pandolfo Petrucci. The Balìa argued that this alteration was based on aesthetic considerations and dictated that from then on the canons would have to make use of the "chapel behind the altar."[13]

The cathedral inventories give some indication of the spatial arrangement from the profane to the sacred. In the fifteenth century the presbytery comprised two sections: an antechoir for the office in the nave and a chapel for mass on the other side of the high altar.[14] The antechoir was decorated on the inside with inlaid wood and on the outside with

93

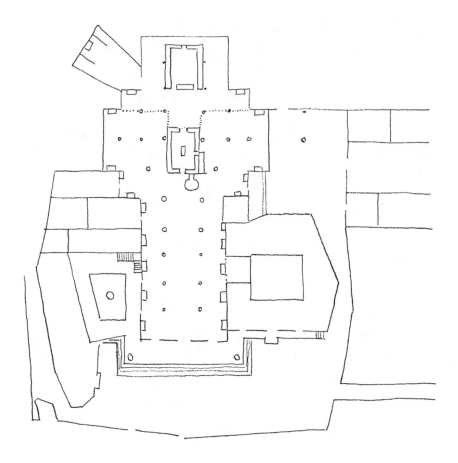

Figure 4.3. Reconstruction of Siena Cathedral, its choirs, and its adjacent buildings, ca. 1400–1506. (Drawing by Bram Kempers.)

worked marble.[15] The importance of a choir on the nave side of the altar is also apparent from the draft plans for the new cathedral, drawn up in the 1320s.[16] Francesco del Tonghio and his son Giacomo worked on the choirs between about 1362 and 1396. The antechoir was renovated with a lectern and new seats and after 1378 a monumental second section was newly constructed around the high altar in the *cappella maggiore*.[17] The alteration of 1506 entailed the demolition of the antechoir in the nave and far-reaching modifications to the choir around the high altar. The whole presbytery was relocated right behind the high altar, now occupying the entire space, including the former ambulatory, which was to serve for both the choir office and the canons' mass (see Figure 4.3).

In the early fourteenth century the cathedral was much smaller than it appears on the plan of about 1658. Prior to the 1370s the presbytery was considerably smaller. Around 1260 the east end of the duomo was in the shape of a right angle two bays deep.[18] In the twelfth century the cathedral was even more moderate in size: a semicircular apse, a smaller dome, and a separate baptistery facing the main entrance.[19]

The appearance and use of the cathedral in the early thirteenth century are described in the *Ordo officiorum ecclesie Senensis*, which was written by Canon Oderic since the 1140s.[20] It is a remarkably detailed ordinal, containing numerous theological elucidations, which, however, have no bearing on the interior arrangement of the cathedral. It is in this very respect that the text is summary, since Oderic passes over things that would have been well known to his fellow canons.

Oderic's most detailed account is naturally of the procedure relating to divine office and mass. Antiphonal and responsorial chants were sung on either side of the high altar dedicated to the Virgin Mary. The majority of the singers were positioned on the nave side, while a cantor and sometimes two other soloists stood in the apse.[21] The clergy used the space that extended from the apse into the nave for the singing of office and the celebration of mass; the presbytery comprised an elevated choir in the apse and an antechoir in the nave (see Figure 4.4).

A crucial part of the liturgy, which often was performed after sunset, was the "creation" of light. The cathedral clergy processed into the church to cense the altars and light the candles. At Whitsun the bishop, when present, the canons, and all the clergy of the city (*totius civitatis*) left the cathedral after mass and communion to process through the city, and on the feast of Saint James they also visited the church of that saint. Song was not the only method used to add luster to the ceremonies. The cathedral bells were frequently rung and stressed the hierarchy in the ritual events.[22] The choir was the domain of the chapter, but on feast days the bishop or a priest celebrated a mass for the laity.[23]

In addition to the high altar there were a number of other altars. The most important ceremonies took place at the altar of Saint Crescentius in the presence of both cathedral clergy and the rest of the Sienese priests. Constructed like the high altar, it could be used on both sides. This altar stood in the middle of the crypt and contained a relic of Saint Crescentius, whose feast day was celebrated on a grand scale, *cum Majori referentia*.[24] Canon Oderic mentions other sanctuaries as well. So, apart from the high altar and the one in the crypt, there were several side altars. Two were located in the elevated choir and the other altars were in the nave. The altar of Saint Savinus contained the main relic of Siena's first bishop, the head of Saint Victor, and other relics. It was at this altar that the feasts of Saints Savinus, Victor, and the latter's wife Corona were celebrated. The archangel Michael had an altar dedicated to him, as did Silvester, John, and Bartholomew. The cult of several saints was combined in one altar. The cathedral, moreover, possessed the body of Saint Ansanus, whose feast was traditionally celebrated *devotissime*.[25]

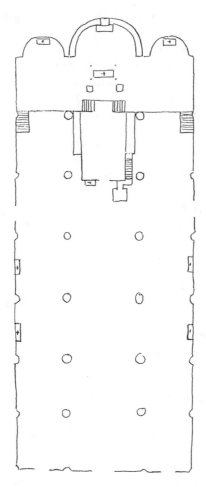

Figure 4.4. Reconstruction of Siena Cathedral with the altars, choirs, and pulpits, ca. 1200. (Drawing by Bram Kempers.)

Not only the altars, but also the pulpits, constituted an important element in the church interior and its liturgy. A raised pulpit for singing, reading, and preaching on the occasion of special ceremonies was part of the presbytery: the dean could read the gospel and the singer, with three brothers, could perform from this raised platform. The solemn pulpit was supplemented by two small lecterns on both sides of the high altar. The altar of the Blessed Virgin formed the focal point of the church. Behind the high altar were seats for priests and a bishop's throne, although these elements were not mentioned in Oderic's description of the canons' office. Within the antechoir the bishop had a special seat as well. The antechoir was on the nave side, some steps down and surrounded by a low wall against which the solemn pulpit was placed.[26]

This ensemble provided the spatial framework for the canons' liturgy as it was codified by Oderic. However, this ceremonial space was not an intimate domain exclusively reserved for the clergy. City processions fell outside the scope of an *ordo* written by a canon, but other texts testify to their importance. In such processions icons were often borne by the populace. The entire civic community gathered in the cathedral on Christian feast days. The processions were a supplement to the office and mass and constituted together the highlights of cathedral ritual.

An important element in the public ceremonies was the offering of candles and tribute money. An example of such an act of submission was performed by three brothers, the Lords of Montepescali (near Lucca), in 1147. They were obliged to offer candles to the cathedral. Similar acts of feudal obedience are recorded: the Lords of Asciano in 1175, the counts of Frosini in 1178, the men from Montelaterone in 1205, and those of Montalcino in 1212.[27] The citizens of Siena attempted to adapt feudal ritual in their commune. They copied the practice of offering tribute to a lord and the ceremony of triumphal processions in order to create a new civic ritual.

The size of the offering was proportional to the status of the nobles, as a statute in 1200 decreed. On the eve of the Assumption, Sienese citizens were to go to the cathedral with simple candles, the use of candlesticks being reserved to members of the city government, the Concistoro. Three groups were represented in a hierarchical order: nobles from the *contado*, Sienese citizens, and the elite of merchants and bankers. Besides the candles, the subject villages, castles, and towns brought banners to the cathedral, which were bound to the pillars of the nave.[28]

The commune further elaborated the civic ritual. Civic authorities purchased wine and paid for town criers who summoned the people to the feast. They financed standards and pennons, garlands and the transport of candles, together with vermilion cloth for the trumpeters who accompanied the procession. Jesters and jugglers entertained the people.[29] The commune increased its expenses from the mid–thirteenth century onward and took great care that it was present as the main sponsor of the event. In 1298 the commune offered a candle of a hundred pounds, while twelve other candles were given by the civic officials individually. Moreover, it was the government's privilege to donate decorated candles.[30] The civic community gathered in the cathedral not only on the eve of Assumption but also in times of war.

2. Tradition: Icons, Processions, and War

On 2 September 1260 the Florentine ambassadors came to Siena for final negotiations, as the city chronicles, which were compiled in the fifteenth century, relate.[31] The Sienese civic authorities, the Council of Twenty-four, received them in San Cristoforo, their usual meeting place.

The day before the battle took place a solemn mass was celebrated in the cathedral, and the citizens made large offerings to the Virgin Mary.[32] The keys of the city were laid on the altar of the Blessed Virgin, to whom the city was then dedicated. The learned bishop of noble birth played a considerable role in these ceremonies.[33] "And by these actions and by means of prayers offered to the Mother of *Misericordia* the city defended itself against such danger."[34] During the night the Sienese saw an apparition of the Virgin; it was as if night had turned into day, so that the whole of Siena was covered as if by a canopy.[35] On 4 September 1260, the feast day of Saint Boniface, the Sienese gained an unexpected victory, which was celebrated with a procession in the presence of men, women, and children who knelt and gave thanks to God and the Virgin Mary.[36]

According to a second, more elaborate account, written by Paolo di Tommaso Montauri, the participants in the processions were Bonaguida Lucari, the man who had been elected *sindaco*; the bishop; the canons of the cathedral; all the citizens in order of rank and precedence; then the people; and finally the women, *grandi en picole.* They begged for succor, sang litanies, and recited prayers, alternating between *pater noster* and *ave marie.*[37] The bishop caused the bells to be rung and preached a short sermon. He implored the Virgin to liberate Siena, descended from the pulpit, and processed, singing and praying, through the duomo. Lucari, too, appealed to Mary to free Siena from the lions and dragons that sought to devour it.[38] He knelt at the foot of the choir, where he met the bishop. Together they went toward the high altar and continued to address supplications to the Virgin.[39] Lucari laid the keys of the city gates on the altar and entrusted Siena to the Virgin's protection. In the ensuing procession all the clergy walked behind the carved crucifix of the cathedral, followed by a banner and a "panel painted with the likeness of Our Lady under a canopy" (see Figure 4.5).[40] In the thanksgiving processions following the victory, the flag and cross were borne at the head, followed by the monks and friars, the bishop, the canons, and the city council.[41]

Yet another account reveals more exactly which icon was borne in the procession and the precise nature of the civic rituals. In December 1442 Niccolò di Giovanni di Francesco Ventura completed his extensive text and a large series of miniatures illustrating the history of the battle of Montaperti.[42] Ventura introduced the subject of his chronicle in the first sentence: the victory of the Sienese at Montaperti and its circumstances.[43] Not much is known about the painter and writer Ventura.[44] Upon the completion of his manuscript he was registered in 1448 as one of the *pizzicaoli* who received a concession from the master of the cathedral works in connection with the use of candles.[45] Ventura states that his sources include both new observations and old accounts.[46] In

Figure 4.5. "Procession with the Madonna Icon in 1260." Chronicle by Niccolò di Giovanni Ventura, 1442, fol. 5r, Biblioteca Communale degli Intronati, Siena. (Photo, Testi Siena.)

his chronicle he both described and illustrated the main episodes: the beginning of the war, the rituals in the cathedral together with the processions through the city, the battle, the victory celebrations, and, lastly, concluding events.

In the first series of illustrations, the Florentine army that marches on Siena carried banners with the city arms above a red lily; the initial letter encloses the Virgin Mary who protects Siena (fol. 1r). The Florentine ambassadors go to San Cristoforo, above the door of which the Virgin and Child and two saints are portrayed, while inside the authorities are engaged in urgent consultation (fol. 1v). The Sienese civic council meets in San Cristoforo, which is depicted as an "open" church with the bell tower on the extreme right (fol. 2r; see Figure 4.6). Feudal nobles from the *contado*, led by count Giordano d'Anglano, come to offer military assistance, while the citizens are in conference (fol. 2v). Bankers led by Salimbene Salimbeni come with a cart filled with money (fol. 3r; see Figure 4.7).[47]

The bishop preaches a sermon at the third bay of the cathedral nave (fol. 3v).[48] On the steps of the presbytery he encourages the kneeling people, while the clergy stand behind him (fol. 4r; see Figure 4.8). Lucari gives the keys to the bishop, who is pointing to the altar and an altarpiece; it is depicted as a Gothic triptych whose central panel shows the Virgin and Child on a throne, flanked by three representations of several

Figure 4.6. "The Florentine Ambassadors and the City Authorities of Siena in San Cristoforo," Chronicle by Ventura, fol. 2r.

Figure 4.7. "The Sienese Bankers Bring Money to Finance the Battle of Montaperti," Chronicle by Ventura, fol. 3r.

Figure 4.8. "The Bishop and the Clergy, the *Sindaco* and the *Popolo* in the Cathedral," Chronicle by Ventura, fol. 4r.

Figure 4.9. "Lucari Gives the Keys to the Bishop in front of the High Altar," Chronicle by Ventura, fol. 4v.

101

figures; a cleric holding a staff stands next to Lucari, the people and clerics are assembled behind the *sindaco,* and to the right a notary draws up a deed of the transfer of the keys (fol. 4v; see Figure 4.9). In the procession an icon is borne along, representing the Virgin with the infant Jesus on her lap. The Sienese civic arms are depicted on the canopy carried by some of the citizens, the image is followed by the bishop and the people, and at the head march clerics bearing a crucifix (fol. 5r; see Figure 4.5). An illustrated account of the battle follows.[49]

The fourth series of illustrations shows the victory rites.[50] The Sienese return to their city garlanded with oak leaves, taking with them their carts and banners (fols. 18v–19r; see Figures 4.10 and 4.11). They go to the cathedral accompanied by their prisoners (19v). Still wearing their oak-leaf wreaths, the knights process to San Cristoforo, taking with them one of the prisoners, who is carried upside down on an ass (fol. 20r). Siena celebrates victory (fol. 20v). The civic authorities assemble in San Cristoforo (fol. 21r). During the thanksgiving procession on 7 September (fols. 21v–22r), the bishop walks beneath a baldachin, preceded by four canons in copes carrying a chest containing relics, a bust, and two more relics, one of which is contained in a Gothic ostensorium; four crosses with banners are also carried in the procession, which is headed by a cleric bearing a bleeding, carved crucifix to which a large red banner is attached (see Figures 4.12 and 4.13).[51] The fifth group of illustrations shows concluding events.[52]

Like others before and after him, Ventura describes the bishop's sermon from the pulpit, during which he announces that a procession and a confession will take place the following day.[53] A *stendardo* was carried in the procession along with the carved crucifix, which in his day was kept near the bell tower.[54] Ventura provides further information about the images of the Virgin. A new *tavola* depicting the Virgin and Child was painted immediately after the battle of Montaperti. In a passage inserted subsequently, Ventura makes clear that this new panel was confused with a smaller and older *tavola,* namely, the icon before which the vow of Montaperti was made. He describes its location: attached to the tower in the duomo, next to the Porta del Perdono and without an altar. Moreover, Ventura indicates that the icon of the vow possessed a quality that distinguished it from the other, later images: it was *di mezo taglio, cioè di mezo rilievo.*[55]

The description "in middle relief," or *di mezo rilievo,* leaves no doubt that the panel painting used in the processions can be identified with the Virgin in the Cathedral Museum that is referred to as the "Madonna degli occhi grossi" (see Figure 4.14). The current theory, that this panel was originally an antependium that was later (about 1215) placed on the altar as an altarpiece, is not confirmed by any written or pictorial source. The hypothesis that the relief panel is a traditional icon, con-

Figures 4.10 and 4.11. "The Victorious Sienese Return to the Cathedral," Chronicle by Ventura, fols. 10v–19r.

Figures 4.12 and 4.13. "The Thanksgiving Procession with Relics and Cross," Chronicle by Ventura, fols. 21v–22r.

Figure 4.14. "Madonna-in-relief" ("Madonna degli occhi grossi"), Museo dell'Opera del Duomo, Siena. (Photo, Grassi.)

cerning which the above-mentioned Sienese chronicles provide important information, is much more credible. Such panel paintings usually had four characteristics before the mid–thirteenth century: they were located near a door, they were not directly related to an altar, they were carried in processions, and they were only temporarily placed in the choir near the high altar. Comparison with other cities shows this to be plausible for the Sienese Madonna-in-relief, about which contemporary sources remain silent.

Since the seventh century, icons were carried in processions relating to battles, especially by emperors.[56] When war threatened, the sacred image of Maria, the *Hodegetria*, was carried along the city walls in Constantinople. Emperors offered thanks to the portrait for subsequent victories: Emperor Michael VIII Paleologus took it on his triumphal procession through Constantinople on 15 August 1261.[57] This custom of carrying icons in processions has been depicted extensively. A miniature in a chronicle shows how in the tenth century Emperor John Tzimisces captured an icon that was reputed to have performed miracles and carried it in his triumphal procession.[58] In Arta, in northern Greece, a thirteenth-century fresco portrays the celebrated *Hodegetria* being carried in a procession on a palanquin covered with precious fabrics. A fourteenth-century fresco depicts the procession in the same way: a palanquin covered with costly fabrics on which the sacred image is borne.[59] This custom is shown in illustrations up to and including the seventeenth century, for example in Crete and in Venice.[60] Rome was the city toward which Siena might look for inspiration. Since the eighth century the pope had taken part in processions marking the most important festivals of the Virgin: Purificatio or Candle Mass (2 February), Annuntiatio (25 March), Nativitas (8 September), and Dormitio, later rechristened Assumptio (15 August). In the most important procession, that of the eve of Assumption in the night from 14 to 15 August, participants had borne an icon of Christ since as far back as the ninth century.[61] The most important festival took place in Santa Maria Maggiore, which housed a very old icon of the Virgin, a painting attributed to no lesser artist than Saint Luke himself, but which probably dates from the fifth century.[62] The main procession to this church took place on the eve of the Assumption.[63] A canon of Saint John Lateran describes the processions with the icon in 1170.[64]

The ceremonial's high point was the meeting of the Virgin and Christ. An icon of Christ the Redeemer, which was kept in the palace chapel of Saint John Lateran, the Cappella Sancta Sanctorum, was carried to Santa Maria Maggiore in solemn procession. It was there, according to a tradition that dated back to the eighth century, that Christ was reunited with his mother after their dramatic parting on earth. This encounter was the "ratio" of the Assumption procession. During the twelfth and thirteenth centuries the civic authorities and the populace took an active part in these ceremonies.[65]

The image of the Virgin hung above the baptistery door, *supra limen baptisterii*, as Bishop Durand records in his *Rationale divinorum officiorum*.[66] Its link with the Virgin's image, which was named "Regina" or "Regina Coeli," caused the door to be known as the Porta Regina.[67] Shortly after Durand had remarked upon this, the icon in question was placed under a monumental canopy, the companion piece of an older ciborium containing a holy relic, to which an altar was added in 1378.[68] When the processions of the Assumption arrived in Santa Maria Maggiore, the icons of Christ and his mother were placed on either side in the antechoir near the pulpits and ciboriums, the icon of the Virgin on the north side opposite the icon of the Redeemer, and the kneeling pope in between.[69]

Carrying icons in processions was as much a standard practice in the fourteenth century as in the seventeenth century. In Orte the panel painting of the Virgin by Taddeo di Bartolo was removed from the cathedral on the eve of the Assumption to be reunited with Christ after a journey through the city.[70] A Sienese painting depicted the procession bearing the icon of the Virgin, enshrined on a covered baldachin, from Provenzano to the new church dedicated to her in 1610. Clerics followed by members of the civic authorities accompanied the translation of the miraculous image.[71] Processions such as these were customary in Siena well into the seventeenth century, as is apparent from a painting by Agostino Marcucci.[72]

It is thus that we must also imagine the processions that had taken place since the twelfth century with an icon of the Virgin. In Siena the relief panel, now displayed in the Museo dell'Opera del Duomo, was carried in the great civic processions. As one might deduce by analogy with Santa Maria Maggiore, the panel hung next to the Porta del Perdono. The account of Ventura and the inventories, which I will deal with later in the chapter, confirm this hypothesis. The Madonna *di mezo rilievo* was not originally attached to the high altar as an antependium, but hung next to or above the church door, probably in a tabernacle covered by a cloth and wings. It did not have a principal function in the canons' office and mass, but was carried through the city as a *Kultbild* on the eve of the Assumption and during processions on special occasions, to be worshiped temporarily in the antechoir in front of the high altar.

3. Innovation: An Altarpiece and a Chapel

The civic authorities wished to commemorate the victory at Montaperti with a new monument to the Madonna, who had, on that occasion, become the city saint of Siena, as the later chronicles suggest. The new civic constitution of 1262 described plans for a chapel as part of a series of provisions regarding the cathedral and other churches. The civic statute proclaimed that a new chapel was to be built to the honor of God, the Blessed Virgin, and those saints (such as Saint Boniface) to whom Siena owed its victory, and thus to commemorate permanently the victory over the city's enemies. Work was undertaken at the initiative of the bishop and at the expense of the Opera del Duomo.[73]

The first, anonymous chronicle postulates that Duccio's Maestà had replaced the Madonna delle Grazie and that the latter was the same painting known as the "Madonna with the bulging eyes," which was the Madonna that had played a role in 1260 in connection with the prayers before and immediately after the battle of Montaperti.[74] A first sign of confusion becomes manifest here.

The chronicler Angelo Tura records that after the Maestà was placed in position, the old altarpiece was given a home in the chapel of Saint Boniface.[75] Ventura confirms Tura's account, but interrupts his historical narrative in an attempt to clarify the connection between the Madonna of the vow of Montaperti, that is, the Madonna-in-relief, and the Madonna delle Grazie, as he calls the *tavola* commissioned immediately after the victory on 4 September 1260, the feast of Saint Boniface (see Figure 4.15).

Ventura presents himself as a contemporary observer whose duty it is to clear up an ancient misunderstanding. After describing the processions preceding the battle, Ventura relates that a new painting had been executed: "To commemorate the donation made to her [the Virgin] of the city of Siena and its surrounding domains a *carta* has been painted in the hand of the Child."[76] In this way, Ventura attempts to give an explanation for the unusually conspicuous *carta*, which in fact was derived from the *Hodegetria* tradition. This Madonna type existed in Roman churches and gained a new popularity through Byzantine influence since 1204. Guido da Siena introduced it in Siena at the festive occasion of the victory at Montaperti. Ventura notes the relocation of this panel from the high altar to "the altar that is now known as that of Saint Boniface, in the cathedral near the tower, which is called the Madonna delle Grazie." Realizing the potential for confusion, he praises its beauty and the devotion to the painting and adds, "But before I continue, I should like to point something out to you, namely that the Madonna that stood on the high altar of the cathedral, in the place where the said bestowal took place, was a panel that was smaller, and very old, showing the likeness of Our Lady, half carved, that is to say in half relief, as were the surrounding figures, which is attached to the tower in the cathedral, next to the Porta del Perdono without an altar, and that is the Madonna before which the said bestowal took place. At a later date was painted the one that we referred to earlier as the Madonna

Figure 4.15. "Madonna delle Grazie," Guido da Siena, ca. 1261, Cappella del Voto, Duomo, Siena. (Photo, Grassi.)

delle Grazie, and subsequently the beautiful panel was made, surrounded by the beautiful decorations, so as to honor Our Lady fittingly as a well-deserved expression of gratitude for what she has done to the city of Siena and its citizens."[77] Ventura concludes that both the second panel (the Madonna delle Grazie) and a third (the Maestà) were painted as a mark of gratitude for what the Virgin had done for the city and its citizens.

The above facts allow two hypotheses about the earliest Madonna paintings in the cathedral. The Madonna delle Grazie was made for the high altar within the renovated choir. The Cappella delle Grazie was to be the new home for the Madonna-in-relief. Yet, it could be that the

Madonna delle Grazie was intended for the Cappella delle Grazie, which the commune ordered to be constructed as a mark of gratitude to the Virgin and her contribution to the victory at Boniface's day. None of the chroniclers gave direct information about the original location of the Madonna delle Grazie on the high altar. The relevant passages date from long after the 1260s and, therefore, are only speculative.

In any case, the old Madonna-in-relief was the panel before which the city of Siena had been solemnly dedicated to the Virgin in 1260, and this image played a crucial role in the civic ritual after the victory. As an expression of gratitude concerning the victory, the new chapel was built in 1262 at the instigation of the civic authorities and the bishop. A new representation of the Virgin was created, not the traditional *Sedes sapientiae* (a seated Madonna, frontally depicted, with Christ on her lap), but the new *Hodegetria* type (a Madonna with Christ on her arm): the Madonna delle Grazie. This image added to the devotion for Mary as a source of victory to the commune as a whole, without, of course, replacing the old one that had miraculously saved the Sienese citizens. The second panel was later referred to as the "Madonna degli occhi grossi," as the fifteenth-century inventories indicate: another source of confusion.

4. Synthesis: Duccio's Maestà and Civic Processions

The role of the Virgin's images in civic ceremonies became so important that late in 1308 a third painted Madonna was commissioned, one of an unusual format that explored the advantages of altarpieces: their size, their place, and their liturgical function. Icons reached a larger public because they could be carried around, but they were small and did not occupy a central location. Altarpieces could be much bigger and offered scope for more elaborate representations. The advantages of both could be combined by organizing processions past a monumental altarpiece. This was the accomplishment that the Sienese achieved in commissioning the Maestà.

In 1308 Duccio was commissioned to paint a panel to be placed on the high altar (see Figure 4.16).[78] The civic authorities turned the installation of the Maestà into a spectacular civic event. The anonymous chronicler and Tura extensively recorded how all the clergy and citizens (women and children as well as the commune authorities) carried the altarpiece to the cathedral with flaming torches in their hands, while bells pealed and the Gloria was sung.[79] This ritual confirmed the Virgin's role in preserving and augmenting peace and the *buono stato* of Siena *e sua jurisditione* and emphasized her role as the city's *avocata e protetrice*.[80] In June 1311 one of the tax services, the Biccherna, paid four musicians from the Sienese commune "to meet the panel of the Virgin Mary."[81]

Figure 4.16 "Maestà," Duccio, 1308–11, Museo dell'Opera del Duomo, Siena. (Photo, Grassi.)

The processions on the occasion of the Assumption were the main reason for commissioning such an unusual altarpiece. New civic ordinances made participation in the festivals of the Virgin, particularly that of the Assumption, compulsory.[82] The religious festivals were seen as a means of cementing the city-state's peace and prosperity. Civic authorities used the cathedral rites to make clear that the merchants and bankers enjoyed a dominant position vis-à-vis the bishop and chapter and the feudal nobility. All the inhabitants of the city and of the surrounding satellite towns were required to take part in the collective ritual and finally to make an offering to a new state symbol.[83] The order of precedence in the procession, the size of the offerings, and the banners emblazoned with coats of arms (kept all year in the cathedral and borne in the procession) provided an annual public manifestation of the city-state's social structure.[84]

The identity of the republic was more elaborately visualized than in the two preceding Madonna images. The four male patron saints of Siena—from left to right, Ansanus, Savinus, Crescentius, and Victor—kneel beside a monumental throne, and a choir of angels sings in the background. The enthroned Virgin is a combination of the *Sedes sapientiae* and the *Hodegetria*. Duccio created a new image and added a number of elements to both traditions.

All except bandits, convicted criminals, swindlers, rebels, and traitors were required to offer up candles in the cathedral. On the eve of the Assumption and also on the feast of Saint Boniface (the day of the victory at Montaperti), the commune authorities took charge of candles offered by subordinate towns and castles and themselves offered a gigantic foliated candle.[85] In 1310, as a further mark of honor to the Virgin, civic authorities organized, on a grand scale, the *palio,* a horse race named after the banner that was bestowed upon the winner, "in onore de la Vergine Gloriosa."[86]

The visual effect of light and darkness played a crucial role in the civic ritual. The procession occurred at night to enhance the effect of the candles. The very expensive wax made the candles into a useful status symbol, clarifying the republic's social stratification. This effect was further exploited by the golden background of the altarpieces, in particular the Maestà, the apotheosis of the festivities. The image of choirs, pulpits, altars, icons, and polyptych must have made an enormous impression on all participants.

Siena was distinct from other cities in the far-reaching influence that the civic authorities exercised on rituals that derived on the one hand from the chapter liturgy and on the other from feudal festivals celebrating victories or rituals of surrender. The *signori Nove governatori et difenditori del comune et del popolo di Siena* added their own touches to the service of the secular clergy, such as those recorded by Canon

Oderic, and used feudal elements to turn it into an urban pageant with the Maestà as a divine pièce de résistance.

5. Confusion: Renovation and Extension

In the fifteenth century the Sienese appear to have fallen victim to a number of mistakes about the oldest images of the Virgin from their illustrious past. The descriptions, chronicles, and inventories given of the cathedral and its interior are confused, partly because of the many alterations that had taken place. All panel paintings changed places during the new campaign of renovations that began in 1362. Some returned to their former chapels, but all of these were thoroughly remodeled. New patrons emerged, like the *operaio* of the cathedral, his family, other wealthy families, and guilds. They gave commissions for frescoes, altarpieces, and tombs, sometimes changing the chapel's titular saint. Confusion sprang from the numerous renovations and, paradoxically enough, from an increasing awareness of history in an age that was less glorious than the preceding one.

Around 1382 the building campaign, which included the extension of the transepts and eastern end above the new baptistery, came to an end. The construction of a new choir and new chapels followed soon. Therefore, an inventory was needed. The 1389 inventory lists the altars in largely arbitrary order.[87] At that time the cathedral had some twenty altars, not counting the high altar. Besides the latter, there were two other altars dedicated to the Virgin: *laltare dele gratie* and *laltare di santa maria dala porta*.[88] This suggests that the Madonna delle Grazie was made for the altar *dele gratie*, and that the Madonna-in-relief had always been located near the door.

From then on, each new director of the cathedral works ordered a new inventory to be made. The 1420 inventory, which is more detailed than its predecessor, gives a different picture and a more detailed one. Certain altars had disappeared and new ones had been erected. Overall the cathedral had fewer altars. Three chapels next to the choir had been cleared and their altarpieces sold.[89] The inventory mentions *Uno altare di Santa Maria dele Grazie, chon tavola,* and *Uno altare e tavola di Santo Bonifazio*.[90] The chapel of Saint Boniface was elaborately furnished.[91] The inventories of 1423 and 1429 record "la chapella di Santo Bonifatio" as well as "the altar of the Blessed Virgin of Thanks next to the Porta del Perdono," implying a change since 1389. Reference is made to a *tavola antica* in the chapel of Saint Boniface.[92]

In the 1420s the arrangement of the cathedral was as follows. Taking the main entrance as a starting point, the first bay on the south side had no altar. The second bay contained the chapel of Saint Niccolò.[93] Then came the altar of Saint Boniface and that of Saint Anthony. The fifth and last bay in the nave housed the small chapel of Saint Jacomo Interciso.[94] In the transept next to the Porta del Perdono there was a chapel dedicated to Mary. Then, successively, came the "Chapel next to the crucifix" (also called Four Crowned Martyrs), the chapel with the crucifix, the chapel of Saint Crescentius, the chapel of Saint Victor (within the presbytery), the high altar, the chapel of Saint Ansanus (also within the presbytery), and that of Saint Savinus. A series of chapels followed: Saint Catherine and Saint Thomas, the altar of the shoemakers' guild, the Magi, Saint Peter, and, last of all, back at the main entrance, the chapel of Daniel.[95]

At the beginning of the fifteenth century the duomo contained two ancient panels. One was near the door, "Porta del Perdono" serving as an unambiguous specification here. The other panel was situated in the nave. The icon near the door was described as being *di mezzo rilievo*.[96] However, by 1446 it had been transferred to the rebuilt oratory of Sant' Ansano; civic authorities had conferred its rights of patronage upon the cathedral works.[97] The first reference in the cathedral inventory appendix concerned an "old relief panel."[98] This *tavola antica* remained in Sant' Ansano throughout the fifteenth century.[99]

The relocation of the "old relief panel" was connected to a sequence of alterations in the cathedral. The 1435 inventory records a new *tavola* next to the Porta del Perdono. This panel painting of the Virgin, dating from 1432 and now in the Contini Bonacossi collection in Florence, proves to be important in connection with the relocation of images in the cathedral. The widow of a former *operaio* of the cathedral, Turino di Matteo, commissioned Sassetta's "Madonna della Neve" (Madonna of the Snows).[100] The payments and subsequent descriptions indicate that it was placed on the altar next to the Porta del Perdono, which received a new dedication: the Blessed Virgin of the Snows.[101]

The 1429 inventory reveals that the feast of the Virgin of the Snows had been entered in the calendar as one of four new feasts.[102] In the 1435 inventory the altar dedicated to the Virgin of the Snows was next to the Porta del Perdono and incorporated a painted altarpiece depicting the Virgin, saints, and the legend of the miracle of the snow. The old relief icon hung close by.[103] But not for long. The 1439 inventory mentions "la cappella di Santa Maria della Nieve" but not the old icon of the Virgin. Someone other than the original scribe wrote in the remaining space and in the right-hand margin that the latter panel was in the oratory of Sant' Ansano.[104]

The transfer of the *mezzo-rilievo* icon of the Virgin from the cathedral to the oratory (near the old castle of Siena, where the city reaches its highest point) led the civic authorities to undertake an even more drastic alteration. On 28 December 1447 the Concistoro allocated 250 gold florins for the refurbishment and painting the Chapel of the Virgin.[105] On 20 October 1448 it was decided to saw some side pieces off the panel depicting the Virgin because it was too big and heavy to be carried in processions.[106] This was put into effect in 1455. The Madonna delle Grazie was thus made smaller in order that she might take over the functions that up to about 1430 the *rilievo* icon had fulfilled. The Concistoro minutes reveal that in 1447 and 1448 civic authorities no longer knew that the Maria delle Grazie had not played a role in the vow of Montaperti. Ventura tried in vain to correct this misconception.[107]

After the completion of alterations between 1362 and 1396, numerous attempts were made to give the old icon and the first altarpieces special standing and thus to invest them with added mystique and supernatural power.[108] In the second half of the Trecento all panel paintings changed places temporarily or permanently; a new wave of modifications followed soon.

The altar in the third bay came to be described in much more detail than any other in the cathedral. Between 1451 and 1454 the chapel was rebuilt and refurbished.[109] One of the new features was costly sculpture depicting scenes from the life of the Virgin in colored marble.[110] In 1449 it was described as "La chapella della nostra Donna, detta di Sancto Bonifatio." The dedication to the Virgin and to Saint Boniface was a double one, both patron saints corresponding to the commemoration of the victory at Montaperti. In the same period plans were made for a separate chapel to Saint Boniface.[111] In 1458 and 1467 the words *delle Gratie* were added after the name *nostra Donna*, after which followed *detta di San Bonifazio*. The connection between Saint Boniface and the Chapel of Thanks was by no means odd, as the victory of Montaperti fell upon Saint Boniface's Day. After 1480 the name of Boniface disappeared from the inventories, leaving only that of Our Lady of Thanks.

The Chapel of Thanks was refurbished in stages. On 22 August 1449 the silversmith Francesco di Antonio was paid for a silver crown for the Madonna delle Grazie and for supplying vermilion and ultramarine pigment. Later payments were made for a green altar cloth and for an antependium made of gold brocade.[112] By degrees, more and more votive offerings were attached to the icon. These took the form of eyes fashioned from silver, giving the image the descriptive name of the "Madonna with the bulging eyes" used by the cathedral inventories.[113] The 1423 inventory, which apart from the spelling is almost identical to that of 1429, provides the following information: The chapel of Saint Boniface contains an old icon of the Virgin and Child, which is popularly called the "Madonna degli occhi grossi." It is seen as the most important of the church's old panels. The predella shows scenes from the life of Saint Boniface. Near it were images depicting Saints Francis and Anthony and the Virgin Mary.[114]

By 1449 the collection of silver eyes had swelled to 34, by 1458 to 42, and the inventory of 1467 lists a total of 56. In 1473 space was left in order that a number (80) might be filled in at some later date, and in 1480 there were so many that counting was given up.[115] According to the inventory, the panel was furnished with two silver crowns, one for Mary and one for Jesus, and with stars of precious metal.[116] The panel of the Virgin was placed in a tabernacle covered with a costly fabric.[117] In 1457 the Balìa ruled that the old image of the Madonna could only be unveiled with the consent of the canons and the chaplain.[118]

6. Multiplication: Many More Madonnas and Saints

The cover of the Gabella's annual report for 1483 and the 1482 inventory show clearly that the Virgin who is receiving the keys comes out of her frame in the chapel (see Figure 4.1). In the fifteenth century the painted image that corresponds to this holy vision was known as the "Madonna degli occhi grossi." About 1446 it had taken over the function of a *Kultbild* being carried in processions rather than the older Madonna icon, which had been transferred to Sant' Ansano.

The antependium in *La cappella della nostra Donna delle gratie* bears the civic coat of arms, which can also be found on the spandrels of the frame: the white lion on a red ground, and the black and white colors of Siena. The chapel contains "an altar with a painted panel *all' antica*, showing the likeness of Our Lady with her son on her arm, with a crown decorated with *rame*, with a silver star and a crown on the child's head." Silver eyes have been attached to the representation of the Virgin and Child, which is why it is popularly known as the "Madonna degli occhi grossi." Other chapel furnishings include a silk cloth with which to cover the panel. Before it stand two iron candlesticks and a wooden step. Two small angels with candlesticks, a large candle, and a large quadripartite lamp provide further lighting. A chest containing candles and a chest for offerings stand near the chapel. Sculpted scenes from the life of the Virgin decorate the chapel periphery and the lunette depicts the Virgin and Child. An iron screen closes off the chapel.[119]

The twelve representations of the apostles were placed against the pillars, and four of them were depicted on the Gabella cover. Behind the Chapel of Thanks was the chapel of Saint Anthony, which housed "a painted panel, small and old" (see Figure 4.17).[120] It was executed in 1381 by Maestro Nanni del Maestro Francesco del Tonghio.[121] Saints were depicted on the altarpiece, above a predella portraying scenes from the life of Saint Anthony.[122] Behind this were frescoes by Taddeo di Bartolo dating from 1400 and 1401.[123]

Backing on to the altar of Saint Anthony was that of Saint Jacomo Interciso, with a Virgin and Child in colored marble. A carved crucifix was placed above the chapel.[124] According to the fifteenth-century tradition, this crucifix was carried in procession before and after the battle of

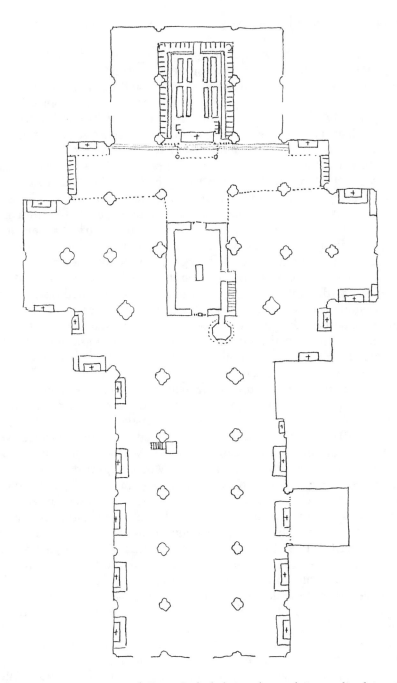

Figure 4.17. Reconstruction of Siena Cathedral, its altars, choirs, and pulpits, 1483. (Drawing by Bram Kempers.)

Montaperti.[125] Behind this altar were frescoes by Andrea di Bartolo from 1398.[126]

In the background of the Gabella panel the artist depicted part of the iron gate around the monumental pulpit by Pisano at the front of the antechoir, facing both the Porta del Perdono and the main entrance in the nave.[127] Behind the stone pulpit, which was draped in a black cloth bearing the civic coat of arms, one can see the right-hand section of Duccio's Maestà on the high altar and the stained glass window with the Coronation, Assumption, and Dormitio made to his design.

The Maestà stood at the center of other altarpieces, also depicting scenes from the lives of the patron saints of Siena. In 1382 it had been placed on a new marble altar, which, like its surroundings, was lavishly decorated.[128] Above the altarpiece was a canopy supported by four iron poles. The Maestà was lit on either side by two little carved angels holding iron candlesticks.[129] An iron lamp comprising forty-one small lamps provided yet more light. An ostrich egg was suspended before each side of the altarpiece. The altar, predella, and the polyptych itself could be covered with silk cloths. The sacred images were unveiled only on festive occasions. Three tabernacles housed three little carved and gilded angels that descended bearing the host, the cups, and the covering for the hands required by the officiating priest during mass. Next to this altar stood a chair for the bishop and a tripartite one for the celebrants. Offertory boxes were placed on the other side of the altar.

The choir around the high altar had an impressive repertoire of images.[130] Statues of Saints Peter and Paul and the four patron saints of Siena were placed on the stalls that were extensively decorated. On feast days the tabernacles of the statues were opened while the altarpiece was unveiled. Statues of the angel Gabriel and the Madonna stood in front of the Maestà, forming an Annunciation.[131] Moreover, on the feast of the Sagra, 8 November, four statues representing the seated patron saints were placed on the altar in front of the Maestà.[132] These statues, with the relics of the saints in boxes on their knees, were normally kept in the sacristy, where Benedetto di Bindo painted the shutters of the Arliquiera with scenes from the life of Christ.[133] The altarpieces, frescoes, statues, and other items in sacristy and presbytery formed an impressive ensemble. Further multiplication of images in the nave and transepts enhanced the devotion to the Virgin and the male city saints.

Sassetta's altarpiece depicting the Madonna of the Snows was situated in the southern transept, next to the Porta del Perdono.[134] Then came the altar of the Visitation (with the altarpiece by Gregorio di Cecco, now in the Cathedral Museum) and that of the crucifix, which did not possess an altarpiece, but was adorned by a group of statues, a painted crucifix with shutters and frescoes.[135] On the altar Mary, John, and Mary Magdalen were mourning the dead Christ: Mary and Saint John flanked the crucifix.[136] To the left and right of the high altar were the organs; the small one was situated above the door to the sacristy behind the altar of Saint Ansanus.[137] On the wall above the door were Old and New Testament figures painted by Taddeo di Bartolo, who decorated the whole eastern part of the cathedral.[138]

The high altar was flanked by the chapels of the four patron saints of Siena and their polyptychs. Ambrogio Lorenzetti had painted Saints Crescentius and Michael next to the Purification, and Bartolomeo Bulgarini had painted Saints Victor and Corona to the left and to the right of the Nativity of Christ (see Figure 4.18). Opposite are Simone Martini's Annunciation, flanked by Saints Ansanus and Massima, and Pietro Lorenzetti's Birth of the Virgin with Saints Savinus and Bartholomew.[139] The citizens saw the life of the Virgin in a chronological order from her birth, on the altar of Savinus, to her purification, on the altar of Crescentius.

In each altarpiece the lateral figure to the left is the city saint to which the altar was dedicated. The predella depicted scenes from the saint's life and the miracles ascribed to him. The four polyptychs, then, were of a common type: a large-scale narrative from the life of Mary as the central image, two full-length standing saints for the laterals, and small-scale narratives from the saint to the left on the predella. These chapels, too, are decorated with frescoes depicting scenes from the lives of and miracles performed by the male patron saints of the city. The frescoes representing Saint Victor were executed in 1405 by Andrea di Bartolo di Fredi, and the lives of Saints Crescentius and Savinus were subsequently portrayed by Martino di Bartolomeo.[140]

Saint Sebastian's altar, which stood opposite that of Saint Savinus, bore a painted representation of the titular saint's martyrdom. A group of marble figures above had the patron in prayer for the Virgin and Child: bishop Antonio Casini, introduced by Anthony Abbot. The marble figures, sculpted by Jacopo della Quercia, were placed in the lunette above the altarpiece. Furthermore, the chapel had four images, two on panel and two on linen, with the Magi, Joseph, and Saint Ambrogio. Like the chapels of the four patron saints, there were iron gates, wooden seats, and marble steps, which added to the monumentality of the structure.[141]

The chapel of Saint Bernardino, containing a statue of the titular saint (*rilevato et dipento connuno quadro in mano*), adjoined the chapel of Saint Sebastian and the as-yet-unfinished chapel of Saint John.[142] The entrance of the new chapel was constructed near the site of the chapel of Saint Catherine, which housed the tomb of cardinal Riccardo Petroni and a small altarpiece with a crucifix and saints.[143] Just as in the case of the Cappella della Grazie and the chapels of Saints Victor and Ansanus, both these chapels contained reliefs by Umberto da Cortona.[144]

The rights of patronage to the first of the series of altars in the nave,

Figure 4.18. Central panel of Purification altarpiece by Ambrogio Lorenzetti, 1343, Galleria degli Uffizi, Florence. (Photo, Anderson.)

dedicated to Saint Thomas Aquinas, had been conferred upon the guild of shoemakers. The altarpiece portrayed the titular saint, and there were also depictions of the Virgin and Saint Leonard.[145] The following altar was dedicated to the *Natività della vergine Maria*. The center of the altarpiece depicted the Assumption, painted by Luca di Tomè, Bartolo di Fredi, and Bartolo di Fredi's son Andrea.[146] In the nave was an additional pulpit for preaching.[147] The chapel of the Magi contained an altarpiece portraying the Adoration and frescoes by Nastaggio di Guasparre.[148] The altarpiece in the chapel of Saint Peter represented the Presentation of the Virgin in the temple and was painted by Paolo di Giovanni Fei.[149] The cathedral was not only a monument to the Sienese saints and citizens but also to its most excellent painters.

After the Chapel of Saint Peter came the altar by the door, formerly dedicated to Daniel, now to the Four Crowned Martyrs, who are portrayed next to the Virgin.[150] Opposite is the altar of Saint Callistus, built in 1458, with the Virgin, saints, and angels on the marble altar.[151] Then came the chapel of Saint Niccolò, with figures including the titular saint, and finally the artist of the Gabella panel resumed his work by allowing his gaze to rest once more on the most imposing structure: the Chapel of Thanks.

7. Repetition: Church Ritual and Its Political Significance

The Gabella panel painter depicted only part of the cathedral's interior, with its impressive repertoire of altars, altarpieces, statues, marble walls, iron gates, wooden seats, pulpits, stained glass windows, lamps, and candles. He added a grand ceremony, recalling that of 1260. Supplementary information may be found in a diary kept by a Sienese citizen between 1479 and 1483 and in some of the commune's minutes.[152] Siena's period of wealth and glory was followed by one in which its citizens struggled to maintain their position in a political scene increasingly dominated by the large states surrounding the city-state: the republic of Florence, the Papal States, and later the states of the French king, the king of Spain, and the German emperor. The shift in balance of power between Siena and other states and within the cathedral left its traces in ritual, in *Kleinarchitektur*, and in the imagery.[153]

In mid-September 1482 a new war threatened.[154] The various factions in Siena tried to set aside their differences, but internal peace was constantly disturbed through exiles' interference. The external pressure forced the political parties (*Monte*) to adopt a unified position.[155] On the eve of the battle a procession of prayer was organized. The citizen's diary refers to the tradition that the civic authorities, the committees, and the various ranks of citizenry went to the cathedral "because the people and the city of Siena have always received infinite favors by virtue of the intercession of the city's Mother and Advocate the Blessed Virgin." Led by the cardinal, they processed to *la nostra Donna delle Gratie* in the cathedral, where men and women of all ranks together received a blessing after a prayer. In a ceremony presided over by an Augustine monk, the city and its authorities were placed under the protection of the Virgin.[156] Success in the battle occasioned thanksgiving processions. In the first the *chiovo di Cristo* from the hospital was borne along. "The Blessed Virgin of Thanks, who is kept in the Duomo and very much venerated there" was carried in the second.[157] In the third the Sienese bore the Sacred Host, just as on the feast day of Corpus Christi, "with very much honor, devotion, and respect, and in the presence of a very great number of men and women."

During a ceremony on 21 March 1483 the cardinal, speaking on behalf of the pope, proclaimed an indulgence in the Cappella delle Grazie.[158] Once again there had been a threat. During the night of 1 February banned members of the Nove attacked the castle of Montereggione. They were hiding in the Maremma, an uncultivated stretch of coastal land, where they had assembled an army of five hundred cavalrymen and some two thousand foot soldiers. The internal and external threats inspired the civic authorities with a desire to reinforce internal cohesion and peace. As a result they decided to repeat the ritual of dedication. In a surge of historical awareness it was adduced that in 1399, during the temporary suzerainty of the duke of Milan, the Virgin had been formally ousted from her role as the patron of Siena.[159] It was unanimously resolved that Siena should be "restored and anew given and conceded to the Most Glorious Virgin, than whom there can be no more effectual or stronger protection and safeguard." Meetings of the Consiglio della Campana and of the Consistoro led to the drafting of a new notarial deed in which the Virgin was proclaimed "vere domina, custos, defensio et presidium nostrum."[160]

This decree was confirmed in the cathedral on 24 August 1483, with a repetition of the ritual offering of the keys and dedication of the city to the Virgin, at which ceremony the controlling civic administration declared itself the Virgin's direct vassal and representative.[161] The Magnificent Lords and the Captain of the People went in procession from their palace to the cathedral. They were accompanied by both the magistrates and the citizens. The civic authorities and the clergy met at the choir, as had been the custom since the days of the battle of Montaperti. The bishop and cardinal, Francesco Piccolomini, offered a prayer composed for the occasion. After the solemn mass Master Mariano da Ghinazano ascended the pulpit and preached a sermon in praise of Our Lady. "The prior of the lords, Andrea di Sano Battelori, speaking on behalf of the Commune, dedicated the city and its domains once again to the Blessed Virgin, the *avvocata* of the people."[162] The notary of the

Consistoro formally published the contract of the presentation of the keys, stipulating that no one had any right by reason of the sacred ceremony, save only the Virgin herself. After the prayer the prior rose and, as the choir behind him commenced singing the Te Deum, reassumed with his own hands the keys of the city from the altar. The cover of the Gabella annual report of late 1483 depicted the repetition by Andrea di Sano and Francesco Piccolomini of the 1260 ritual as it was reconstructed in the fifteenth century.

The degree to which the ceremony in the Cappella delle Grazie and the apparition of the Virgin as the protectress of Siena during time of war dovetailed, and the length of time for which this image persisted, can be seen from Biccherna and Gabella covers from 1476 to 1552. The concept of the Virgin as a source of miracles was an integral part of religious perception and of the binding effect of devotional images, a concept that clarified and reinforced the social order. The whole Sienese community saw the Virgin and found it a consoling and heartening experience.

In 1527 both tax services—Biccherna and Gabella—commissioned a representation of the ritual and the war. The first, painted by Beccafumi, depicts the ceremony before the Cappella delle Grazie in the cathedral. The point of view differs from that in 1483, so the relocation of choir, pulpit, and altarpiece (in spite of the canons' opposition) was left unrecorded. The second cover shows the miracle performed by the Virgin in her capacity as Siena's patron saint: the victory near the Porta Camollia (see Figure 4.19).[163] A large banner showing the Assumption waves above the city gate; to the left is a banner of Siena's former ally, Charles V. On the outer gate is a fresco showing the Virgin as the Queen of Heaven in a golden light.

A contemporary chronicle recounted that in 1526 the Virgin appeared once again in heaven to the Sienese in order to support them in their battle against foreign domination. The allied papal and Florentine troops, aided once again by the exiles or *fuorisciti*, advanced on the walls of Siena, just outside the Porta Camollia.[164] The Virgin's cloak covered the city like a cloud or canopy and an unearthly beam of light fell on the representation of the Virgin on the Porta Camollia. A ceremonial rededication of the city to the Virgin took place, with the keys being bestowed upon her as they had been in 1260 and in 1483. On Sunday, 22 July 1526, the civic authorities and the people processed to the cathedral with a great silk standard showing the Assumption of the Virgin in the skies above Siena. The magistrates went to the altar of Our Lady of Thanks, bestowed the keys of the gates according to the ancient rite upon the Virgin, declared her the protectress of the city and its domains, and begged her to free them "from the hands of the enemies, the Florentines and Clement VII."[165] The subsequent sortie was successful, their

Figure 4.19. "The Victory at the Porta Camollia," Biccherna panel, 1527, Archivio di Stato, Siena. (Photo, Grassi.)

enemies were routed on Wednesday, 25 July, and the Sienese led the foreign soldiers into the city as they had done before with the captive Florentines after the battle of Montaperti. According to the chronicler, the victory was due "firstly to the fact that there was a repetition of the solemn ceremony of *il vasallagio* which had been pledged to the Queen of Heaven 266 years ago," together with the confession, veneration of the Virgin, the bearing of banners emblazoned with her image, and the offering of the keys of the city.[166]

The companion cover shows the civic ceremony in the cathedral on

22 July 1526, which deliberately repeated the great ritual of "266 years ago." In a variation of the 1483 painting, which formed the point of departure of this chapter, Beccafumi's painting depicts the grand display that still fascinates us today.[167]

Notes

I am very much indebted to Sible de Blaauw, Monica Butzek, Eva Frojmovič, and Gerhard Wolf for sharing their ideas and expertise with me, as well as to the Dutch and German institutes in Florence and Rome. I should also like to thank the universities of Amsterdam and Groningen, which provided me with all manner of assistance, and the archives and libraries referred to below. The following abbreviations are used in the notes: ASS, Archivio di Stato di Siena; OM, fondo Opera Metropolitana in ASS; AOMS, Archivio dell'Opera Metropolitana di Siena; BAV, Biblioteca Apostolica Vaticana; BCIS, Biblioteca Communale degli Intronati di Siena; CS, "Cronache Senesi," in *Rerum Italicarum Scriptores*, edited by I. Fabio and A. Lisini, new series 15, 6 (Bologna: Nicola Zanichelli, 1931–37); RRIISS, *Rerum Italicarum Scriptores*.

1. E. B. Garrison, "Towards a New History of the Siena Cathedral Madonnas," in *Studies in the History of Medieval Painting*, 4 vols. (Florence, 1960), 4: 5–22, quotation on p. 5. It is a work to which art historians nearly always refer.

2. See for these themes B. Kempers, "Gesetz und Kunst: Ambrogio Lorenzettis fresken im Palazzo Pubblico in Siena," in *Malerei und Stadtkultur in der Dantezeit*, edited by H. Belting and D. Blume (Munich: Hirmer Verlag, 1989): 71–85, and B. Kempers, *Kunst, Macht und Mäzenatentum: Der Beruf des Malers in der italienischen Renaissance* (Munich: Kindler Verlag, 1989); also B. Kempers, *Painting, Power and Patronage: The Rise of the Professional Artist in the Italian Renaissance* (London and New York: Penguin, 1993). With regard to Siena Cathedral, this article is more explicit than my book about the choirs and the different Madonna paintings.

3. U. Morandi, ed., *Le Biccherne Senesi* (Siena: Monte dei Paschi di Siena, 1964), p. 112. The panel is in the museum of the Archivio di Stato, Siena. The image is accompanied by the description "L'unione delle classi e l'offerta delle chiavi della città alla Vergine." The date on the cover gives an indication of the date when the panel was painted: "INCOMINCIATO A DI PRIMO DI GENNAIO MCCCCLXXXII ET FINITO A DI VLTIMO DI DICEMBRE MCCCCLXXXIII."

4. The inscription reads, "APREXENTATIONE DELE CHIAVI QVANDO TUTTI EQVATRO EMONTI S'ADVSSENO ADVUNO."

5. The title is given on the plaque under the painting in the exhibition room known as the "Sala dalla Madonna degli occhi grossi." Compare H. Hager, *Die Anfänge des italienischen Altarbildes: Untersuchungen zur Enstehunsgeschichte des toskanischen Hochaltarretabels* (Munich: Anton Schroll Verlag, 1962), p. 92. See also E. Carli, *Il Duomo di Siena* (Genoa: SAGEP Editrice and Monte dei Paschi di Siena, 1979), pp. 79–80, who proposes that the painting be referred to as the "Madonna del voto di Montaperti"; and H. W. van Os, *Sienese Altarpieces 1215–1460*, 2 vols. (Groningen: Bouma's Boekhuis, 1985 and 1990), pp. 10–12. Part 1 (1985) has a contribution by K. van der Ploeg and Part 2 (1990), a contribution by G. Aronow. See also A. Riedl and M. Seidel, eds., *Die Kirchen von Siena*, 3 vols. (Munich: Bruckmann Verlag, 1985), p. 334 and n. 133.

6. Garrison, *Studies*, pp. 5–58; Hager, *Anfänge*, pp. 83, 106–7 and 134–36; J. H. Stubblebine, *Guido da Siena* (Princeton, N.J.: Princeton University Press, 1964), pp. 72–75; Carli, *Duomo*, p. 81; van Os, *Sienese Altarpieces* 1:15–18; H. Belting, *Bild und Kult: Eine Geschichte des Bildes vor dem Zeitalter der Kunst* (Munich: Beck Verlag, 1990), p. 439.

7. Carli, *Duomo*, pp. 65–75; J. White, *Duccio: Tuscan Art and the Medieval Workshop* (London: Thames and Hudson, 1979), pp. 80, 179 n. 1; van Os, *Sienese Altarpieces* 1:39–46.

8. Both traditions are dealt with more extensively in the Introduction of Kempers, *Painting, Power and Patronage.*

9. See, for example, P. Burke, *Tradition and Innovation in Renaissance Italy: A Sociological Approach* (London: Fontana, 1974), and *Culture and Society in Renaissance Italy* (London: Bataford, 1972). Another example, focusing more on anthropology, is R. C. Trexler, *Public Life in Renaissance Florence* (New York and London: Academic Press, 1980).

10. BAV, Chigi P. VII 11, fols. 38v–39r, one of the drawings; in van Os, *Sienese Altarpieces* 1:119 and 2:228. The new plan entails the demolition of the archiepiscopal palace, the building of a new "Sagristia," building a new chapel between the new sacristy and the old door and modification of the side wall. This and other draft plans in the volume show that the new chapel was originally dedicated to Saint Ansanus and to Christ (fols. 38v, 42v, 44v, 48v).

11. BAV, Chigi P. VII 11, fols. 42v–43r, indicates that the house of the master of the cathedral works was built against the canonica, facing the piazza and the hospital. The canonica's buildings comprised a cloister around a "Cortile" with a well in the center. The canons' palace had a loggia, as did the master's house (fols. 32r and 50v).

12. Sigismondo Tizio, "Historiarum Senensium libri X," BCIS B III 12, fols. 3–5. The passage is cited in G. Aronow, *A Documentary History of the Pavement Decoration in Siena Cathedral, 1362 to 1506* (Ph.D. diss., Columbia University, 1985; Ann Arbor, Mich.: University Microfilms Int.), pp. 495–97, after the copy in BAV, Chigi G. II 37, fols. 8v–11r.

13. ASS, Balìa 52, fols. 58r, 59r–v. Cited by A. Lisini, "Notizie di Duccio pittore e della sua celebre ancona," in *Bulletino senese di storia patria* 5 (1898) and by Aronow, *Pavement Decoration*, p. 499. Aronow's suggestion that a choir might have existed in the nave is not consistent with the reconstructions in van Os, *Sienese Altarpieces* 1, diagrams 12, 14, 16, proposed by van der Ploeg, and Aronow's plan in van Os, *Sienese Altarpieces* 2:226.

14. The 1420, 1423, and 1435 inventories refer to these two sections separately and distinguish them from one another in that they are given separate entries and described differently. See ASS OM 28, fol. 13v, and ASS 29, fol. 16r, as well as the 1435 inventory, ASS OM 30, fols. 17r–v. See also AOMS 867, 1420 (1), fols. 18r–v and 1429 (2), fol. 14v. Some extracts are quoted in Lisini, "Notizie di Duccio," and Aronow, *Pavement Decoration*, p. 38.

15. ASS OM 29, fol. 17r, and AOMS 867, 1467 (8), fol. 15v: "El coro di mezzo del legnamine intarsiato bellisimo et di fuore lavorato di marmo."

16. BAV, Chigi P. VII 11, fol. 37r. The chapels on either side of the high altar are described as being dedicated to Saints Crescentius and Savinus to the left, and Ansanus and Gregory to the right. The original drawing is in the Museo dell'Opera del Duomo, Siena number 154. See B. Degenhart and A. Schmitt, *Corpus der italienischen Zeichnungen: Süd und Mittelitalien*, 4 vols. (Berlin: Gebr. Mann Verlag, 1968), 1: 89–97. See also Carli, *Duomo*, p. 23, and van der Ploeg in van Os, *Sienese Altarpieces* 1:142.

17. See CS, p. 634, and G. Milanesi, *Documenti per la storia dell'arte senese*, 3 vols. (Siena: Onorato Porri, 1854–56), 1:328–83.

18. Carli, *Duomo*, pp. 12–20; for the choir by Tonghio, pp. 91–92.

19. More material will be presented in my forthcoming article, "The choirs of Siena Cathedral."

20. *Ordo officiorum ecclesial Senensis*, in BCIS G V 8, published by J. C. Trombelli (Bologna: Longhi, 1766), the edition used in this article; for the date of the unpublished *tabula* (1139), see fol. 7v; and for a later, abridged *Ordo*, G V 9.

21. Canon Oderic, *Ordo officiorum*, pp. 9, 34–37, 45, 122, 123, 178, 220, 410, 418. *Ante Altare* is used to indicate "in the choir," that is to say the antechoir of the nave. The *Ordo* was used extensively by van der Ploeg in van Os, *Sienese Altarpieces* 1:131–39, 152–53, but with other conclusions and reconstructions, the main difference being that he

does not take into account a choir in the nave and hence gives a different reading of *ante* and *post altare.*

22. Oderic, *Ordo officiorum,* pp. 9, 12, 13, 20, 46, 116, 117, 180–81, 234, 410, 484. For the bells, pp. 44, 116, 315.

23. Ibid., pp. 440–41, 444–48, 454–66, 471, 474.

24. Ibid., pp. 147, 363–65, 371.

25. Ibid., pp. 54–55, 106, 132, 273–75, 288, 291, 322, 325, 337, 357, 373–76.

26. Ibid., pp. 34, 106, 148, 220, 293, 450.

27. G. Cecchini and D. Neri, *The Palio of Siena: The Palio and the Contrade—Historical Evolution* (Siena: Monte dei Paschi, 1958), p. 15. For the Palio see also W. Heywood, *Our Lady of August and the Palio of Siena* (Siena: Enrico Torrini, 1899), reprinted in W. Heywood, *Palio and Ponte: An Account of the Sports of Central Italy from the Age of Dante to the 20th Century* (Siena: Enrico Torrini and London, 1904).

28. Cecchini and Neri, *Palio,* p. 16.

29. Ibid., p. 19.

30. Ibid., pp. 19–29.

31. One of the oldest descriptions can be found in the anonymous chronicle concerning the period 1202–1384. However, the oldest available copy dates from 1689 in ASS 55; see *RRIISS,* p. 40. The edition in *RRIISS,* pp. 41–162, is based on various versions.

32. CS, pp. 57–58.

33. The bishop who played this historic role was Tommaso Balzetti, who held office from 1254 to 1273. See G. A. Pecci, *Storia del vescovado della città di Siena* (Lucca, 1748), p. 216: "[A]ntichissima di origine, e Nobilissima di sangue, fu ancor esso Religioso Domenicano, e Prelato di gran Dottrina."

34. CS, p. 58.

35. Ibid.

36. Ibid., p. 59.

37. Ibid., p. 202, derived from the chronicle written by Paolo di Tommaso Montauri in the third quarter of the fifteenth century, in BCIS A VII 44. The chronicle concerns the periods 1170–1315 and 1381–1432. The period 1316–80 is a compilation of earlier texts. It survives in a copy dating from around 1490, published in *RRIISS,* pp. 179–252.

38. CS, p. 201. The pulpit is described as *in pergolo* or *in sul pergolo.* See also the Aldobrandini and Ventura chronicles in G. Porri, ed., "La Sconfitta di Montaperti secondo il manoscritto di Niccolo di Giovanni Francesco Ventura," in *Miscellanea storica senese* (Siena: Onorato Porri, 1844), pp. 8, 44.

39. CS, p. 202. The location for the meeting of bishop and *sindaco,* who entered through the *porta del perdono,* is specified as *a piei el coro del Duomo.* Together they proceeded *a l'altare magiore.* The oration and the song for the Virgin took place *dinanzi a la Vergine Maria.* See also Porri, ed., "La Sconfitta di Montaperti," pp. 8, 43.

40. CS, p. 202. ("E stando ordinato la procisione, e prima pigliaro uno crocefisso di rilievo di legno, el quale è a lato al canpanile in Duomo, el quale crocefiso è conposto con tutte le congegniture, ed è molto divoto, e questo andava innanzi a ognuno, di poi seguè tutti li religiosi e poi uno stendardo overo padiglione tuto di sciamito rosso, e poi una tavola dipenta co' la figura de la Nostra Donna sotto el baldachino....")

41. Ibid., p. 218.

42. The original manuscript is in BCIS A IV 5. See G. Garosi, ed., *Inventario di manoscritti della Biblioteca Communale degli Intronati di Siena,* 3 vols. (Florence, 1978), 1: 256–59. The text has been published by Porri, ed., "La Sconfitta di Montaperti," pp. 33 98, using as a basis copy BCIS A IV 6, which is less damaged at the edges, as well as another version. The transcription of Porri contains many errors, but, as far as I have checked the original, none are relevant to the main themes dealt with here. As far as I know only some of the miniatures about the battle have been published in *RRIISS.*

43. "Comincia la storia per ordine, come e Sanesi isconfissero e Fiorentini a Monte Aperto, con tutte le circostanze appartenenti."

44. In 1403 Niccolò Ventura completed the *Guerra di Troja* (Garosi, ed., *Inventario* number I VII 12). In 1428 he was registered in the guild of painters (Milanesi, *Documenti* 1:49). The illustrations that accompany the account of the battle of Montaperti were completed in July 1443 (Porri, ed., "La Sconfitta di Montaperti," p. 98). Ventura died in 1464 (ibid., pp. xviii–xxii). In 1412 Francesco di Giovanni Ventura was baptized. He became chancellor of the Republic in 1477 and died in 1499 (see *RRIISS*, p. xxvii n. 2).

45. CS, p. xxx; and Garosi, ed., *Inventario*, p. 259.

46. These included the chronicle of Villani, who does describe the battle against the Florentines, but not the rituals in Siena. The Sienese tradition cannot be precisely traced. Ventura's text is particularly important, as the original manuscript is the only original text that has been preserved. Compare Garosi, ed., *Inventario*, p. 259.

47. For the text see Porri, ed., "La Sconfitta di Montaperti," pp. 33–41.

48. See Porri, ed., "La Sconfitta di Montaperti," pp. 41–50, for the ceremonies.

49. For Ventura's text see Porri, ed., "La Sconfitta di Montaperti," pp. 50–76. The information provided by Ventura and Montauri is similar, although their formulation is far from identical. A herald summons the army to advance into battle in the direction of Montaperti (fol. 5v). Count Giordano and his troops march under the banner of Saint Martin, the patron saint of the city quarter of that name from which this regiment has been recruited (fol. 7r). The rest of the army follow, and in their midst is a *caroccio* from which a large white flag flutters (fol. 7v). The Florentines have set up their camp on the other side of the river (fol. 8r). The Sienese organize their food supply (fol. 8v). They are positioned opposite the Florentines at the Arbia (fol. 9r). The Sienese make a large fire (fol. 9v). The Florentines hold a council of war in their army camp (fol. 10r). The Sienese take position around their carriage and their other insignia (fol. 10v). They advance, led by Count Giordano (fol. 11r). Count Aldobrandini encourages his troops (fol. 11v). Count d'Arese, too, advances (fol. 12r). The entire Sienese army follows (fols. 12v–13r). The cavalry of both armies engages, as shown on another double illustration (fols. 13v–14r). The Sienese attack the Florentine army camp and capture standards (fols. 15v–16r). The city populace rejoices at the victory (fol. 16v). The army slays fleeing Florentines (fol. 17r). The mounted knights fight for their lives (fol. 17v). Some are captured (fol. 18r).

50. Ibid., pp. 77–87 and 87–99.

51. See ibid., pp. 86–87. ("E fu fatto uno gonfalone, che si porta ora alle processioni, vermiglio grandissimo di zendado con una croce piccoletta in capo dell' asta, e così andava innanzi a tutte le reliquie. E poi andava quello Crocifisso che è in Duomo, come dinanzi e detto....") These are most probably the relics of the city's four patron saints as mentioned by Canon Oderic and described in the inventories to be referred to below. After the bishop and the canons come the *Ventiquattro* with Lucari, the *capitano* with some *cavalieri*, *cittadini*, Count Giordano and his German soldiers, the people, monks, and priests. After processing through the city, the bishop heard their confession and blessed them, whereupon all returned to their homes.

52. Ibid., 87–95. The Florentines pay a ransom (fol. 22v). Siena advances toward Montalcino (fol. 23r). This city is besieged and taken (fol. 23v). Montalcino is set alight and its people driven off (fol. 24r). The castles of the Florentines are also set on fire (fol. 24v). The Sienese return through the city gate, which bears the sign of the she-wolf, the Roman symbol that Siena had adopted (fol. 25r). The pictorial narrative is concluded with a representation of Saint George slaying the dragon (fol. 25v).

53. Ibid., pp. 41–44.

54. See ibid., p. 44. ("A la quale processione innanzi a ogni cosa andava lo Crocifisso, che è scolpito in Duomo, e lo Crocifisso è quello che sta sopra all' altare di S. Iacomo Interciso a lato al campanile. E poi seguiva tutti e religiosi, e poi andava uno stendardo, e sotto esso stendardo era nostra madre vergine Maria. Di presso era Misser lo Vescovo ed era scalso, e a lato aveva Buonaguida incamici [. . .] poi seguitavano tutti canonici del Duomo

scalsi...."] Porri (pp. 3–29) also publishes the Aldobrandini chronicle, which differs only slightly from Ventura's version, this episode on p. 9, the rituals and the use of images on pp. 6–10.

55. Ibid., p. 46.

56. Belting, *Bild und Kult*, pp. 209–11.

57. G. Wolf, *Salus Populi Romani: Die Geschichte römischer Kultbilder im Mittelalter* (Weinheim: VCH Acta Humaniora, 1990), p. 142.

58. Belting, *Bild und Kult*, p. 209, illustration 107.

59. Ibid., pp. 63, 215–17.

60. Ibid., illustrations 123–24; and Wolf, *Salus Populi Romani*, illustrations 11, 39, 47, 49, 82.

61. S. de Blaauw, *Cultus et decor: Liturgie en architectuur in laatantiek en middeleeuws Rome: Basilicae Salvatoris Sanctae Mariae Sancti Petri* (Delft: Eburon, 1987), pp. 214–15, with an Italian edition forthcoming in *Studi e Testi della Biblioteca Apostolica Vaticana* 355; Belting, *Bild und Kult*, pp. 554–55; and Wolf, *Salus Populi Romani*, pp. 14, 44–45. To the elaborate procession belonged a "carmen in Assumptione sanctae Mariae in nocte, quando tabula portatur."

62. Wolf, *Salus Populi Romani*, pp. 11, 13, 23–28.

63. De Blaauw, *Cultus et decor*, 215–16; Belting, *Bild und Kult*, 83; and Wolf, *Salus Populi Romani*, 44–49. Liturgically, the night of 14 August belongs to the feast of Assumption, as the new day started after sunset.

64. Wolf, *Salus Populi Romani*, pp. 31–33. The prayers to the Virgin were codified in the ninth century.

65. Sources in Wolf, *Salus Populi Romani*, pp. 37, 52, 65. For the role of the Roman commune, see pp. 73–75.

66. Ibid., pp. 98–100. For the *Aufstellung* of icons see also Belting, *Bild und Kult*, pp. 590–92, 598–99, and illustration 24, of a thirteenth-century miniature that portrays the position of the *Hodegetria* in Constantinople. With regard to the Sienese Madonnas, Belting arrives at conclusions that differ from the hypotheses proposed here.

67. Wolf, *Salus Populi Romani*, pp. 102–6, 113.

68. De Blaauw, *Cultus et decor*, p. 196; and Wolf, *Salus Populi Romani*, pp. 102, 223–27.

69. As recorded by the papal masters of ceremony in the beginning of the sixteenth century. These sources will be dealt with in a forthcoming article about the Masolino-Masaccio altarpiece, which was located on the canon's altar in Santa Maria Maggiore.

70. Information provided by G. Solberg on the basis of her Ph.D. dissertation.

71. Morandi, ed., *Biccherne*, pp. 200–201. The transfer took place on 23 October 1611; the illustration appears shortly afterward in the Biccherna annual account.

72. Depicted in Carli, *Duomo*, p. 17.

73. ASS, Constitution of 1262, Dist. I, section xiv, is entitled "De inveniendo loco pro cappella construenda ad honorem dei et beate virginis." The text runs: "Et teneantur priores xxiiiior et camerarii et iiiior provisores comunis Senarum et consules utriusque mercantie, si exinde fuerint requisiti a domino episcopo Senarum, invenire et videre et ordinare locum unum, in quo eis videretur magis conveniens, pro construendo et faciendo fieri, expensis operis Sancte Marie, unam cappellam ad honorem et reverentiam dei et beate Marie Virginis et illorum Sanctorum, in quorum solempnitate dominus dedit Senensibus victoriam de inimicis cum oportet cappellam sancti Iacobi destrui pro ornatu episcopatus. Et in illo loco, quem predicti ordines approbaverint et ordinaverint, dicta cappella fiat expensis Operis Sancta Marie." Published in L. Zdekauer, *Il costituto del Comune di Siena dell' anno 1262* (Milan: Hoepli, 1897; reprint, 1974), p. 29.

74. "E anco nel detto tenpo e della signoria predetta, si fornì di fare la tavola dell' altare magiore e fu portata a Duomo e posta al detto altare magiore, e funne levata quella la quale sta ogi a l'altare di S. Bonifazio, la quale si chiama la Madonna degli occhi grossi, e Madonna delle Grazie. E questa Madonna fu quella, la quale esaudì el populo di Siena,

quando furo rotti e Fiorentini a Monteaperto" (CS, p. 90). Montauri is on this point less elaborate than the anonymous chronicle and does not mention the earlier Madonnas (ibid., p. 236).

75. "E la tavola vechia che era all' altare magiore fu levata e posta all' altare di San Bonifatio la quale ogidì si chiama la Madonna de le Gratie" (CS, p. 314). The text, which covers the period 1300–1352, comes from BCIS A XI 42, and is published in *RRIISS*, pp. 255–564. It is ascribed to Angolo di Tura del Grasso; see *RRIISS*, pp. xiv–xv and xxvi–xxvii, for uncertanties about the time when this chronicle was written, which parts are by Tura himself, and who he was.

76. Porri, ed., "La Sconfitta di Montaperti," p. 46. The Aldobrandi chronicle, too, refers to the *carta in mano* to commemorate the *donazione di Siena*; see ibid., p. 9: "... una carta in mano a significazione della donazione di Siena." The *carta* was not an exceptional symbol, but in this context the Sienese historians gave, in retrospect, a special interpretation to it.

77. The text is in the BCIS A IV 5, fols. 4r–5v; Porri, ed., "La Sconfitta di Montaperti," pp. 45–46. For the purposes of the information relevant here, the differing versions of the manuscripts are, as far as I can see, not important. Incompletely cited by Hager, *Anfänge*, p. 106; and Carli, *Duomo*, p. 79, who arrive at different conclusions.

78. White, *Duccio*, pp. 192–97.

79. CS, pp. 90, 313.

80. Tura, in CS, p. 313.

81. White, *Duccio*, pp. 196–97; also pp. 80–134.

82. ASS, Constitution of 1309–11, Dist. I, section dlxxxiii. This long section, "Di guardare la festa de la beata vergine Maria del mese d'agosto," dates from 30 October 1309. The decision was taken by the General Council, the people, and all the leading magistrates. "Denanzi a voi signori Nove governatori et difenditori del comune et del popolo di Siena, si propone et si dice, ad onore et reverentia de la Vergine Maria, la quale fue, è et sarà per la sua gratia capo et difenditrice de la città di Siena, che conciò sia cosa che la città di Siena et li cittadini d'essa sieno tenuti e debiano guardare et onorare le feste de la beata Vergine Maria, et specialmente la festa la quale del mese d' agosto a sua reverentia si celebra." See A. Lisini, ed., *Il Costituto del Comune di Siena*, 2 vols. (Siena: Tip. e Lit. Sordmuti di L. Lazzeri, 1903), p. 361.

83. "Acciò che la città di Siena in buono e pacifico stato si conservi piaccia a voi fare ponere et a consèllio mettere che la festa de la beata Vergine Maria, la quale si celebra del mese d' agosto per tutti et ciascuni mercatanti et artefici et altri homini tutti de la città di Siena et de' borghi solennemente con diligentia et reverentia sia onorata et guardata et guardare si debbia." See Lisini, ed., *Costituto*, p. 361.

84. The banners are referred to in the last section of the inventories; see, for example, S. Borghesi and L. Banchi, *Nuovi documenti per la storia dell' arte Senese* (Siena: Enrico Torrini, 1898; reprint, Soest: Davaco, 1970), pp. 319–26.

85. Section xxxvi in Lisini, ed., *Costituto*, pp. 64–68.

86. "Di correre el palio ne la festa di Sancta Maria del mese d' agosto," Section dlxxxvi in Lisini, ed., *Costituto*, p. 366.

87. AOMS 864. This inventory lists the following dedications in addition to the high altar, differing in a number of respects from those mentioned by Canon Oderic in 1215: John the Baptist, Savinus, delle Grazie, Catherine, Mary Magdalene, Guild of Shoemakers, Magi, Daniel, Peter, Messer Cione, Agnes, Jacomo Interciso, "Sancta Maria dala Porta," Anthony, Quattro Coronati, Crescentius, Victor, and Michael. The inventories of 1391 (AOMS 865) and 1397 to 1410 (AOMS 866) do not add much, as they do not list the altars.

88. AOMS 864, fol. 12r. As far as the altars are concerned, the inventories of 1391, 1397, 1404, 1405, and 1408 are extremely brief, or give no information whatsoever concerning the saint to which they are dedicated or their arrangement. See AOMS 865 and 866.

89. Aronow in van Os, *Sienese Altarpieces* 2: 230, for the meeting of 10 July 1404

concerning the removal of "gli altari che erano appoggiati al coro, cioè a le more del decto coro." The inventory of 1408 (AOMS 866) suggests a reduction to seventeen altars. They were originally furnished with altarpieces, as witness the sale in 1408 of "una tavolla anticha dipinta di Santa Maria e altri santi" (Aronow in van Os, *Sienese Altarpieces*, nn. 12 and 13). There were thus three altars adjoining the choir.

90. ASS OM 28, fols. 14v–15r. Also AOMS 867, 1420 (1), fols. 14v and 15r. Between these altars the altars of Saints Jacomo Interciso and Antonio are mentioned.

91. In 1400 payment was made: "A maestro Martino di maestro Agustino dipentore, per metitura in oro de la tavola di S. Bonifazio." In 1402 the following took place: "Agnolo di m. Vanni zondadaio fa 'l davanzale all' altare di S. Bonifazio." See V. Lusini, *Il duomo di Siena*, 2 vols. (Siena, 1911 and 1939), 1: 319 n. 63, for the gold that was added and the *davanzale* that was made. In 1401 "maestro Sano," architect and sculptor, made a marble figure in the chapel of Saint Boniface (Milanesi, *Documenti* 2: 24).

92. "L'altare di Sancta Maria dele Gratie alato ala porta del Perdono con una tavola antica ala figura di Nostra Donna; con predelle da piei e ferro di tende senza tenda" (ASS OM 29, fol. 18v); AOMS 867, 1429 (2), fols. 18r–18v, with the *cappella di Santo Buonifazio*.

93. ASS OM 29, fol. 19r; similar information in all inventories.

94. ASS OM 29, fol. 18v, and AOMS 867, 1429 (2), fol. 18r. This range of chapels is described as such in all inventories.

95. This reconstruction accords with that of Aronow in van Os, *Sienese Altarpieces* 2: 226–27.

96. Porri, ed., "La Sconfitta di Montaperti," p. 46: "cioè di mezzo rilievo."

97. Repeatedly referred to at the end of the inventories in AOMS after 1446, following the description of the cathedral itself. See AOMS 867, 1446 (5), fol. 44r, the section "la cappella di Sancto Sano in Castelvecchio." In 1446–47 Luca di Bartolo (*scarpellino*) and Pietro Paolo di Giovanni (*legnaiuolo*) were paid by the *Comune di Siena* to do work in the "chapella beati sancti Ansani in castel veteri" (Milanesi, *Documenti* 2: 233–35).

98. "Una tavola antica, con la predella, con figura di Nostra Donna di mezo rilievo e più figure di più Santi" (AOMS 867, 1446 (5), fol. 44r—apart from the spelling, identical to 1467, fol. 22r, which adds "e predella con l' arme dell' opera").

99. See also AOMS 867, 1449 (6), fol. 36r, and 1458 (7), fol. 42v. In the latter half of the sixteenth century the icon qualified as *di mezo rilievo* has evidently been replaced by Simone Martini's Annunciation from the cathedral; in the seventeenth century it hung in the tower of Sant' Ansano. See also Lusini, *Duomo* 2: 64, and Riedl and Seidel, eds., *Kirchen*, pp. 334–36.

100. See J. Pope-Hennessy, *Sassetta* (London: Chatto and Windus, 1939), pp. 26–27. In the document of 25 March 1430 commissioning the work, there was talk of it being located "on the altar of the chapel of Saint Boniface, the said chapel being next to the entrance to the great church, which is referred to and described as the porta del perdono" ("ad pingendum unam tabulam ad altare cappelle Sancti Bonifatii, que cappella est prope portam ecclesie maioris prefate, que vocatur et dicitur la porta del perdono"; cited by Pope-Hennessy, p. 45, and Carli, *Duomo*, p. 80).

101. Pope-Hennessy, *Sassetta*, p. 51. In the report of his visit in 1575, Archbishop Bossio wrote that the *mensa* of the altar dedicated to the Madonna of the Snows had been removed, that it was no longer used for celebrations, and that the altar was plagued by a severe draft emanating from the door. "Visitavit Capellam Ste. Marie ad Nives prope una ex portis d. ecclesie [...] et ventus qui ex ea vehementer spirat" (cited by Pope-Hennessy, p. 52 n. 64). In 1591 the altarpiece was removed and sold by the *operaio* (see p. 52 n. 65).

102. "Uno libro grande, basso nuovo, coperto con tavole a cuoio rosso, coppe di ferro, nel quale sono quatro uffici nuovi solfatta la spirito santa, l'Eternità, il Corpo di Cristo, Santa maria de la Nieve" (AOMS 867, 1429 (2), fol. 3v).

103. "L'Altare di Santa Maria della Nieve, alato ala porta del Perdono si è l'Altare suvi la tavola dipenta, messa a oro, di Nostra Donna e altri santi col miracolo della Nieve, con

predella dappiei et ferro con tenda vermeglia, con due candelieri di ferro in su l'altare. E rincontra al detto altare si è la tavola antica di nostra Donna, che stava prima al detto altare" (AOMS 867, 1435 [3], fol. 19r). Canvases depicting the Annunciation and the birth of Christ were also hung near the Madonna of the Snows altar, and candles were sold there (variant in ASS OM 30, fol. 19r).

104. "La deta tavola è ala cappella di santo Sano in Castelvecchio" (AOMS 876, 1439 [4], fol. 19r).

105. Borghesi and Banchi, *Nuovi documenti*, pp. 158–59. ("Ad ornatum et devotionem cappelle et altaris ipsius gloriosissime Matris et Virginis, cui donata fuit civitas hec Senarum.")

106. The Deliberazione del Consistoro runs: "Predicti Magnifici Domini [...] intendunt facere quamdam processionem per civitatem, et portari facere ad dictam processionem tabulam cum figura gloriosissime Virginis Marie ad quem civitas nostra fuit data et donata, et claves ipsius presentate. Et cum dicta tabula sit magne latitudinidis et magni ponderis et difficile esset ipsam, eo modo, portare prout ad presens est, decreverunt [...] qui possint, si eis videbitur, secari facere dictam tabulam et figuram Virginis Marie portare ad dictam processionem sine aliquo corum preiudicio aut damno" (ASS Concistoro, 496, fols. 31v–32r; cited by Borghesi and Banchi, *Nuovi documenti*, p. 159, and by Hager, *Anfänge*, p. 107, with different conclusions).

107. The confusion was exacerbated by the demolition of the Chapel of Thanks, which took place in conjunction with the demolition of the archiepiscopal palace. The Madonna delle Grazie was installed in a new chapel, the Cappella del Voto, built by order of Alexander VII. See G. A. Pecci, *Relazione delle cose più notabili della città di Siena, sì antiche come moderne* (Siena: Stamperia di F. Quinza ed. A. Bindi, 1752). Pecci writes that this chapel was built "in honor of the very old painting, which is believed to be of Greek origin," and states that it was before this very icon that the vow of 1260 was made, and that it had stood on the high altar up to 1311. In his time in the third bay there was a chapel dedicated to St. Francis of Sales.

108. In 1367 payments were made for "due predelle che fecie a l' altare di santa Maria de le Grazie e l' altra a l' altare di S. Bartholomeio," and in 1379 for "tre colmi e due colonegli e una predella di lengniame, civorati e'quagli fecie per la tavola de l' altare de le Grazie." In 1380 the masters Francescho and Andrea were paid for "lo frusto de la tavola e sua fadigha, ala Madona de le Grazie in duomo." See Lusini, *Duomo* 1: 319 nn. 61–63. Paolo di Giovanni Fei and others were paid for the cleaning and restoration of the panel paintings, which were reinstalled around 1380.

109. Milanesi, *Documenti* 2: 271–74, referring to the commissioning of Urbano di Pietro and his brother Bartolomeo, both of Cortona, to do this work; on the space for the Porta del Perdono, see pp. 269–70.

110. AOMS 867, 1458 (7), fol. 27r, mentions that the chapel is *nove fornito* and that *indulgentie* are to be obtained next to the chapel. AOMS 867, 1467 (8), fol 15r, gives a lengthy description of the old *tavola dipenta* and goes on to describe the chapel itself: "Coruna chapella grande bellissima di marmo con più figure et intagli con più figure et istoria di nostra donna tutte intagliate di marmo et messe a oro fino e più colori." For the marble decoration see P. Schubring, *Urbano da Cortona: Ein Beitrag zur Kenntnis der Schule Donatellos und der sieneser Plastik im Quattrocento* (Strasbourg, 1903); and E. Carli, "Un tondo di Urbano da Cortona," in *Antologia di Belle Arti* 21–22 (1984): 11–14.

111. In 1454 it was decided to decorate a chapel dedicated to Saint Boniface with images, inter alia, of the titular saint. Mariano Bargagli, as operaio, acquired the rights of patronage to the chapel. It was agreed that he would be responsible for furnishing the chapel, would contribute the sum of two hundred florins, and would, together with the bishop and the cathedral works advisers, be allowed to choose the chaplain (Lusini, *Duomo* 2: 81 n. 3). This agreement related to a new chapel in the first, then still empty, bay. In 1463 work was indeed carried out there, but ultimately the altar was dedicated to Saint Callistus.

112. Lusini, *Duomo* 2: 72 n. 2.

113. In the inventory of 1420, AOMS 867 (1), fol. 14v, this name does not appear. There is a reference to "uno altare di Santa Maria delle Grazie, con tavola," and to "Uno altare et tavola di Santo Bonifazio."

114. The description runs: "La cappella di Sancto Bonifatio, con una tavola a figura di Nostra Donna col suo Figluolo in collo, antica, che volgarmente si dice e chiama la Madonna degli Occhi Grossi, la quale fu la tavola antica e principale nela decta chiesa, cola predella a la storia di sancto Bonifatio; con ferro e tende vermigle, con predelle a II gradi da piei; con l tavola dalato e figure di Sancto Francesco, e l piccola di Nostra Donna in uno telaio in panno lino ala figura di Sancto Antonio da lato." See ASS OM 29, fol. 19v. Another version, differing only in respect of spelling, is to be found in AOMS 867, 1429 (2), fol. 18v.

115. See AOMS 867, 1449 (6); 1458 (7), fol. 27r; and 1467 (8), fol. 15r. An annotated version of the 1467 inventory has been published in a French translation; see J. Labarte, *L'Eglise Cathédrale de Sienne et son trésor d'après un inventaire de 1467* (Paris: Librairie Archéologique de Didron, 1868), a reprint from an article in *Annales Archéologiques* 25 (1865).

116. AOMS 867, 1449 (6), fol. 22v.

117. AOMS 867, 1458 (7), fol. 27r. See also AOMS 867, 1467 (8), fol. 15r.

118. Lusini, *Duomo* 2: 81 n. 1. On 2 April 1457 gold brocade for the altar was purchased in Florence.

119. Borghesi and Banchi, *Nuovi documenti*, p. 318.

120. In AOMS 867, 1458 (7), fol. 27r, it was described thus: "Uno altare con tavola dipenta di più Sancti, piccola et anticha." This was replaced by the altarpiece by Matteo di Giovanni, now in the Museo dell'Opera del Duomo.

121. He was a relative of the woodworker who designed and made the choir around the high altar. See Lusini, *Duomo* 1: 319 n. 59.

122. "La cappella di Sancto Antonio conuna tavola di nostra donna con IIIIor Sancti da lato, cola predella ala storia di Sancto Antonio con ferro e tende azzure e predelle con II sedi dale latora a II gradi da piei con due figure di Sancto Antonio rilevate dale latora con II tabernacoli al detto Sancto Antonio con ferri da candeli intorno." AOMS 876, 1429 (2), fol. 18r, or ASS OM 29, fol. 18v. Labarte, *L'Eglise de Sienne*, p. 26, is incorrect in his identification of the altarpiece by means of a payment to Paolo di Giovanni Fei.

123. Milanesi, *Documenti* 2: 5–6.

124. It was described as follows in ASS OM 29, fol. 18v: "La cappella di Sancto Jacomo interciso una nostra donna di marmo col suo figluolo in collo rilevata messa doro con uno crocifixo da capo rilevato con ferro e tenda vermigla e predelle da piei a II gradi con una lampana pendente e con uno Sancto Giovanni grande rilevato messo a oro che sta in sul detto altare." In 1398 and 1400 Andrea di Vanni was paid for painting (Milanesi, *Documenti* 1:305–6). The 1482 description is given in Borghesi and Banchi, *Nuovi documenti*, p. 317. The Madonna and child by Jacopo della Quercia are today in the Piccolomini chapel (Carli, *Duomo*, p. 101).

125. Porri, ed., "La Sconfitta di Montaperti," pp. 9, 46. Both chroniclers state that the crucifix is located above the altar of Saint Jacomo Interciso.

126. Labarte, *L'Eglise de Sienne*, p. 26, with reference to the payment.

127. ASS OM 28, fol. 13v, makes a clear distinction here between "uno choro intorno a detta altare" and "uno choro dove si chanta chontinouo el divino ufizio intarsiatto e belo, e chon uno legìo in mezo, grande e bello e l'etratta da piei, e chon uno ucio di gratichola di fero."

128. Lusini, *Duomo* 1: 322–23 and nn. 81–87.

129. See AOMS 867, 1429 (2), fol. 15v. The goldsmith Piero d'Angolo and the painter Lippo di Vanni were paid for the angels in 1375 and 1376. See P. Bacci, *Francesco di Valdambrino: Emulo del Ghiberti e collaboratore di Jacopo della Quercia* (Siena: Istituto Comunale d'Arte e di Soria, 1936), pp. 82–83.

130. "Uno coro bellissimo fermo rilevato intorno al detto altare intarsiato e bene lavo-rato con più civori intorno e da capo a esso le figure di sancto Pietro e sancto Pauolo e IIIIor Martiri tutti grandi e belle rilevate" (ASS OM 29, fol. 16r). Already in 1386 Taddeo di Bartolo did work on the choir statues. The information is culled from the 1423, 1429, and 1435 inventories. Extracts have been published in Lisini, "Notizie di Duccio," pp. 23–24, 37 n. 1. See also Milanesi, *Documenti* 1: 285, 312–15, 347–83, and 2: 37, 108; and Borghesi and Banchi, *Nuovi documenti*, pp. 313–14, 318.

131. Tizio, "Historiarum Senensium," fol. 5.

132. "Quatro figure rilevate grandi di legno cole casette in mano medesimi Santi cioè Ansano Vettoria Crescenzio e Savino in essi a oro pongensi [...] la sagra in su laltare." AOMS 867, 1429 (2), fol. 5r. Ventura shows how these relics could be borne in processions separately. Canon Oderic reports that in the thirteenth century these relics were kept in altars.

133. These were made in 1409 by Francesco di Valdambrino. Andrea di Bartolo di Fredi painted two saints. Benedetto di Bindo painted saints Savinus and Victor (Milanesi, *Docu-menti* 2:110; and Bacci, *Valdambrino*, pp. 152–212, in particular pp. 163, 168, 173, 199). The four wooden figures were commissioned by the operaio Caterino di Corsino in 1408. See also Carli, *Duomo*, pp. 101–2, and figures CLI-CLII with the remaining parts of the saints.

134. "La cappella di Sancta Maria della nieve. Uno altare con tavola dipinta con figura di nostra Donna at miracolo de la nieve, una tenda azzura, con due candelieri di ferro, con uno banchetto et goffano covertato di tavole, dove si vendano le candele, et tre sedi d'intorno al campanile et più uno goffano dove si vendano i candeli" (Borghesi and Banchi, *Nuovi documenti*, p. 317).

135. Lusini, *Duomo* 1:318 nn. 49–52. In 1370 Andrea Vanni was paid for the shutters. Bartolo di Fredi repainted a crucifix in 1375.

136. In 1421 Maestro Alberto di Betto da Assisi made the Pietà, which was commis-sioned by the operaio Turino di Matteo (Milanesi, *Documenti* 2:101–2; and Carli, *Duomo*, p. 102 and figure CLIV).

137. Borghesi and Banchi, *Nuovi documenti*, p. 314; for a detailed description of the sacristy, pp. 261–314. For the sacristy frescoes, made between 1409 and 1411, see also Pope-Hennessy, *Sassetta*, p. 42 n. 41.

138. Milanesi, *Documenti* 2:6–8, 15–16. These frescoes were executed between 1401 and 1405.

139. See Lusini, *Duomo* 1:256–65; H. W. van Os, *Marias Demut und Verherrlichung in der sienesischen Malerei, 1300–1450* (The Hague: Kunsthistorische Studiën van het Ned-erlands Instituut te Rome I, 1969), pp. 6–7; van Os, *Sienese Altarpieces* 1:77–89; K. M. Frederick, "A Program of Altarpieces for the Siena Cathedral," *Rutgers Art Review* 4 (1983):13–18; and J. Steinhoff-Morrison, *Bartolomeo Bulgarini and Sienese Painting in the Fourteenth Century* (Ph.D. diss., Princeton University, 1990; Ann Arbor, Mich.: Universi-ty Microfilms Int.), pp. 62–101. The identifications of the lateral saints are based on the inventories, although these are not consistent.

140. Milanesi, *Documenti* 2:26 and 31; for frescoes in other chapels, 1: 263–64, 305, and 2: 36.

141. Antonio Casini, whose titular church was San Marcello in Rome, acquired the rights of patronage to the chapel of Saint Sebastian and the Virgin around 1430. The frag-ments depicting Casini, his name saint and the Virgin, still survive, and form part of the collection of the Museo dell'Opera del Duomo. See the inventories, the relevant parts of which have been published in P. Bacci, *Jacopo della Quercia: Nuovi documenti e com-menti* (Siena: Libreria editrice Senese, 1929), pp. 295–350.

142. See AOMS 867, 1458 (7), fol. 25v. Tommaso di Paulo made the silver statue of Saint Bernardino in 1453 (Milanesi, *Documenti* 2:278). It was decided on 12 March 1453 to build the chapel of Saint Bernardino next to that of Saint Sebastian, and this was dedicated on 10 September (Lusini, *Duomo* 2:81 n. 2).

143. Borghesi and Banchi, *Nuovi documenti*, p. 315.

144. Lusini, *Duomo* 2:96–105, 119–26.

145. See Borghesi and Banchi, *Nuovi documenti*, p. 316, describing "la cappella di Sancto Tommaso d'Aquino ogi de' Calzolari." In 1410 Bartolo di Fredi's heirs received payment for a *tavola* that was "a l'altare di san Tomaso" (Milanesi, *Documenti* 2:37–38). In 1442 Domenico Cristofano and Agostino di Marsiglio were paid for decoration work: "per dipentura d' una chapella anno dipenta in duomo a chapo a l' altare di Santo Tomaso" (Lusini, *Duomo* 1:319 n. 66).

146. The rights of patronage had previously been enjoyed by the guild of shoemakers but had been transferred to cardinal Antonio Casini (Borghesi and Banchi, *Nuovi documenti*, p. 316). Milanesi, *Documenti* 2:36, refers to the contract of 15 April 1389 between the *Università de' Calzolari* and the painters; the payment is cited in Borghesi and Banchi, *Nuovi documenti*, p. 28. Also Labarte, *L'Eglise de Sienne*, p. 23, and van Os, *Sienese Altarpieces* 2:136.

147. ASS OM 29, fols. 17r–v, 19r; and 30, fols. 18r, 29r; and Carli, *Duomo*, p. 107.

148. Labarte, *L'Eglise de Sienne*, p. 24.

149. AOMS 867, 1429 (2), fol. 17v, states: "La cappella di Santo Piero coruna tavola dipenta di santo Piero e santo Pauolo e inmezo l' Offerta di Nostra Donna." ASS 33 (1458), fol. 26r, contains the following entry: "La chapella di Sancto Pietro. Uno altare con tavola dipenta colla ripresentationi al tenpio di Nostra Donna et di sancto piero et di sancto pauolo et di più altri sancti e sancte." See Borghesi and Banchi, *Nuovi documenti*, p. 316, for a similar description. M. Mallory, *The Sienese Painter Paolo di Giovanni Fei (c. 1345–1411)* (Ph.D. diss., Columbia University, 1965; New York and London: Garland, 1976), pp. 116–28, was the first to connect the descriptions with *The Presentation of the Virgin in the Temple* in the National Gallery of Art in Washington, D.C. Mallory, pp. 126–27, argued that the 1392 payment to Bartolo di Fredi "per la tavola di san Piero che fa" is not related to this altarpiece. Payments to Paolo di Giovanni Fei "per la tavola di sco. Piero e sco Pauolo" were made in 1398. A little before, the woodworker Barna di Turino was paid for the altarpiece by Paolo. The payment made in 1392 to Bartolo di Fredi is recorded in Milanesi, *Documenti* 2:37. See also van Os, *Sienese Altarpieces* 2:136.

150. Borghesi and Banchi, *Nuovi documenti*, p. 316.

151. Labarte, *L'Eglise de Sienne*, p. 27.

152. The part of the *Diario di Cristoforo Cantoni* that runs from 11 Nov. 1479 to 13 Oct. 1483 is published in *RRIISS*, pp. 879–944.

153. This is dealt with more extensively in Kempers, *Painting, Power and Patronage*.

154. *Diario*, in *RRIISS*, p. 920.

155. Ibid., pp. 896–900.

156. Ibid., p. 900.

157. "Nella seconda lo sabbato fu portata la madonna delle Gratie, che sta in duomo con grandissima devotione" (ibid., p. 926).

158. Ibid., p. 936.

159. Heywood, *Our Lady of August*, pp. 67–68.

160. The documents in A. Toti, *Atti di votazione della Città di Siena e del Senese alla Vergine madre di Gesu Cristo* (Siena: Lazzari, 1870).

161. Heywood, *Our Lady of August*, pp. 70–71. Documents in ASS, Consiglio Generale 239, fol. 119, and Balià 26, and Toti, *Atti*.

162. See also O. Malavolti, *Dell' historia di Siena* (Venice, 1599), p. 88.

163. In 1467 the illustration on the cover of the Biccherna accounts portrays the Virgin appearing above the city in order to protect it against an earthquake. In 1552 the Virgin appears on the covers of the annual accounts of both tax services, this time succoring the Sienese in their battle against the Spanish, who had built a stronghold outside Siena; see Morandi, *Biccherne*, pp. 98–99, 144–47.

164. A. Borghia, E. Carli, et al., eds., *Le Biccherne: Tavole dipinte delle magistrature Senesi (secoli 13–18)* (Rome, 1984), pp. 226–29. The panel is Chatsworth Devonshire Inv.

32. Its date is given with a question mark and so is its provenance, Biccherna, while the *Vittoria di Camollia* is dated 1526, *post quem,* and its provenance as Gabella (?).

165. Heywood, *Our Lady of August,* pp. 75–78, also based on Toti, *Atti.*

166. M. Callegari, "Il fatto d'armi di Porta Camollia nel 1526," *Bulletino senese di storia patria* 15 (1908): 351–52. The ceremony was repeated in 1550, 1554, and 1699 (355). As a mark of thanks for the victory of 25 July 1531 and in commemoration of an apparition of the Virgin, a church dedicated to Saint James was founded (ibid., pp. 380–81).

167. Borghia, *Biccherne,* pp. 226–27. The ritual is described in ASS Consistoro 959, fols. 8–9.

CHAPTER 5

The Liturgy of the Count's Advent in Bruges, from Galbert to Van Eyck

James M. Murray

On an April day in 1127, Galbert, a notary of Bruges and chapter scribe of Saint Donatian's Church, wrote of the "Joyous Advent" of a new count of Flanders:

> On April 5 ... at twilight, the king with the newly elected Count William, marquis of Flanders, came into our town at Bruges. The canons of Saint Donatian had come forth to meet them, bearing relics of the saints, and welcoming the king and new count joyfully in a solemn procession worthy of a king. On April 6 ... the king and count assembled with their knights and ours, with the citizens and many Flemings in the usual field where reliquaries and relics of the saints had been collected. And when silence had been called for, the charter of liberty of the church and of the privileges of Saint Donatian was read aloud before all.... There was also read the little charter of agreement between the count and our citizens.... Binding themselves to accept this condition, the king and count took an oath on the relics of saints in the hearing of the clergy and people.[1]

On another April day more than two and a half centuries later, the Bruges notary and chapter secretary of Saint Donatian's Church, Peter van Eyck, wrote an account of the *Adventus Iocundus* of the first Burgundian count of Flanders:

> In the year of our lord 1384, on the twenty-sixth day of April, Lord Philip, duke of Burgundy, and Lady Margaret, duchess of Burgundy, entered the city of Bruges around midday. And our deacon, chapter, and all the choir, clad in silk robes, went out in procession to meet and accompany them to the gate of the Burg that opens on the market square, where they [duke and duchess] entered and dismounted. Then the deacon sprinkled holy water and burned incense, and after this the singers began to sing "Honor, Virtus, etc." and they followed the procession until it reached the main altar of our church. And there, after many prayers, the deacon brought to the

duke and duchess the book of privileges in which the count's oath is written, which they both swore, and then first the duke opened a Gospel book and by chance he picked the Gospel, "But when the Counselor comes"; then, the said Gospel book being closed, the countess opened the book and discovered the same Gospel. After this the deacon read the prayer and collect that are traditionally read at the Joyous Advent of the count. Then the duke proceeded to the altar and offered a cloth of gold and twenty-eight pieces of gold.... After this the duchess offered one piece of gold. And at the end of the responsory, the organist began to play a motet, and all the candelabra were lit as on Christmas day, and the choir joined in ... and all the church bells rang.[2]

There is a timelessness in the two passages that belies the centuries separating what are, to my knowledge, the only eyewitness accounts of the count's advent ceremony in Bruges before the fifteenth century. Based on van Eyck's description, Bruges seems much the same as it was in Galbert's time, with the Burg—the site of the count's first castle and fortifications—and its church, Saint Donatian's, still firmly at center stage of the greatest of urban spectacles. In reality, van Eyck was reporting what he saw through the distorting lens of the chapter of Saint Donatian's, for the true center of social and economic life had long since shifted to what Galbert called the "*suburbium*," the teeming market-places, workshops, and *hôtels* of the *poorters* of Bruges.[3] Even the counts had long since abandoned their residence in the Burg—the Love—which at the time van Eyck wrote, was serving as prison to dozens of rebels awaiting execution as the penalty for their support of Ghent in its revolt against their count and king. But to view the spectacle of Philip the Bold's "Joyous Entry" into Bruges as an exercise in illusion or anti-quarianism would be to miss the hard core of realpolitik being acted out before the main altar of Saint Donatian's Church. For beneath the liturgical flourishes of incense, music, and holy water, a political bargain was being struck between two eager, even desperate, parties. Achieving rapprochement between ruler and ruled after much bloodshed and economic disaster was the goal of that urban spectacle of 1384, but the antique and comforting forms of the advent liturgy could hardly disguise the anxiety on both sides.

Bruges, on the one hand, was a twice-conquered city with its economy in shambles and a huge war indemnity to pay. Duke Philip, on the other, was struggling to establish his authority over a war-ravaged country, whose most populous city, Ghent, still defied him.[4] The English remained allied with the Gentenars in their rebellion, despite the complete failure of the English "crusade" of 1383, but even in failure there was still much to fear from the English alliance. Philip had already seen ten years of careful political planning and patronage destroyed in this so-called Ghent War of 1379–85, and he was determined to win back the loyalty of the richest city of Flanders—Bruges.[5]

For Philip the Bold, Bruges was a rich prize. Not only was it a wealthy commercial capital, but it alone, of the three largest cities of Flanders, had been a more or less pliant partner to comital ambitions after 1340. Turning its back on more than half a century as the spearhead of revolution in Flanders, Bruges was the first city to receive Louis of Male (Philip the Bold's father-in-law) as count in 1348 and remained his most loyal ally even during the disastrous civil war that marred his last years. This turn from violence to coexistence, even cooperation, reflected the profound change in the economic orientation of the city as Bruges was transformed from Flanders's leading port into a genuine world market-place. As a commercial center, Bruges was the place where, as one Florentine businessman wrote, "most of the resident merchants dwell to do business and change currency."[6] Business, of course, depended on political stability without and social peace within, so it is no surprise that the goals of Bruges's magistrates meshed with the count's on foreign (that is, outside Bruges) policy and left the task of ensuring domestic tranquility to a new social and political elite. That elite was in turn liberally laced with brokers, hostelers, bankers, and merchants whose money and interests both reshaped the urban economy and repressed the revolutionary aspirations of many urban artisans. So successful was this victory of commerce and capital in Bruges that the textile industry itself was transformed by the 1360s. Even when the genie of urban revolution escaped from the bottle, as it did in Bruges in 1359 and 1382, this was the exception that proved the rule that Bruges seldom opposed comital centralization before 1436.[7]

Philip already knew Bruges well. He had made lengthy visits to the city since his marriage to the heiress of Flanders, Margaret of Male, in 1369, particularly in 1375–76, when he was an intermediary in the English-French peace negotiations held in Bruges. By the 1370s he had come to share his father-in-law's preference for Bruges over Ghent, for even when Philip organized jousts in Ghent in conjunction with the peace negotiations, he and his company returned to Bruges for serious work at the earliest opportunity.[8] During the years of civil war, Philip had repeatedly aided both Louis of Male and Bruges through hard and dangerous times. Perhaps most crucial for the Brugeois had been Philip's role as intercessor for the Flemish with Charles VI after the crushing defeat of the Flemish militias by the French army at Westrozebeke in November 1382. At a time when nothing stood between Bruges and the pillaging hordes of French soldiers, Philip had helped negotiate a deal sparing the city in return for a large "gift" paid to the French. But if the sum was large, the terms were moderate, giving the Brugeois time to squeeze part of the money from the smaller towns and countryside of the Franc (castellany) of Bruges. The French army then left West Flanders, with the most feared of their soldiers, the Bretons, muttering about the loss of such a rich prize. Philip crowned his diplomatic efforts in 1383 by forgiving the balance of the fine Bruges owed in return for the city's support of the campaign against the English invasion led by the Bishop of Norwich.[9] If Philip was indeed "sage, froid et imaginatif,"[10] as Froissart described him, his actions on behalf of Bruges amounted to a conscious and careful courtship of the city whose success was crowned by the "Joyous Entry" of 1384, just three months after the death of Louis of Male.

The people of Bruges were no less anxious on that April day. Bruges had been a reluctant rebel in the Ghent war, remaining loyal to Louis of Male until defeated and occupied by the Ghent militia in May 1382. A reign of terror ensued, fueled by the Ghent captain Philip van Artevelde's penchant for viciousness and by accumulated social and political hostilities within Bruges.[11] The bodies had scarcely been buried when the great massacre at Westrozebeke occurred, where men from Bruges perished alongside those of Ghent. The news of the defeat caused panic in a city recently denuded of fortifications at van Artevelde's order. But there followed in rapid succession the fine negotiated by Philip the Bold sparing Bruges from pillage, the struggle to pay the first installment, and numerous executions and confiscations. Between January 1383 and September 1384, 224 persons were beheaded, including the former town executioner, and the possessions of at least 281 persons were confiscated. Adding to the trauma of war and repression was an economic crisis caused by the cessation of trade and the flight of foreign merchants from Bruges. The Brugeois desperately needed peace in order to rebuild their prosperity, but it had to be peace without debilitating terms, and preferably with a full return of their former privileges.[12]

Cultural historians have long recognized the importance of the "Ruler's Advent," the ceremonial first entrance of a new ruler into his most important cities. For Huizinga such "Blijde Inkomsten" came third on the list of examples of " 's Levens Felheid"—the violent contrasts of life, after a city's soundscape, shaped by its bells and religious processions marking anxious times. He recognized that the "Entry" was in reality a simultaneous staging of many urban spectacles, "prepared with all the sensory pyrotechnics one could command."[13] Ernst Kantorowicz, influenced by Huizinga, pointed out the manifold liturgical and theological layers of the advent ceremony. In a classic article, Kantorowicz noted the important theological message of the advent: "Time and again it has been announced on these occasions that the comer is the Expected One and that accordingly the city ... is another Zion. For whenever a king arrived at the gates of a city, celestial Jerusalem seemed to descend from heaven to earth." In other words, the *adventus* liturgy was the symbolic meeting ground of the eternal city and its eternal ruler—past, present, and future.[14]

Recent scholarship has focused on the political and contextual aspects of the Entry ceremony. Hugo Soly, writing specifically about the Burgundian Low Countries, noted that "Intochten" were particularly sensitive moments in the duke's relations with his cities, forcing him to "try to accomplish two nearly incompatible goals: stimulate the loyalty of the citizens and demonstrate his ducal authority." The city had its own agenda for such spectacles, wishing to win favor and confirmation of privileges from the duke, while overawing the local populace with a civic display of wealth and power.[15] For Sabine MacCormack, writing about the *adventus* ceremony in late antiquity, the *adventus* "remained a ceremony of persuasion, integration and consent. . . . [It] acts on several levels, each capable of interpenetrating the other, thereby enhancing and extending visible and historical reality and giving it universal significance and comprehensibility. . . . History makes sense because it is continuous, and one of the ways of highlighting such continuity is the use of the ceremony of adventus."[16] The Bruges advent of 1384 shows many of the characteristics described above, but with some significant variations, which justify a more careful analysis of the setting and meaning of the event.

Given the drama of the moment and the strong motives of the participants, we must look for a moment at the stage itself. Why does so much of the action take place in the Burg square and its church, Saint Donatian's? In this respect, some things had changed since the twelfth century, for while Galbert describes the procession of canons that met the king and count, the ceremonial oath-taking took place at the customary meeting place for public assemblies, well away from the church, on the day after the entry. In the intervening centuries, as the city grew to fill and overflow the city wall of 1127, building a second encircling wall in 1297, the Burg, the old center of the city, became in effect ceremonial space. It became the place of execution, procession, election, administration, with its own gates, its own church, its own ancient past.[17]

Part of Saint Donatian's power lay in its role as keeper of the dynastic memory of the counts of Flanders. The church's origins lay, according to twelfth-century legend, with the first count of Flanders, Baldwin Iron Arm, who built a chapel to house the relics of his patron saint, the holy bishop of Reims, Donatianus. The church that later arose on the square formed by the count's castle symbolized the aspirations of the Flemish dynasty, for it was modeled after Charlemagne's chapel in Aachen, proclaiming the link to the Carolingians through Baldwin's wife, Judith. Its construction, dating from about 960, was probably the work of Count Arnulf I, who desired a grander building to house a growing collection of relics, as well as a growing dynastic reputation, with both to be tended by twelve canons he established in the church.[18] Saint Donatian's continued to be endowed richly by Arnulf's successors, notably Robert II, who in 1089 added to his ancestors' endowments and made the church's provost the hereditary chancellor of Flanders and head of the comital administration.[19] In addition, the chapter had the Saint Basil Chapel, also called the Chapel of the Holy Blood, in its gift; thus canons of the church led the Holy Blood Procession, Bruges's most important procession and one of the most important in Flanders.[20] But it was the murder of the saintly count, Charles the Good, as he knelt in prayer in Saint Donatian's that both gave Galbert the subject of his history and sealed the relationship of the church and the comital dynasty as the center of the cult of Charles the Good.[21] It is clear that Philip the Bold, who, as Froissart put it, "saw far where his interests were concerned," was looking both to the past and to the future as he joined in the advent ceremony, acting a role that had been written for him. He knew that his acceptance as legitimate successor would depend in part on the essential paradox of invoking the memory of dead counts to gain the loyalty of living subjects.

The last but not the least anxious actors in Philip the Bold's Joyous Entry were the clerics of Saint Donatian's itself. The chapter, too, had known dark days in the recent past, including large loss of income from church properties outside the walls laid waste in the civil war and English invasion. They had also experienced violence and disorder during the dictatorship of Philip van Artevelde when the houses of both the provost and the deacon were occupied by "ruffians and harlots," who were expelled with help bought from van Artevelde. Other trials followed: a tax on all church property in Bruges, a canon forced on the chapter by van Artevelde and his hand-picked aldermen, and ever-deepening financial losses.[22] The extent of such losses ranged from the case of Jan Dierard, who in September 1384 informed the chapter that he could no longer afford to be buried in their church because of the losses he had suffered at the hands of the Gentenars on "that evil Saturday," to the complete absence of merchants who customarily hawked their wares in stands in front of and alongside the church rented out by the chapter.[23] The church's desperation bordered on pathos when a servant was ordered to plant banners bearing the church's insignia on church properties outside the walls in the vain hope that they would be spared destruction in the aftermath of van Artevelde's takeover.[24] The chaplains, canons, and choristers of Saint Donatian's who marched out to greet Philip and Margaret were certainly hoping for better days. Perhaps a few even dared to dream of a return to prominence for the chapter as in the days of Galbert. The key was to gain favor with the new count. And as if to give substance to these hopes, the chapter ordered its secretary to write down his brief account of the ceremony among the dry legal documents of the *Acta Capituli.*

In short, there was a multitude of ambitions and expectations among the participants and spectators of Philip the Bold's entry into Bruges, and all these were somehow joined in the ceremonies of that day in April. But how could the ceremony described by van Eyck serve so many purposes, from symbolizing the advent of Christ to representing a return of peace, from proclaiming the advent of a new dynasty in Flanders to helping a church chapter repair its shattered dignity and finances? Only by penetrating into the message of the rituals, their sights, smells, sounds, and offerings and the role all parts played in the whole, can we even approach an understanding of the political overtones of this many-voiced event.

The initial impression given us by van Eyck is of an overwhelming sensory experience: the sight of the magnificent silk robes worn by the canons and choir, the smell of incense, but above all the sounds of music and bells. Huizinga's insights come to mind here, when he wrote that bells were the most arresting element of a city's soundscape, and with the six bells of Saint Donatian's ringing, accompanied by those of all the other churches of Bruges, the din must have been deafening.[25] But van Eyck is also careful to describe the music produced by the church choir and the great organ—the interior soundscape, as it were. Thanks to recent research on music in Bruges, we now know that Saint Donatian's was an important center for the composition and performance of polyphonic music, so the singing and playing were of an extraordinarily high order. In fact, the music was so much to Philip's taste that he hired away the church organist soon afterward. From this time on, Saint Donatian's would be a rich source of musical talent and support for Burgundian court music, both as a training ground for promising talent and as a source of sinecures for Burgundian court musicians.[26]

Hardly less arresting than the soundscape was the landscape—the confined space of the Burg and its square with the oldest and holiest buildings of Bruges—Saint Donatian's on one side, Saint Basil's Chapel housing the relic of the Holy Blood on another. The former comital castle, built in Galbert's time, stood on the east side of the square, and the Steen, perhaps the most ancient comital residence in Flanders, still stood beside Saint Basil's.[27] This was a sacred space for all the participants in Philip's entry ceremony, yet, paradoxically, for one and different reasons. For Philip and the chapter the association with the Flemish dynasty was clear, but the Burg was also the government square of the day, where aldermen of both the castellany around Bruges (the Franc) and of the city itself held court. The *stadhuis* that still graces the south side of the Burg of Bruges was just under construction at the time of Philip's accession, and a more magnificent monument to urban pride can scarcely be imagined. The building was not completed until 1420, when its impressive facade held statues of the counts of Flanders. Another van Eyck, the painter Jan, would polychrome six of these statues (perhaps including that of Philip the Bold) in 1434–35.[28] Clearly, as

the original role of the Burg declined, its ceremonial role increased, symbolized by the incense and holy water with which Philip and Margaret
were greeted upon entering the gate. The procession then continued the
short distance to the main altar of Saint Donatian's. It was there, within
sight of the tomb of Charles the Good, that the ancient liturgy would
take place.

It might be useful to pause a moment and consider a typology of the
adventus liturgy. Kantorowicz identified basically two liturgies, representing two concepts of advent. First was a reference to the historical
entry of Christ into Jerusalem with the biblical text "Benedictus qui
venit in nomine Domini" as the antiphon. Second was the eschatological Advent, dominated by the figure of John the Baptist as the precursor
of Christ with the text "Ecce mitto angelum meum, qui praeparabit
viam tuam ante faciem meam." Not coincidentally, the latter text was
the first lesson read on the first Sunday of Advent.[29] The biblical text
employed in the Bruges advent, however, is related only thematically
and not literally to the above, for neither text appears in the liturgy. The
thematic link is the shared prominence of prophecy and *Christomime-
sis.* For example, the Gospel opened by both Philip and Margaret is
taken from John 15:26: "Cum venerit Paraclitus, quem ego mittam
vobis a Patre, Spiritum veritatis, qui a Patre procedit, ille testimonium
perhibebit de me." This is clearly a prediction of Pentecost rather than
the second coming of Christ, yet it still links the new rulers to Christ,
for "he [they] will bear witness to me."[30] The element of prophecy is
reinforced by the "random" opening of the gospels by both rulers, resulting in the selection of the same text.[31]

Linking the new count with Christ seems audacious at first glance,
particularly given the fact that the count was neither king nor emperor,
the typical rulers who invoked Christ and the prophetic tradition. But
the counts of Flanders had never let the niceties of nomenclature limit
dynastic ambitions, and the Burg of Bruges itself shows attempts of
Flemish counts to identify with Christ. After all, the nearby chapel of
Saint Basil contained the relic of the Holy Blood of Christ, brought from
the Holy Land, according to legend, by Count Dirk of Alsace. It became
the most venerated relic in Bruges and perhaps in all of West Flanders.[32]
A second example of imitation of Christ was even closer at hand—
Charles the Good, whom Galbert described as "devout and strong,
Catholic, the supporter of the poor, the protector, after God, of the
churches of God, the defender of the fatherland, and one in whom the
residue of earthly authority assumed the form of ruling well and the
substance of serving God."[33]

The sights and sounds within the church also take up the twin
themes of Advent and prophecy. The music for the antiphon "Honor,
Virtus" does not survive, but its text is drawn from Apocalypse 7:12,
itself part of a hymn of praise to God the Father in the presence of "the

lamb."[34] An explicit link with the most visionary and prophetic book of the Bible, describing a scene with striking parallels with what was taking place in Saint Donatian's that day, is extremely suggestive. The sight of all the "great candelabra being lit as on Christmas Day" forms the visual link of the ceremony with the holy day that is the fulfillment of the Advent season. Thus van Eyck makes quite explicit the juxtaposition of an earthly ruler and the Redeemer. And although van Eyck omits the text of the motet struck up by the organist as a recessional, most likely it too was linked thematically with Advent.[35]

Unfortunately, we know nothing about the prayers or collect "traditionally read at the Joyous Advent," for the library of Saint Donatian's disappeared during the French occupation of Bruges in 1793.[36] Lost as well was the *liber statutorum*, or book of privileges, containing the oath sworn by the ducal pair. It is probable that the texts quoted at length in Galbert's chronicle of 1127 were contained in this book. If that is true, Philip and Margaret swore to confirm and honor the privileges of the church, especially in the election of the provost.[37] The book must have been a beautiful object in its own right, for it had recently been rebound and contained ornamented rubrics and illuminations. If the manuscript was typical of those that have survived from Bruges workshops of the time, it would have more than held its own in that opulent company.[38]

Finally, it was the turn of Philip and Margaret to make an offering to the church, and the language used to describe this maintained the tone of solemn liturgy. Philip "processed" to the main altar and did not "give" (*dare*) his gift of gold but "sacrificed" (*immolare*) it. This very biblical verb of consecration was also used to describe Margaret's gift of the single gold piece. The worth of this gift was noted down to the very type of coin given, for van Eyck indicated that of the twenty-eight gold pieces, eight were *moutons*, and their total value amounted to thirty "shields," or *écus*.[39] This is extraordinary precision for a short chronicle entry, pointing out in effect that some of the coins were obsolete and giving their equivalent value in current coin. As a gauge of financial anxiety, such minute attention to money is eloquent.

There is one notable omission in van Eyck's description of Philip the Bold's entry: the oath sworn by Bruges's burghers to their new count. Galbert's chronicle shows a close identification of the privileges of Saint Donatian's with those of the urban *coniuratio* or commune. In fact, Galbert's account of William Clito's entry summarized above not only gives a detailed description of the church's privileges, but also summarizes the "little charter of agreement" (*chartula conventionis*) between the new count and the citizens of Bruges. This document was the foundation charter for Bruges as a commune, granting rights of self-government and freedom from the toll.[40] William Clito simply swore to uphold both the liberties of the church and the newly granted privileges to the Brugeois. By 1384, a new count swore two oaths, one in Saint Donatian's, the second on the Burg square in front of the *stadhuis*, facing Saint Donatian's. We know from the charter of confirmation issued by Philip that he and Margaret left the church and proceeded to the square where they both received the oath of fealty by all gathered there and took an oath themselves. Although the oath sworn by the ducal couple on that day does not survive, it was probably similar to that sworn at Ypres: "We swear that we will be good and loyal lords of Ypres and her citizens, and that the said city of Ypres and our subjects there will be kept, defended, and secure in their laws, privileges, freedoms, liberty, and good customs and usages, with God's help and all the saints of paradise."[41]

Unfortunately, we do not know what happened immediately before or after the ceremonies van Eyck describes. If the example of later tradition holds true for 1384, then the ducal party entered the city through the Kruispoort, where it was met by delegations of aldermen and other important burghers and the procession from Saint Donatian's.[42] Townspeople no doubt thronged the streets, although only a relative few could have squeezed into either the Burg or Saint Donatian's church. Feasting and drinking probably followed the last oath, but it is unlikely that wine flowed from the public fountains as it would in future festivities. The lay masters of the church fabric of Saint Donatian's, however, presented the count and countess with wine worth twenty-eight pounds groot Flemish, a considerable sum, and the city government no doubt followed suit.[43]

More important than the depth of drink were the long-term implications of this advent ceremony for the new dynasty of Burgundian counts and its relations with the Brugeois. Did it fulfill the hopes of those involved? For Philip the Bold the outcome of his Joyous Entry in Bruges was heartening. He had succeeded in replacing his late father-in-law in the affections of the Brugeois; he had furthered his policy of isolating rebel Ghent from the rest of Flanders, a policy that would finally bring Ghent to negotiate a treaty with the count; and he had established contacts within the Bruges community that would aid him in the future. For all these reasons, Bruges became a place where the Burgundian counts would often visit, sometimes dwell, and always draw upon the city's wealth of money, luxury goods, and specialized talent.

That Bruges would suit the Burgundians was almost predictable, given the city's social and economic patterns of the fourteenth century. One of these "patterns" was the popularity of jousts and other forms of chivalric display. As early as 1305, the town accounts mention "Shrove Tuesday, for jousters, burghers, and Easterlings (Germans), who jousted on the market." By 1392 Bruges had a permanent tournament society, the "White Bear," consisting of knights and notables, who preferred to stage their tourneys on Shrove Tuesday. In 1394, a Shrove Tuesday parody of a tourney was performed at Bruges in the presence of the count himself by Jan van Hulst and his companions, who formed a brotherhood known for literary and musical activities. These men later formed the nucleus of a chamber of rhetoric, that of the Holy Ghost.[44] So thoroughly did the chivalric ethos penetrate the upper classes of Bruges that the society of the White Bear was given a permanent meeting place in the "Poortersloge"—the house of the association of Bruges's social elite—and allowed to put their emblem on the front of the building.[45]

Even the commercial, financial, and manufacturing sectors of Bruges complemented the craving for chivalric display and honor so characteristic of the Burgundian dynasty and their developing state policy. As the great entrepôt of northern Europe, Bruges offered nearly every imported luxury, and its own workshops produced luxury cloth, finely tailored furs and clothing, jewelry, and of course art and music to dazzle any eye or ear.[46] The bankers and merchants of Bruges also did their part. As the wars against the pagans in Prussia reached their height between 1350 and 1400, many knights from the west journeyed east to join the crusade. Bruges, as the largest Hanseatic outpost in the west, became the natural point of embarkation and financial center of the Prussian crusade. To cite but one example, the Bruges banker, Collart de Marke, acted in cooperation with a local hosteler to provide a line of credit to Jean of Blois, lord of Gouda and Schoonhoven, during his crusade in the east in 1369.[47] It is also not surprising that beginning with Philip the Bold, the Burgundians hired their financial talent from the Bruges business community.[48]

Philip the Bold also began the dynastic pattern of residing in Bruges, although it was Philip the Good who made Bruges a favorite residence. Already by 1396, the apartments of Louis of Male in the city had been expanded into a much grander palace. Philip the Good enlarged and remodeled this "Prinsenhof" in 1429 and founded the Order of the Golden Fleece there a year later. Charles the Bold completed work on the complex in preparation for his marriage to Margaret of York in 1468. All this building activity was both earlier and more extensive than was the case in most other Flemish cities, with the possible exception of Lille.[49]

Both the city and the chapter of Saint Donatian's profited from the auspicious beginning of the Burgundian dynasty. Bruges's privileges were restored nearly intact, and a relatively peaceful time of cooperation with the Burgundians began.[50] Of course the interests of the city and the counts could never be identical, particularly where relations with England were concerned, yet to an unusual extent, Philip the Bold worked to restore Bruges's damaged commerce, and the city rewarded him and his successors with financial subsidies. Canonries in Saint Donatian's became a much-coveted source of prebends with which the Burgundians rewarded their clerics, and in turn the chapter enjoyed the favor of the Burgundians throughout the fifteenth century, particularly as the scene of Philip the Good's funeral.[51]

To a remarkable degree the hopes of 1384 were fulfilled as the Burgundian period commenced in Bruges, and, almost as a sort of musical accompaniment, the traditional ceremony as described by Peter van Eyck was repeated at the Joyous Entry of each successive Burgundian prince.[52] The successful continuity from Galbert's time and before down to the current count of Flanders was always made manifest. The joining of past to present, memory to expectation, heaven to earth, all accomplished in the *Adventus Iocundus*, remained crucial to both count and people.

Notes

1. I have used the translation of J. B. Ross, *The Murder of Charles the Good* (New York: Harper and Row, 1967), pp. 201–4. The preferred edition of the text is that by Henri Pirenne, *Histoire du meurtre de Charles le Bon* (Paris: Alphonse Picard, 1891), pp. 86–87: "Nones aprilis, feria tertia Aqua sapientiae, in crepusculo noctis, rex simul cum noviter electo consule Willelmo, Flandriarum marchione, Bruggas in suburbium nostrum venit, cui obviam processerant canonici Sancti Donatiani, reliquias sanctorum afferentes, et in sollempni processu regio more regem et comitem novum cum gaudio suspicientes. Octavo idus aprilis, feria quarta, convenerunt rex et comes cum suis et nostris militibus, civibus et Flandrensibus multis in agrum consuetum, in quo scrinia et reliquiae sanctorum collatae sunt. Et silentio indicto, lecta est charta libertatis ecclesiae et privilegiorum beati Donatiani coram universis.... Lecta est quoque chartula conventionis inter comitem et cives nostros.... Sub hac ergo conditionis compositione juraverunt rex et comes super sanctorum reliquias in audientia cleri et populi." Pirenne believed that Galbert wrote soon, even immediately after, the events he saw (Pirenne, *Histoire*, p. x).

2. The translation is my own and is somewhat edited from the original, which is *Bischoppelijk Archief te Brugge* (hereafter BAB), A48, *Acta Capituli*, fol. 111r: "Anno domini 1384, die vicesimasexta mensis aprilis, dominus Philippus dux Burgondie et domina Margareta ducissa Burgondie et comitissa Flandrie intraverunt villam Brugensis circa horam prandii. Et dominus decanus et capitulum cum totum (sic) chori processionaliter invenerunt eis obviam, induti cap(p)is sericatis, usque ad portam Burgi versus forum et ibidem intra portam descenderunt. Et dominus decanus dedit aquam benedictam et incensam, et hoc facto, cantores inceperunt Honor, Virtus, et cetera. Et sic cantandes [ms: cantands] processionaliter subsequebantur processionem usque ante maius altare ipsius ecclesie. Et ibidem, fusis orationibus, dominus decanus obtulit eis librum statutorum in quo scriptum est iuramentum domini comitis, quo ambo iuraverunt. Et aperuit primo dominus dux ewangeliarium in quo casualiter aparuit hoc ewangelium, Cum venerit paraclitus.... Et subsequenter, dicto libro ewangelii clause, domina comitissa aperuit dictum librum, et inveniebatur etiam idem ewangelium. Hoc facto, dominus decanus legit orationem et collectam consuetam legi in adventu iocundo cuiuslibet comitis. Et tunc dictus dominus dux processit ad altare et immolavit unum pannum aureum et xxviii peciis auri, inter quas erant viii mutones que faciebant summam xxx scutorum auri. Et postea domina immolavit unam peciam auri. Et finito responsorio, organista luset in organis unum motetum. Et erant accens(s)a omnia luminaria maiora, sicut in nativitate domini, et ornatus chorus ... et ominino campane sonabantur solenniter." This text has remained virtually unknown until now. Van Eyck is the literal translation of "De Quercu," the name used by the author in his Latin writings, but he also used the variant "Van der Eeke" from time to time. See L. Gilliodts–van Severen, *Inventaire des archives de la ville de Bruges. Section premier. Inventaire des Chartes* (Bruges: Gaillard, 1871–85), vol. 3, p. 237: "Meester Pieter van der Eeke, capitel clerc van Sinte Donaes." The term *Adventus Iocundus* (Joyous Advent) refers to a medieval tradition of celebrating the accession of a new ruler with a

ceremonial entry into his new cities and awarding him certain gifts. In France, where this tradition was most common, it became the occasion for both ceremony and taxation; in Brabant, on the other hand, the *Adventus* referred also to rights and privileges of the ruler vis-à-vis his new subjects. For a fine discussion of these traditions, see Lawrence M. Bryant, *The King and the City in the Parisian Royal Entry Ceremony: Politics, Ritual, and Art in the Renaissance* (Geneva: Librairie Droz, 1986), esp. chap. 1.

3. Ross's translation of *"suburbium nostrum"* as *"our town"* is a problem. It is clear that Galbert made the distinction between the "Burg" or *"urbs"* and the sub-urbs, the area outside the gates of the count's original fortifications. It is likely that holding the entry ceremony and the oath-taking outside the Burg was quite unusual, done only because rebels still held out in a part of the church itself. Of course it was this area outside the Burg that experienced tremendous growth in the twelfth and thirteenth centuries. For this period in Bruges, see J. A. Van Houtte, *De Geschiedenis van Brugge* (Tielt, Belgium: Lanoo, 1982).

4. Even though Philip the Bold held power in Flanders as count and not as duke, I have preferred to refer to him as duke for the purposes of this paper.

5. The Ghent War has never been the subject of a thorough study. Helpful are Fritz Quicke, *Les Pays-Bas à la veille de la période bourguignonne (1356–1384)* (Brussels: Editions universitaires, 1947); R. de Muynck, "De Gentse Oorlog (1379–1385): Oorzaken en Karakter," *Handelingen der Maatschappij voor Geschiedenis en Oudheidkunde te Gent*, n.s. 5 (1951): 305–18; and J. Van Herwaarden, "The War in the Low Countries," in J. J. N. Palmer, ed., *Froissart: Historian* (Totowa, N.J.: Rowman and Littlefield, 1981), pp. 101–17.

6. Francesco Pegolotti, *La practica della mercatura* (Cambridge, Mass.: Medieval Academy, 1936), p. 236 ("Cioe Bruggia e Guanto e Ipro e Lille e Doagio, ma parlereno il pui di Bruggia pero ch'ella a quella terra ove piu stanno i risedenti mercatanti a fare la mercatantia e cambi in Fiandria").

7. The term "worldmarketplace" was applied to Bruges by R. Häpke, *Brügges Entwicklung zum mittelalterlichen Weltmarkt* (Berlin: Curtius, 1908), p. 4n. I am currently engaged in research on the implications of economic and social change in Bruges in the fourteenth century. Two preliminary results are James M. Murray, "Cloth, Banking and Finance in Medieval Bruges," in *Textiles of the Low Countries in European Economic History*, ed. Erik Aerts and John H. Munro (Leuven: Leuven University Press, 1990), pp. 24–31, and "Family, Marriage and Moneychanging in Medieval Bruges," *Journal of Medieval History* 14 (1988): 115–25.

8. *Oeuvres de Froissart, publiées avec les variantes des divers manuscrits*, ed. Baron Kervyn de Lettenhove, 26 vols. (Brussels: Devaux, 1867–77; reprint, Osnabrück: Biblio Verlag, 1967), 8: 373.

9. For the relations of Bruges and Philip the Bold before 1384, see Richard Vaughan, *Philip the Bold* (Cambridge, Mass.: Harvard University Press, 1962), pp. 17–19, 30. The degree of panic within Bruges after the defeat at Westrozebeke can be gauged by the large numbers of burghers who fled the city just on the rumor of the French army's approach, and by the unfortunate woman who drowned herself for fear of the approaching *Bertoenen* (Van Herwaarden, "War in the Low Countries," p. 111).

10. Quoted in A. Van Nieuwenhuysen, *Les finances du Duc de Bourgogne Philippe le Hardi, 1384–1404* (Brussels: Editions de l'Université de Bruxelles, 1984), p. 45.

11. David Nicholas, *The Van Arteveldes of Ghent* (Ithaca, N.Y.: Cornell University Press, 1988), pp. 172–73.

12. Van Houtte, *Geschiedenis*, p. 121.

13. Johan Huizinga, *Herfsttij der Middeleeuwen* (Groningen: Wolters-Nijhoff, 1919), p. 3; my translation.

14. Ernst Kantorowicz, "The King's Advent and the Enigmatic Panels in the Doors of Santa Sabina," *Selected Studies* (Locust Valley, N.Y.: Augustin, 1965), p. 42. Kantorowicz's admiration for Huizinga is shown not only in his review of Huizinga's collected essays in

the *American Historical Review* 60 (1955): 853–55, but also by a project he undertook in the mid-1930s on "the history of the Dukes of Burgundy of the Valois race." I owe this reference to the kindness of Professor Robert E. Lerner.

15. Hugo Soly, "Plechtige intochten in de steden van de Zuidelijke Nederlanden tijdens de overgang van de Middeleeuwen naar Nieuw Tijd: Communicatie, propaganda, spektakel," *Tijdschrift voor Geschiedenis* 97 (1984): 343.

16. Sabine MacCormack, *Art and Ceremony in Late Antiquity* (Berkeley: University of California Press, 1981), p. 53.

17. Van Houtte, *Geschiedenis*, p. 262. Despite the construction of the walls of 1127 and 1297, the Burg retained both its walls and gates until the eighteenth century.

18. The early history of Saint Donatian's has been a subject of some controversy, especially since the chapter foundation charter of 961 was proven to be a forgery. The best summary of both the controversy and the reconstruction presented above is G. Declercq, "Wanneer onstond het Sint-Donaaskapittel te Brugge?" *Handelingen van het Genootschap voor Geschiedenis* 122 (1985): 145–57.

19. This office quickly became more honorific than of any real importance, except during the reigns of Charles the Good and Thierry of Alsace (d. 1167). On this point see David Nicholas, "Of Poverty and Primacy: Demand, Liquidity, and the Flemish Economic Miracle, 1050–1200," *American Historical Review* 96 (1991): 20 n. 16; and Ellen Kittell, *From Ad Hoc to Routine: A Case Study in Medieval Bureaucracy* (Philadelphia: University of Pennsylvania Press, 1991), p. 7.

20. Van Houtte, *Geschiedenis*, pp. 250–51. The procession took place on May 3 each year and was not only the highlight of the processional year, but also heralded the beginning of the Bruges fair.

21. B. Janssens de Bisthoven, "Het Kapittel van Sint-Donatiaan te Brugge," in *Sint-Donaas en de Voormalige Brugse Katedraal* (Bruges: Jong Kristen Onthaal voor Toerisme, 1978), pp. 51–59.

22. Nicholas, *The Van Arteveldes*, pp. 173–74.

23. BAB, A48, *Acta Capituli*, fol. 99r; for financial losses, BAB, G1/4 (accounts of the Fabric of Saint Donatian's, 1381–82), fol. 2v: "[received] de ostio occidentali ecclesie hoc anno propter paucitatem mercatorum, nichil."

24. BAB, G1/4, fol. 7r: "Item datum domino Jacobo de Zaemte ad procurandum vexilla pro defensione terrarum nostrarum extra villam. 32s."

25. Huizinga, *Herfsttij*, pp. 2–3. Saint Donatian's had six bells each of a different pitch; see Reinhard Strohm, *Music in Late Medieval Bruges* (Oxford: Oxford University Press, 1985), p. 104.

26. Strohm, *Music in Medieval Bruges*, pp. 18–19. The organist hired by Philip was Jean Visée. Among the Burgundian court musicians who held prebends in Saint Donatian's in the fifteenth century were Gilles Binchois, Guillaume Dufay, and Gilles Joye.

27. Van Houtte, *Geschiedenis*, p. 41.

28. Ibid., p. 268.

29. Kantorowicz, "The King's Advent," pp. 52–53.

30. Thus this passage of John is strikingly similar to the "Ecce mitto angelum meum" text, for it also constructs a "twofold" role of the ruler. Either he is the one sent by God to bear witness to Christ, or, more likely, the Holy Spirit precedes and directs the ruler as the anointed of God. See Kantorowicz, "The King's Advent," pp. 52–53.

31. Richard Kieckhefer, *Magic in the Middle Ages* (Cambridge: Cambridge University Press, 1989), p. 88. Divination by opening a book was a time-honored form of fortune-telling throughout the Middle Ages and beyond.

32. Van Houtte, *Geschiedenis*, pp. 247–48. The identification of the Holy Blood and Dirk of Alsace is certainly false, and most historians now believe that the relic was plundered from Constantinople during the Fourth Crusade and brought to Bruges in the early thirteenth century. This count did, however, rebuild his palace chapel (Saint Basil's), creating four chaplaincies attached to the chapter of Saint Donatian's.

33. Ross, *Murder of Charles the Good*, p. 81.

34. The scene is one where all the angels stand before the divine throne and chant a hymn of praise to God: "[D]icentes: Amen. Benedictio, et claritas, et sapientia, et gratiarum actio, honor, et virtus, et fortitudo Deo nostro, in saecula saeculorum. Amen." This is all done "in conspectu Agni."

35. We are also told that both the choir and the church bells joined the organ in the unnamed motet. It is thus possible that the motet was to begin with solo organ and then swell to a crescendo of choir and bells much like a medieval *1812 Overture*. See Strohm, *Music in Medieval Bruges*, p. 4, for the Netherlandish art of motet composition employing church bells.

36. On the library of Saint Donatian's, see A. Derolez, "De bibliotheek van het Kapittel van Sint-Donatiaan te Brugge in de Middeleeuwen," *Koninklijke Zuidnederlandse Maatschappij voor Taal- en Letterkunde en Geschiedenis* 15 (1961): 159–74.

37. Ross, *Murder of Charles the Good*, p. 202; and Pirenne, *Histoire du meurtre*, p. 86.

38. In the church accounts of 1379 BAB, G/2, 1379, fol. 24v: "item pro libro statutorum capituli religando et aliquibus scripturis ac picturis in eo factis 6 lb." For the Bruges book industry of the later Middle Ages, see the essays in *Vlaamse Kunst op Perkament* (Bruges: Stad Brugge, 1981).

39. "Moutons," or in Flemish *mottoenen*, were Flemish gold coins struck by Louis of Male from June 1356 to March 1364 but in circulation far longer. The shields (scuta) referred to by Van Eyck were probably the "nieuwe schilden" (*écu* in French) struck by Louis from June 1373 to the end of his reign and into the first few months of the reign of Philip the Bold. The best source for information on coinage in this period remains Hans van Werveke, *De Muntslag in Vlaanderen onder Lodewijk Van Male* (Brussels: Paleis der Academiën, 1949), p. 22. I am indebted to Professor John Munro for information on this point.

40. Pirenne, *Histoire du meurtre*, p. 87; Ross, *Murder of Charles the Good*, p. 203.

41. J. Bartier and A. Van Nieuwenhuysen, eds., *Ordonnances de Philippe le Hardi, de Marguerite de Male et de Jean sans Peur, 1381–1419*, vol. 1: *Ordonnances de Philippe le Hardi et de Marguerite de Male du 16 octobre 1381 au 31 décembre 1393* (Brussels: Recueil des Ordonnances des Pays-Bas, 1965), pp. 21–22.

42. A. Dewitte, "Twee Keer Blijde Intrede te Brugge: 1468, 3 Juli, Margareta Van York; 1515, 18 en 22 April, Karel Prince des Hespaignes," *Biekorf* 89 (1989): 260. This was the route followed by the procession at the wedding of Charles the Bold and Margaret of York.

43. BAB, G/2, 1384, fol. 6v. Although the Bruges town accounts do not survive for 1384, in 1385, after the peace accord with Ghent, Philip and Margaret were honored with a festive escort into the city and a gift of wine worth 5 pounds groot Flemish. See Gilliodts–van Severen, *Inventaire*, vol. 3, p. 63. Presents of wine were frequent upon such occasions and throughout the year. They were a regular budget item in both the Ghent and Bruges accounts (Marc Boone, *Geld en Macht: De Gentse stadsfinanciën en de Bourgondische staatsvorming (1384–1453)* [Ghent: Maatschappij voor Geschiedenis en Oudheidkunde, 1990], pp. 92–94).

44. Herman Pleij, *Het gilde van de Blauwe Schuit: Literatuur, volksfeest en burgermoraal in de late Middeleeuwen* (Amsterdam: Meulenhoff, 1979).

45. Van Houtte, *Geschiedenis*, pp. 160–61.

46. Strohm, *Music in Medieval Bruges*, pp. 11 and 18; and Wim Blockmans and Walter Prevenier, *The Burgundian Netherlands* (Cambridge: Cambridge University Press, 1986), pp. 88–89.

47. The transaction is recorded in *Stadsarchief, Brugge, Koopmansboeken Collart de Marke*, Ledger 5, fol. 86v; it will appear in vol. 2 of the series edited by Professor Werner Paravicini, *Die Preussen reisen des europäischen Adels* (Sigmaringen, Germany, forthcoming). See also Maurice Keen, *Chivalry* (New Haven, Conn.: Yale University Press, 1984), p. 172; and W. Paravicini, "Die Preussenreisen des europäischen Adels," *Historische Zeitschrift* 232 (1981): 25–38.

48. Two notable examples were Dino Rapondi, a long-time member of the Bruges financial community, originally from Lucca, who was Philip the Bold's financial adviser even before he became count of Flanders, and Pieter Bladelin, who was councillor and treasurer to Philip the Good. See Van Nieuwenhuysen, *Les finances du Duc de Bourgogne Philippe le Hardi*, p. 49; on Rapondi, L. Mirot, "La société des Raponde: Dino Raponde," *Bibliothèque de l'Ecole des Chartes* 89 (1928): 299–389; and Van Houtte, *Geschiedenis*, p. 160.

49. Van Houtte, *Geschiedenis*, p. 160.

50. Part of the ceremony of 1384 was a confirmation of the city privileges as granted by Louis of Male in 1358; the text is printed in full by L. Gilliodts–van Severen, *Inventaire*, vol. 3, p. 1. Philip also worked to bring back the foreign merchants who had fled Bruges during the Ghent war; see A. Van Nieuwenhuysen, *Les finances du Duc de Bourgogne Philippe le Hardi*, pp. 168–69.

51. Vaughan, *Philip the Good*, p. 91.

52. Strohm, *Music in Medieval Bruges*, p. 97.

CHAPTER 6

The Spectacle of Suffering in Spanish Streets

Maureen Flynn

Every year on the evening of Holy Thursday, between the hours of twilight and midnight, city residents came out of their homes into the open air to express grief. It was a grief inherited from their religion, from the sacred narrative of the Christian faith. Spanish Catholics in the Late Middle Ages were commemorating the last hours before Christ's death, including his last supper, his agony in the garden, and his journey to Calvary for crucifixion. Men and women who were old, weak, and feeble, young men in their prime of life, and girls just entering the age of puberty filled the streets to witness this annual reenactment of Christ's sacrifice.

The biblical tale of suffering and humiliation, of crowns of thorns and bloody floggings, captured the Spanish imagination in a bond of affective ties to a past that seemed never to atrophy with the passage of time. The collective memory of these Spanish Catholics in the late medieval period clung tenaciously to images of Christ's martyrdom. Harboring no doubts about the historical veracity of biblical events concerning the passion and crucifixion, the Spanish people remembered them with a sorrow that penetrated the privacy of their own emotional experiences. What rendered these crucifixion episodes significant and valid sources of religious inspiration for these people, it appears, was not so much their biblical authority, as the "mood" that memory of such events inevitably created. By remembering the suffering of the absent Christ, personal and familiar sensations of grief surfaced from the depths of the imagination and were expressed in visual scenes of theatrical pain. Private agonies and daily hardships that had remained until now inaccessible to public expression were made manifest in the collective symbolism of this reenactment. The power and potential of the Holy Thursday myth was to condense unconscious emotional energy and impose upon these emotions chains of signifiers attached to the lacerated and exhausted body of Christ. The story of Christ's suffering spoke to Spanish Catholics of their own psychic needs, offering an explanation for their pain and articulating for them a meaning about the many diverse and unique experiences of life.

Castilian laypeople from early childhood heard preachers and parish priests relate the story of how a young man, Jesus Christ, felt constrained on Thursday evening to meditate upon the prospects of mortality and to anticipate in his imagination the death of the body. The events that occurred that evening in the Garden of Gethsemane as Jesus considered the violence that would soon end his own life on earth was told most powerfully in the gospels of Matthew and Luke. With a heavy heart, they said, Jesus left his friends in order to contemplate the afflictions that would soon rend his flesh and fatally exhaust his physical strength. It is said in Luke that his despair was so great that "sweat became like drops of blood, falling down upon the ground" (22:44). At this point in the narrative, death is just being anticipated in the mind, anticipated with such force that the body itself begins to respond. For Christ's followers, asked to bear with him a short while in these thoughts, this was the single, unparalleled opportunity to share completely in his suffering. It was the moment when their imaginations could leap across the singularity of his later bodily suffering and empathize with his agony in its entirety. For this reason Holy Thursday represented to Christians of all ages the focal point of belief and the arena into which religious commitment was directed.

In Spain the story of Christ's agony in the garden provided the opening theme to the public's participation in the saga of redemption. It was reenacted by groups of young men and women called *disciplinantes*, wandering storytellers who reproduced the mournful scriptural tale in their imaginations and inscribed on their flesh the blood that was thought once to have been shed by Christ. Initially, the people who chose to participate in the public performances met together privately in parish churches and local monasteries to contemplate Christ's suffering and share in evening meals. They extended to one another signs of affection and goodwill and offered apologies for past offenses.[1] Wedded in this state of grace and freed of animosity, they silently journeyed out onto dirt and cobblestone streets, walking barefoot through the narrow stone corridors of their neighborhoods for distances of some two to three leagues.[2] On the way they scourged themselves, flailing long knotted and waxed-tipped ropes across their backs until blood drenched their linen tunics and spilled over onto darkened pavements.[3] They were all under the age of fifty, and it was required by corporate law of the confraternities of the Vera Cruz in which they claimed membership that they be in good health.[4] This was necessary because the activity of the *disciplinantes* demanded enormous physical strength and endurance in order to perform in front of the public with unwavering resolve.

The way in which the Spanish people reenacted Christ's sacrifice, in processions that riddled the surface of their streets with the blood of the inhabitants, exposes for us with perfect clarity the function of ritual in the religious experiences of traditional oral communities. Mircea Eliade has observed that ritual is a means of spanning the chronological distance between present and past and perpetuating memories of a community's supernatural origins.[5] Among Christians in medieval Spain, such ritual flagellation was done precisely as a memorial to an act of sacrifice that occurred centuries in the past, a sacrifice that was supposed to have won for them life beyond the grave. This commemorative function of ritual was made perfectly clear to spectators in public pronouncements. In Palencia, for example, two small boys holding candles in procession before flagellants cried out loudly for all those present to hear that "this is done in memory of the Passion of Our Redeemer Jesus Christ."[6] Spectators in the small village of Arlanzón heard a similar message from a group of young men as they solemnly raised scourges over their heads. As the lashes flickered through the torchlit night, they announced that "this is done in honor and reverence of the shedding of His precious blood, and in honor of the five thousand lashes that they gave Him in order to redeem and save us."[7]

Those lashes, it must be emphasized, were reenacted not merely symbolically, but literally, upon the shoulders and backs of the Vera Cruz *disciplinantes*, tearing into the flesh and exposing at the same time layers of psychic experience that must have run much deeper than the mere memory of Christ's sacrifice. As much as a pound of coagulated blood was sometimes shed by each flagellant—more than enough, one might think, to stimulate recall. Indeed, a Portugese visitor watching some fourteen hundred participants proceed in this manner through the streets of Valladolid found the daunting portrayal of pain nearly incomprehensible as a commemorative rite. He compared it with horror to more modest memorials performed in his own home territory of Lisbon.[8]

The extreme behavior of the Castilians suggests that ritual flagellation was not simply or exclusively a mnemonic device designed to facilitate the recall of an abstract historical event, although it may be true that memories are triggered more by bodily sensations than by factual details of an occurrence, and that pain, the twinge of the skin as it ruptures with blood, may have served, as the smell of the *petite madeleine* did for Proust, to stimulate recollection. But it is at least equally useful, in our exploration of the collective meaning of ritual flagellation, to look beyond the mnemonic function and consider the emotional purposes of bodily mortification. For Maundy Thursday celebrations in Castile were undoubtedly something more than historical simulations of an absent past, more than street plays of the variety staged on the feasts of Corpus Christi and Christmas. They were also very real and personal productions of human pain and suffering performed by men known to have been of great courage and physical endurance. The genuinely painful manner in which biblical reenactment was practiced in Castile suggests a critical phenomenological difference between the operation of historical memory and the operation of ritual memory.[9] Spaniards did not commemorate the past by imagining it as a passage of events recorded in a history text, but rather with a release of psychic energy that laid claim to their immediate concerns with bodily pain. They were rehearsing a past that continued to live on in their own emotional appreciation of the world, watching blood past and blood present mingle with theatrical ease over human backs bent in actual agony and fatigue.

The explanation for this ritual bleeding was to be found by Spanish participants in the realm of theology. It was the theological meaning attributed to Christ's suffering that was articulated in confraternal ordinances and announced to spectators by torch-bearing criers in procession. Very young boys, boys who had only recently acquired the powers of language, were commissioned to convey with their lithe little voices the symbolic content of bodily suffering. Consistent with official church teachings, these public oracles explained to spectators that Christ's suffering was an offering that had secured mankind's salvation by serving as atonement for individual offenses against God and by satisfying divine justice.[10] In accomplishing this task, Christ's pain had to be regarded as sanctifying pain. It was pain that was endowed with the power to cleanse, to heal, and to restore moral order.

Outside the theater of ritual flagellation, the Catholic church taught that only Christ's blood had the potential to earn eternal life for mankind. Within the theater of public scourging, however, this message was amplified beyond the bounds of official propriety to admit of the sanctifying power of all people's suffering. Indeed, as one bewildered visitor from France, Antonio Collet, observed after watching Holy Thursday events in Castile, Spanish celebrants practiced their imitative actions with such zeal that each of them seemed to be personally claiming the power of sanctification. He had been participating in paschal ceremonies in the 1570s and was taken before the Inquisition of Toledo for critically remarking that it was quite enough, in order to recall the redemption, simply to carry the image of Christ in procession. Collet had argued with participants that there was no need to discipline the flesh, which was "a great vanity and foolishness," for "Christ had suffered and died for our sins once and for all in the past." As native participants enthusiastically upheld the imperative of a continual and personal involvement in the primordial act of salvation, he offered the sober opinion that believers need not reenact for themselves this already consummated moment in sacred history. Despite his attempts to subject the meaning of ritual to historical time, Collet was no Protestant. He had not accepted Luther's theology about the utter passivity of man before God, and he accepted fully the idea that personal penance was necessary to bring about forgiveness of sins. What he resisted in the Spanish rites was the idea that flagellation of the human body held supernatural significance. He told Inquisition officials in his own native language of French that it was his understanding of Christian theology that *contrition* is all that is needed for salvation. Spaniards were behaving, he complained, as if they believed that their own physical suffering were efficacious in spiritual purification. As Christ suffered physically to redeem mankind of sin, so every member of his church in Spain seemed to feel the need to endure chastisement in order to atone for iniquities of the soul.[11]

The Frenchman's argument contained more than a little truth. This attitude about suffering had become, in fact, a crucial dimension in popular soteriology in Spain by the end of the Middle Ages. Among the pious activities of lay confraternities, in particular, the role of bodily mortification had come to equal and even to surpass the role of prayer and good works such as charity in corporate programs for the salvation of the soul.[12] Clearly the activity of mortifying the flesh had been regarded as an effective means of sanctification by the monastic orders for a long time, but it was not until the thirteenth and fourteenth centuries in certain parts of Europe,[13] and not until this latter period in Spain,[14] that it became a prominent element of lay spirituality.

The impulse for this extension of asceticism undoubtedly derived from the imposition upon the laity of the sacrament of penance in 1215, when the Fourth Lateran Council ordered that all Christians annually confess their sins to trained members of the clergy.[15] In the following centuries, as laypeople in Spain became accustomed to admitting before religious superiors their responsibility and guilt for moral transgressions, the role of pain acquired grave importance in their response to sin. Penitents were required, as the most important part of their duties as Christians, verbally to express remorse and sorrow for having violated God's commandments. It was this *emotional* element in the performance of penance, a sense of sorrow proceeding within from love of God, that was supposed to produce for them forgiveness of sins.[16]

Without an internal feeling of contrition, contemporary theologians stressed, no sinner would be absolved of guilt. Antoninus of Florence stated in his prominent confessional manual that "confessions must be tearful and filled with great pain."[17] The best-selling author of lay spiritual guides in Spain during the sixteenth century, Juan de Dueñas, declared that confessions ought to be "tearful and lachrymose [*lloroso y lachrimosa*] because it is through weeping that the stains of the soul are cleansed."[18] The exact nature of contrition appears to have deeply concerned lay penitents seeking genuinely effective confessions. Francisco de Villagracia speaks in his *Arte de bien confesar* about penitents who worried that they were not able to feel the same degree of sorrow for sins as they might feel for temporal misfortunes.[19] Antoninus of Florence too talks about anxious penitents who admitted that they felt more intense sorrow about the death of parents and friends, and more concern about material hardships, than they did about the sins that they committed.[20] On the advice of Thomas Aquinas and Bonaventure, these late scholastic theologians tried to console penitents about their perceived moral inadequacy by distinguishing between mental and bodily suffering.

Only mental suffering, they explained, was required in the sacrament of penance. "The pain of contrition," Villagracia said, "is not of a sensual nature, of a kind that might be felt in our physical being." "It is," he said, "a pain of the mind."[21] Antoninus of Florence called the pain of contrition "intellectual pain" and defined this as "a feeling of perfect rational repugnance of sin."[22] The Franciscan Juan de Dueñas called this superior expression of sorrow "voluntary" or "rational" pain because "it is a deliberate act of consciousness or reason."[23] Martín de Azpilcueta added that this pain was not experienced in the same way that grief was expressed in the death of someone loved, for it did not reach into our flesh and affect the body's humors. As he saw it, "perfect" contrition occupied a realm independent of human physiology, unconnected with natural feelings of depression and melancholy and bereavement.[24]

So frequently do the confessional manuals insist on a distinction between intellectual and bodily pain in contrition that it can be surmised that lay penitents, for whom the manuals were written, had difficulty in conceiving of an act of sorrow that was entirely unrelated to the life of the body. Be that as it may, the penitential literature reveals incontestably that it was extremely important to churchmen that contrition be envisioned as an intellectual experience. Trained in a classical understanding of human nature that placed reason in a preeminent position among the powers of the human soul, they believed that suffering of the intellect carried with it more merit than suffering of the body. In privileging the intellect in this manner, late scholastic theologians were merely adopting the values of the most renowned philosophers of the Western world, from Aristotle to Aquinas, who had always maintained that it was reason that gave man access to things divine. Compared to pain governed by reason, or rational pain, all other kinds of suffering were inferior, particularly "sensual pain," or feeling, in the words of Antoninus of Florence, "that comes from the sensitive part of man as a result of alterations and afflictions of the flesh."[25] Sensual pain of this sort was held to be unnecessary for forgiveness of sin because it was of an order that even animals experienced. Although most theologians admitted that physical pain might accompany and even deepen the intellectual experience of sorrow, they consistently warned penitents not to become preoccupied with sensations of a bodily nature because these alone were ineffective in remitting their guilt and saving them from eternal punishment.[26]

It would appear, from this description of medieval penance, that church theologians had all but banished the body as a source of influence in the process of forgiveness of sin. But contrition was only one step in the three-tiered structure of sacramental penance. The penitent seeking pardon for sin was expected, after experiencing this initial inner sense of regret and sorrow for sin, to reveal the content of the soul orally before a priest—this was the second requirement and the actual "act of confession" in penance. And then finally, the penitent was obliged to perform some act of expiation or atonement before God. It was in this third and last requirement of sacramental confession that the body played a role. Theologians asserted that while contrition and confession were essential in obtaining God's pardon and relieving the sinner of personal guilt, these two subjective expressions of remorse did not succeed in appeasing divine anger. This could only be achieved, they argued, by enduring bodily punishment. The "acts of satisfaction" constituting punishment could be expiated either on earth, in fulfillment of obligations prescribed by priests, or in purgatory, in fulfillment of God's bill of suffering.

In the late medieval period, ecclesiastical prescriptions of penitential punishment usually took the form of prayer, charity, and fasting. In Spain the popular confessional guide of Pedro Ciruelo, for example, recommended prayer as a perfect form of compensation for sins of pride, for it is a manner, he said, of humiliating the heart before God. Charity, or the sharing of wealth, he suggested, offers adequate compensation for sins of avarice. For sins of lust and greed, he advised fasting because hunger makes the body suffer directly from its excesses of pleasure.[27] The widely circulated confessional manual of Azpilcueta also recommended that penitents think of prayer, charity, and fasting as means of atoning, respectively, for sins of the heart, of the hand, and of the mouth. This short little mnemonic device, associating forms of atonement with the bodily instruments of sin, undoubtedly shaped the penitential experiences of thousands of Castilians in the sixteenth century, encouraging them to engage in acts of atonement that did indeed "afflict the flesh."[28]

But we should not suppose that mortification exercises were imposed unilaterally by the clergy upon an unwilling and passive laity. Considerable evidence exists, both direct and indirect, that attests that bodily punishment was taken up eagerly by laypeople. By the sixteenth century the sanctifying powers of pain had acquired such prestige among lay members of society that voluntary mortification surpassed in severity and frequency the penitential obligations that the church hierarchy had attempted to impose upon the flock at confession. The hagiographical literature of this period, in the first instance, is filled with examples of private individuals secretly practicing flagellation and wearing hair shirts against the better judgment of their confessors.[29] It was during this time as well that priors and prioresses were constrained to draw up special statutes for their orders specifying that mortification exercises be practiced modestly to preserve the health of novices.[30]

Confessional manuals for priests also issued warnings intended to protect the physical well-being of lay penitents. Azpilcueta wrote that "the sentient pain of repentance and other corporal afflictions like fasting and sleeping on bare floors ... are not to be so excessive that they damage one's physical disposition and deprive one of the strength necessary to perform daily tasks."[31] Juan de Segura's *Confessionario* offered the suggestion that a state of melancholy and discomfort was not always conducive to spiritual perfection. "During repentance," he said, "one must not harm one's health, and it should be taken into account that discipline, when it is inflicted, is not to be directed onto the shoulders because this is damaging to the eyes. As for hair shirts, they should not be worn in their entirety, because in this style they can be very cumbersome and create severe lesions in some people. In order to moderate these harmful effects, it is recommended that *cilicios* be taken off the waist periodically and not worn many days in succession." Continuing his advice, Segura states that "the belt should be worn very low so that it does not touch the kidneys, and the part touching the liver should be padded with linen."[32]

Even in such precautionary prescriptions, we note that a remarkable amount of energy and attention was focused on the human body. Penitents were being asked to avoid excessive rubbing of their skin against goat's hair, and they were cautioned about seriously damaging bodily organs with tight bindings around the waist. In these warnings, but also more cogently and forcibly in the lists of taxes imposed on sin, the human body occupied a critical position in the pursuit of religious purity. Intercourse with one's spouse on Sunday was penalized with seven days of fasting;[33] blasphemy incurred one hundred lashes with a whip;[34] and erroneous statements about the nature of God's divinity could provoke a penalty of standing for long periods of time at novena services.[35] We recognize, within the praxis of medieval penitence, a culture that was by no means ignoring the flesh in its search for the transcendent, but making use of the flesh's sentient qualities in that quest. Pain was the touchstone of sanctity in late medieval Spanish society, the human means of transport to an extrahuman, and extracorporeal, world. It was through the endurance of sentience, of the extreme limits that bodily sentience can reach in pain, that God was discovered. This method of piety, extending beyond Spain to all Christian parts of Europe in the medieval period, has been made abundantly clear to us by professors Carolyn Walker Bynum and Peter Brown in their intimate and extensive examinations of saints' lives. They have demonstrated that religious asceticism impinged upon nearly every sensory experience of the body and laid the foundation for the construction of sanctity in traditional Christian society.[36]

The Italian scholar Giulia Calvi, moreover, has offered us an account of beatification proceedings in Italy that goes a long way toward explaining the cultivation of suffering in the Christian world. The case that Calvi raised involved the public affirmation of sufferings endured by a young Dominican nun by the name of Domenica da Paradiso. During the plague year of 1527, Domenica offered to substitute the suffering of her own body, through a ritual exchange, for that of the residents of her beloved city of Florence. According to contemporary accounts, she asked God to gather all of the Florentine plague into her body and to accept all her contaminated blood, to be purged from her veins, as an offering in exchange for their collective suffering. After making this vow with God, Domenica became fatally ill and shed her blood copiously in natural wounds and wounds inflicted through the hands of attending physicians. Domenica was quickly recognized as a saint in Counter-Reformation Florence, and Calvi told us in graphic detail how her exhumed and theatrically displayed corpse became for the anxious and pest-ridden Florentines a sensuous symbol of the religious virtues of bodily suffering. Calvi explained thoroughly that what made Domenica holy in the eyes of the Florentines was not merely the fact that she endured great physical pain, but that she voluntarily took on this pain, like Christ, for the sake of the city.[37]

At a time when bodily pain was an unavoidable fact of life for all residents, the voluntary espousal of suffering came to be regarded as an act of great valor and moral strength. What is perhaps most noteworthy in the Florentine's approach to pain is the notion that one person's suffering could be transferred imaginatively onto another. Pain could be exchanged from one man to another man, from many men to one woman, circulating as a costly currency in the purchase of spiritual goods. This attitude toward pain was the basis, in fact, of the entire medieval system of suffrages, of the prayers and charitable offerings made by the living for the sake of suffering souls in purgatory. Men and women who were illiterate, unskilled in trades, and destined to lives of poverty believed that they could attain for themselves and for their departed loved ones special sanctifying graces by embracing physical pain.

In this regard it is useful to take into account the many examples of voluntary mortification recorded in the proceedings of the Spanish Holy Office. One such case involves a simple working woman named Isabel Briñas, the daughter of a tailor, who was brought in the early seventeenth century to inquisitors in Madrid for questioning about extraordinary gifts that she claimed to enjoy from God. Isabel had attracted a great deal of attention from her neighbors for her abilities to cure diseases and tell the future. It was thought that she had acquired these powers as a result of an impeccably pious lifestyle that involved frequent fasting on bread and water and the wearing of hair shirts for periods of up to five weeks. The trait that she herself held in the highest regard, the sign most indicative of her special status in the eyes of God, was the incredible physical pain that she could endure. Isabel was convinced that her periodic headaches were divine omens of Christ's crown of thorns, for she had asked God to allow her to share in the divine passion. A second, more elusive, sign of her exalted spiritual condition that was revealed to inquisitors were the *suspensiones,* or out-of-body experiences, that "were granted her." One year, it is recorded, she had *suspen-*

siones two or three times a day, sometimes when kneeling in prayer and other times when washing or standing on her feet. They would last, she said, about an hour or half an hour, although occasionally they passed very quickly. Her confessor had tried to warn her about these experiences, but they would always return despite her attempts at suppression. Isabel tells us little about the exact nature of these *suspensiones* except to say that on one occasion they came back accompanied with such great agony that she thought her head might fracture and that this physical pain lingered long after the *suspensiones* had ceased.

Isabel associated her suffering with the fact that she had been praying at the time for the safe delivery of souls to heaven. At one point in her testimony, after describing her afflictions, she said, "I was praying for the souls of those in purgatory and for the souls of those of us still living with such intensity that I must have asked for the whole world!" Isabel interpreted her agony as an empathetic transfer to herself of the sufferings of all humanity. With her pain Isabel had taken on the penitential work of all those people whom she held in her imagination. Like the redemptive life of Christ, and like the contemporary cult of Domenica da Paradiso in Florence, Isabel's role was to relieve other people of the burdens of their sins. Isabel's own confessor was convinced of her sanctifying powers, and he went to her once after the death of a friend, a sacristan from the Colegio of Atocha, and asked her to commend the dead man's soul to God. Taking on the request, Isabel spent two or three days in awful pain and discomfort. When the feelings subsided, she suspected that the sacristan had escaped his penalties in purgatory. Her proof came moments later when she saw, "not with my corporal eyes but with the eyes of my soul that the friar had risen to heaven."[38]

It was within the context of a civilization that regarded pain as the principal currency of exchange with God that the Spanish flagellant groups operated. Their special duty was to endure bodily pain, voluntarily, as a means to rectify the wrongs of others and appease the wrath of God. In their statutes, the Vera Cruz and other Christological confraternities publically promised to conduct flagellation exercises not only on Maundy Thursday but whenever asked of them by communal authorities for protection against plague, famine, flooding, or other scourges "that our Lord, as a result of our sins, has sent us." Vera Cruz ordinances in the Zamoran village of Arguhillo, for example, enjoined its members to mortification at such times because this service "is of great merit in supplicating his divine majesty to placate his anger and lift the scourge."[39] What is essential in the meaning of flagellation rites to these people are two concepts that already have been expressed in the private lives of both Domenica da Paradiso and Isabel Briñas. First, physical pain was believed to be instrumental in human communication with divine providence, and, second, these communicative powers of physical pain were believed to be transferable from one individual to another.

On the night of Holy Thursday, these expiatory functions of pain were expressed for the public in theatrical performances that filled the eyes of spectators with extravagant and emphatic images of corporal punishment. While most penance in the late medieval period was performed privately, in a state of humility and shame in accordance with the decrees of the Fourth Lateran Council, the paschal ceremonies of the Vera Cruz confraternities brought all these covert feelings of repentance into the open, in ostentatious display. Urban and rural residents as well as some foreigners poured into the streets of Castile, forming a tearful lining for a ritual flow of blood designed to reestablish metaphysical equilibrium between man and the divine. That which appears most bizarre and horrendous to us today—the grandiloquent manner in which the body was penalized—was the precise value of flagellation ceremonies to contemporaries and the common form in which tragic theater of all kinds is presented. For the Spanish people this open-air spectacle served the same function as tragic theater in ancient times. It exaggerated in gesture and mime a specific set of human emotions that captured the private moments of their lives. The public wanted to see the spirit of contrition and repentance in excess, a tragedy of tremendous potential that left no intellectual doubt about the transcendent value of corporal pain. This is why the staging was so exact, the gestures endowed with such rhetorical flourish. On that stagelit night of Maundy Thursday, candles and torches revealed only a small dimension of the universe to the spectator's imagination. The public witnessed small gestures raised to magnificent meaning as a wooden crucifix carried by two men introduced this tragic procession of mourners draped in long white tunics. Somewhere close by a bell ringing urgently signaled the white figures "to bend down to their knees, spatially separated in such a manner that they could do each other no injury." The public then observed these prostrate men "take up scourges with great devotion and discipline their exposed backs, asking that these efforts be received in payment for all the sins of the Christian people."[40]

The key to the whole spectacle was to be seen in the bodies of the actors. With their heads covered in hoods as tokens of modesty,[41] their knees bent in humility, their moist flesh streaked with blood, they were the consummate image of passion. The orchestrated movements of their bodies, like masks worn in a tragedy, were designed to amplify the sufferings of man. Flesh and blood, offered in rhythmic gestures to the tune of the Miserere, demonstrated with emotional eloquence the ideal of Christian repentance. The message of all these theatrical movements was ultimately a moral one. The flagellants who cried out under the weight of their own scourges offered an excessive portrayal to the community, not of violence and cruelty, but of the ordered nature of repentance. They were offering their blood voluntarily and heroically. It was clear to the public that their pain was not inflicted upon them by anyone, not even, symbolically, by God. It was self-imposed punishment taken on by a new community of believers whose moral disposition was being shaped by the conscience, or what Freud might have called the superego, rather than by external powers. Flagellation was above all meant to portray the ordeal of justice and the voluntary workings of the conscience. The idea of paying for sin was essential to the commemoration. It was as if each stroke of the lash announced, "This much we must pay for our sins." Ritual flagellation on Maundy Thursday was nothing more than the theatrical production of private practices in a narrative format that reiterated the moral message of compensatory suffering.

Notes

1. The Vera Cruz confraternity of Briviesca describes the ceremony this way: "[D]espues de comer y estando asi juntos unos a otros nos perdonamos qualesquier injurias y ofensas de forma que no quede rencor" (Archivo Histórico Nacional, Briviesca, *Legajo* 944, *Estatutos de 1585*. Statutes of the Vera Cruz in Villalpando (1580) describe group pardons in the following manner: "damos colación y allí juntos nos perdonemos los unos a los otros todas nuestras injurias y malquerencias" in Luis Calvo Lozano, *Historia de la Villa de Villalpando y su Tierra* (Zamora: Diputación Provincial, 1981), p. 241.

2. Ordinances of the confraternities of the Vera Cruz are held in the various ecclesiastical archives of the Spanish dioceses. The collections called *Libros Parroquiales* (hereafter referred to as *L.P.*) are particularly rich in information on these local parish corporations. For a brief description of the origins of these archives and a summary of the sources available, see Jose Luis Martínez Sanz, "Una Aproximación a la documentación de los archivos parroquiales de España," *Hispania* 46, no. 162 (1986): 169–94. The confraternity of the Vera Cruz in Barcena de Cudón, Santander, walked five leagues in procession on Holy Thursday (Archivo Diocesano de Santander, Barcena de Cudón, Parroquia de Santa María-Barcena de Cudón; see also regulations in the Archivo de la Catedral de Burgos, Frandovine, *L.P.* 5, *Libros de la Vera Cruz*, statutes of 1536). Statutes of the Cofradía de la Vera Cruz in Cañezal of 1570 describe the route taken from the parish church to a rural hermitage and church and then back to the pueblo (Archivo de la Catedral de Burgos, Cañezal, *Estatutos, capitulo* xiii). A drawing of the itinerary taken by the Cofradía de San Francisco in the city of Palencia, according to its *Libro de Reglas*, is available in Rafael Angel Martínez González, *Las cofradías Penitenciales de Palencia* (Palencia: Caja de Ahorros y Monte de Piedad, 1979), *lamina* 15.

3. The Cofradía de la Vera Cruz in San Felíz de la Vega of the province of Astorga stated in its statutes of 1623 that wounds would be washed in warm wine by the abbot after processions (*L.P.* 3/13). Descriptions of instruments are also available in Archivo Histórico Nacional, Clero, *Libro* 19491, Guadalajara, Escariche, Iglesia de San Miguel Archangel, *Libro de la Cofradía de la Vera Cruz*; Archivo de la Catedral de Burgos, Escalado, *L.P.* 4, *Libros de la Cofradía de la Vera Cruz*; and Archivo Diocesano de Santander, Isla, Parroquia de San Julián y Santa Basilisa, *Cofradía de la Vera Cruz, signatura* 6281, statutes of 1615.

4. Men and women over the age of fifty were allowed to walk in procession with candles but they were not permitted to flagellate. They were called "cofrades of light" (Archivo Diocesano de Palencia, Alba de Cerrato, Parroquia de Nuestra Santa María; Archivo de la Catedral de Burgos, Las Balbases, *Libros de la Cofradía de la Vera Cruz de los disciplinantes*, statutes of 1551, *L.P.* 26; Archivo de la Catedral de Burgos, Altable, *L.P.* 2, *Libro de la Cofradía de la Vera Cruz*, statutes of 1591; Archivo de la Catedral de Burgos, Cascajares de Bureba, *L.P.* 5, *Libros de la Cofradía de la Vera Cruz*, statutes of 1590; and Archivo Diocesano de Santander, Villaverdes de Pontones, Parroquia de Santo Tomás

Villaverde de Pontones, *Cofradía de la Vera Cruz*). Constitutions of 1608 stipulated that *cofrades* must all be twelve years old or older, and that no *cofrade* under the age of thirty may enter if he does not flagellate. Everyone must continue this practice until the age of fifty. The same stipulations prevailed for the Cofradía de San Sabastián y Fabián (Archivo Diocesano de Santander, San Andres, Parroquia de San Andres, *Signatura* 3121).

5. Mircea Eliade, *The Sacred and the Profane* (New York: Harcourt, Brace and World, 1959), pp. 68–113.

6. Archivo Diocesano de Palencia, Cofradía de la Vera Cruz of the monastery of San Pablo, Statutes of 1524. Almost identical statements are made by Vera Cruz confraternities in Archivo de la Catedral de Burgos, Las Balbases, *Libros de la Cofradía de la Vera Cruz de los disciplinantes* of 1551; and Archivo Histórico Nacional, Clero, *Libro* 19606, *Ordenanzas de la Vera Cruz de Malaguilla.*

7. Archivo de la Catedral de Burgos, Arlanzón, *L.P.* 5, *Libros de la cofradía de la Vera Cruz* of 1584.

8. Cited in J. Meseguer Fernández, "Las Cofradías de la Vera Cruz," *Archivo Iberoamericano* 8 (Madrid, 1968): 203.

9. The widening gulf between the two in modern times has been explored by Pierra Nora in "Between Memory and History: *Les Lieux de Mémoire,*" *Representations* 26 (Spring 1989): 7–25. In Nora's words, "Memory is unself-conscious, commanding, all-powerful, spontaneously actualizing, ... vulnerable to manipulation and appropriation ... a bond tying us to the eternal present.... History, on the other hand, is the reconstruction, always problematic and incomplete, of what is no longer." It is "an intellectual and secular production [that] calls for analysis and criticism" (pp. 8–9).

10. The phraseology was nearly identical among the Vera Cruz confraternities. The statutes of the Vera Cruz of Argoños of 1597 stated, for example, that "in the evening they all leave the church in procession, some flagellating and others bearing candles, all barefoot, dressed in tunics with shoulders exposed and eyes covered, and every once in a while they say, 'This is in memory of the passion of our Lord Jesus Christ and in remission of our sins'" (Archivo Diocesano de Santander, Argoños, Parroquia de El Salvador, *Cofradía de la Vera Cruz, signatura* 5887, *pagina* 49).

11. Archivo Histórico Nacional, *Inquisición de Toledo, Legajo* 33, *numero* 44. Jakob Gretser (1562–1625) defended flagellation against Protestant objections of this sort in *De disciplinis,* included in *Opera omnia* 4/1 (1606).

12. I have shown that testators in the city of Zamora demonstrated an increasingly strong preference for the attendance at their funerals of members of penitential confraternities rather than members of charitable confraternities in the second half of the sixteenth century. See Maureen Flynn, *Sacred Charity: Confraternities and Social Welfare in Spain, 1400–1700* (Ithaca, N.Y.: Cornell University Press, 1989), pp. 126–35.

13. The first public flagellant processions on record occurred in Bologna in 1260. The account of Saint Justina in Padua can be found in Jean Louis de Lolme, *The History of the Flagellants, Otherwise of Religious Flagellation among Different Nations, and Especially among Christians* (London: Robinson, 1733), pp. 346–50. In this book is included a translation of the entire *Historia Flagellantium, de recto & perverso flagrorum usu apud Christianos* (Paris: Aniffon, 1700) of Abbé Boileau. In the mid–fourteenth century, this public manifestation of penitence spread to Greece, Germany, and Poland. Jean Delumeau argues that monastic asceticism became commonplace among the laity in *Le péché et la peur: La culpabilisation en Occident, XIIIe–XVIIIe siècles* (Paris: Fayard, 1983).

14. See my own examination of Spanish penitence in *Sacred Charity,* pp. 127–34; and Gabriel Llompart, "Desfile iconográfico de penitentes españoles," *Revista de Dialectología y tradiciones populares* 25 (Madrid, 1969):31–51.

15. "Omnis utriusque sexus fidelis, postquam ad annos discretionis pervenerit, omnia sua solus peccata confiteatur fideliter, saltem semel in anno proprio sacerdoti" (J. Alberigo et al., eds., *Conciliorum oecumenicorum decreta,* 3rd ed. [Bologna: Instituto per le scienze religiose, 1973], p. 245, column 21). The historical impact of this decree has been empha-

sized by the two most prominent English-speaking scholars of the medieval penitential system, Henry Charles Lea and Thomas Tentler. Other modern scholars affirm that the laity obeyed this rule reasonably well in the following centuries. See Henry Charles Lea, *A History of Auricular Confession and Indulgences in the Latin Church* (Philadelphia, 1896; reprint, New York: Macmillan, 1968), 1:230 and 2:73–101; Thomas N. Tentler, *Sin and Confession on the Eve of the Reformation* (Princeton, N.J.: Princeton University Press, 1977), pp. 20–22; John Bossy, "The Social History of Confession in the Age of Reformation," *Transactions of the Royal Historical Society*, 5th ser., 25 (1975): 21–38; and Lawrence G. Duggan, "Fear and Confession on the Eve of the Reformation," *Archiv für Reformations-Geschichte* 75 (1984): 158–61.

16. On the gradual enhancement of the subjective force of sorrow in the doctrine of penance, see Bernhard Poschmann, *Penance and the Anointing of the Sick*, trans. Francis Courtney (Freiburg and London: Herder, 1964), pp. 157–58.

17. Antoninus of Florence, *Summa de confessión llamada Defecerunt Compuesta por Fray Antonino Arcobispo de Florencia* (Medina del Campo: Pedro de Castro, 1550), fol. 17v.

18. Juan de Dueñas, *Remedio de peccadores por otro nombre llamado confessionario que habla de la sacramental confessión* (Valladolid: Juan de Villaquirán, 1545), fol. 52. In the *Espejo de consolación: En el qual se veran muchas y grandes hystorias de la sagrada escriptura* (Burgos: Juan de Junta, 1546), Dueñas says, "What is penitence but crying about sins already committed, and by crying, not to commit them anew" (*Parte* 2, fol. 88).

19. Francisco de Villagracia, *Arte de bien confesar. En el nombre de Jesuchristo ... comiença un saludable devoto dialogo entre un penitente y un confesor: en el qual se contienen doctrinas necessarias y muy provechosas: para recta y catholicamente confessar* (Medina del Campo: Pedro de Castro, 1544), Biblioteca Nacional, R. 8. 392.

20. Antoninus of Florence, *Confesionale de S. Antonino: Quia ta scientiam* (Mantova, 1475), fol. 30v.

21. Villagracia, *Arte bien confesar*; see also Domingo de Valtanas, *Confessionario*: "[T]he pain of contrition is not sensual pain but pain of reason" (Sevilla: Sebastián Trugillo, 1555), fol. 6.

22. Antoninus of Florence, *Defecerunt*, fol. 19v.

23. Juan de Dueñas, *Remedio*, fol. 23.

24. Martín de Azpilcueta, *Manual de Confessores y Penitentes, que clara y brevemente contiene la universal y particular decision de quasi todas las dudas que en las confessiones suelen occurrir....* (Salamanca: Andrea de Portonarijs, 1557), p. 9. Antoninus of Florence similarly drew a distinction between feelings caused by temporal misfortunes and feelings of contrition over moral issues (*Confesionale* [1475], fol. 30v).

25. Antoninus of Florence, *Defecerunt*, fol. 19v.

26. For a thorough discussion of penitential punishment, see Tentler, *Sin and Confession*, pp. 318–40.

27. Pedro Ciruelo, *Confessario compuesto per el ... maestro Ciruelo ... Es arte de bien confessar: Muy provechose al confessor y al penitente* (Zarogoza: George Coci, 1541), fol. xxv(v). So also the anonymous guide, *Espejo de lego*, fol. 130v (Biblioteca Nacional, MS. 18465) recommends these three forms of satisfaction.

28. Azpilcueta, *Manual*, p. 23.

29. Carolyn Walker Bynum examines over eighty *vitae* of female saints in her immensely influential book, *Holy Feast and Holy Fast: The Religious Significance of Food to Medieval Women* (Berkeley: University of California Press, 1987). A thoughtful examination of the *vitae* as well as a recent bibliography on primary and secondary sources is provided by Jane Tibbetts Schulenburg, "Saints' Lives as a Source for the History of Women," in *Medieval Women and the Sources of Medieval History*, ed. Joel T. Rosenthal (Athens: University of Georgia Press, 1990).

30. Teresa of Avila, *Camino de perfección*, ed. Padre Silverio de Santa Teresa (Burgos: El Monte Carmelo, 1916), book 3, chap. 39, p. 188, requests that confessors and superiors

take careful notice of all acts of mortification practiced by their nuns and that they be especially watchful of signs of pride accompanying these activities. Rules of the order of Concepcionistas in Toledo stated that "todas sean obligadas a manifestar llana y abiertamente a la Perlada el perjuycio que reciben con la disciplina o con el ayuno en la salud. Silicio no se permite sino raríssimas vezes y nunca muchos días arreo porque quita la salud. Tengase gran cuenta con que los días que estuvieren con la indisposición del mes ni quatro días antes ni quatro días despues no tomen disciplina" (Biblioteca Nacional, MS. 1111, *Regla de los Concepcionistas*, fols. 20v and 21). Statutes of the Vera Cruz confraternity in the monastery of San Pablo in Palencia ordered in 1572 that some cofrades moderate their "dangerous" flagellation exercises on Holy Thursday (Palencia, Archivo de San Pablo, *Cofradía de la Vera Cruz*).

31. Azpilcueta, *Manual*, p. 9.

32. Juan de Segura, *Confessionario: Assí útil para los confessores y para saberse los penitentes examinar y confessar: como para conoscernos en algo, y tomar caución y aviso, contra vicios y defectos* (Burgos: Juan de Junta, 1555), fols. 112–13.

33. Andreas de Escobar, *Modus confitendi ... Interrogationes ... Canones penitentiales* (Nuremberg, 1508), C3b–E2a. Thomas N. Tentler considers Andreas's brief manual listing sins as one of the most popular penitential manuals in fifteenth-century Europe, equal only to the *Confessionale* of Saint Antoninus of Florence. He has identified eighty-six printings in twenty-three different cities prior to the sixteenth century, in *Sin and Confession*, pp. 40–41.

34. In addition to sacramental penance, late medieval Spain had a second institution, the Inquisition, that dealt with sin through bodily punishment. Public whipping through the streets was the most common form of punishment inflicted by the Spanish Inquisition on lay men and women accused of blasphemy. In 1523, for example, Francisco Tebero, identified as a "trabajador" from the village of Belmonte, maligned the Virgin Mary while drinking and was required as punishment to sit on an ass, naked from the waist up, with a muzzle across the mouth and there to receive one hundred lashes (Archivo Diocesano de Cuenca, *Inquisición, Legajo 83, numero 1193*).

35. In 1527, Martín de Sanzedo was penalized for denying God's omnipotence with an Inquisitorial sentence of "standing on his feet without a hat and with a wax candle lit, and to pray the rosary during nine days of novena services at a monastery, and to give charity" (Archivo Diocesano de Cuenca, *Inquisición, Legajo 99, numero 1439*). In the case of Axenxo Palacios of 1580, a fine was levied and the tongue mutilated (Archivo Diocesano de Cuenca, *Inquisición, Legajo 707, numero 595*).

36. Bynum, *Holy Feast and Holy Fast*; and Peter Brown, *The Body and Society: Men, Women, and Sexual Renunciation in Early Christianity* (New York: Columbia University Press, 1988). Their reassessment of Christianity's attitude toward the body is shared by an ever growing number of medieval scholars. See especially Gedaliahu G. Stroumsa, "*Caro salutis cardo*: Shaping the Person in Early Christian Thought," *History of Religions* 30 (1990): 25–50; and A. Rousselle, *Porneia: De la maîtrise du corps à la privation sensorielle* (Paris: Presses universitaires de France, 1982).

37. Giulia Calvi, *Histories of a Plague Year*, trans. Dario Biocca and Bryant T. Ragan, Jr. (Berkeley: University of California Press, 1989), pp. 199–253; originally published as *Storie de un anno di peste* (Milan: Bompiani, 1984).

38. Archivo Histórico Nacional, *Inquisición, Legajo 102, numero 5*: "El Fiscal de Santo oficio contra Isabel de Brinas (Beata) Vecina de Madrid, Acusada de raptos fingidos, revelaciones afectadas, apariciones de Jesu-Cristo, y falsas profecias."

39. Archivo de la Mitra de Zamora, *Libro 66, Ordenanzas de la Confradía de la Cruz*. In Susilla's parish church of San Miguel in the province of Santander, the Vera Cruz offered to propitiate God for water (Archivo Diocesano de Santander, Susilla, P. S. Miguel, *Cofradía de la Vera Cruz*, Statutes of 1538, *Signatura 1140*).

40. Archivo de la Catedral de Burgos, Moduba de la Custa, *L.P. 3, Libros de la Cofradía Vera Cruz*, 1584.

41. Ordinances of the Cofradía de la Santa Vera Cruz in the Zamoran village of Villan-campo (1534) ordered members to attend Holy Thursday processions with scourges and shirts and warned them specifically not to carry *"señales conocidas"* (Archivo Histórico Provincial de Zamora, *Protocolos,* no. 7, fol. 164). According to the seventeenth-century statutes of the Santa Cruz confraternity in Toral de Fondo, province of Astorga, "We walk barefoot and naked, wearing only our tunics and coverings over our faces, without any sign with which we might be recognized, because the devil can tempt us with vainglory" (Astorga, Toral de Fondo, 3/24).

PART III

Harmony and Dissonance in the Urban Ceremonial Community

CHAPTER 7

Ceremony and Oligarchy
The London Midsummer Watch

Sheila Lindenbaum

D uring the eventful London summer of 1521, Lodovico Spinelli, the secretary of the Venetian ambassador in England, took time to record an important ceremonial event: a procession of Londoners on the Midsummer Eves preceding the feasts of Saint John the Baptist and Saints Peter and Paul (24 and 29 June). Describing the bands of halberdiers and other armed men in the procession, Spinelli records their numbers from first to last, together with the appearance of a spectacular giant and seven gorgeous pageants: Pluto, the Tree of Life, a besieged castle, the Assumption, Saint George, Saint John the Evangelist, and John the Baptist. Toward the end of his account, between the pageants of Saint George and Saint John the Evangelist, he notes a group of morris dancers attending the chief officers of the city. All of this Spinelli takes to be a sign of collective "rejoicing," of festivity that has drawn spectators of both sexes "in very great number."[1] Here, we might conclude, is one of those celebrations of community that unified late medieval English towns and cities.

A second eyewitness gives us a rather different version of the event, however. In his list of expenses for the show, the recorder of the Drapers' Company confirms Spinelli's account in almost every detail; but for him the entire event centers on the mayor and two sheriffs, figures Spinelli merely mentions in passing. For the draper, this is no general "rejoicing" but specifically "my lord the Mayres Watche," a spectacle in honor of the officers who, with the twenty-four aldermen and the masters of the merchant guilds, constituted London's ruling elite.[2] For him, what matters is that five of the pageants honor the mayor, John Brugge, a draper, while the other two honor the sheriffs: John Skevington, a merchant tailor, and John Kyme, a mercer. Here, we might say, is not a celebration of community but a celebration of London's oligarchy.[3]

I want to stress the draper's version, not because it is superior to Spinelli's as a historical source (later I shall draw on both) or because I wish to focus on his view of the world. My purpose will be to show how ceremony reproduces power relations rather than how it reflects a given mentality or set of beliefs. I cite the draper mainly because in highlighting the merchant oligarchy's central role, he calls into question those modern studies that have emphasized the collective nature of civic cere-mony—studies in the tradition of Charles Phythian-Adams's classic essay, "Ceremony and the Citizen: The Communal Year at Coventry." For Phythian-Adams, the function of civic ceremony was to "promote cohesion within the community." To this end, ceremonies like the Mid-summer Watch emphasized the "welth and worship of the hole body." Although the ceremonies visually mirrored the social hierarchy, the im-pulse behind them was democratic. The towns and cities sponsoring them were "remarkable chiefly for the evident intermixture of all types of person," and the ceremonies accordingly involved the "community in its entirety." Only with the Reformation and the development of class loyalties in the mid–sixteenth century did these socially integrative spectacles disappear.[4]

A new generation of scholars has suggested that we need to revise this paradigm. Historians of medieval English towns have begun to question the Durkheimian notion that these were "traditional commu-nities" unified by a common religion and set of values. Although not always clear about the implications of their research, historians have clearly begun to give greater importance to the exclusion of a large propor-tion of town dwellers, including women and artisans as well as common laborers and servants, from meaningful participation in local govern-ment. Simultaneously, there has been a greater stress on the centraliza-tion of power in burghal elites, and a growing tendency to see this change beginning in the late fourteenth century, much earlier than the period assumed by Phythian-Adams.[5] Stephen Rigby, for instance, has discovered in a wide range of towns at this time a pattern of "restric-tions on who could stand as mayor, the replacement of burgess assem-blies with councils, the appointment of officers from above rather than by election, and the introduction of office for life." As a result of studies like Rigby's, historians have been more willing to recognize that the portrayal of a town as a "whole body" is not a description of social real-ity but a construction of a particular social group. As Caroline Barron says for London, the "normal voice of the city" making such representa-tions was not that of a "homogeneous body" but that of "its wealthy governing minority."[6]

Hence my attempt in this essay to shift the focus from Phythian-Adams's "Ceremony and the Citizen," with its associations of social wholeness and democracy, to "Ceremony and Oligarchy." In making this shift, I want particularly to question the notion that civic ceremonies were "collective effervescences," instances of heightened group feeling and social integration based on shared values. No doubt the Midsummer bonfires and neighborhood feasting nostalgically recalled by John Stow signified mutual "amitie" and "familiaritie" to many medieval inhabitants of the city, as they did to him. But this does not mean that we should accept that interpretation. In important ways, these were not spontaneous popular celebrations, but customs strictly regulated by the merchant oligarchy. During a royal visit of 1525, for example, the "ffires after the maner of midsomer fyers" and "neybourly drynkyng" were a matter of mayoral decree. At the watch itself, festivity was limited by orders to close victualler's shops and taverns at an early hour and to light bonfires in officially designated places. Such neighborhood feasting as did take place was supposed to occur under the aegis of "the wealthier sort," as Stow himself notes, and the religious feasts on the days after the watch were celebrated most conspicuously not by ordinary people but by the elite guilds dedicated to Saint John the Baptist and Saints Peter and Paul.[7] In all these respects, the watch was a practice that helped to consolidate and extend the oligarchy's political dominance. As such, it needs to be considered in relation to other practices—police surveillance, the use of honors and titles, and the making of wills and corporations—that had the same effect.

The first step will be to show that civic ceremonies helped London's oligarchs lay claim to what Michel de Certeau calls a "proper place"—a sphere of influence where their political will could operate and a stable base from which to deal with outside threats.[8] Later we will see how claiming such a place enabled them to accumulate other "property," both material goods and an intangible cultural capital, as a basis for extending their power into the future. The point is not that the rulers consciously and cynically exploited less powerful groups within the city, or that they always acted in perfect unison in relation to these groups, but that rulers and ruled alike became implicated in a web of habitual social practices through which the oligarchy's power was exercised and simultaneously disguised. The focus will be the 1521 Midsummer Watch, but much of the discussion will apply to the entire period between the late 1370s and 1530s when the ceremonial watches regularly took place.

"Watch and Ward"

The Midsummer Watch was part of the ordinary system of surveillance by which London's rulers controlled the city. Although the ceremonial form of the watch magnified this activity to spectacular proportions, it still retained the main features of the everyday "watches" or police patrols conducted by the city constables. A mayor proclaiming a Midsummer Watch always gave orders not only for the marching watch through the principal streets, for which marchers were supplied mainly by the guilds, but also for a standing watch in the wards under the supervision of the aldermen. The aldermen deployed armed householders throughout the city to keep "very strict watch," as Spinelli tells us, lest "some tumult" occur during the festivities. In these provisions, moreover, the Midsummer Watch was closely akin to the extensive emergency watches ordered by the mayor when the city was threatened by foreign invaders, rebels, or rioters from within the walls.[9]

The term used in official documents for all these forms of the watch was "les veilles et les geytes"—watch and ward. As the term indicates, the watches combined surveillance of the city's inhabitants with measures to guard property. The earliest recorded watches, dating from the thirteenth century, were ordered as a protection against midsummer fires, and the mayor's announcement of a ceremonial watch was still accompanied by an order to place a tub of water outside each house in the city.[10] In later years, however, the watchmen seem to have concentrated on the houses of the rich. They kept a special lookout for thieves who made "nightly inuasions vpon houses of the wealthie, to the intent to rob them." In this way, the watches helped conserve the physical property that was the basis of the oligarchs' political power. They also guarded mercantile assets of a less tangible nature, for the chronic fear was that if order was not kept, the king would step in, as his predecessors had sometimes done, and suspend the liberties and trade privileges on which the merchants' business relied.[11]

In June 1521, the need for a "very strict" Midsummer Watch was particularly acute. Two events had recently stirred the populace: the burning of Luther's books by Cardinal Wolsey, performed in great splendor at Saint Paul's in May,[12] and the public execution of the duke of Buckingham, who had often resided in the city and had a popular following there.[13] Popular protests against the duke's execution (over which sheriffs Kyme and Skevington were forced by virtue of their office to preside) recalled the Evil May Day of 1517, when two thousand apprentices sacked the shops and houses of London's aliens, who they thought were unfairly privileged by the king, and the king retaliated by sending an army of a thousand men into the city.[14] The protests of 1521 gave the king an excuse to intervene in civic affairs once again, and he threatened to remove the merchants' customary right to appoint certain officials— an important source of their income as well as one of their means of controlling commerce. Just a few days before the initial performance of the watch on Saint John's Eve, Henry seized the important office of the Great Beam for one of his favorites, and the merchant guilds had cause to fear further erosion of their commercial privileges, especially if they were unable to restrain the local population.[15]

Against these threats to the merchants' property and privileges, the Midsummer Watch provided the dual protection of "watch and ward." First of all, the marchers parading through the center of the city together with the standing "watchmen" in the wards provided ample surveillance.[16] Since the watch took place at night (from 11 until 2 on the eves of the two holidays, according to Spinelli), surveillance was aided by hundreds of torches and cresset lights carried by the marchers, in addition to lanterns ordered outside each house and bonfires throughout the city. The watch was therefore a spectacle in which the marchers and the "watchmen" in the wards, rather than the people gathered in the streets, were the most important spectators. Even the great giant who preceded the mayor in the march functioned as a kind of watchman, turning about "from side to side, looking in every direction."[17]

In addition to surveillance, the standing watch also provided a "ward" or guard by erecting barriers in the streets, manning the city gates, and committing any offenders against the peace to the Compters, the sheriffs' prison.[18] The barriers restrained insiders while preventing outsiders from entering the city. Meanwhile, in the marching watch, the armed castle described by Spinelli and the drapers' recorder manifested a similar containment and exclusion. Some soldiers barricaded themselves within a castle, while others stood on its walls "with stones in their hands for its defense," fighting off an exotic "Soldan" who was pursuing them on horseback with a "very long tin sword tinged with blood." The fortified castle was a familiar way of representing London in civic pageantry; and this pageant, one of those produced in honor of the mayor, highlighted his role as "custos" of the city, responsible for guarding the walls against invaders.[19]

The pageants' significance was not always so transparent, however. Especially in defining threats to the city's stability, the pageants worked by means of displacement and substitution, so that the exotic "Soldan" could become a way of representing not only foreign invaders but also the resented foreigners within the walls. The pageant Spinelli calls "Pluto" (called "The King of Moores" by the drapers) featured another exotic persona who alluded to aliens in this way, his riches making the connection with the wealth amassed by alien merchants in the city. Such figures were always threatening—Pluto emitted "xlv reedes of wyld fyr," and it took twenty-eight pounds of gunpowder to repel the Soldan—but their blustering was also funny and firmly contained within the procession, so that they, too, emphasized the magistrates' control of civic space.[20]

It was by riding in the watch themselves, however, that the mayor and sheriffs most decisively asserted their rights over the local terrain, as if to claim all the property in the city as their own. This was not a legal claim, nor was it self-consciously articulated, but it was a powerful symbolic gesture. The mayor affirmed his territorial interests as irresistibly when he paraded in civic ceremonies—a Corpus Christi procession, his own inauguration, a royal entry, or a Midsummer Watch—

as when he rode out to confirm his legal right to hunt in the suburbs, or when the city was threatened with actual invasion, and the "mair with the Shireffes, Constables, and other officers of the City kept grete Wacche," riding "abowte the City daily . . . accompanyed with [1000] men or thereaboute well and sensible arayed."[21]

The visual splendor of the mayor's "riding" enforced his claim to the civic terrain. The mayor was preceded by his swordbearer (Spinelli reminds us that the mayor was "never wont to go abroad unless preceded by the sword") and accompanied by armed and mounted members of his household—an imposing array in the narrow streets of a city, and more so when it was supported by the massed bands of infantry that joined the marching watch in the course of the fifteenth century. How impressive the display could be is clear from a comment by the unseated king of Denmark when he saw the 1523 watch: "I would to god I had so many Archers, Pikes, and halberders, as I sawe this night, then I trust I would ponishe suche, as haue wrongfully dispossessed me, of my realme and countrey."[22] What the Dane does not see is that the ceremony of the watch itself, and not just the potential fighting force it put on display, was a powerful territorial strategy. Like all ceremony, the watch was ritualized violence; it could be as effective as actual force in securing the oligarchs' control of the city and protecting their material investments within the walls.

Symbolic Capital

The Midsummer Watch thus helped secure a safe place where London's rulers could invest their capital, earning profits from commerce and rents from the properties held by individual merchants and guilds. The merchants alluded indirectly to these and other material benefits of ceremony when they spoke of it as yielding them a "profit" and when they treated the properties of the watch as a kind of capital. The decorated wagons were stored along with the woolsacks at Leadenhall, and the smaller properties were kept in one of the companies' great chests, similar to the Renters' Box where rents were saved for future investment or to the great chests where merchants stored the money they would leave to their heirs.[23]

Yet whatever material advantages the ceremonies brought to their producers, these advantages could not be explicitly stated. It was important that the oligarchs' exploitation of the lesser crafts and the unliveried members of their own companies be disguised, from themselves as well as others; otherwise, the political system that guaranteed their power would reveal itself as a human arrangement that could be changed, rather than the natural and inevitable way of the world. The profit the rulers earned from the ceremonies was therefore euphemistically construed as the "honor" and "worshyppe" the governed owed to them and their guilds. Pierre Bourdieu calls this kind of honor "symbolic capital"—an accumulation of intangible debts and obligations among the governed that can later be transmuted back into material advantages. The symbolic capital that the Midsummer Watch produced for the mayor, sheriffs, and aldermen eventually permitted them to collect substantial fees in the performance of their official duties and ensured obedience to the ordinances by which they regulated the city's commercial life.[24]

It was mainly through the aristocratic trappings of the watch that the rulers' acquired advantages were expressed as an intrinsic "honor" and dignity. The mayor became one of noble lineage, "my lord the Mayor," taking precedence in the city over every other person except the king. A magnificent figure, he wore a gown of "rede Crymsyn velvett, and a grete hatte furred royally"; those attending him and the sheriffs wore the parti-colored clothing identified with servants of the nobility. In a similar transformation, the services of men hired for the event were interpreted as gestures of personal loyalty to a prince. The "harnessed men" paid to march with the mayor and sheriffs were given coats bearing the officers' badges or crests, as if they were their personal retainers. The ceremony thus duplicated the process by which the rulers customarily constituted their dependents as clients and placed them within a system of patronage where they could incur debts and obligations. This process was so fundamental to civic ceremony, as to other areas of life, that the personal entourage was the first arrangement made for a watch. In 1521, before ordering their five pageants, the drapers commissioned "xx iiij harnest men . . . for the Mair" and eighteen others as their contribution to the two sheriffs' trains.[25]

The need to euphemize the rulers' material advantages explains why merchant oligarchies in many towns and cities were willing to expend vast resources of money and time on civic ceremony, even in periods of severe economic decline. In 1521, for example, the London companies were notably lacking in funds, having just paid a royal subsidy and designated one thousand pounds for famine relief. The mercers' funds were so low that they reported "no money remaynyng in our Comen boxe" and appealed for personal contributions to complete their new hall, "or ellys it must stonde undone." Individuals were also hard pressed: two of the mercers who marched in the 1521 watch—the sheriff, John Kyme, and an alderman, Michael Englysshe—were later reported to be "reduced to extreme poverty" by the financial demands of their offices.[26] Yet the companies continued to produce ever more elaborate Midsummer Watches, the drapers spending over five times as much in 1521 as they had in 1477, when the mayor was also one of their company. None of the explanations usually given—a desire for status for its own sake, an addiction to conspicuous consumption, or a strong sense of civic pride—satisfactorily accounts for such financial profligacy in men usually known to be highly "conservative and cautious." After all, these were the same men who, when presented with a chance to finance a voyage to the New World, could think only of "dangers and shoals" and wish for "less jeopardy in the adventure."[27] It may be that the merchants' vast investment in ceremony is best explained not as a result of a collective decision or self-conscious reflection, as these usual explanations suggest, but as a habitual activity that continued and became elaborated because it produced a desired social effect.

The prodigal spending on ceremonies becomes understandable if we think of it as generating the kind of honor that translates effectively into political and economic power, rather than simply satisfying personal vanity or civic pride. Indeed, the financial outlay and the pleas of insolvency that often followed were necessary to staying in power, since they concealed the profits of officeholding by making it look altruistic. Thus, while the protestations of poverty were not calculated lies, they may have been more conventional than true: the mercers were not really so insolvent that they had to abandon their hall, and Sheriff Kyme was not so "reduced to poverty" that he could not leave a substantial estate at his death.[28] Moreover, the more exclusively power was concentrated in an oligarchy, the more spending was needed to disguise their material gains. This axiom would explain the steady growth of urban ceremony from the late fourteenth century, when power began to be concentrated in an oligarchy in London and other places. Certainly, the expenses of ceremony were great, but the oligarchs' need for the symbolic capital that the ceremonies produced was also great and became increasingly pressing as time went on.

Strategies of Reproduction

We have seen how ceremonies like the Midsummer Watch helped enforce the oligarchs' power, first by securing their territory, and then by earning them a profit in the form of symbolic capital. It remains to show how the watch helped perpetuate their political dominance. For although the "honor" acquired in civic ceremonies was intangible, it could be objectified in a number of forms—names, precedents, legends, and legal incorporations—that could be stored in memory and passed on to the future. By helping to objectify honor in these ways, the watch became an important strategy for prescribing the behavior of future Londoners, thereby reproducing the political and economic relations that guaranteed oligarchic power.

Such a strategy was particularly important in a city where the political order was not passed on through established lineages. Throughout the period of the Midsummer Watches, London lacked great merchant dynasties. Suffering from epidemics and high infant mortality, in addition to losing those of their numbers who became country gentry, the merchants did not produce enough children to replenish their ranks. Of the twenty-four aldermen in the 1521 watch, for example, four apparently died in an epidemic of the "sweat" later that year, and none left children who would serve in public office. None of the chief officers— Brugge, Kyme, or Skevington—left children who figured in London politics either; of the three, only Brugge was from a London family, and while his son or relative, George Brugge, was admitted as a draper in 1531, we hear nothing of him thereafter.[29]

Yet London merchants like Brugge, Kyme, and Skevington were greatly preoccupied with inheritance, and in the absence of heirs they often found alternative ways of perpetuating their line. Brugge's fellow draper, Thomas Howell, for example, endowed a school for forty illegitimate children, thirty boys and ten girls, to be recruited if possible from his kin or his home town in Wales. The children were to wear "bills [signs] in front and on their backs with the word Howell inscribed in great letters" and were "for ever after to bear the name of Howell."[30] Howell compensated for the missing heirs of his body by creating a "perpetual body" in his school. Through the cultural mechanism of the will, he was able to devise a legal corporation that could inherit and pass on his wealth. To make sure his will was carried out, moreover, he literally recorded it on the bodies of his dependents, not only prescribing rules to govern their future behavior, but writing his name on their "front" and "backs" in the form of the specified signs.

In their civic ceremonies, London's rulers had inherited similar, if less self-consciously deployed, strategies for perpetuating themselves as an institution. In the 1521 watch, for instance, they represented themselves as a "perpetual body." Two of the men honored in the watch, Brugge and Kyme, had been struggling for some years to portray the city officers this way in Parliament, after the Crown tried to limit the power of magistrates to act as a corporation.[31] In the watch, the perpetual body took the form of a giant who accompanied the mayor as he marched (in some years, but not in 1521, each of the sheriffs also had a giant). This was a canvas creature on a wickerwork frame, heavily armed, with jointed limbs moving "as if they were alive," and it clearly represented generative power. It sometimes appeared with a female giant or, as seems to be the case in 1521, with baby giants played by puppets. These creatures were also associated with procreation through legend, for they were the children of Albion's lustful sisters, who mated with "men of air" to produce the giants and populate Britain.[32] The giants thus identified the merchant rulers with whom they marched as procreative figures, making their authority seem natural (since the giants were represented as being "alive") and undying.

The "Jesse" and "Assumption" pageants worked in much the same way. Despite their religious subject matter, these too were powerful images of procreation. Spinelli describes the tree of Jesse as "sprouting from the belly of a recumbent male figure," and the Assumption pageant featured the Virgin's carnal body, the "vessel of lyf" that gave birth to Christ.[33] Both of these pageants substituted a myth of Christ's divine lineage for the lineage the mayor and sheriffs lacked; and through their place in the procession, following the civic officer they honored, they neatly inserted that figure into the divine lineal scheme.

More than this was needed, however, to ensure the success of the watch as a reproductive strategy. In the watch, as in Thomas Howell's will, it was also necessary to regiment the bodies of the governed in order to ensure their compliance in the proceedings. Even though certain occupations (notably the armorers, but also the tallow-chandlers and painter-stainers) profited financially from a ceremonial watch and large numbers of marchers were paid to participate, these had to be recruited: the drapers alone, as the mayor's company, had to find some 126 armed men, 95 entertainers, and 36 laborers and craftsmen for the 1521 show.[34] An even larger number of politically disempowered citizens had to be persuaded to give their services gratis. Thirty-seven lesser companies—companies who had no members at all among the aldermen—contributed to the watch, and it was the politically disenfranchised branch of the drapers, the Bachelors, that produced the Assumption pageant for John Brugge.[35] Recalling the orphans in Howell's will, some of the recruits were children from London's choir schools, acting in pageants (John the Evangelist and John the Baptist) that followed the tradition of commemorating the city officers (John Brugge and John Skevington) by name.[36]

The records of the watch show masses of these performers, from the greater and lesser city companies, paid and unpaid marchers, caught in a web of official directives. These directives worked like an elaborate etiquette, binding on both rulers and ruled, and compelling because they codified what seemed to be the natural (because customary) way to move and dress in a public procession. Each company produced a specific number of marchers, in accordance with official charts in the city records. The companies issued further minute instructions for what to do in the standing watch, where to assemble for the march, and especially what uniforms they all were to wear. In 1521, for example, the drapers ordered sixty-six white cotton coats with red crosses, in addition to straw hats with specially made white bands, for its group of fifty "moryspykes," fourteen gunners, and two accompanying minstrels.[37]

The effect was to make each rank of marchers a single disciplined body. For example, the halberdiers with their axe-headed pikes "presented a body rather like a moving porcupine," advancing slowly to the beat of drums. These marchers did not reflect the social order, as Phythian-Adams would have it: some groups were too overrepresented (the military) or underrepresented (the clergy) for that. Rather they presented a living tableau of the *orders* that had been issued for their behavior.[38]

What made this a reproductive strategy as well as a disciplinary one—a strategy ensuring the perpetuation of the oligarchs' will—was that the orders were recorded in the form of "precedents." When they stored their properties for the watch in a box, the goldsmiths also included records of the event "entred into a booke" so that the pageants could be reproduced in "tymes hereafter."[39] Similarly, guilds inscribed in their ordinances a system of fines for those members who failed to take part in the watch; they wrote down rules governing the wearing of ceremonial livery and indicated where the various guilds were to stand and march. These ordinances call to mind the *Liber Albus*, in which John Carpenter recorded London's customs for the youth who would govern the city when their elders were carried off by plague. Through the practices and routines they perpetuated, the ordinances had the effect of a powerful will prescribing the behavior of future generations. Sometimes interpretation of a precedent produced debate within the oligarchy itself, as when the skinners and merchant tailors argued over who would march first in civic processions, or the mercers objected to contributing more than their customary share to the procession of a mayor from a rival guild.[40] But the authority of the precedent itself was seldom challenged by either rulers or ruled. On the whole, the precedents helped to perpetuate the subordination of the lesser to the greater guilds and the system of patrons and clients in which all were implicated.

Such practices did not make London's ruler invulnerable, however. True, there was little sustained objection to the idea of oligarchic rule among ordinary people—for instance, the crowds of men and women Spinelli noted at the 1521 watch. As Sylvia Thrupp remarks, "Conflicts of interest failed to detach any permanent opposition theory that was entirely free from the dominant assumptions." But there was a hidden side of the watch in the "nightwalking" that the torchlight ceremony was supposed to put down. Even as the oligarchs were asserting their control of city space in practices like the watch, a "mobile and ingenious" criminal element established its own headquarters in the city, founding an underground world that would present a continuing challenge. In 1521, for example, the Midsummer Watch was preceded by an order condemning certain vagabonds to the pillory, but neither the pillory nor the power represented in civic ceremony could be entirely effective against the underground's elusive threat.[41]

Moreover, the tendency to objectify power in the form of corporations and books of precedent may have made that power easier to appropriate by those who understood this kind of strategy. Certainly, Henry VIII found it remarkably easy to commandeer the Midsummer Watch for his own purposes. Not only did he preempt the 1509 watch with his coronation procession through the city; in the following year, he used the watch to exercise his own surveillance, witnessing the procession from the King's Head in Cheapside in the guise of a halberdier. In the 1520s, he had watches canceled in favor of royal entertainments or used them to entertain visiting royalty like the king of Denmark. In 1535, the pageants were used to show Henry triumphantly "cutting off the heads of the clergy." Finally, in 1539, Henry canceled the watch in favor of a muster in Saint James Park, so that the pageants eventually had to be transferred to the lord mayor's inaugural show.[42] The watch thus took its place with the other civic resources that Henry usurped as part of his own patrimony. Like the rulers of London, Henry had difficulty producing reliable heirs of his body, but he outdid them in the use of ceremonial practice to perpetuate his political will.

Notes

1. Rawdon Brown, ed., *Calendar of State Papers, Venetian*, vol. 3 (London: Longmans, Green, 1869), pp. 136–37. This is one of Spinelli's letters to his brother Gasparo at his diplomatic post in France, given by Brown in English translation.

2. Records of the 1521 watch in the Drapers' Repertory Book 7, Wardens' Accounts, and Renters' Accounts are printed in *A Calendar of Dramatic Records in the Books of the Livery Companies of London, 1485–1640*, ed. Jean Robertson and D. J. Gordon, Malone Society Collections 3 (1954), pp. 5–11. I cite the Robertson edition but am indebted to Anne Lancashire for additional details from her edition of London craft guild records, to be published in the Records of Early English Drama series. The clerk of the drapers' company at this time was Thomas Richardson, who kept the Repertory Books on behalf of the company's court of assistants.

3. Caroline Barron concisely describes London's late medieval government in *The British Atlas of Historic Towns*, vol. 3 (Oxford: Oxford University Press, 1989), pp. 43–44. See also Sylvia Thrupp's discussion in *The Merchant Class of Medieval London* (Chicago: University of Chicago Press, 1948), pp. 80–92. Prior service as sheriff was a requirement for the mayoralty, and the sheriffs and mayors were elected (by an indeterminate body of electors summoned for the purpose) from among the twenty-four aldermen, who in this period always were masters of the greater merchant companies. The aldermen served for life, and their terms (at least in the fifteenth century) averaged over a dozen years. They were elected in the wards, but nevertheless came from a small pool of candidates: in 1521, only eight companies were represented by the twenty-four aldermen; twelve aldermen were either drapers or mercers. The process of electing the London aldermen and the Common Council, which had some fiscal responsibility, needs further study.

4. Charles Phythian-Adams, "Ceremony and the Citizen: The Communal Year at Coventry, 1440–1550," in *Crisis and Order in English Towns, 1500–1700*, ed. Peter Clark

and Paul Slack (London: Routledge and Kegan Paul, 1972), pp. 75, 58, 65, 64. Another repeatedly cited article that makes similar assumptions is Mervyn James, "Ritual, Drama and Social Body in the Late Medieval English Town," *Past and Present* 98 (1983): 3–29. James stresses the contrast of late medieval "communal" governments with later "urban authoritarianism," as does Michael Berlin in "Civic Ceremony in Early Modern London," *Urban History Yearbook* (1986): 17–25. Berlin's comments on the Midsummer Watch derive mostly from the nostalgic description in John Stow, *A Survey of London*, ed. C. L. Kingsford (Oxford: Clarendon, 1908), 1:101–4. This, and his debt to Phythian-Adams, explains Berlin's view of the watch as a communal celebration. Susan Brigden also refers to the "communal spirit" of the Midsummer Watch in *The Reformation in London* (Oxford: Clarendon, 1989), p. 26. See also Michael D. Bristol in *Carnival and Theater* (London: Methuen, 1985), p. 5, where he assumes that the watch was a "collective celebration" that "took place outside any formal administrative apparatus." An assumption that medieval and Renaissance festivity was unregulated underlies many studies that focus on the carnivalesque.

5. Phythian-Adams, "Ceremony and the Citizen," also lists these exclusions, but he then goes on to treat civic ceremony as if it includes all the "basic divisions of humanity." In contrast, Lyndal Roper shows how "community" is constituted in different contexts to include and exclude selected social groups; see Roper, "The Common Man, The Common Good, Common Women: Gender and Meaning in the German Reformation Commune," *Social History* 12 (1987): 1–21. On burghal elites, see, for example, Robert S. Gottfried, *Bury St. Edmunds and the Urban Crisis* (Princeton, N.J.: Princeton University Press, 1982), chapter 4; and Marianne Kowaleski, "The Commercial Dominance of a Medieval Provincial Oligarchy: Exeter in the Late Fourteenth Century," *Mediaeval Studies* 46 (1984): 355–84.

6. Stephen Rigby, "Urban Oligarchy in Late Medieval England," *Towns and Townspeople in the Fifteenth Century*, ed. John A. F. Thomas (Gloucester: Alan Sutton, 1988), p. 76. This is an excellent study that takes into account the recent work on a number of towns. Noting Susan Reynolds's objection to the use of the term "oligarchy" as implying undue self-interest among the rulers, Rigby uses the term to represent the opposite of "democracy" (not of moral worth). Still, he does tend to see town rulers as self-interested; he describes urban government as "often little more than an executive committee for managing the common affairs of the richer townsmen" (Rigby, "Urban Oligarchy," p. 74). A very different view of London's government, one that stresses an open elite and the considerable participation of ordinary citizens in government, appears in Steve Rappaport's *Worlds within Worlds: Structures of Life in Sixteenth-Century London* (Cambridge: Cambridge University Press, 1989). However, Rappaport's study applies primarily to the period after 1531, when an act of parliament dramatically extended the privileges of citizenship by reducing the guilds' enrollment fees; and I would agree with Ronald M. Berger that Rappaport tends to misinterpret the rulers' hegemony as communal harmony (*Journal of Economic History* 50 [1990]: 457). As Ian Archer points out in *The Pursuit of Stability* (Cambridge: Cambridge University Press, 1991), pp. 2–9, the issue is not London's political stability in the sixteenth century, which few would question, but what produced that stability. For the voice of the city, see Caroline Barron, "London and the Crown, 1451–61," in *The Crown and Local Communities*, ed. J. R. L. Highfield and Robin Jeffs (Gloucester: Alan Sutton, 1981), pp. 88–90.

7. Steven Lukes criticizes the notion of "collective effervescences" in "Political Ritual and Social Integration," *Sociology* 9 (1975): 299. Midsummer customs, including the well-documented London custom of decorating church doors with birch, are summarized in John Brand, *Observations on the Popular Antiquities of Great Britain*, vol. 1 (London: Bohn, 1848), pp. 298–338. For the royal visit, see Corporation of London Record Office, Journal 12, fol. 329a. For the regulation of bonfires, see Journal 12, fol. 9a (10 July 1519). The annual order for the watch typically specified the closing of victuallers' shops and tav-

erns; for an example in English, see Corporation of London Record Office, Journal 4, fol. 30b. The livery of the merchant tailors, whose patron saint was John the Baptist, held its annual religious services and feast on 24 June. For this and other information about commemoration of the feast in London, see J. L. Andre, "Saint John the Baptist in Art, Legend, and Ritual," *Archaeological Journal* 50 (1893): 1–19. For the Feast of Saints Peter and Paul as celebrated by the elite guild of Saint Peter at Cornhill, see *Sixth Report of the Royal Commission on Historical Manuscripts*, part 1 (London: Eyre and Spottiswoode, 1877), appendix, p. 413.

8. Michel de Certeau discusses the "proper place" ("le lieu propre"), a concept taken from Bourdieu, in *The Practice of Everyday Life*, trans. Steven Rendall (Berkeley: University of California Press, 1984), p. 55.

9. For the standing watch, see Spinelli's description in Brown, *Calendar of State Papers, Venetian*, p. 137, and Stow, *Survey* 1:101–2. A proclamation of 1517 provided for one half of the wards' constables to attend on the mayor and the other half to keep watch in the wards from 8:00 P.M. to 3:00 A.M. (Corporation of London Record Office, Repertory 3, fol. 146b).

10. For the origins of the watch and the practice of "watch and ward," see Henry T. Riley, ed., *Liber Albus* (London: Longman, 1859), Rolls Series, no. 12, vol. 1, pp. 118–19, 280, 284; and Mary Bateson, "A London Municipal Collection of the Reign of John," *English Historical Review* 17 (1902): 502. Midsummer watches are recorded in the earliest records, at the beginning of the thirteenth century, and they were always ceremonial in that they took place annually according to formal procedures, but in the late 1370s there are indications of an enhanced ritual and the introduction of a marching watch through the center of the city to supplement the standing watches in the wards. For the Midsummer Watches of 1378 and 1379, the city prescribed colorful garb and lances for the aldermen and men of their wards, together with directions to pass through the city in groups. See Corporation of London Record Office, Letter Book H, fols. lxxix, cxi; translated in H. T. Riley, *Memorials of London and London Life* (London: Longmans, 1868), pp. 419–20, 433. The earliest decorated "pageant" that I have found (on the Nine Worthies) was put on by the drapers in 1477; see A. J. Johnson, *The History of the Worshipful Company of the Drapers of London*, 2 vols. (Oxford: Clarendon, 1915), 2:273–74. However, pageants may have been introduced earlier by guilds whose records do not survive.

11. Stow, *Survey* 1:100. Thrupp, *Merchant Class*, discusses property as the basis of political rights in the city (p. 102) and the chronic fear of royal interference (p. 99).

12. Spinelli called this "Luther's festival." Carl S. Meyer, "Henry VIII Burns Luther's Books, 12 May 1521," *Journal of Ecclesiastical History* 9 (1958): 186.

13. On May 8, the duke's indictment had been laid at the guildhall before John Brugge, the mayor honored in the 1521 watch (J. S. Brewer, ed., *Letters and Papers, Foreign and Domestic, of the Reign of Henry VIII*, vol. 3, pt. 1 [London: HMSO, 1867], p. cxxvi). See Brigden, *Reformation in London*, p. 155, for emergency watches later that summer.

14. Brigden, *Reformation in London*, pp. 129–33.

15. Brigden, *Reformation in London*, p. 164; and Helen Miller, "London and Parliament in the Reign of Henry VIII," *Bulletin of the Institute of Historical Research* 35 (1962): 141.

16. For the mercers' supervision of their men in the watch ("going with theym alle the Wache time as yn the comyng home with theym"), see Laetitia Lyell, ed., *Acts of Court of the Mercers' Company, 1453–1527* (Cambridge: Cambridge University Press, 1936), p. 728. Stow, *Survey* 1:102, gives the route of the marching watch, from West Cheap through Cornhill to Aldgate, and then back through Fenchurch Street to Gracechurch before returning to West Cheap.

17. Stow, *Survey* 1:101, and Brown, *Calendar of State Papers, Venetian*, p. 137 (cresset

lights); Riley, *Memorials*, p. 582 (lanterns); and Brown, *Calendar of State Papers, Venetian*, p. 136 (giant).

18. Riley, *Memorials*, p. 35; Reginald R. Sharpe, *Calendar of Letter Books ... of the City of London: Letter Book H* (London: John Edward Francis, 1907), p. 373.

19. Robertson, *Calendar of Dramatic Records*, pp. 5–9. For the mayor as "custos," see Riley, *Liber Albus* 1:16, and Richard Maidstone's report of Richard II's reconciliation with London, quoted in Glynne Wickham, *Early English Stages*, vol. 1 (London: Routledge, 1966), p. 67. In the 1470s, the mayors had been obliged to undertake major repair of the walls. The giants who accompanied the mayor may also have been associated with his custody of the city. Compare the London entry of Henry VI, where giants held a chain inscribed with the names of his dominions: "in tokennyng thatt the emperour is able to holde all those domynyons by pour and strength as the seyd gyauntys holde the same cheyne by pouer and strength" (Robert Withington, *English Pageantry*, vol. 1 [Cambridge: Harvard University Press, 1918], p. 176).

20. A Sultan appears in several Midsummer Watches between 1519 and 1524, perhaps alluding to the Turkish leaders whose threat to Europe had in 1519 inspired Henry VIII to call for a crusade. In August 1521, Sultan Solyman finally took the castle of Petra Varadin near Belgrade by blowing up the walls with gunpowder (Brewer, *Letters and Papers*, vol. 3, pt.1 [London, 1867], pp. 603–4, 615). The drapers' records mention that one child was paid extra in the 1521 watch "be cavs he was hurt with gonpowder" (Robertson, *Calendar of Dramatic Records*, p. 7). This was not the only such accident to occur in the ceremonial watches.

21. In 1460, the mayor, sheriffs, and aldermen rode out to the suburban property of the abbot of Stratford to assert their hunting rights (Betty R. Masters, "The Mayor's Household before 1600," in *Studies in London History*, ed. A. E. J. Hollaender and William Kellaway [London, 1969], p. 100). For the 1458 watch, see T. F. Reddaway, *The Early History of The Goldsmiths' Company* (London: Arnold, 1975), p. 132.

22. *Hall's Chronicle* (London: Johnson, 1809), p. 658.

23. For the "profit" derived from the watch, see, for example, Lyell, *Acts of Court*, p. 97 ("the Wardens bought Clothe for Jakettes entendyng the more profitt of the felyshipp"). See Robertson, *Calendar of Dramatic Records*, p. 35, for a properties' chest. A photograph of the chest in which the draper Thomas Howell kept money for his heirs appears in Johnson, *History of the Drapers* 1:257.

24. Pierre Bourdieu, *Outline of a Theory of Practice*, trans. Richard Nice (Cambridge: Cambridge University Press, 1977), pp. 175–84.

25. Barron, *British Atlas of Historic Towns*, p. 44, notes that a petition was addressed to "My Lord Mair" as early as 1414; Thrupp, *Merchant Class*, p. 149; Lyell, *Acts of Court*, pp. 98, 371; and Robertson, *Calendar of Dramatic Records*, p. 5.

26. Corporation of London Record Office, Journal 12, fols. 75–76, cited in Reginald R. Sharpe, *London and the Kingdom*, vol. 1 (London: Longmans, 1894), p. 365; and Lyell, *Acts of Court*, pp. 516, 513. For the poverty of Kyme and Englysshe, see the document of 1535 in Alfred B. Beaven, *The Aldermen of the City of London*, vol. 2 (London: Fisher, 1913), p. xxxvii.

27. Johnson, *History of the Drapers* 2:273–74 (1477); and Robertson, *Calendar of Dramatic Records*, p. 10 (1521). In 1541, the drapers record a debate about the expense of the watch, stating that "for euyry grot in tyme past [the wardens] ar now ffayne to gyve v" (Robertson, *Calendar of Dramatic Records*, p. 32). The drapers' accounts confirm that this statement is accurate. For the "conservative and cautious" nature of the rulers, see Barron, "London and the Crown," p. 90. For the expedition, see Johnson, *History of the Drapers* 2:16.

28. Kyme's goods were assessed at 500 pounds (low for an alderman but still substantial) for the subsidy of 1523 (S. T. Bindoff, *The House of Commons, 1509–1558* [London: Secker and Warburg, 1982], 2:485); and over 1,000 pounds were collected from his debtors

after his death (James Gairdner, ed., *Letters and Papers, Foreign and Domestic, of the Reign of Henry VIII*, vol. 11 [London: HMSO, 1888], pp. 592–93). His finances were complicated, however. According to the drapers, the "Worshipful Citezens were never wars served" than at his inauguration feast, so there may have been some initial truth to his plea (Johnson, *History of the Drapers* 2:7).

29. Thrupp, *Merchant Class*, pp. 191–206. See also p. 311: "New families were constantly appearing for a generation or two, by the end of which time either they were physically extinguished or else surviving members had moved to new scenes and a different social position." Information about the aldermen comes from Beaven, *Aldermen of the City of London*, passim. George Brugge may be the dead son to whom Brugge refers in his will; Brugge left property to two other sons, who are not recorded as mercers in the livery or aldermen (Bindoff, *House of Commons* 2:533). Skevington bequeathed property to a minor son who similarly never became an alderman or company officer (J. S. Brewer, *Letters and Papers, Foreign and Domestic, of the Reign of Henry VIII*, vol. 4, pt. 1 [London: HMSO, 1870], p. 411). Thrupp, *Merchant Class*, p. 203, gives statistics for the high mortality of minor children mentioned in wills.

30. Johnson, *History of the Drapers* 2:256, 85.

31. Brugge was an MP in 1510, when London seems to have attempted to have the "acte concernyng corporacions" of 1504 repealed, and Kyme was an MP in 1512 and 1515, when the city sought the repeal actively. For London's troubles with this act, see Miller, "London and Parliament," passim. The act imposed on all corporate bodies the duty of having their ordinances approved by the king's chancellor, rather than by the municipal authorities who had been approving them up to this time. The effect was to question the powers of the municipal authorities, who sought until the late 1520s to repeal the act.

Like myself, Lawrence M. Clopper connects civic ceremony with the incorporation of towns, but, in line with Phythian-Adams, he sees incorporation as signifying civic independence and a new sense of "corporate lay responsibility." See his "Lay and Clerical Impact on Civic Religious Drama and Ceremony," *Contexts for Early English Drama*, ed. Marianne G. Briscoe and John C. Coldewey (Bloomington: Indiana University Press, 1989), p. 107. It seems clear, though, that the incorporation of towns brought them no new freedoms; in fact, during the great period of incorporation, the king extended his control over civic oligarchies (Rigby, "Urban Oligarchy," p. 78).

32. Withington, *English Pageantry* 1:156, 176; and 2:377 (index); and Frederick W. Fairholt, *Lord Mayors' Pageants*, vol. 1 (London: Percy Society, 1843), pp. xx–xxvii. For "popys" (puppets?) in the 1521 watch and a reference to the giant as lord "moryspykes," see Robertson, *Calendar of Dramatic Records*, pp. 9, 11. The giants of Albion are described in Friedrich W. D. Brie, ed., *The Brut*, Early English Text Society (EETS), o.s. 101 pt. 1, p. 4. Londoners could have read the legend of the giants in Caxton's edition of this work, the *Chronicles of England* (1480).

33. Brown, *Calendar of State Papers, Venetian*, p. 136. Gail McMurray Gibson discusses Assumption pageants in *The Theater of Devotion* (Chicago: University of Chicago Press, 1989), p. 168. The drapers frequently staged the Assumption of Our Lady, their patron saint. In 1523, they paid "Gleyns daughter," presumably to play the Virgin, in an Assumption pageant for the watch (Robertson, *Calendar of Dramatic Records*, p. 14).

34. Robertson, *Calendar of Dramatic Records*, pp. 5–11, and the transcript by Anne Lancashire.

35. Forty-eight companies are listed in order of precedence in a processional list of 1515 reproduced by William Meade Williams in *Annals of the Worshipful Company of Founders* (London: privately printed, 1876), p. 213. The number of men each contributed to the Midsummer Watch must be estimated by consulting a range of sources; however, the number of bowmen (as opposed to halberdiers and other personnel) they sent to the marching portion of the watch is specified in a list of 1518, which names forty-six guilds

and their contributions of between 2 and 8 men, 210 bowmen in all (Corporation of London Record Office, Journal 11, fol. 347v). Most of the extant guild records for the watch of 1521 concern these bowmen. The drapers paid 8 bowmen, the number specified on this list, in addition to the 50 halberdiers and 14 gunners they supplied because the mayor was of their company (Robertson, *Calendar of Dramatic Records*, p. 10). Also in 1521, the vintners, eleventh in precedence, spent 19s. 9d. on white cotton coats for their 6 men (British Library MS. Egerton 1143, fol. 70). The founders, the thirty-second guild in order of precedence, ordered eight yards of white cotton to uniform their men (*Wardens' Accounts of the Worshipful Company of Founders*, ed. Guy Parsloe [London: Athlone, 1964], 61). The carpenters (twenty-sixth) ordered a similar amount for their 4 men, as they had been doing since at least 1503 and as they did for the revival of the watch in 1548. This was the same number as the torches they contributed for royal funerals (Edward Basil, *An Historical Account of the Worshipful Company of Carpenters* [London: Pickering, 1887], pp. 40–44). As for the standing portion of the watch, an order for an emergency watch in July 1521 lists three groups of wards with the watchmen's routes and standing places in the city and asks each ward to supply 6 to 10 good and able men (Corporation of London Record Office, Journal 12, fol. 119); it is possible that a similar number of men from the wards participated in the ceremonial watch in June. Given the figures available and the inability to confirm Stow's reference to 700 cresset bearers from other sources, his estimate of 2,000 men in the marching watch alone seems somewhat high. He may have been recalling the elaborate revival of the watch in 1549. But there may well have been 2,000 persons involved in the entire 1521 watch, with its standing and marching components. For the Bachelors' pageant, see Robertson, *Calendar of Dramatic Records*, pp. 5–11.

36. For the children in 1521, see Robertson, *Calendar of Dramatic Records*, pp. 5–11. In Brown, *Calendar of State Papers, Venetian*, p. 137, Spinelli identifies some as choristers. A number of the Midsummer pageants referred to the names of the officers: for example, in 1534, the mayor's name was William, and one of his pageants was William the Conqueror; the Castle of Monmouth was produced for Mayor Monmouth in 1535.

37. Lyell, *Acts of Court*, p. 728; information on the drapers' uniforms courtesy of Anne Lancashire.

38. This is Malcolm Vale's description of halberdiers marching, in *War and Chivalry* (Athens: University of Georgia Press, 1981), p. 154. In "A Bourgeois Puts His World in Order," Robert Darnton also notes that a civic procession "could not be taken literally as a model of society, because it exaggerated some elements and neglected others." I would not agree, however, that the processions still "expressed the essence of society." See Darnton, *The Great Cat Massacre* (New York: Vintage, 1985), pp. 122–23.

39. Robertson, *Calendar of Dramatic Records*, p. 35. In 1542, the drapers complained that the mercers in their pageants were setting "precedents" no other craft could meet (Robertson, *Calendar of Dramatic Records*, p. 32). In 1510, the mercers complained that Mayor Capell (a draper) had demanded too many men for his watch and asked that he put in writing that this was *not* a "precedent" (Lyell, *Acts of Court*, pp. 371–72).

40. In 1513, the fine for a mercer not attending the watch, if he had been assigned to do so, was 6s. 8d. (Lyell, *Acts of Court*, p. 413). In 1521, two constables had to pay 20s. to those who substituted for them in the watch (Corporation of London Record Office, Repertory 5, fol. 204). For the mercers' complaint, see note 39 above. For Carpenter, see Riley, *Liber Albus* 1:3.

41. Thrupp, *Merchant Class*, pp. 99, 100; and Corporation of London Record Office, Repertory 4, fol. 76b.

42. J. J. Scarisbrick, *Henry VIII* (Berkeley: University of California Press, 1968), pp. 17–18. For the King's Head, see Roman Syboski, ed., *Songs, Carols, and other Miscellaneous Poems*, EETS, e.s. 101 (1907), p. 156; and Stow, *Survey* 1:257–58. For heads of the clergy, James Gairdner, *Letters and Papers, Foreign and Domestic, of the Reign of Henry*

VIII, vol. 8 (London: HMSO, 1885), p. 373. For the cancellation, Stow, *Survey* 1:103–4, 284 n. and Muriel St. Clare Byrne, ed., *The Lisle Letters*, vol. 5 (Chicago: University of Chicago Press, 1981), p. 542 ("some of the citizens, having prepared for the same, are not very well pleased"). For revivals, see Stow, *Survey* 1:103–4. The Midsummer bonfires were also appropriated by Henry VIII's court for an ambassadorial visit at Midsummer 1519 (Sharpe, *London and the Kingdom* 1:363) and, it might be argued, for the burning of Luther's books.

CHAPTER 8

Unity or Division?

The Social Meaning of Guild Ceremony in Urban Communities

Benjamin R. McRee

Scholars who have studied the public culture of English towns and cities during the late medieval period have emphasized the sense of unity that communal celebrations could foster among urban residents. In otherwise stratified and faction-ridden communities, men and women put their differences aside long enough to share communal meals, engage in neighborhood games, and march through the streets shoulder to shoulder in processional demonstrations of fraternity. One commentator has even gone so far as to speak of the "social wholeness" that public pageants nurtured within the medieval community.[1] Such interpretations of urban ceremony, appealing as they are, tell only part of the story, however. As some observers have noted, much urban ceremony produced just the opposite effect, promoting not wholeness but separateness, not unity but division. Perhaps most familiar are the disorders that arose out of Carnival observances. Researchers have discovered that these pre-Lenten celebrations could easily get out of hand, resulting in assaults, murders, and, on some occasions, full-scale riots.[2] More mundane ceremonies could also lead to trouble, however, as students of Corpus Christi processions have discovered.[3] These spectacles periodically produced bitter disputes over questions of status and precedence as competing groups jockeyed for position in the march. Indeed it is remarkable how often urban unrest in preindustrial Europe was associated with ceremonial observances.

Ceremony did not have to produce violence to discourage social unity, of course. Even when riots did not result, public ceremony could be insidiously divisive, drawing attention to the lines separating different social groups within the community rather than working to erase those lines. Nowhere was this more apparent than in the multiform guild ceremony that pervaded the public life of English towns and cities during the Middle Ages. Religious guilds in particular furnish a valuable source for investigating the impact of ceremony on the urban community. These fraternal organizations enjoyed tremendous popularity during the late Middle Ages, and the processions and other spectacles they sponsored accounted for a substantial portion of the public celebrations that took place in medieval towns and cities. Most significantly, religious guilds were independent corporations with their own clientele, their own rules, and their own images to maintain. As the material that follows will show, the ceremonies they sponsored, both public and private, were meant not to draw the inhabitants of their communities together, but instead to secure their own places within the local, hierarchical order.

The character of guild ceremony grew, at least in part, out of the social needs of these organizations. In large communities where numerous fraternities competed for members and status, each had to find a way to distinguish itself from the others and so to create a niche for itself. For some groups a unique social definition was easy. Those practicing the same trade, for example, shared common economic interests and work experiences. An individual's profession determined, to a large extent, his relative wealth, his colleagues, his contacts during the day, and his opportunities for social and political advancement. Organizations that drew their members from a particular parish or city ward, likewise, were drawn together by proximity of residence and common interests in sanitation or the maintenance of the parish church. But many religious guilds did not limit membership to the practitioners of one craft or the residents of a single parish and were not unified by such obvious mutual concerns. Building a distinct identity was a challenge for these guilds, one that they had to overcome if they were to achieve prominence in their communities or even if they were to attract sufficient members to survive from one generation to the next.

An urban religious association thus had a twofold task. First, it had to forge a sense of common identity among its members. Those who belonged had to believe that their participation in the guild made them part of a group whose members shared a unique bond. Second, the guild had to project that sense of unity to the population at large. Guilds employed a variety of techniques to achieve these goals. By carefully screening initiates, for example, they could shape the social character of their organizations, moving them closer to the sense of common identity they needed; in a parallel fashion they could advertise their shared values by contributing candles, stained glass, religious images, or other objects to the parish church. Such steps constituted no more than a beginning, however. It was the ceremonial repertoire of medieval urban life that provided guilds with the most effective tools for defining their place in the community. Successful organizations thus made liberal use of the ceremonial language of late medieval life to establish social boundaries that emphasized both internal unity and social exclusivity. Initiates thus became members of a select group that was distinguished socially and sometimes politically from the rest of the populace.

For the men and women who belonged to religious guilds, the process of separation began with the initiation ceremony. By establishing ties of loyalty that lay outside the usual network of family, civic, and professional bonds, the induction ritual helped to build the special identity that fraternal institutions needed and members wanted. Such rites did not have to be elaborate to be effective; it was only necessary that they provide an established procedure for recognizing new members and integrating them into the existing group. Guild initiation rites commonly focused attention on the creation of two relationships, one vertical and the other horizontal. The vertical relationship subordinated the new member to the guild officers' authority. The recital of an oath of loyalty, in which the initiate pledged to obey the leaders of the fraternity and to conform to its statutes, typically established the lines of authority. The horizontal relationship placed the new member in a state of equality with the existing body of members. It stressed the bonds of brotherhood that tied one member to another, often through some symbolic act such as the exchange of a kiss. Initiation into the Guild of Saint Barnabas and Saint Lawrence in Horncastle provides an illustration of the way in which guilds could use ceremony to separate their members from the general populace. The initiation process had three distinct steps. First, in a practice reminiscent of the feudal ceremony of homage, the brother-to-be placed his hands between the guild alderman's to signify his acceptance of that officer's authority. Next, the initiate swore an oath of loyalty, invoking Christ, the Virgin, the patron saints of the guild, and all saints. Having offered both physical and oral submission, the initiate was admitted to the brotherhood. The guild marked his acceptance in the third and final step by giving him "une gerland" to signify his new status and by obliging him to exchange a kiss with each of the other members.[4] This ceremony stressed acceptance of the guild laws, obedience to the alderman, and the importance of maintaining peaceful relations among members—goals shared by most guilds. It also bound members into a group with a distinct social identity. Only the members of this organization had placed their hands in the alderman's, sworn their oaths, and accepted one another with a kiss. Each time an individual joined and the ceremony was repeated, the guild's unique social identity was reaffirmed for the assembled members.

The communal feeling engendered by admission ceremonies would have been pointless without the support of additional activities that reinforced guild solidarity. One of the most popular, and perhaps ancient, ways of sustaining the spirit of fraternity was the holding of annual feasts.[5] At commensal gatherings members rekindled feelings of brotherhood and renewed their sense of identification with the guild. In Oxford the Guild of Saint Thomas the Martyr explained that the purpose of its feast was the promotion of brotherly love within the organization.[6] Similarly, Stratford-on-Avon's Holy Cross Guild expected its communal meal to encourage fraternal spirit, bring an end to malicious speech, and preserve peace among the members.[7] Feasts made this possible because they separated members of the fraternity from the general populace and placed them in an environment far removed from the familiar surroundings of their daily lives. Indeed, the "apartness" of the feast was its principal strength. Isolated from the rest of the community in time and space, guild members were encouraged to leave their worries and their connections to the outside world behind as they were temporarily transported into a new and better world featuring rich food, drink-enriched entertainment, and a reminder of shared values. A feeling of camaraderie among the feasters as well as a renewed sense of corporate identity were natural products of guild commensalism. Such, at least, were the results for which guild leaders hoped, and no doubt their expectations were often fulfilled. But private gatherings at most achieved internal solidarity; guilds also needed public recognition as distinct social bodies.

An ideal way to obtain public exposure was to march together in a procession. A fraternity's annual march was its most visible activity, affording the organization a unique opportunity to shape its public image. As town residents looked on, members of the guild marched past in what the organization hoped would be an impressive show of strength. Ordinances and practices drawn from a number of fraternities suggest that a carefully choreographed, properly managed procession could help to achieve three organizational goals. First, it could emphasize the social unity of the membership, a crucial task when guild brothers and sisters might be drawn from different professions, different neighborhoods, and different social strata. Second, it could establish a unique public identity for the organization, a significant goal in large towns and cities when dozens of religious guilds competed for attention. Third, it could promote the dignity of the organization, an important aim where "worshipfulness" and respect for commonly held values were vital to a group's status in the community.

The language of processions was, of course, a visual one, and so it is not surprising that guilds used visual means to achieve their goals. The most telling indicator of fraternal unity, for example, was the ornamental costume or livery worn by marchers. To emphasize the ties that bound their members together, many guilds required those joining in the procession to dress in a common livery.[8] Such a policy resulted in a sight imposing to the eye—many urban guilds, after all, enrolled over one hundred members—and also provided a colorful confirmation of the link that tied guild brothers and sisters together. The use of common clothing was not limited to processions, of course; members also donned their liveries for funerals, feasts, religious services, and fraternity business meetings. At all of these gatherings the livery served its purpose by setting members apart from those who did not belong to the organization. As one fraternity put it, the function of the livery was "to kennen ye bretheryn an systeryn."[9]

A fraternity's livery typically comprised a gown and hood made of high-quality cloth dyed in bright colors. To ensure an impressive appearance many guilds cautioned members to take good care of their liveries, and some even enacted regulations requiring them to renew the clothing every year or two. In Norwich members of the Guild of Saint George owned both a gown and a hood made from red or mixed red and white fabric. Members alternated use of the two pieces during the early fifteenth century, wearing the gown one year and the hood the next. Regulations restricting the purchase and sale of these liveries underscored their importance as an exclusive mark of guild membership. The guild maintained complete control over the manufacture of the garment, selecting the cloth, choosing someone to cut it, and pricing it so that the guild could make a profit. No member could sell his or her livery, or even give it away without first dyeing it so that it no longer identified its wearer as a member of the guild.[10] A livery did not have to be made of rich or elegant fabric to be effective, however; it did not even have to be a piece of clothing in the traditional sense. A guild in Lincoln signaled its corporate identity in an unusual and inexpensive way by asking members to don distinctive garlands during its march.[11] Apparently any material would do as long as it was worn by all of the members.

Many guilds moved beyond the provision of common clothing to create a more memorable trademark for themselves by adding a dumb show or special religious representation to their annual march. This step not only imparted a dramatic flair to the procession, but, as the symbols used were usually inspired by the guild's dedication, it also gave the march a unique identifying stamp. In Beverley, for example, the Guild of Saint Helen depicted the legendary discovery of the cross by its patron saint. Two men marched at the front, one carrying a cross and the other the tool used to unearth it, a spade. Behind them followed a boy, elegantly garbed, playing the part of Helen.[12] The Guild of the Purification in the same city directed that one of its members, dressed as the Virgin Mary, walk at the head of the column carrying a child in her arms. She was accompanied by others who played the parts of Joseph, Simeon, and a pair of angels. When they arrived at the church, Mary handed the child to Simeon at the high altar, just as the biblical story of the Purification related.[13] Corpus Christi guilds, naturally enough, made the host the focal point of their processions. In Grantham, for example, the Corpus Christi Guild directed that two chaplains dressed in their vestments bear the consecrated host while a pair of youths clothed in albs walked alongside with candles.[14] The principal concern of the Corpus Christi Guild in Lynn was the provision of sufficient candles to honor the host. Three men had founded this organization after the Black Death, the guild claimed, when they noticed that the body of Christ was being carried through the streets with only a single, poor candle accompanying it. They decided that the host deserved a better escort and decreed that it was henceforth to have thirteen torches in its train, each torch being ten feet long and weighing ten pounds.[15]

The representations employed by these guilds served as emblems that visually proclaimed the sponsoring organizations' identities. When residents of Beverley saw the cross and spade, they knew that the Guild of Saint Helen was staging its annual march. In Lynn the host and its train of torches identified the Corpus Christi Guild. Theatrical demonstrations were, of course, more than mere labels; they also had entertainment value, and they provided a ready outlet for creative expression. This side of processions, in fact, caused some anxiety among guild leaders who worried lest exuberance be carried too far and threaten the dignity of the undertaking. They had worked hard to create impressive shows and did not want unseemly conduct or inattention to detail to spoil their efforts.

In an attempt to discourage inappropriate behavior, many guilds laid out precise instructions for the conduct of their processions. Ordinances covered every aspect of the march, beginning with the selection of a suitable starting point. Guild regulations usually left the determination of this location to the officers, warning, however, that it ought to be an honest and reputable place.[16] Because arrangement of the members into marching order could not have been an easy task, leaders were encouraged to avoid crowded public places when selecting an assembly point. The confusion of daily business in a crowded square would have complicated the process and projected an undesirable image of disorder. A suitable starting point allowed the marchers, once properly assembled, to pass through the town's busiest streets, affording them maximum public exposure. It also permitted them to stop along the way at any shrines important to the guild. Since many organizations had their members carry candles during the march, they may have followed the practice of a Norwich craft guild and assembled at the shop of a chandler so that each member could be supplied with wax.[17]

Notions of hierarchy and order were also prominent in rules governing the march. Ordinances sometimes divided the sexes, placing the women in the less desirable front position and instructing the men to follow behind. Officers of the guild marched at the rear of the column, in the most prestigious position.[18] Most guilds favored a column in which members lined up two by two, one pair behind another, in what the British today call a "crocodile." Such an arrangement was easy to organize and manage, since two members, walking side by side, could stay abreast while three or four might make an uneven line. Of course the slim column also made it easy to negotiate the narrow streets of a medieval city center.[19] Some guilds added admonitions stressing sober demeanor during the parade. A pair of Cambridge guilds instructed their members, for example, to march slowly, hoping to impress onlookers with their dignified cadence.[20] The Guild of Saint Mary and Saint George in Lynn was one of a number of guilds that warned its members to go "honestly and decently" as they processed to the parish church.[21]

Through regulations such as these religious guilds sought to preserve the dignity of their processions and protect the public image of their organizations.[22]

Guild processions, however simple or elaborate their external trappings, were, at heart, public declarations of autonomy. They announced that the marchers were part of an independent body with its own goals, its own rules, and its own corporate identity. Even if stripped of banners, candles, representations of saints, and other paraphernalia, guild processions would still have presented their members to the public as socially distinct groups. As the marchers paraded through the streets in well-ordered columns, the division between those who were members and those who were not was made explicit. This division was not necessarily a dangerous one. It might have done no more than underscore existing social groupings, such as those of neighborhood or parish. As long as the groups delineated by guild membership were in accord with local notions of proper social organization, it is unlikely that ceremonial expressions of such divisions would cause trouble. Even in these benign cases, however, guild processions were hardly conducive to civic unity. They emphasized not the wholeness of the community, but its division into separate, semiautonomous subgroups. Such compartmentalization of the populace might be described as *passively* divisive. It focused attention on the lines separating different elements within the local community, but it did not seek to exploit the division among those elements for partisan gain.

Guild processions could also be *actively* divisive, seeking to undermine the existing order and widen rifts between social groups. Unfortunately it is not easy to discover examples of this type of procession; except in cases of violence or serious disorder, a procession's impact on the community usually remains hidden by a lack of appropriate documentation. Without court records or detailed comments by observers, it is impossible to know just how a particular procession was perceived. Through a judicious use of those records that do survive, it is sometimes possible to build a circumstantial case, however. A revealing example of this sort comes from the city of Norwich, where the Guild of Saint George gained prominence during the first half of the fifteenth century. A close study of conditions in that city, coupled with an attentive analysis of details of the fraternity's procession, suggests that the guild's seemingly innocent march became actively divisive during the 1430s and 1440s. The balance of the present investigation will be devoted to an examination of this case.

The procession mounted by the Guild of Saint George took place twice each year: once on 23 April, the feast day of Saint George, and again on the following day. It started from the Church of Saint Peter Mancroft, located on the city's western side, and moved east toward the cathedral where members attended services for the souls of deceased brothers and sisters.[23] The earliest evidence of the procession appears in a set of ordinances drawn up in the first quarter of the fifteenth century. The statutes called for guild officers to choose one of the members to play the part of Saint George, another to bear a sword before him, a third to carry his banner, and two more to carry torches. The rest of the members were instructed to ride on horseback, wearing the guild livery.[24] The first surviving guild account roll, covering the year that ran from April 1420 to April 1421, recorded payments for a procession organized in precisely this manner. The guild spent roughly £2 for costumes, torches, a fee for the man who played the part of Saint George, and refreshments for the participants.[25]

Later records provide more concrete information about the appearance of the saint and his attendants. Saint George entered on horseback, dressed in the elegant clothing of a well-to-do knight. He wore a scarlet gown, lined with green tartan and trimmed with fur. The guild owned a suit of armor, beaten with silver, for him as well. He may have worn this over the gown or, as was the custom in later years, it may have been carried for him by attendants.[26] From time to time the guild renewed his clothing. It bought him a new outfit made of tawny and crimson-purple velvet in 1537; three years later it lined a crimson robe with red satin for his use. The material for this apparel was expensive. The velvet needed for the robe in 1537 cost the guild £7 7s. In 1540 the bill came to £11 10s., an extraordinary expenditure for an organization with an annual income of only £20.[27] To allow Saint George to appear in different outfits without exhausting the treasury, the guild occasionally borrowed clothing from the local gentry. In 1478, for example, it paid 8d. to use the robe of William Calthorp, a knight and former sheriff of Norfolk and Suffolk. It also borrowed a hat from one of the city's former mayors in the same year. The guild ventured further up the social ladder in 1520 when it borrowed a coat and gown from the duke of Suffolk.[28] Besides being an inexpensive way to provide Saint George with elegant dress, borrowing clothing from local magnates helped to solidify regional political alliances.[29]

The horse ridden by the saint helped to complete his image as a wealthy man-at-arms, the premier fighting man of the fifteenth century. The horse's caparison, consisting of reins, cruppers, headstalls, and pectorals, complemented the saint's attire. All of the equipment was lined with red cloth and decorated with gilt bosses that displayed the saint's arms. In addition, a chaplet attached with a copper clasp was provided for the animal.[30] A pair of attendants, called henchmen, rode with Saint George. They wore red "jakettes" or "jacks" with crosses and roses worked into the surface. A kind of doublet, the jack was the armor traditionally worn by valets who attended men-at-arms as well as by soldiers who could not afford the protection of more expensive armor. Many of the fighting men that Norwich supplied to the king wore this type of armor. The military jack was made of leather or quilted fabric reinforced with metal studs. When worn in the procession, however, it was made from red fustian and buckram, heavy fabrics usually reserved for clerical vestments and ceremonial wear. The henchmen also wore gloves, and their horses were draped in white cloth.[31]

The column included a dragon, Saint George's legendary opponent. Postmedieval sources, together with information gleaned from the fraternity's account rolls, provide useful hints about the appearance of this creature. Known to residents as Snap, it survived long after sixteenth-century religious reformers insisted that Saint George be dropped from the procession; indeed, several dragon costumes from the eighteenth and nineteenth centuries still exist at the museum in Norwich.[32] The oldest, dating from about 1795, was constructed of canvas stretched over a basketwork frame. It had a barrel-shaped body into which a man could insert his head and operate the monster's mouth and batlike wings. One of the nineteenth-century dragons had a hinged jaw with a metal plate on the lower gum. When the operator pulled a cord, the jaws banged together with a loud snap. The medieval version of the dragon was probably similar. Guild account rolls reveal that it too was covered with canvas, and a basketwork body would have protected the man inside the costume from blows delivered by Saint George.[33]

The saint probably jousted with the dragon as the column moved through the streets. The main battle took place, however, near the cathedral where the march came to an end. This was the highlight of the procession, and the guild strove to make the combat as dramatic as possible. The saint, mounted on horseback, attacked the monster with a lance, doing enough damage to require regular repairs to the creature's canvas covering. The dragon, played by a member of the guild wearing the costume already described, was not defenseless. On at least one occasion the guild supplied it with gunpowder, presenting the saint with a fire-breathing adversary.[34] After the combat came to its conclusion and the creature had been slain, Saint George and the other marchers entered the cathedral, where the saint made an offering at the altar and members of the guild heard a mass for the souls of their deceased brothers and sisters.[35]

Other details of the procession included torches, a ceremonial sword, and banners identifying the guild. Four torches were carried by poor men who received small payments for their labor. Occasionally the guild also employed boys to carry torches around the guild's banner.[36] Ceremonial swords frequently appeared in civic processions, usually being carried before the mayor or some other city official. The guild's sword, reputedly given to it by Henry V, preceded the saint. It was made of wood, with a latten-covered pommel and hilt. The handle, appropriately, had a dragon's head carved upon it. A scabbard, decorated with velvet and studded with latten bosses, was worn by the man who bore the sword.[37]

The guild also owned several banners that were carried at the front of the column. Four of the banners were for trumpeters who must have hung them from their instruments; each of these banners depicted the arms of the guild's patron saint. Two other banners appeared in the guild's inventory; one displayed an image of Saint George while the other contained a silvered image of his arms. The guild used only one of the two during a procession and probably alternated them for the two marches it conducted each year.[38]

The processional details recorded in the guild accounts and other documents appear to have been harmless enough. Indeed, during the 1410s and 1420s, the period from which the earliest evidence of the march survives, the evidence suggests a unifying display of pride in the wake of England's recent military victories in France. The warrior saint, preceded by his sword and banner and accompanied by armor-clad attendants, would have reminded onlookers of English military might and imparted a patriotic flavor to the march. This aspect of the display may even have helped to attract the handful of knights and gentlemen who enrolled in the fraternity, men such as Thomas Kerdestoun, Henry Englose, William Paston, Simon and Roger Felbrigge, Roger Boys, and John Fastolf.[39]

During the 1430s and 1440s, however, the procession acquired a second layer of meaning, one that was less likely to have evoked a sympathetic response from some onlookers. The procession's new meaning arose from political events taking place in the city. During the 1430s, Norwich witnessed the emergence of a controversial political faction led by Thomas Wetherby, a wealthy merchant who became mayor of the city in 1432.[40] In the following year Wetherby and his allies came into conflict with other prominent citizens over electoral issues. They fared poorly in the clashes that resulted, and finished by being stripped of power and banned from city offices. In 1436, however, Wetherby staged a comeback, and managed to gain the support of the region's most powerful nobleman, the duke of Suffolk, and two of his henchmen, John Heydon and Thomas Tudenham. Suffolk supported the rehabilitation of Wetherby and his friends and later played an important role in furthering lawsuits against the interests of Wetherby's enemies. These actions led to riots in the city in 1437 and 1443 and, on each occasion, a temporary revocation of the city's liberties by the king. Wetherby's opponents naturally came to resent the interference of Suffolk and his allies in the city's affairs, believing that without the help of these powerful figures Wetherby would not have been able to cause them any further trouble after his initial defeat in 1433.

Norwich's political troubles touched on the Guild of Saint George, because Wetherby and most of his local supporters were fraternity members. Suffolk too belonged to the guild, and, at the height of the disturbances, Heydon and Tudenham were also admitted. These developments brought the organization under political suspicion and, I believe, added a new, partisan layer of meaning to the symbolism of its annual procession. This meaning can best be appreciated in the context of the legendary story of Saint George's conquest of the dragon. The saint had originally won his fame by coming to the aid of the Libyan city of Silene, which was being terrorized by a monster that lived in a pond outside the gates. To pacify the dragon, residents sacrificed sheep to it. When they ran out of sheep, they began offering children and adolescents, chosen by lot, to the monster. Just as a young princess was about to be sacrificed to the creature, Saint George appeared on the scene. The saint charged the dragon, stunning it with his lance. He then instructed the maiden to tie her girdle around the beast's neck and lead it back into town. Overcome by the bravery of Saint George and the purity of the maid, the dragon followed meekly. Once inside the city the saint beheaded the dragon before the assembled populace, freeing them from their devilish oppressor.[41]

The legend of Saint George thus glorifies the beneficent intervention of a member of the warrior class in the affairs of a beleaguered city. If it had not been for the timely arrival of the saintly man-at-arms, a young princess would have lost her life and Silene would have remained at the monster's mercy. The lesson of the story would appear to be that cities could not protect themselves and so required the beneficent intervention of powerful outsiders in order to survive. How did this message apply to Norwich? The city did not, after all, have to contend with the dragon. It did, however, face serious political problems during the 1430s and 1440s. Amid the turmoil of those decades, the story of St. George and the dragon might well have implied to the residents that the city needed the assistance of figures such as Suffolk, Heydon, and Tudenham. They too were men-at-arms, and even if they lacked saintly qualities, they too were eager to assist helpless citizens. Wetherby and his followers would have recognized the truth of this message in the restoration of their authority; without Suffolk's support they would most likely have remained powerless in Norwich. Wetherby's enemies would not have been so sanguine. For them the procession must have served as a reminder of their inability to silence Wetherby after his initial defeat and of the tribulations that they had suffered as a consequence. The march thus became a partisan political statement that could only have inflamed tempers and hardened divisions within the city.

Despite its provocative character the procession mounted by the Guild of Saint George never resulted in a riot. Indeed, no direct evidence that its imagery ever generated hostility survives. Hints that the march did foster tensions appeared later, however, when the guild underwent a major restructuring; the evidence on this point is not conclusive, but it is sufficiently intriguing to warrant further examination. In 1452 guild leaders and city officials agreed to reform the fraternity in an effort to eliminate its factional character. The most important changes were those affecting governance and membership. Henceforth, the outgoing mayor of the city was automatically to become alderman of the guild each year, and all city officers were to be admitted freely to the fraternity. These changes would have brought many of Wetherby's former opponents into the fraternity, and so it should not be surprising to discover that the procession also underwent important alteration. The most dramatic change was the apparent disappearance of Saint George and the dragon from the march. The first mention of either character after the 1452 restructuring did not occur until fifteen years later, in 1467–68.[42] Then, in 1471, guild leaders found it necessary to pass an ordinance that required the saint's inclusion in the procession and mandated his combat with the dragon.[43] The regulation apparently proved effective during the 1470s and 1480s when guild accounts regularly recorded the activity of the saint and his opponent. Then in 1491 a new exhortation to include both characters was made.[44] What are we to make of the disappearance of the saint and his adversary in the aftermath of the 1452 reforms and of the hints that they were subsequently readmitted only with reluctance? It is possible, of course, that a change in tastes or a reluctance to bear the expenses associated with the two characters resulted in their temporary removal from the march. Given the events of the 1430s and 1440s and the restructuring of the guild in 1452, however, it seems more likely that some of the guild's members, particularly its recent matriculants, found the procession's implication of urban dependence on powerful outsiders offensive and applied pressure to keep the two figures out of the parade. An additional piece of circumstantial evidence supports this view. Local records reveal that the year in which the saint and the dragon reappeared in the procession was the same one during which Robert Toppes died.[45] Toppes had been one of the leaders of the opposition to Wetherby during the 1430s and 1440s, and, more important, his death in 1467 removed the last of Wetherby's major opponents from the ranks of the guild. He may have been the last member to oppose the saint's presence in the parade.

The changes described above were not the only alterations to the procession after 1452. During the same period the guild added a number of religious elements to the march, perhaps attempting to shift attention away from Saint George and the dragon and diffuse earlier political implications. In 1467, the fraternity included half a dozen chanting clergymen from the city's cathedral church in the column.[46] This was, of course, the year in which Saint George and the dragon regained their places in the procession. Whether or not these moves were coincidental, clergymen quickly became a regular feature. The guild passed an ordinance several years later that required each of the city's aldermen and some of the sheriffs and former sheriffs to send a priest, outfitted in the guild's colors, to the procession. The measure was evidently difficult to enforce and had to be repeated in 1472. A few years later the guild itself began to pay for the priests, indicating its failure to persuade the alder-men to take responsibility for providing the clergymen. Nevertheless, the guild continued to sponsor anywhere from a dozen to two dozen priests until it was secularized in 1548.[47] Although the participating clergymen were secular priests, not the cathedral clergy it had started with in 1467, the shift did not reflect unhappiness with the latter group. They contin-ued to serve the guild by ringing the cathedral bells during the proces-sion and storing costumes and equipment throughout the year.

By 1500, Saint George's place in the annual procession had once again become secure as the memory of the troubles that had made his inclu-sion controversial faded. During the sixteenth century, the guild elabo-rated its march in ways that revealed just how comfortable citizens had become with the saint and his retinue. Some of the changes were minor, such as the addition of a man bearing a cross, another carrying a basin filled with holy water, and attendants garbed in vestments rented from a local monastery. Other additions were more striking. A canopy carried by four men dressed in albs covered Saint George's head after 1520, while three other men, dressed as angels, carried his helmet and armor.[48] The most interesting change, however, was the inclusion of a new char-acter in the drama acted out by Saint George and the dragon. In 1530 the guild bought clothing for a "mayde" who rode with Saint George. A group of female attendants accompanied her, and, like Saint George, she occasionally supplemented her wardrobe with clothing and jewelry bor-rowed from local magnates. After the combat with the dragon she entered the cathedral with Saint George and made an offering at the altar. The lady was identified as Saint Margaret in 1533 and was known by that name until she and Saint George were banned from the proces-sion in 1548.[49]

The legend of Saint Margaret, like that of Saint George, involved a dragon. As a girl of fifteen living in Antioch, Saint Margaret had been imprisoned by an official who lusted after her. He hoped that confine-ment would induce her to abandon her Christianity and be more recep-tive to his advances. While in prison she prayed that God would reveal her true adversary so that she could deal with him directly. The devil promptly appeared in her cell in the shape of a dragon and lunged at her. She successfully defended herself, making the sign of the cross and caus-ing the creature to vanish. She later died a martyr's death, guarding both her religious convictions and her chastity to the end.[50]

Although records are silent about Saint Margaret's role in the Nor-wich procession, her presence must have added considerable drama to the battle with the dragon. Perhaps Saint George rescued her from the dragon's clutches before he slew the monster. Or she may have helped Saint George defeat the dragon by taming it with her girdle so that he could attack it without danger to himself. A notation in the 1530 guild account presents another possibility. The guild paid for the construction of two dragons in that year, the same year that Saint Margaret made her first appearance in the march. This may have been a coincidence. On the other hand, Saint George and Saint Margaret may have faced twin dragons, each confronting one of them. As Saint George dispatched the first monster with his lance, perhaps Saint Margaret slew the second by making the sign of the cross.

The addition of Saint Margaret to what had, by the early sixteenth century, become an increasingly lavish procession was the last flourish for a spectacle that was shortly to undergo sharp modification. In the reformist climate of Edward VI's reign there was no place for such ceremony, and the guild was compelled to remove the "superstitious" elements from its procession. Ordinances drawn up in 1548 specified that in the future the mayor, city aldermen, and guild members should make several trips between the guildhall and the cathedral during the week of Saint George's Day. No mention was made, however, of Saint George, Saint Margaret, the dragon, or the other elements that had recently been part of the procession.[51] In 1550 the guild sold some of its possessions, notably the procession paraphernalia and costly costumes for which it no longer had a use.[52] Although the procession continued in altered form, it was henceforth a truncated affair that lacked the color and style of the medieval march.

Every procession expressed a particular vision of the community. Even seemingly innocent parades called attention to social divisions, at the very least articulating the split between privileged "in" groups of members who appeared in the column and "out" groups of strangers who stood to the side, watching or going about their business. Processions thus proclaimed fundamental social divisions, divisions that had the potential for causing trouble. Why then did some parades become actively divisive while others did not? The answer lies in the interplay between ceremony and local circumstance. It seems reasonable to conclude that as long as general agreement existed about the appropriateness of the ordering depicted in a procession, problems were unlikely to arise. Where the ordering became controversial, however, a procession could be provocative. The history of the Norwich procession illustrates this theme. Until the 1430s the march appears to have been relatively innocent, proclaiming the status of the fraternity's membership and perhaps expressing pride in the country's military success, but no more. Then in the 1430s and 1440s political events transformed the march into an actively divisive statement about the local order. During this period the procession may have helped to harden divisions between Wetherby and his supporters on one side and the opponents of his policies on the other. Only after the reform of the guild in 1452 and subsequent alterations to the procession that purged it of its partisan imagery did the march return to its more benign status.

By the sixteenth century elaborate religious processions, such as the one sponsored by the Guild of Saint George, were increasingly coming to be seen as too costly, too Roman, and too old-fashioned for a new age. They were accordingly being eliminated or, as in Norwich, scaled down in many communities. One scholar has even argued that it was this ceremonial decline, with its undeniable impact on urban social life, that truly marked the end of the medieval era in towns and cities.[53] It is, in fact, hard to imagine that any settlement could lose its traditional ceremonial reference points without seeing a corresponding decline in community feeling. At the same time it must be recognized that the social impact could not have been entirely negative. While some medieval spectacles, such as the pageants studied by Mervyn James, may have had a unifying effect on the community, the ceremony sponsored by many religious guilds would have had exactly the opposite influence. Guild ceremony carried the message that each organization stood as an independent social body, a miniature community within the larger urban community. This separatist theme helped to affirm and even deepen existing social fractures. The disappearance of religious guilds and their ceremony in the sixteenth century, then, may have actually contributed to urban unity as the ceremonial walls dividing townsfolk into discrete fraternal cells came down.

Notes

1. Mervyn James, "Ritual, Drama and Social Body in the Late Medieval English Town," *Past and Present* 98 (1983): 3–29. See also Charles Phythian-Adams, "Ceremony and the Citizen: The Communal Year at Coventry, 1450–1550," in *Crisis and Order in English Towns, 1500–1700,* ed. Peter Clark and Paul Slack (London: Routledge and Kegan Paul, 1972), pp. 57–85, esp. pp. 64–69; and George Huppert, *After the Black Death: A Social History of Early Modern Europe* (Bloomington: Indiana University Press, 1986), pp. 30–40.

2. John Bossy, *Christianity in the West, 1400–1700* (Oxford: Oxford University Press, 1985), pp. 42–45; and Emmanuel Le Roy Ladurie, *Carnival in Romans,* trans. Mary Feeney (New York: George Braziller, 1979). In the English city of Norwich a Carnival-style procession led to a riot in January 1443 (William Hudson and John Cottingham Tingey, eds., *The Records of the City of Norwich,* 2 vols. [Norwich, 1906–10], 1:lxxxviii–xcii, 340, 345–46, 351–52; Norman P. Tanner, *The Church in Late Medieval Norwich, 1370–1532* [Toronto: Pontifical Institute of Mediaeval Studies, 1984], pp. 148–51; Ben R. McRee, "Bonds of Community: Religious Gilds and Urban Society in Late Medieval England" [Ph.D. diss., Indiana University, 1987], pp. 266–73; and R. H. Hilton, *English and French Towns in Feudal Society: A Comparative Study* [Cambridge: Cambridge University Press, 1992], pp. 117–26).

3. Miri Rubin, *Corpus Christi: The Eucharist in Late Medieval Culture* (Cambridge: Cambridge University Press, 1991), pp. 261–63. My own work has turned up other examples. In Norwich a formal agreement set the order of march for the Corpus Christi procession during the middle of the fifteenth century, suggesting conflict over precedence (Hudson and Tingey, *Records of Norwich* 2: 230; note that the order of march to which Rubin refers, appearing on p. 312 of the same volume, dates from the sixteenth, not the fifteenth century, as both Tingey and Rubin state). More information survives concerning a conflict over the Corpus Christi procession in Shrewsbury between the guild of carpenters and the guild of fletchers, coopers, and bowers that ended with a particular compromise in 1461. The two organizations agreed that their members should be intermingled in the column, with the aldermen of the two guilds marching side by side, followed by pairs of

marchers, each pair consisting of one member from each guild, alternating the left and right sides of the column with each row (David Robert Walker, "An Urban Community in the Welsh Borderland: Shrewsbury in the Fifteenth Century" [Ph.D. diss., University College of Swansea, Wales, 1981], pp. 286–87).

4. Public Record Office, London (hereafter cited as PRO), C.47/40/127. Although the guild clearly included both men and women among its members, the induction ceremony referred only to men as initiates. The new member exchanged kisses with both male and female members. Female members were probably the wives of male members. The "gerland" given to the new member was identified only as "une gerland ensynge de la dite frat'nite." For a description of the more elaborate rites used by some Florentine confraternities, see Ronald F. E. Weissman, *Ritual Brotherhood in Renaissance Florence* (New York: Academic Press, 1982), pp. 90–98. On the importance of civic (not guild) oaths in German towns, see Bernd Moeller, *Imperial Cities and the Reformation,* trans. and ed. H. C. Erik Midelfort and Mark U. Edwards, Jr. (1972; Durham, N.C.: Labyrinth Press, 1982), p. 45.

5. E. Coornaert, "Les ghildes médiévales," *Revue historique* 199 (1948): 31–33, 233, traced the origin of medieval guilds back to early medieval feasting societies. He believed that this was the central activity of any guild.

6. The feast was held "propter amoris incrimentum" (PRO C.47/45/391a,b).

7. In the words of the return, "[I]n septimana Pasche faciendam in tali forma quod fraterna dileccio inter eos augeatur et turpiloquia repellantur set pax semper inter eos reformetur et vera dileccio retineatur" (PRO C.47/46/440a,b). The return is printed in Toulmin Smith, ed., *English Gilds: The Original Ordinances of More Than One Hundred Early English Gilds,* EETS, o.s., no. 40 (1870; reprint, London: Oxford University Press, 1963), pp. 216–17.

8. The requirement of a livery appeared far more frequently among urban than rural guilds. A royal survey of guilds conducted in 1388–89 shows, for example, that only 4 percent of rural guilds whose returns survive mention liveries, while 19 percent of the urban guilds did so (PRO C.47/38–46). For the purposes of this measure, an urban settlement was defined as one for which one thousand or more individuals paid the poll tax of 1377. The figures for both rural and urban liveries are likely to be underestimates because of government suspicion of liveried groups at the time of the survey.

9. The Guild of Saint Mary and All Saints in Norwich (PRO C.47/44/307). This was a craft guild made up of saddlers and spurriers. The guild was uneasy about its livery, fearing that the government would interpret it as a sign that the guild was a band of strong-armed troublemakers. The specification of the purpose of the livery was meant to allay government suspicion.

10. Mary Grace, ed., *Records of the Gild of Saint George in Norwich: 1389–1547,* Norfolk Record Society, vol. 9 (1937), pp. 34, 38.

11. The Corpus Christi Guild in Lincoln (PRO C.47/40/135). Although the garlands are not described, they may have been made of oak leaves, as were those worn by members of the Guild of Saint Peter in the village of Wiggenhall: PRO C.47/45/362.

12. PRO C.47/46/446.

13. PRO C.47/46/448. For the story of the Purification of Mary and the dedication of Christ, see Luke 2:22–35.

14. PRO C.47/40/109.

15. PRO C.47/43/279. The torches were to accompany the consecrated host whenever it was carried through the streets. This would have been done during the visitation of sick persons as well as during the Corpus Christi procession.

16. See, for example, the return of the Guild of the Holy Trinity in Cambridge (PRO C.47/38/10).

17. The Holy Trinity Guild, an organization of carpenters (PRO C.47/44/306).

18. This order of march is taken from Beverley's Guild of Saint Helen (PRO C.47/46/446). Most guilds included both male and female members in their processions,

although only the two Beverley guilds already cited specified the position of the sexes. Other guilds probably followed this arrangement, placing the men at the rear.

19. The English guild returns of 1389 are full of examples of guilds that instructed their members to go "bini et bini," or two by two. See, for example, the Guild of Saint Margaret in Lynn (PRO C.47/43/261). No other formations were mentioned in the returns. All of the advantages of marching in pairs would, of course, have applied even more strongly to a single file column. Such an arrangement would, however, have drawn too much attention to a guild's individual members, detracting from the impression of unity the association wanted to convey.

20. The Guild of the Purification and the Holy Trinity Guild (PRO C.47/38/9 and PRO C.47/38/11, respectively).

21. PRO C.47/43/264.

22. On the importance of order in a different sort of procession, see Edwin Muir's account of Venice's ducal procession in his *Civil Ritual in Renaissance Venice* (Princeton, N.J.: Princeton University Press, 1981), pp. 185–211.

23. No record of the exact route of the procession exists. The march certainly ended at the cathedral, but the starting point is less certain. Mary Grace, editor of a volume of guild records, claimed that the route was unknown (*Records of the Gild of Saint George*, p. 18). A single reference to the Church of Saint Peter Mancroft did occur, however, in the account for 1434–35. Four boys reportedly carried torches around the guild banner from the Church of Saint Peter to the cathedral in that year (Norwich Record Office [hereafter cited as NRO] 8/e).

24. Grace, *Records of the Gild of Saint George*, p. 34. The 1389 return did order members to be "at ye Chaundelers by pryme of ye day," suggesting that there may have been a simple procession of candle-bearing members in the fourteenth century (PRO C.47/43/296).

25. NRO 8/e. The amount paid was 36s. 6 1/2d. The refreshments were probably for the man playing the saint and his attendants.

26. The gown and armor appeared in two inventories of guild possessions, the first in 1441–42 and the second in 1469 (Grace, *Records of the Gild of Saint George*, pp. 30–32). The account roll of 1532–33 describes three angels carrying Saint George's helmet and armor (NRO 8/f).

27. Grace, *Records of the Gild of Saint George*, pp. 140–41, 146. The guild did, however, have large cash reserves, as evidenced by a loan of £150 to the city for new mills in 1531 and later loans for smaller amounts (pp. 132, 149, 152). During the 1530s and 1540s the guild's income ranged from a low of £16 1d. to a high of £30 14s. 9d. (NRO 8/f).

28. NRO 8/e for the 1478 items; NRO 8/f for 1521.

29. As will be related below, the city suffered the disfavor of the region's most powerful figures during the 1430s and 1440s. When relations improved after this stormy period, rulers proudly advertised the success of their fence-mending efforts by clothing the hero of the procession in the garb of important men from time to time.

30. These items appeared in the guild's two fifteenth-century inventories (Grace, *Records of the Gild of Saint George*, pp. 30–32).

31. A man-at-arms was traditionally accompanied by two armed valets like the henchmen of the Norwich procession. For a brief description of various types of late medieval soldiers, see Desmond Seward, *The Hundred Years' War: The English in France, 1337–1453* (New York: Atheneum, 1978), p. 52. In 1471 the guild bought "ij jakettes of fustean and Rede Bukram" for the henchmen (Grace, *Records of the Gild of Saint George*, p. 67). Cloth called "red sarsey" was purchased for them in 1492–93 (NRO 8/e). The crosses and roses appeared in a 1516–17 account (NRO 8/f). Grace claimed that the henchmen also wore yellow and tawny outfits in some years (Grace, *Records of the Gild of Saint George*, p. 17). For the jacks that Norwich supplied to the king, see William Hudson and John Cottingham Tingey, eds., *The Records of the City of Norwich*, 2 vols. (Norwich: Jarrold and Sons, 1906–10), 1:404.

32. An ordinance of 1552 stated that on the feast day of Saint George "there shall [be] neither George nor Margaret, but for pastime, the Dragon to come and shew himself, as in other years." See Benjamin Mackerell, "Account of the Company of Saint George in Norwich from Mackerell's History of Norwich, Ms. 1737," *Norfolk Archaeology* 3 (1852): 343. A woman playing the part of Saint Margaret had been added to the procession in the sixteenth century (see below). After the Reformation, Snap appeared annually with the newly elected mayor and civic officers in a procession ending at the cathedral. A group of men called "whifflers" used swords to clear a path through the crowd for Snap, while spectators tossed coins into his mouth. When the column arrived at the cathedral, the officials went inside for a religious service. Snap waited outside on the "dragon's stone" and then accompanied the officers back to the guildhall when the service was over. The language of the 1552 ordinance provides the best explanation of Snap's survival, explaining that it was "for pastime."

33. Folklorists have taken an interest in the Norwich dragon. The description of Snap and the mayor's procession is taken from four works: Edwin Christopher Cawte, *Ritual Animal Disguise* (Cambridge: Brewer, 1978), pp. 36–39; Enid Porter, *The Folklore of East Anglia* (London: Batsford, 1974), pp. 60–61, 63–65; Jacqueline Simpson, *British Dragons* (London: Batsford, 1980), pp. 95–97, 101–2; and Richard Lane, *Snap the Norwich Dragon* (Norwich: Trend Litho, 1976). None of these authors used the original documents. Simpson's description of the procession before 1548 contains a number of inaccuracies. Lane's pamphlet contains photographs of the surviving dragons and drawings of procession participants from the early modern period.

34. The dragon was mentioned regularly in the guild's accounts, usually because of repairs that had to be made to it. A 1471 ordinance mandated a battle, stating that "the George shall goo [in] procession and make a conflicte with the dragon" (Grace, *Records of the Gild of Saint George*, p. 67). The privilege of playing the part of the dragon may have been a form of relief for impoverished members; several of the men who played the dragon were also named as recipients of guild charity. The 1428–29 account said that a member played the dragon "cum gonne powder" (NRO 8/e). Accounts of other years did not mention the gunpowder, so it may have been a one-time experiment.

35. There is no evidence for the exact time or place of the combat. The 1538–39 account reported that the saint "pleyd atte Tomlond," the city's cathedral district (NRO 8/f). The open area in front of the church would have provided a more suitable arena for the battle than the narrow streets of the city.

36. The poor men who carried torches were mentioned frequently in the guild's account rolls (NRO 8/e and 8/f). See, for example, the account for 1430–31. Payment was 2d. for each of the poor men. Boys were mentioned in 1434–35, and both paupers and boys appeared in the 1461–62 account. The guild may have used paupers one day and boys the other.

37. Grace, *Records of the Gild of Saint George*, pp. 16, 30–32. Latten is an alloy that resembles brass.

38. Ibid., pp. 30–32, 45, 142. In 1428–29 the guild paid 13s. 10d. for three new banners (NRO 8/e).

39. NRO 8/e, 1428–29, 1431–32; and Smith, *English Gilds*, pp. 453–60.

40. A detailed account of the city's political troubles is beyond the scope of this chapter. Those interested in further information will find the following works useful: Hudson and Tingey, *Records of the City of Norwich* 1:xliv–ci; R. L. Storey, *The End of the House of Lancaster* (London: Barrie and Rockliff, 1966), pp. 217–25; Ben R. McRee, "Religious Gilds and Civic Disorder: The Case of Norwich in the Late Middle Ages," *Speculum* 67 (1992): pp. 69–97. I am currently working on a more detailed account of these events.

41. For the tale of Saint George, see Jacobus de Voragine, *The Golden Legend, or Lives of the Saints as Englished by William Caxton*, ed. F. S. Ellis, 7 vols. (London: Dent, 1900; reprint, New York: AMS Press, 1973), 3:125–34. *The Golden Legend* enjoyed tremendous popularity in England during the late fifteenth and early sixteenth century. Whether or not

this version of the tale was current during the 1430s and 1440s, I have not been able to ascertain.

42. In 1467–68 the guild paid for a lance for Saint George (NRO 8/e, 1567–68). References to the saint also appear in the 1468–69 and 1469–70 accounts.

43. Grace, *Records of the Gild of Saint George*, p. 67.

44. Ibid., p. 82.

45. Norwich Consistory Court, Jekkys, fols. 97–99.

46. NRO 8/e, 1467–68. The account did not record how many priests were included. The cost, however, was 2s., enough to pay six priests 4d. apiece, the rate used after 1473.

47. The ordinances are printed in Grace, *Records of the Gild of Saint George*, pp. 64, 69–70. The sheriffs included were those who had not been aldermen. In 1477–78 the guild hired twenty secular priests to appear in the procession and at the mass. The following year it used fourteen, specifically describing them as being dressed in red and white copes. This was how the priests sent by the aldermen were supposed to have been attired (NRO 8/e).

48. NRO 8/f. See the accounts for the following years: 1491–92, 1501–2, 1516–18, 1520–23.

49. Grace, *Records of the Gild of Saint George*, p. 17, said that Saint Margaret first appeared in 1532. She overlooked the reference in the 1530 account, however: NRO 8/f. For other references, see the accounts for the 1530s and 1540s.

50. De Voragine, *Golden Legend* 4:66–72.

51. NRO 17/b, 1452–1602, fols. 168–69.

52. NRO 8/g. As discussed above, the Company of St. George continued to use the dragon.

53. Charles Phythian-Adams, "Ceremony and the Citizen," pp. 79–80; also, by the same author, *Desolation of a City: Coventry and the Urban Crisis of the Late Middle Ages* (Cambridge: Cambridge University Press, 1979), pp. 275–78.

CHAPTER 9

The Politics of Welcome

Ceremonies and Constitutional Development in Later Medieval English Towns

Lorraine Attreed

T wo anecdotes culled from medieval urban archives stand as warning to modern interpreters that royal visits and civic spectacle are perceived in different ways by different societies. For those who study ceremonies and marvel how the strained, late medieval economy stretched to pay for them, the remarks of Henry VI are salutary. In 1449, in granting the city of York various privileges and monetary concessions, the king concluded that the borough's poverty was caused directly by the fact that "[it] has not been relieved for [a] long time by the king's presence, courts, councils or parliaments."[1] Rather than urging civic officials to avoid such costly outlay, Henry understood that the initial expense of hospitality and spectacle could reap long-term financial benefits, a relationship to be analyzed in this study. The second anecdote reminds us that such ceremonies awakened negative feelings as well as cordial and admiring anticipation. In February 1500, Henry VII and his family visited Nottingham and excited the interest of one of its citizens, John Hewick. Hewick later told his neighbors that he was pleased he had not only approached and welcomed the royal family but had exchanged pleasant words with Henry's queen, Elizabeth of York, renowned for her patient and sympathetic demeanor. The visit was not all that Hewick anticipated, however, for he thought he "shuld have spokyn more with hire seid Grace had [it] not bene for that strong whore the kynges moder," Lady Margaret Beaufort, whose termination of the conversation led Hewick to condemn her and the entire visit with "moche oder unsyttyng language."[2]

Despite the stress of the arrangements and the strain of the expenditure, towns regarded visits of royalty and nobility as valuable investments. In a society in which most towns were royal creations, dependent upon the English Crown for the liberties and privileges essential to self-government, it was vitally important to maintain good relations with the source of those privileges. During the fifteenth century the Wars of the Roses made favoring the wrong noble, much less the wrong king, a matter of treason. Bestowing appropriate ceremonial could be vital to town liberties. The monarch and the nobles who had influence with him could be persuaded to take an active interest in a town's welfare, or in contemporary terms exhibit "good lordship" toward it. This essay studies the way in which spectacle and welcoming ceremonies endeavored to establish peaceful relations with monarchs and nobles, to interest them in a town's welfare, and to convince them to assist its borough liberties.[3] A warm welcome, an entertaining pageant, and display and spectacle that praised the monarch and his dynasty were calculated to persuade him and his followers to act sympathetically toward urban officials' complaints and financial requests. For a late medieval English town, a successful visit was one that began with pageantry and expense and ended in the acquisition or reaffirmation of charters, privileges, liberties, and financial concessions so valuable in the strained, postplague economy.[4] Ceremonies and a valuable gift accompanied information about a town's problems and how the visitor could help, even if cries of civic poverty seemed at odds with the presents and pageants displayed.

On a deeper level, these ceremonies were also influential in the way medieval citizens and the officers who represented them understood themselves and wished the outside world to understand them. After all, kings and nobles were not the only individuals welcomed by pageants and processions. Newcomers to civic office were greeted with ceremonies that initiated them into positions of influence and responsibility in the town. Incumbents cherished the ceremonies that accompanied many of their public duties and enjoyed the deference all citizens were supposed to show them. Religious obligations and holy days such as the feast of Corpus Christi inspired elaborate arrangements meant to strengthen both the unity of urban subjects and the precious liberties that gave them a privileged identity in medieval society. Inclusion in such ceremonies, the position one physically took in them, and the garments one wore were all matters of the utmost importance to the individuals who participated and to the society that measured rank and precedence with exceptional care. Ceremonies bore witness to the prestige of the community, they expressed the power relationships of its members, and they permitted a visual reminder of the ordered and unified structure of all the parts of the urban social body. Such ceremonies and the participants who brought them to life celebrated a town's very right to exist and to act in the medieval world with dignity, power, and autonomy. Most important, they were occasions upon which members of the urban community could present and define themselves in relation to a broader society at large.[5]

For this study of the political and constitutional aspects of urban spectacle, the focus of inquiry must be carefully defined. Examples will be confined for the most part to four English provincial towns of varying sizes and states of legal development from the fourteenth through the early sixteenth centuries. York, almost two hundred miles north of London, was considered by contemporaries to be of cultural and economic importance, second only to the capital. Its hold on this status was precarious, however, as its postplague population of about 10,000 was in decline, and its golden age as a major textile city and international trading port ended around 1450.[6] By the early sixteenth century, Norwich had assumed York's position, with a population of over 12,000 and wealth based on profitable cloth manufacture and export. Cloth and continental contacts accounted for Exeter's prosperity as well, although the brightest period in this southwestern town's history lay in the future, later in the sixteenth century. As its population grew from under 2,500 residents in 1377 to around 8,000 by 1500, Exeter surpassed the development of Nottingham, a small town of little over 2,000 souls whose central location nevertheless gave it a strategic military and mercantile importance beyond its size.[7] All four towns are blessed with local and national records tracing their constitutional growth, and all four augmented their capacities for self-government by charters and grants resulting from contacts with the politically influential. The distance of the four from London made the prospects of visits and the spectacles they planned for them more special, more likely to be preserved in local records, and almost certain to provoke reflection on the nature and purpose of the welcoming ceremonies.

What civic spectacle really meant to medieval citizens can be seen most immediately in their comments about the ceremonies performed by and for town residents. Officials such as mayors and aldermen may have been elected in many towns by a small group of wealthy merchants, but they were ultimately responsible to the citizenry at large. Expected to be just, honorable, and industrious, urban officials represented the town to the rest of society and upheld its honor and dignity. To do so effectively, they had to convey an image of that honor and dignity by relying heavily on the use of powerful symbols. Language itself was an influential tool: the chief officers of London and York had acquired the title "lord mayor" by the early fifteenth century, and even small towns imposed heavy fines upon those who attacked by words or blows the personal or professional lives of the officers.[8] An entourage also conveyed power. The major officers of towns, copying the royal and noble households of the time, preferred to go about even mundane chores surrounded by servants and assistants in an informal procession.[9] The ceremonies that expressed urban unity nevertheless delineated the superior and inferior parts of that whole.

These displays gained added power when graced by a town's regalia, another expressive symbol of urban dignity and influence. Swords, maces, and caps of maintenance were often given by monarchs in recognition of a town's status, along with the right and obligation to bear these objects in processions. Sergeants and servants of the mayor and other officers bore the regalia in public ceremonies that emphasized the town's wealth and privilege.[10] So strong were these symbols, not every officer had the right to be in their company. Anxious to fill offices, York's city council nevertheless excused promising candidates if they did not have the wealth or dignity with which to grace their positions.[11] During Richard III's reign, York citizen Thomas Wrangwish was elected mayor while in Westminster attending Parliament. Upon his return, the council ordered the swordbearer with his sword and mace, and all the sergeants with their maces, to escort him into the city's geographic liberties with sword and mace before him. Wrangwish, sensitive that he had not yet taken his oath of office, accepted the escort but "he wald not let [the regalia] be born to fore [him] in so myche as he was unsworn" and thus undeserving of the honor.[12]

Wrangwish's reluctance illustrates the belief that ceremonies and spectacles could become meaningless if they were enacted too often or wasted upon men who did not take them seriously. City records contain numerous entries about the importance of public processions and displays: officers were reminded to attend, to bear the regalia, to quell arguments about precedence, and to remember that these ceremonies preserved ancient custom.[13] Although small in expense and modest in display compared with spectacles arranged for kings and princes, these ceremonies were no less expressive of urban identity. When the town's citizens performed them with respect, they increased the honor and dignity not just of the participants, but of the city itself. As the town records of Beverley expressed it, officers and citizens participated in the ceremonies "for the praise and honour of God and the Body of Christ, and for the peaceful union of the worthier and lesser commons of the town."[14] However impossible the last clause was to achieve, such unity remained an ideal and a guiding principle, allying closely a town population with the peacekeeping duties of royal power.

A town's ideas about its own identity and its relationship with the Crown were magnified when its officers were called upon to welcome individuals of national influence. More often than not, these visitors were nobles who held important positions in the royal government and were thought to have influence with the king. Whether they came from Westminster or were resident in the countryside surrounding a town, noble visitors expected and usually obtained from urban officials an impressive welcome. Town budgets that had difficulty paying the mayor's salary or repairing walls and streets had to be stretched to provide the kind of ceremony that could result one day in added privileges.[15] Patronage is probably too strong a term for the relationship that towns sought and nobles enjoyed. Contemporaries preferred "good lordship" and, moreover, chose not to define too narrowly the kinds of actions that could compose it. The men and women who received the gifts and enjoyed the ceremonies scarcely depended upon urban fish or stipends for survival, and they were not obliged to respond in any way.

Nevertheless, the gifts and the ceremonies contributed to their own high status, which they often chose to confirm further by advancing the town's interests at court. The relationship between borough and patron was a close one, and the enhancement of a town's liberties and privileges could affect the position and influence of the "good lords" so closely identified with it.

The city of Norwich provides a clear example of a constitutional change its officials wanted, and the means by which it identified and rewarded those people best able to achieve it. At the start of Richard II's reign, confirmation of the city's old charter prompted some of the citizens to petition the king for a new grant with broader financial and jurisdictional powers. Having seen a copy of London's charter, Norwich officials envied the capital's powers allowing its mayor and aldermen to change any custom or ordinance they found unsatisfactory. Norwich was still ruled by bailiffs and a council, having not yet acquired the status of incorporation that gave a town a legal identity with extended judicial rights.[16]

While Richard II saw no need to change or broaden Norwich's chartered rights, town officials were not discouraged. A local knight of the county, Sir Thomas Erpingham, took a special interest in the city and was rewarded accordingly. Not only was he consulted by its officials on judicial matters, but also he was willing to bring Norwich's needs to the king's attention. As a member of the retinues of both John of Gaunt and his son, Henry Bolingbroke, Erpingham could also inform the highest princes of the realm of the city's problems. Gaunt's own visits to Norwich received as much attention and spectacle as a royal progress, a fair comparison considering that the city's princely friend had claimed the Castilian throne, had been created duke of Aquitaine, and maintained a stable influence over his nephew the king.[17] When Richard remained immovable about a new charter, Gaunt advised the city to have patience, while his son promised them their grant if ever it were in his power to issue one. Gaunt died in 1399, but that year saw Henry take the crown as the first Lancastrian king, a move instrumentally assisted by Sir Thomas, who became Lord Chamberlain. City gifts to Erpingham began in earnest in 1399, taking the shape of the edible (oats, capons, and wine, often directed to Lady Erpingham as well) and the spendable ("twenty marks to the knight, for bearing his good word to the king, for the honor of the city and for his good counsel").[18] In 1404, Erpingham's influence gained for Norwich officials a significant charter that gave them a mayor, county status, incorporation, and increased financial and judicial independence.[19] As Henry IV's health and power waned, Sir Thomas and the city he advised allied closely with the Prince of Wales, and he may have convinced Norwich officials to extend their patronage to members of the future Henry V's circle. His modern biographer remarks that "[i]t was in adjusting East Anglian society to the change of dynasty that Sir Thomas Erpingham was instrumental," but the knight's shrewd relationship with a developing borough is to the credit of them both.[20]

Deciding how to welcome noble visitors and how much to spend on them produced stress on towns, but this was not the only challenge civic officials faced. Nobility, particularly those resident nearby, could be actively hostile to the town or could be involved in many of the violent and lawless actions that characterized English fifteenth-century government. Exeter and Norwich both suffered from the dilemma of having to welcome and mollify difficult visitors whose very presence in a city engendered danger. Although their experiences were not unique, other towns enjoyed more placid relationships with their noble patrons. Yet civic officials everywhere in medieval England tended to treat and cultivate influential guests similarly. All urban subjects lived in hope that the right amount of wine, fish, processions, and entertainments would convince a guest to take municipal interests to heart. But not all towns had the good fortune to be allied with an Erpingham or a Gaunt.

For Exeter, problems of "good lordship" centered on the earls of Devon and their Courtenay relatives. As the largest landholders in Devonshire and the most powerful lords of the West Country, an earl and his brothers or uncles received gifts and enjoyed ceremonies offered by civic officials almost every year throughout the fourteenth and fifteenth centuries. Strained relations began in the 1240s, when the family launched their campaign of annoyance against Exeter by obstructing the river it relied upon for trade and by holding a rival fair.[21] Although their incomes were small compared with other English lords, the Courtenay earls and their cousins wielded significant power in the west and made their friendship essential to a developing borough. During the 1380s, Edward, the third earl, headed commissions of array and of the peace in the county, and served as a justice of the peace, admiral of the western fleet, and lieutenant of the duchy of Lancaster's lands in Devonshire. He gave his livery to over a hundred men, some of them active in royal government, including county sheriffs, parliamentary representatives, and even some of Exeter's civic officials.[22]

But personal tragedy engendered municipal confusion by the mid–fifteenth century. Earl Edward's blindness during his later years, the early death of his son, the fourth earl (in 1422), and the long minority of his grandson Thomas weakened Courtenay influence in the county and encouraged the rise of a rival family, the Bonvilles. For Exeter, these changes provoked two related problems. The Courtenays and Bonvilles were bitter enemies whose competition for power in Devonshire flared occasionally into violence, making the choice of which one to patronize a difficult one for Exeter. Civic officials wisely chose to reward representatives of both families with an almost equal amount of gifts, deference, and welcoming ceremonies (the earl retained a slight edge). They did not wait for these local patrons to visit the city but occasionally rode out to their estates in ceremonial procession to ask their advice on municipal matters and to try to inspire in both families a sense of responsibility toward Exeter.

Nowhere was the city's success better seen than in the role Courtenay and Bonville played in Exeter's dispute over territorial jurisdiction with the cathedral party. The bishop of Exeter and his dean and chapter claimed legal right to the lands surrounding the cathedral. Civic officials argued that they could best keep the king's peace within the city and consolidate municipal power only if they had control over all the lands within its walls. The dispute began in the thirteenth century, but the 1440s witnessed such an intensification of suits and countersuits that both sides felt it imperative to settle the matter once and for all. After many bitter accusations were exchanged, the city and the cathedral parties agreed to submit the case to arbitration. Chosen to preside and to deliver a final decision were the Courtenay earl of Devon and Sir William Bonville, both considered to be men of influence, local knowledge, and the power needed to impose a verdict and require the two sides to live up to it. Both parties invested healthy sums of money in patronizing the two men, in addition to many of the lawyers and justices involved in the case. The decision the arbitrators made tended to favor the cathedral party, for they decided that the church had jurisdiction in its own precinct. However, many of the rights the bishop claimed were denied him, and it was made clear that tenants of the cathedral were not exempt from the judicial and financial responsibilities all other citizens owed the town. The gifts and special welcomes extended to Courtenay and Bonville over many years did not assure a biased verdict in favor of the city, but the patronage no doubt prevented civic officials from losing more than they did.[23]

By the 1450s, however, no amount of gifts or spectacle could protect Exeter from the lawlessness introduced into the West Country by the Courtenay-Bonville rivalry. The earl's alliance with Richard, duke of York, gave Courtenay added confidence to pursue local enemies such as Sir William, his tenants, and his retainers, some of whom were Exeter citizens. In 1454, the earl's henchmen led a group of armed men into the city, seized the gates, and attacked the mayor and citizens for two days. The violence worsened the next year when the earl's son and over a hundred of his tenants attacked the home of Exeter recorder and Bonville counselor Nicholas Radford, murdered him in cold blood, then occupied the city for the entire autumn. The earl saved his personal enmity for Bonville himself, defeating the knight in a brief battle outside of the city in mid-December. Although Courtenay's actions so shocked the realm that even his ally York turned against him, Exeter had to show more prudence. When the earl returned in victory that night, the city arranged for an elaborate celebration complete with blazing torches and wine for all the Courtenay combatants. Once more, ceremony and spectacle were extended by civic officials with powers of foresight focused solely on the possibility of municipal gains and survival.[24] The gamble paid off, for the city remained safe from further attack. Thereafter, for the rest of the fifteenth century, Exeter dedicated gifts and welcomes to a wider variety of nobles loyal to the Yorkist and Tudor monarchs.[25]

As difficult as it might be to believe, Norwich had an even worse time with vicious local nobles more skilled at harming than helping the city. William de la Pole, earl of Suffolk, was the most important courtier in the vicinity, but civic officials feared the malign influence he and his lawless retainers had on borough and shire alike. The gifts he received and the ceremonies he enjoyed perhaps should be seen as a kind of protection money offered to organized crime bosses. Until his fall from public power and execution in 1450, Suffolk interfered with city elections, encouraged Norwich's ecclesiastical rivals to sue the city over disputed jurisdictions, and permitted his retainers to wreak havoc in city streets.[26] A favorite of Henry VI, Suffolk had little to fear from the royal court. Civic officials felt fortunate when Suffolk ignored Norwich, although occasionally they would have appreciated his attention had he used it beneficently to extend their municipal jurisdiction and give them the additional chartered rights they craved.[27]

The dynastic upheaval we call, however inaccurately, the Wars of the Roses, presented unique problems for towns and the welcomes they were expected to extend.[28] On Palm Sunday 1461, Edward of York's forces defeated at Towton an impressive and numerically superior royal Lancastrian army, prompting Henry VI to flee to Scottish exile. If the city of York, only twelve miles away, had any doubts about how to receive the young victor, they were assuaged by the intercession of the Yorkist Lords Montagu and Berners. The noblemen gained from Edward a pardon for the city's previous loyalty to the Lancastrians and directed civic officials to accept the new situation by greeting Edward "with great solemnity and processions."[29] The ceremonies served as a background for Edward's personal mission at York, namely the removal of his father's severed head from Micklegate Bar, on which it had been placed by the victorious Lancastrians after the battle of Wakefield three months earlier.[30] York's welcome and Edward's filial gesture confirmed the installation of a new dynasty as strongly as any of the coronation ceremonies held months later in London.

A decade later, York faced an even more difficult decision. Upon his return from exile on the continent in 1471, Edward passed by York on his way to ending the readeption of Henry VI. The city's recorder met him three miles outside of town and advised him that he was not welcome. Edward, whose possession of the throne was a matter of debate at this moment, was finally permitted to rest in the city one night, provided he left all his troops outside the walls.[31] Welcoming ceremonies were not extended to this figure of dubious rank, but neither did the city actively reject him in case the wheel of fortune rotated him to power once more. As it happened, Edward regained the throne, and York survived to honor him with spectacle and illuminations on his 1478 visit.[32] Not until the accession of Henry VII did York or any other town face such a dilemma about the kind of welcome a contender for the throne deserved.

York also provides us with the most positive examples of the interaction between spectacle and patronage. The confidence with which its civic officers petitioned local noble Richard, duke of Gloucester, in the 1470s was exceeded only by their delighted anticipation when the duke became King Richard III in 1483. Although far from universally liked by the citizens, Richard took the kind of active, personal interest in York's fortunes that made its significant investment in gifts and greetings worthwhile.

Records of Richard's visits to York before 1475 are lost, but the ones that remain inform us of a city willing to invest in spectacle to influence a leading nobleman.[33] On his first recorded visit in 1476, Richard was met by all the civic officials in their ceremonial gowns. Accompanied by local noble Henry Percy, earl of Northumberland, and an armed force of five thousand men, Gloucester delivered a royal proclamation against unlawful violence.[34] Previous visits had earned him gifts of wine; the links having been established, York's officials wasted no time in providing Richard with opportunities to display his interest in civic welfare. Frequent letters advised the duke of river blockages, criminal officials, civic poverty, and the problems encountered in mustering soldiers for the Scottish campaigns Richard personally led.[35] The duke's visits were treated as state occasions, which officials and guild members attended in their best array or risked bearing a monetary fine. Wine, bread, fish, and game were showered upon Richard and his wife, particularly after he had persuaded the king not to suspend York's liberties following election riots. Responding with positive action to nearly every civic request, Richard earned from York on each visit "a lawde and a thank of his greit labours, gude and benevolent lordship don tofore tyme for the honour and common wele of this cite."[36] In the years before 1483, Gloucester and his duchess spent most of their time at her late father's castle at Middleham, about forty miles from York. They occasionally received delegations from the city, and were members of York's Corpus Christi Guild.[37]

York remained on Richard's mind even during the hectic weeks of his usurpation of the throne in the spring of 1483. Preoccupying the civic officials at that time was the matter of their declining prosperity. They proposed to Richard that he arrange for a decrease in their £160 fee farm, an annual sum the city paid the Crown in recognition of its liberties and autonomy. Tolls levied on visiting merchants composed a portion of the farm, and the city wished to waive the charges in order to encourage trade. In June 1483, Richard wrote to York that he had no time to consider such a matter at the moment, but the city could oblige him by sending troops to defend their good lord against the threats of the widowed queen and her adherents.[38] The soldiers who responded to the call played a considerable role in transforming Duke Richard into King Richard, providing him with the force necessary to make his claim to the throne stick. The city's hopes for maintaining its relationship with him can best be seen in the ceremonial procession made to Middleham shortly after his coronation, to deliver to the king's small son an impressive array of wine and foodstuffs.[39]

The royal progress Richard and his queen embarked upon included York as a significant stop. The spectacle planned for their visit was to be the culmination of the couple's relationship with the city. Arrangements to meet the royal party in proper array began weeks before the king's secretary worriedly addressed a letter to the officials. John Kendal wrote that although he was certain they had everything in hand, he hoped York, like the other towns on the route, would greet the couple with pageants and speeches and that the streets would be hung with cloths and tapestries to impress the nobles from the south who were in the entourage. Further to inspire them to new heights of celebration, Kendal reminded the officials of the king's gratitude to York and of how he planned to grant them privileges greater than any monarch ever had before.[40]

York's elaborate arrangements fulfilled the highest expectations. The "sights" or entertainments planned for the visit cost the city chamberlains so much money, their numbers had to be increased in order to bear the charges.[41] These displays were erected at the gate by which Richard entered the city and on major streets as he made his way on horseback through York. The royal procession trod the same path as the city's annual Corpus Christi play cycle. This literally moving performance wound through the streets on wagons and by the participation of so many disparate groups of citizens represented the social unity and concord to be derived from the veneration of the Eucharist.[42] Although he had missed their performance three months earlier, Richard had timed his visit to a day particularly hallowed within the city. He arrived on 29 August, the feast of the Decollation of John the Baptist, a symbol the citizens understood to be analogous to the Body of Christ worshiped so visibly by their leading guild and the ceremonies it sponsored.[43]

Religious symbolism mounted as high as the costs of all this spectacle. Most of the officials contributed generously to the gifts of money presented to the king and queen, while "the most honest men of every parish" underwrote the performance of the Creed Play for the royal entourage.[44] The mayor and council members accompanied King Richard to the performance, while the dean and chapter viewed the procession of scenes from the Minster gates. Neither as long nor as elaborate as the Corpus Christi cycle, the performance was still impressive, with its use of pageant wagons to bear the costumed actors and sets in twelve scenes enacting the major points of the Creed.[45] The text of this play does not survive, but it was probably similar in form to the Corpus Christi cycle. Both were presented by the city guild of that name, with the purpose of "educating the layman in the basic principles of his faith," although the Creed Play seems to have been regarded as the special property of the citizens, to be performed for their particular honor and benefit when they deemed it appropriate, such as for royal visits.[46]

But even this was not the highlight of the royal visit. Richard planned to honor the city even more by holding in it his son's investiture as Prince of Wales, a move calculated to consolidate support for his line.[47] The investiture ceremony was so lavish, one chronicler believed the royal couple had undergone a second coronation. On 8 September, the feast of the Nativity of the Blessed Virgin Mary, the king and queen donned their crowns and processed through the streets to the Minster with their young son. After mass, the royal family presided over a sumptuous feast in the archbishop's palace, a four-hour event enjoyed by the Minster staff, five bishops, a score of nobles, and the Castilian ambassador.[48]

Unlike other host cities, whose spectacles and welcomes received no concrete rewards, York did not have to wait long for Richard to show his gratitude. On 17 September, the king gathered the civic officials together in the Minster's chapter house and praised them for the generous musters they had provided for recent Scottish campaigns and for his own accession. For these acts, and because of "the dekey and the grete povert[y] of the said cite, of hys most speciall good grace, withowt ony petecion of askyng of any thyng by the said mair or of ony odyr," Richard released all toll charges paid by nonresident merchants in order to promote increased trade in the city. Because that deprived the city of about £58 of revenue each year, Richard granted York an annuity of £40 and gave the mayor £18 5s. per annum for the honor of being his chief sergeant-at-arms.[49] The civic officials were rightfully jubilant; their good lord and former neighbor had not only reached a position in which he could help his friends, but he had not forgotten them or their specific requests. The cost of dazzling the king with spectacles had produced an appropriate response that would bolster their faltering economy. Only after the king had left town did civic officials begin to wonder, with the tolls waived, and tolls having composed part of the city's £160 fee farm, would they still have to pay the entire farm, or a part of it, or none of it at all? Three aldermen were sent to the king's next resting place on his progress, but they returned with no answers.[50] Doubt turned to frustration when the officials discovered the bureaucracy of the central administration did not or would not act upon the king's grant. The king's generous gift was to provide the city of York with over fifty years of aggravation with the royal Exchequer, as neither Richard nor the Tudor kings could unravel the problem of how much the city actually owed the Crown.[51]

Despite the confusion, the city remained loyal to Richard throughout his short reign, a fidelity that caused its officials distress upon the accession of Henry Tudor in 1485. No sooner had the city received word that Richard had been killed in battle, than its officials wrote to Henry Percy, earl of Northumberland, expressing the wish that he be their new "good lord" and that he advise them how to act "at this woofull season."[52] As a neighboring lord, Percy was a reasonable choice, but he was at that moment under Tudor's arrest, and he never fully gained the new king's trust. Before he could reply with advice, York's officials were forced to cope with Tudor's messenger, who demanded admittance to the city. Far from sending out a welcoming party in ceremonial gowns, much less planning processions and greetings, the city could not even guarantee the messenger's safety in a borough still recalling "the moost famous prince of blissed memory King Richard late decesid."[53] Although Henry assured the city that its privileges were secure, he only earned the officials' annoyance by spending the first year of his reign persuading them to accept his candidates for town offices such as recorder (legal adviser) and swordbearer. Not only did they refuse his suggestions, arguing that they had the chartered right to choose their own officers, but they immediately created "ancient customs" denying office to any man who sought the king's help and promptly elected men who had loyally served Richard III.[54] York was playing a dangerous game with an unforgiving king. But once more ceremony and spectacle would play a part in reconciling a monarch to his urban subjects, who continued to seek expansion of their borough rights.

If Henry Tudor could not afford to be forgiving, it was because of the great uneasiness with which he held the crown in the early years of his reign. A young man of twenty-eight upon his accession, Henry had spent half his life in Breton exile, dependent upon the charity and decisions of others; not the best training ground for a king. Throughout the remaining years of the fifteenth century, he faced threats and rebellions, often organized by surviving Yorkist sympathizers and the pretenders they supported.[55] Although it is an oversimplification to suggest that Henry spent most of his reign searching for ways to bolster his claim to power, he never ignored the means by which he could assert his authority. Given the symbolic power of ceremony and display, it should not surprise us to find that spectacle proved to be a strikingly visual and public way to strengthen his position.

Within a few days of the battle at Bosworth, Henry began to emphasize by ceremonial means the justice of his victory and his claim to the throne. In particular, he presented himself as the most recent fulfillment of a long line of heroes from the distant, almost entirely unrecorded, past of Britain. He stressed his Welsh descent and bore the red dragon device and heraldic arms of Cadwallader, the last British king who had prophesied his race's ultimate triumph over the Saxon (English) invaders. Although Edward I and Edward IV before him also claimed British roots, Henry dedicated far more energy in publicizing his ancestry, especially his claimed descent from King Arthur. The first Tudor not only quartered his arms with those of Arthur but rushed his pregnant queen to Winchester Castle, ancient seat of British kings, for the birth of their first child, appropriately named Arthur.[56] So strongly associated was the British monarch with the entire regime that Arthurian symbolism far outlasted the frail prince destined to predecease his father.[57] Henry's use of British myth was tremendously important in its influence on the concept and writing of history under the Tudors. Historians such as Polydore Vergil, John Leland, William Camden, and Edward Hall all interpreted the Middle Ages and the period we know as the Wars of the Roses in ways complementary to Henry's vision of himself as savior of a battered nation.[58] The resulting histories continue to influence our view of the medieval world even today, but for the multitudes who never read the literature, the public acts of spectacle and ceremony made identical points.

The first year of Henry VII's reign was a critical one of establishment and justification. Assisted by joyous events such as his marriage to Yorkist Princess Elizabeth and the birth of their son nine months later, Henry was able to face enemies and doubters with evidence that Divine Providence was on his side. Unlike previous kings, he did not embark upon a royal progress through his kingdom immediately after the coronation. An epidemic of the sweating sickness, the November parliament, the arrangements for his January wedding, and his wife's pregnancy produced sufficient grounds for delay, but what was really keeping Henry at home was rumor of armed discontent in the realm and the survival of many Yorkist supporters. Henry did not begin to plan a progress in earnest until he received word of the death of York's recorder, Miles Metcalf, a supporter of Richard III considered so dangerous he had been especially exempted from the general pardon granted the late king's other supporters.[59]

Henry set off on his first royal progress early in March 1486. He received enthusiastic welcomes in Waltham and Cambridge, and celebrated Easter in Lincoln by washing the feet of twenty-nine poor men and distributing alms. Undeterred by news that Yorkist supporters were gathering in the north at Richard's Middleham Castle, Henry nevertheless added several thousand men to his escort from the retinues of his uncle and the earl of Northumberland and proceeded on to York. The northern capital had prepared for the visit since mid-March, writing to the archbishop of York for advice on how to receive the king and hiring the talents of a local priest to devise the spectacle.[60] Civic officials had been more confident of their own abilities to plan a welcome when their "good lord" Richard was king and had taken no occasion in 1483 to wonder in the pages of their council records whether the king would think they were as glad of his visit as the arrivals of previous monarchs.[61] The poverty of the city, so the civic officials claimed, was such that a monetary gift could not be given; Henry was to be offered bread, wine, and oxen and greeted by the ceremonially gowned officials at the southern limit of York's franchises. This part of the welcome was changed closer to the time of arrival, when it was determined that Henry had better be shown greater honor by twice the usual number of horsemen and all of the officials, greeting him five miles away from York instead of two. Nothing was left to chance: even the children who formed part of the welcoming committee were prompted to cry "King Henry" on cue. The only sign of the city's former self-confidence is found in its response to a letter from Lord Clifford, who hoped the officials would entertain Henry VII well and be as deserving of Clifford's goodwill as their predecessors had been of his ancestors' favor. The officials wrote back that they consulted their records of previous visits for advice, and in those records they could find no evidence at all of the Clifford family's association with York.[62] Nevertheless, the city had reason to be nervous about the visit, not least because the Yorkist rebels gathering to the west might expect Richard III's special borough to assist them. The officials put aside all hopes that the welcome and spectacle planned would gain them additional privileges and prayed instead that they would assure its mere survival.

Here we enter the realm of theory, for York's records of the ceremonies were all written in the future tense, delineating what was supposed to happen but failing to comment at all on how the spectacle really turned out. As in the spectacles performed at Hereford and Bristol, and planned but not given at Worcester, York's ceremonies intended to stress Henry's suitability for the throne. The characters chosen to perform, and the speeches they made, argued that Henry was king by hereditary right, divine election, providential victory in battle, personal virtue, and popular assent. At York, Henry was to be greeted just inside the first gate by a pageant depicting heaven. Under the celestial roof was planned a garden of trees and flowers, the blooms bowing down to a red rose (symbolizing Henry and his Lancastrian ancestry) and a white rose (the badge of the house of York and symbolic of the queen). The two flowers would then be united, as Henry and Elizabeth had been in marriage, and covered with a crown that descended from heaven. The happy union brought life into the world, as the garden set was then filled with people and turned into the city of York itself. Ebrauk, the legendary founder of York, then came on stage to greet the king and give him the keys of the city, his title, and his crown. He recited a poem, which not only flattered Henry but reminded him to be compassionate to the city that derived so much joy from his visit. Henry was then to pass through the streets hung solidly with cloth and tapestries. If the weather were fair that day, the city planned to run devices raining rose water and candy hailstones upon the crowd. Closer to the center of the city, Henry would encounter the heart of the spectacle, a royal throne bearing six kings, specifically the monarchs who had shared his name. The six Henrys were directed to give a scepter to the actor playing King Solomon, who offered it to Tudor as a symbol of wisdom and justice. Solomon's speech revealed that the six previous Henrys had been looking forward to the seventh of their name, and all of them were fully approving of what he had done since the start of his reign. They urged him to keep up the good work, and concluded with a stanza requesting the king to show the city a little of his "bountevous Benevolence."[63] In front of the Guildhall, the center of York's civic government, was planned a show starring the character of King David accompanied by citizens in the Tudor colors green and white. David compared Henry favorably to Charlemagne, gave him a sword of victory, and reminded the king that York had always been loyal to his family and had often suffered for it. After a shower of fake snow, the royal entourage would have come to the last pageant, presided over by the figure of the Virgin Mary. Her speech was York's most self-serving, telling Henry outright that Christ believed the city to be trustworthy and that she would always intercede on the king's behalf for Christ's grace.

York's pageants craftily ignored the city's relationship with Richard III and other Yorkists and concentrated instead on those elements of antiquity and religion that flattered both the town and the monarch. If the speeches and performances went off as planned, Henry would have had every reason to believe that York delighted in his rule, rejoiced in his marriage, recognized the role Divine Providence had played in his accession, and looked forward to continuing a long and happy relationship with the Lancastrian-Tudor dynasty. How close the reality conformed to the plan is something we will never know, but it is true that unlike Richard, Henry gave the city no grants or privileges after the visit.

Henry left York with the good news that the Middleham rebels had dispersed, but he was forced to head for another center of treason in Worcester.[64] This town had also prepared pageants and displays but never performed them, perhaps because of the threat of Yorkist insurrection. The Worcester pageant's leading character was Henry VI, already in possession of a saintly reputation and believed to have possessed mystic powers of prophecy bestowed by God. Thus the pageant king would have spoken with particular power when he praised his descendant Henry Tudor and urged him to forgive Worcester its trespasses.[65] Another character was then to have coyly mistaken Henry for Noah and other biblical individuals, for Jason, Julius Caesar, Scipio, and King Arthur, which would have led to a confirmation of Henry as Cadwallader's lineal descendant.

From Worcester, Henry traveled to Hereford, whose pageants introduced the characters of Saint George, King Ethelbert of East Anglia (whose relics were in the town's cathedral), and the Virgin Mary. At Gloucester, Henry had some respite from pageants, but Bristol performed five of them, presided over by the figure of the mythical British king Brennius, said to be Bristol's founder. Some stanzas about the city's decline from greatness had the desired effect: later in the visit, Henry questioned the civic officials about their poverty and urged them to develop their shipping. His advice was not accompanied by any monetary grant, but his words seemed to cheer them up, for the mayor remarked that "they harde not this hundred yeres of noo king so good a comfort." Henry left for London on 26 May and arrived at Westminster Abbey just two months after his departure.[66]

Henry's second visit to York was recorded after the fact, so we have a more accurate idea of what actually occurred. This visit followed closely upon the king's victory over pretender Lambert Simnel and the Yorkist adherents who prompted him.[67] Set for late July and early August 1487, the spectacles included performances of the Corpus Christi plays, postponed from earlier in the summer by royal command. These joyous ceremonies were far outnumbered, at least in the records, by public proclamations to keep the peace, directives for the fair pricing of food, and warnings to maintain the watch against invaders. The lineage themes of the first visit were abandoned in favor of a stress on law and order, culminating in the vivid spectacle of the public beheading of a citizen who had admitted some of the king's rebels through York's gates. The visit concluded with the knighting of the lord mayor and an alderman for their services against the rebels in June. This unsurpassed boon to two leading governors of the city increased the honor of York but did not begin to solve some of its basic problems. During this visit, as at other times, the civic officials begged for a clarification of their financial difficulties, but to no avail.[68]

There is no surviving evidence that the court dictated the content of the urban pageants, but it is interesting to observe how rapidly civic officials caught on to the more flattering elements of royal propaganda. Although it was natural for them to include characterizations of their ancient, often mythical founders, in doing so they had tapped into a source of vital importance to the first Tudor. That so many of these founders were of British descent only reinforced Henry's own claims of descent from Cadwallader and Arthur and gave the towns a unique relationship with the Tudor dynasty. On the other hand, the rose symbols were new elements in the royal propaganda and still in flux: the hybrid we recognize as the Tudor rose slowly developed out of the images of white and red roses, often depicted as growing from the same plant.[69] At first only a symbol of Henry's marriage to the heiress of York, the rose came to be associated with the entire dynasty and the success it had had in ending internecine strife. York's use of the flower as a centerpiece of a pageant confirmed the importance and popularity of the symbol. Likewise, the town of Worcester was particularly shrewd in discerning the important role Henry VI played in the Tudor worldview. Often called Henry VII's uncle, the sixth Henry was actually a half-cousin of the first Tudor, and was considered to be a saint and mourned as a victim of Yorkist ambition. For years following the Worcester pageant, court poets depicted Henry VI as spokesman for the convocation of saints in heaven, a visionary who prophesied that young Tudor would take up the crown and bring peace to England.[70]

Few of the pageants gained more for their towns than the kind of supportive advice Henry freely gave to Bristol. In York's case, Henry turned a deaf ear to pleas of poverty, fee farm difficulties, and tradition of self-government, and after returning to Westminster he continued to promote his own candidates for local office.[71] The fairs, swords, and charters acquired after other royal visits and spectacles are nowhere in evidence in the first Tudor's progress.[72] But most civic officials probably breathed a sigh of relief that Henry at least had not taken retaliatory action against them. They may have been unaware of the most important results of Henry's first visits, namely the influence their pageants and spectacles had upon the formation of royal propaganda and the concept of the divinely blessed Tudor dynasty. Their acceptance of symbols and themes that Henry was just trying out confirmed their popular and persuasive power and helped him overcome his shaky start in politics.

This brief overview of the role of spectacle in urban development reveals one aspect of the reciprocal nature of town relations with the royal government. Most English towns, being royal creations, could not survive or mature without the cooperation of the monarch and the privileges of self-government only he could grant. When the king, or a noble close to him, visited a town, civic officials spared no expense in expressing their loyalty and delight by devising spectacles and pageants of welcome. Even if no gift or grant was immediately forthcoming after a visit, a town usually relied upon such ceremonies to give it a good reputation with national leaders and to make clear the social unity and autonomy of the borough. But it is also true that the monarch needed alliances with his urban subjects and depended heavily upon the general tone their loyal, unified expressions set. Throughout the Middle Ages, kings had delegated many responsibilities to towns, the chief one being the need to uphold the king's peace among urban subjects. For all their financial problems, towns remained important sources of wealth, power, and culture in medieval society, and to have them on one's side gave a king significant influence. Richard III's urgent need for support during his short reign explains much of his generosity to York after his accession.

Henry VII survived early threats to his rule largely because of his own confident demeanor, supported in great part by royal propaganda and the towns like York, which accepted its tenets and broadcast its claims. The welcoming spectacles that town leaders devised and national leaders watched bound all of them together in a sharing of status, honor, and unity, which with any luck would last longer than the show.

Notes

1. *Calendar of Patent Rolls, 1446–52* (London: His Majesty's Stationery Office, 1910), p. 221; and Francis Drake, *Eboracum* (London: Bowyer, 1736), p. 105.

2. William Henry Stevenson, ed., *Records of the Borough of Nottingham*, 5 vols. (London: Bernard Quaritch, 1882–1900), 3:300–301. For such frankness, Hewick was accused of treason by one of the neighbors who heard the report and who repeated his sentiments to the mayor and common council.

3. It should be noted early on that the focus of this study is not the Corpus Christi cycle of plays dramatized by many of the towns mentioned here. The plays will be referred to only when their performance coincided with a royal or noble visit. The feast and its processions constitute an important element in urban spectacle and deserve more specialized treatment than can or should be given in an essay about the legal and constitutional results of urban welcoming ceremonies.

4. For the role of towns in the late medieval economy, see R. B. Dobson, "Urban Decline in Late Medieval England," *Transactions of the Royal Historical Society*, 5th ser., 27 (1977 for 1976): 1–22; and David Palliser, "A Crisis in English Towns? The Case of York, 1460–1640," *Northern History* 14 (1978): 108–25. The visiting papal legate received a ceremonious welcome from the civic officials of York in 1486, after which he promised them he would "report ther demenaunce and humanitee in this partie unto the kinges highnesse, that his grace shuld be rather inclined graciously to here there peticions to be ministred unto hyme herafter" (Lorraine Attreed, ed., *York House Books, 1461–1490* [London and Gloucester: Alan Sutton, 1991], pp. 470–71).

5. Mervyn James, "Ritual, Drama, and Social Body in the Late Medieval English Town," *Past and Present* 98 (1983): 12.

6. David Palliser, "Richard III and York," in *Richard III and the North*, ed. Rosemary Horrox (Hull: University of Hull Centre for Regional and Local History, 1986), p. 52; and J. N. Bartlett, "The Expansion and Decline of York in the Later Middle Ages," *Economic History Review*, 2d ser., 15 (1962–63): 423–37, and passim.

7. Charles Phythian-Adams, *Desolation of a City: Coventry and the Urban Crisis of the Late Middle Ages* (Cambridge: Cambridge University Press, 1979), p. 12; W. G. Hoskins, "English Provincial Towns in the Early Sixteenth Century," *Transactions of the Royal Historical Society*, 5th ser., 6 (1956): 72; and Josiah Cox Russell, *British Medieval Population* (Albuquerque: University of New Mexico Press, 1948), p. 142.

8. F. B. Bickley, ed., *The Little Red Book of Bristol*, 2 vols. (Bristol: Hemmons, 1900–1901), 1:149–53; Maud Sellers, ed., *York Memorandum Book*, 2 vols., Surtees Society, vols. 120, 126 (Durham, England: Andrews and Co. for the Society, 1912, 1914), 2:viii; Attreed, *York House Books*, pp. 122–23, 305, 511 (£10 fine for striking any of the officials); and Susan Reynolds, *An Introduction to the History of English Medieval Towns* (Oxford: Oxford University Press, 1977), pp. 179–80. York's mayor received the title from Richard II after his 1387 visit (J. H. Harvey, "Richard II and York," in *The Reign of Richard II: Essays in Honour of May McKisack*, ed. F. R. H. Du Boulay and Caroline Barron [London: Athlone Press of the University of London, 1971], p. 205).

9. For example, beating the bounds of a city's liberties (that is, defining its physical limits) required the mayor to be accompanied by council members and representatives

from the craft guilds, not just to act as witnesses but to confirm the dignity in which the officers were held (Attreed, *York House Books,* pp. 281, 355–56).

10. Exeter acquired four maces as early as 1385, but did not achieve the right to a sword and cap until Henry VII's visit in 1497 (Devon Record Office [hereafter cited as DRO], Receivers' Rolls, 9–10 Richard II, 13–14 Henry VII; DRO, Book 51, fol. 329v; and H. Lloyd Parry, "The Exeter Swords and Hat of Maintenance," *Transactions of the Devonshire Association* [hereafter cited as *TDA*] 64 [1932]: 421–28). In 1404, Henry IV gave Norwich the right to have both a mayor and a sword to be borne before him in procession (William Hudson and John Tingey, eds., *The Records of the City of Norwich,* 2 vols. [Norwich and London: Jarrold and Sons, 1906–10], 1:lxi, 32, 77, 103; Norwich and Norfolk Record Office [hereafter cited as NNRO], 7-c, Treasurers' Rolls, 8–9, 9–10, 11–12 Henry IV).

11. Attreed, *York House Books,* pp. 137, 573–74.

12. Attreed, *York House Books,* pp. 301–2, 426.

13. Attreed, *York House Books,* pp. 4–5, 40, 135–36, 257, 388.

14. A. F. Leach, ed., *Beverley Town Documents,* Selden Society 14 (London: Selden Society, 1900), p. 34.

15. See James, "Ritual, Drama, and Social Body," p. 13 n. 39, for sixteenth-century references to increased trade and prosperity resultant upon such ceremonies and the strangers who came to see them.

16. For a full definition and an analysis of why a charter of incorporation meant more at the end of the Middle Ages, see Reynolds, *An Introduction,* pp. 113–14. The charters issued during Richard II's reign are edited in Hudson and Tingey, *Records of the City of Norwich* 1:27–30.

17. NNRO, 18-a, Chamberlains' Account Book, 1384–1448, fols. 21v–22, 31v–32v; Francis Blomefield, *A Topographical History of the County of Norfolk,* 2nd ed., 11 vols. (London: William Miller, 1805–10), 3:113; James Thompson, *An Essay in English Municipal History* (London: Longman, Green, 1867), p. 131; *History of the City and County of Norwich, from the Earliest Accounts to the Present Times* (Norwich: John Crouse, 1768), p. 99; and Roger Virgoe, "The Crown and Local Government: East Anglia under Richard II," in *The Reign of Richard II,* ed. Du Boulay and Barron, p. 226. Civic officials and leading citizens were required to provide Gaunt with a mounted escort into town, wearing livery or risking being fined two shillings.

18. *Records of the City of Norwich* 2:52–53 (1399–1400), 54 (1405–6), 55 (1408–9), 56 (1409–10), 58 (1411–12), 63 (1420–21).

19. *Calendar of Charter Rolls,* vol. 5, *1341–1417* (London: His Majesty's Stationery Office, 1916), p. 421.

20. Blomefield, *History of Norfolk* 3:125; *Records of the City of Norwich* 2:56; and Trevor John, "Sir Thomas Erpingham, East Anglian Society and the Dynastic Revolution of 1399," *Norfolk Archaeology* 35 (1970): 99.

21. John Hoker (alias Vowell), *The Description of the Citie of Excester,* ed. W. J. Harte, J. W. Schopp, and H. Tapley-Soper, 3 vols., Devon and Cornwall Record Society (Exeter, 1919, 1947), 3:647–52; Frances Rose-Troup, "The Lady of the Isle: Isabella de Fortibus, Countess of Albemarle and Devon," *TDA* 37 (1905): 217, 227; W. G. Hoskins, *Two Thousand Years in Exeter* (Exeter: Townsend, 1960), pp. 49–50; and A. M. Jackson, "Medieval Exeter, the Exe, and the Earldom of Devon," *TDA* 104 (1972): 57–72.

22. Martin Cherry, "The Crown and the Political Community in Devonshire, 1377–1461" (Ph.D. diss., University College of Swansea, University of Wales, 1981), p. 128; and Cherry, "The Courtenay Earls of Devon," *Southern History* 1 (1979): 75.

23. The cathedral party also sent gifts to Courtenay and Bonville, both of whom are listed in the bishop's registers as patrons of local churches and presenters of chaplains and clerks to their ministry. The cathedral had far more peaceful relations with the two men than had the city. For details of the dispute, see Muriel Curtis, *Some Disputes between the City and the Cathedral Authorities of Exeter,* History of Exeter Research Group,

Monograph 4 (Manchester: Manchester University Press, 1932); and Lorraine Attreed, "Arbitration and the Growth of Urban Liberties in Late Medieval England," *Journal of British Studies* 31 (1992):205–35.

24. Emma Louise Radford (Lady Radford), "The Fight at Clyst in 1455," *TDA* 44 (1912): 255–57, 260–62; Radford, "Nicholas Radford," *TDA* 35 (1903): 252–53, 256, 264, 270; J. G. Bellamy, *Crime and Public Order in England in the Later Middle Ages* (London: Routledge and Kegan Paul, 1973), pp. 55–57; and DRO, Receivers' Roll, 34–35 Henry VI, Book 51, fol. 310v.

25. Edward IV's sister Anne, married first to Henry Holand, duke of Exeter, and second to Thomas St. Leger, received some attention from the city, probably in the hope that she could influence her royal brother. Lord Robert Willoughby de Broke received gifts and welcomes as one of Henry VII's chief military organizers in the West Country (G. E. Cokayne et al., eds., *The Complete Peerage of England, Scotland, Ireland, and the United Kingdom*, new ed., rev. V. Gibbs, 12 vols. [London: St. Catherine Press, 1926], 12:683–86; Charles Ross, *Edward IV* [London: Eyre Methuen, 1974], p.184; and DRO, Receivers' Rolls, 1488–93, 1496–99, 1501–6).

26. R. L. Storey, *The End of the House of Lancaster* (1966; reprint, Gloucester: Sutton, 1986), pp. 54–56; *Records of the City of Norwich* 1:348–49. See Public Record Office (hereafter cited as PRO), London, KB.9/272, membrane 3, for details of violence waged by Suffolk retainer Sir Thomas Tuddenham and the earl's counselor John Heydon between 1434 and 1450.

27. May McKisack, *The Parliamentary Representation of the English Boroughs during the Middle Ages* (Oxford: Clarendon Press, 1932), pp. 161–63. Another local noble, John Howard, fourth duke of Norfolk, should have been the natural alternative to de la Pole, but Howard's exclusion from court circles and lack of national importance were noticed even by contemporaries. Instead, his duchess received the bulk of the attention from Norwich, accepting civic delegations bearing gifts of wine, spices, venison, and even a porpoise, not least because she was related to the rising duke of York. Norfolk fortunes were tied to the House of York. Eleanor, duchess of Norfolk, was the duke of York's niece. Her husband died in 1461 and was succeeded by their son John. The fifth duke's only heir, his daughter Anne, married Edward IV's younger son while still a child but died soon after the ceremony in 1481. In 1483, Richard III gave the title to a cadet branch of the family whose members had to work very hard to win the trust of Henry Tudor. The sixteenth-century dukes, once secure in Tudor favor, successfully represented the city to the central government and were treated almost as royal figures, with gifts and spectacles presented upon their visits. The history of the family can be found in *Complete Peerage* 9:600–12. The Norwich Account Rolls for the 1440s through 1480s contain various records of gifts given to the local nobles and petitions made to them for help with the royal government and its financial and military demands. See also NNRO, Chamberlains' Book, 2, fols. 7v–8r, for Norwich's 1469 petition to the duke to excuse them from sending the king troops.

28. A. J. Pollard, *The Wars of the Roses* (New York: St. Martin's Press, 1988), pp. 5–19, discusses the derivation of the term and the "compelling historiographical grounds as well as sound historical reasons for retaining it."

29. Ross, *Edward IV*, pp. 36–37. The phrase comes from a 4 April 1461 letter of William Paston II describing York's welcome five days earlier (Norman Davis, ed., *Paston Letters and Papers of the Fifteenth Century*, 2 vols. [Oxford: Clarendon Press, 1971, 1976], 1:165–66 [letter no. 90]).

30. J. H. Ramsay, *Lancaster and York*, 2 vols. (Oxford: Clarendon Press, 1892), 2:237–38. Legend, reinforced by a near-contemporary chronicle, insists that York's head was adorned with a paper crown to mock his failed pretensions to the throne (Ross, *Edward IV*, p. 30 n. 3). Shakespeare expands on the scene in *Henry VI, Part 3*, in which Queen Margaret orders, "Off with his head, and set it on York gates; / So York may overlook the town of York" (act 1, scene 4, lines 179–80). In 1476, Edward had his father's

remains and those of his younger brother Edmund, also a victim of Wakefield, moved from Pontefract priory to the collegiate chapel at Fotheringhay, in a sumptuous ceremony intended to assert the power of the dynasty.

31. Polydore Vergil, writing in the early sixteenth century, recounted that the citizens threatened violence against Edward if he forced his way into York. They gave way after Edward made numerous promises to benefit them once he regained the throne, but "the whole day almost was spent in this parley" (Henry Ellis, ed., *Three Books of Polydore Vergil's English History*, Camden Society, old series 29 [London: John Bowyer Nichols and Son, 1844], pp. 138–39). The Yorkist-sponsored *Historie of the Arrivall of Edward IV in England*, ed. J. Bruce, Camden Society, old series 1 [London: John Bowyer Nichols and Son, 1838), pp. 4–7, sensed no overt Yorkist sympathy in the city's actions but stressed instead Edward's right to rule, his piety, and his love of peace.

32. R. B. Dobson, *York City Chamberlains' Account Rolls, 1396–1500*, Surtees Society 192 (Gateshead: Northumberland Press, 1980, for 1978 and 1979), pp. 165, 169–70. The city spent 16*d.* on illuminations for Edward's visit and £36 3*s.* 7*d.* for wine, cloth, and bread given the king and other important lords who accompanied him. It was during this visit that the city hoped for royal confirmation of the traditional jurisdictional relationship between York and the royal castle inside its walls. Wine worth twenty pence was provided the mayor, an assize justice, and the county sheriff for their discussion of the city's liberties during the royal visit.

33. City chamberlains' rolls record gifts of wine in 1468 and 1470, almost certain proof that Richard visited the city in those years (Dobson, *York Chamberlains' Accounts*, pp. 126, 137).

34. Attreed, *York House Books*, pp. 8–9. The number is, of course, suspect.

35. Attreed, *York House Books*, pp. 9–10, 128–30 (fishgarths in the River Ouse); 46–48 (former common clerk dismissed for embezzlement and immoral acts); 696–97, 703 (fewer soldiers than usual because of the city's poverty).

36. Attreed, *York House Books*, pp. 78, 233–34, 248–50, 254, 259, 279. Although one citizen complained that Richard did nothing for the city "but grin [at] us," and another that he unfairly influenced city elections, most residents took pride in Richard's interest in York and the many ways he accurately depicted its problems to the king (Attreed, *York House Books*, pp. 696, 707).

37. Richard and Anne Neville joined the guild in 1477; it is not known whether they attended any of the ceremonies and processions (R. H. Skaife, ed., *The Register of the Guild of Corpus Christi in the City of York*, Surtees Society 57 [Durham: Andrews, 1872 for 1871], pp. xii, 101; and York City Archives, C.99:5).

38. Attreed, *York House Books*, pp. 282, 284–86, 712–14. Richard's letter of 10 June arrived in York five days later. The troops were expected to be arrayed and gathered at Pontefract by the eighteenth. In fact, they did not leave town before the twenty-first, and could not have arrived in London for a few days after that. Since it is hard to believe Richard called them to deal with an emergency, we must conclude he probably mustered them to arrive by 25 June, the date set for Edward V's first parliament, during which Richard would need all the strength he could find to remain lord protector of the young king (the office customarily lapsed after a coronation). As it turned out, they arrived in time to witness Richard claim the throne from his nephew (P. W. Hammond and Anne F. Sutton, *Richard III: The Road to Bosworth Field* [London: Constable, 1985], p. 103).

39. Attreed, *York House Books*, pp. 286–87.

40. Attreed, *York House Books*, pp. 287–89, 713.

41. Attreed, *York House Books*, pp. 289, 300. The number increased from three to four in 1484, "to bere soch great chargez as is to be born in thys cite." Between 1484 and 1500, the number varied between four and six. York often succumbed to deficit spending, and exacerbated the situation by forcing the chamberlains to cover some city expenses out of their own pockets. Chamberlains leaving office had to hope that the city then experienced

a good year so they could be repaid. For details of their responsibilities, see Dobson, *Chamberlains' Accounts*, pp. xxiv–xxvi, xxxvii–xxxviii.

42. Pamela Tudor-Craig, "Richard III's Triumphant Entry into York, August 20th [*sic*], 1483," in *Richard III and the North*, ed. Horrox, p. 111; and James, "Ritual, Drama, and Social Body," p. 10.

43. Tudor-Craig, "Triumphant Entry," p. 113. Events had kept Richard in London during the May feast of Corpus Christi; the August date was second in importance on York's religious calendar. For an analysis of the bodily elements in the cult of Corpus Christi and the role they played in urban societies, see James, "Ritual, Drama, and Social Body," pp. 3–29 and passim. Miri Rubin, "Corpus Christi Fraternities and Late Medieval Piety," in *Voluntary Religion*, ed. W. J. Sheils and Diana Wood, Studies in Church History, vol. 23 (Oxford: Basil Blackwell, 1986), pp. 97–109, provides the background of the personal meaning of the cult.

44. Attreed, *York House Books*, pp. 290–92. The king was to have five hundred marks in a pair of silver-gilt basins, and his consort one hundred pounds in gold in a piece of plate. A gift of foodstuffs was also offered to the earl of Northumberland, who had become the leading local noble upon Richard's accession (Attreed, *York House Books*, p. 289).

45. The Creed Play was about one-third the length of a full performance of the York Corpus Christi cycle, so Richard's patience was not as tried as that of Margaret of Anjou, who sat through an entire cycle while visiting Coventry in 1457, except for one play that could not be performed "for lak of day" (Mary D. Harris, ed., *The Coventry Leet Book*, 2 vols., Early English Text Society, o.s. 134–35, 138, 146 [1907, 1913; reprint, Millwood, N.Y.: Kraus, 1971], 1:300; and Lucy Toulmin Smith, ed., *York Plays* [Oxford: Oxford University Press, 1885; reprint, London: Russell and Russell, 1963]).

46. Alexandra F. Johnston, "The Plays of the Religious Guilds of York: The Creed Play and the Pater Noster Play," *Speculum* 50 (1975): 58, 64; Eileen White, *The York Mystery Play* (York: Ebor Press, 1984), p. 29; and Attreed, *York House Books*, pp. 289–93. The Creed Play was performed every twelve years, except in the case of special visits such as Richard's, until 1568. The Corpus Christi cycle was performed annually until 1569. The twelve scenes (each perhaps introduced by an apostle) of the Creed Play include God enthroned, Christ enthroned, the Navitity, the Crucifixion, the Resurrection, the Ascension, the Second Coming, Pentecost, a representation of Church and State, penance, resurrection of the dead, and the Coronation of the Virgin (Johnston, "Plays of Religious Guilds," 68–69).

47. Richard announced his intention to create his son Edward Prince of Wales in letters to the archbishops dated 24 August. The letters do not choose a site for the ceremony, but on 31 August Richard sent to London for cloth and banners (including 13,000 livery badges bearing the device of Richard's White Boar) to be sent him in York (Rosemary Horrox and P. W. Hammond, eds., *British Library Harleian Manuscript 433*, 4 vols. [Upminster and London: Sutton, 1979–83], 1:81–83; 2:42).

48. Hammond and Sutton, *Richard III*, pp. 140–41, citing the Bedern College Statute Book held in the York Minster Library. It was the writer of the Croyland Chronicle who believed Richard and Anne had had a second coronation: Nicholas Pronay and John Cox, eds., *The Crowland Chronicle Continuations, 1459–1486* (London: Sutton, 1986), p. 161. Three weeks after the king's visit, the mayor was to be given ten marks to cover the expenses he incurred in providing dinners for various bishops, barons, a chief justice, and members of the king's council (Attreed, *York House Books*, p. 296). The entertaining probably occurred as part of the royal progress, but the entry does not definitely say so.

49. Attreed, *York House Books*, p. 729.

50. Attreed, *York House Books*, p. 295. The king was in Pontefract in late September.

51. For a full discussion of York's problems with the fee farm, see my two articles, "The King's Interest—York's Fee Farm and the Central Government," *Northern History* 17 (1981): 24–43, and "Medieval Bureaucracy in Fifteenth-Century York," *York Historian*

6 (1985): 24–31. A. J. Pollard of Teesside Polytechnic has wondered whether Richard had any intention at all of acting on his promise to York, and perhaps never told the Exchequer to excuse the city. Without doubting that any medieval king was capable of such duplicity, I would argue that Richard probably intended the gift sincerely. Before leaving York, he arranged for a change in the annuity of Sir John Savage, an important supporter in the Welsh marches. Savage had previously derived his annuity from York's fee farm, but now the money was to come from another source. As Richard explained in a new grant, "It is soo that now of late at oure being in oure said Citee for gret causes us specialy moving, We have disposed the said Fee ferme aswelle to the Releeff and socouring of the said Citee as otherwise, so that the saide annuite ne may be paiable there" (Horrox and Hammond, *Harleian 433* 2:18). York was no less important a source of support than Savage, and it is unlikely that Richard intended to confuse or offend either one.

52. Attreed, *York House Books*, pp. 368–69, 734–38.

53. Attreed, *York House Books*, pp. 373–74, 734–36. The mayor and his brethren had to meet the messenger at an inn called The Sign of the Boar (an ironic reminder that they still respected the king who carried the badge of the white boar?). He assured them that Henry VII would be as generous a king to York as any of his predecessors. On 23 August, the city council records declared that "King Richard late mercifully reigning upon us was thrugh grete treason of the duc of Northfolk and many othre that turned ayenst hyme, with many othre lordes and nobilles of this north parties, was pitiously slane and murdred to the grete hevynesse of this citie" (Attreed, *York House Books*, pp. 368–69). Although few members of the public would have had access to these records, it was brave of the officials to express their loyalty this boldly in the face of Henry VII's accession.

54. Attreed, *York House Books*, pp. 371–72, 383–87, 391–92, 398, 466–67, 471–73, 475–76, 479, 487–88.

55. For analysis of the pretenders' threats to Henry's rule, see my article "A New Source for Perkin Warbeck's Invasion of 1497," *Mediaeval Studies* 48 (1986): 514–21.

56. Sydney Anglo, "The 'British History' in Early Tudor Propaganda," *Bulletin of the John Rylands Library* 44 (1961): 18, 35 n. 4, 38; Roger Loomis, "Edward I, Arthurian Enthusiast," *Speculum* 28 (1953): 114, 126; J. S. P. Tatlock, "The Dragons of Wessex and Wales," *Speculum* 8 (1933): 223–35; and A. H. Thomas and I. D. Thornley, eds., *The Great Chronicle of London* (1938; reprint, Gloucester: Sutton, 1983), pp. 238–39.

57. For the uses of Arthurian symbols in the reigns of Henry VIII and Elizabeth, see Hugh A. MacDougall, *Racial Myth in English History* (Hanover, N.H.: University of New England Press, 1982), pp. 17–26; *Calendar of State Papers, Spanish, 1531–1533* (London: Her Majesty's Stationery Office, 1882), pp. 22–28.

58. For a detailed analysis of Tudor historiographical concepts of medieval society, see my article "England's Official Rose: Tudor Concepts of the Middle Ages," in *Hermeneutics and Medieval Culture*, ed. Patrick J. Gallacher and Helen Damico (Albany: State University of New York Press, 1989), pp. 85–95.

59. John C. Meagher, "The First Progress of Henry VII," *Renaissance Drama*, n.s., 1 (1968): 46; Attreed, *York House Books*, pp. 372, 466–67. Metcalf died at the end of February 1486, after which both Henry and the earl of Northumberland immediately began to remind the civic officials that his replacement should be a man loyal to the new regime (Attreed, *York House Books*, pp. 469–70, 471–73).

60. Attreed, *York House Books*, pp. 474–75, 479. Sir Henry Hudson was parish priest of the church of Spofford. He had also been hired in 1483 to design the welcoming ceremonies for Richard III (Attreed, *York House Books*, pp. 288, 298–99). In anticipation of the 1469 visit of Queen Elizabeth Woodville, Norwich authorities hired a man named Pernall from Ipswich, who created at least two presentations on scaffolds and used huge leather-covered giants (NNRO, Chamberlains' Book 2, fols. 10r–13v).

61. Attreed, *York House Books*, p. 478: "[H]is highnesse may the rather be movid to to [*sic*] think that the said maier, aldermen, sheriffes and othre inhabitances heyr be gladdid and joifull of the same his commyng as thei have be in tymes past of seing commyng of

othre kinges ther soverain lord." Late in 1485, York's officials sent a long letter to the king, describing the history of their loyalty to the Lancastrian house and blaming their poverty on Edward IV's vindictiveness over that fidelity (Attreed, *York House Books*, pp. 390–91).

62. Attreed, *York House Books*, pp. 478, 480–82.

63. The last stanza is not included in the city council records' report of the spectacle but was written by a herald who recorded the scene (Sydney Anglo, *Spectacle, Pageantry, and Early Tudor Policy* [Oxford: Clarendon Press, 1969], p. 26). The account of Henry's visit can be found in Attreed, *York House Books*, pp. 482–85. The herald's account is found in *De rebus Britannicis Collectanea*, John Leland, ed., published by Thomas Hearne, 6 vols. (London: Richardson, 1770), 4:187–90. For the parallels between the pageant speeches and scenes from various Corpus Christi plays, see Meagher, "First Progress," pp. 53–55, and Smith, *York Plays*, pp. 10–11, 18, 20.

64. In the following two paragraphs, I examine towns other than the four originally selected, but I believe the examples they offer excuse such a diversion.

65. Anglo, *Spectacle*, pp. 29–30, 37–41.

66. Anglo, *Spectacle*, p. 34.

67. The most recent and complete treatment is Michael Bennett, *Lambert Simnel and the Battle of Stoke* (New York: St. Martin's Press, 1987), esp. pp. 89–103. For York's archival interpretation of Stoke, see Attreed, *York House Books*, pp. 571–73.

68. Attreed, *York House Books*, pp. 584–89.

69. Illustrations of roses accompany the poetry of court writers Pietro Carmeliano (British Library, Additional MS. 33736, fols. 1 and 2) and Giovanni de Gigli (British Library, Harleian MS. 336, fol. 70). Their poems celebrated Henry's victories in battle and in the bedchamber, taking particular pleasure in the rapid production of Prince Arthur. The birth was described as the major blessing Henry brought to the land by his accession, an act fully in accord with God's plan.

70. Henry VII urged his cousin's canonization, an act he believed would bring increased renown to his line, but for complex reasons he was not able to achieve it. Anglo, *Spectacle*, p. 43 n. 1, reviews the various theories and concludes that when the task fell to Henry VIII to fulfill, the young king simply was not interested.

71. Attreed, *York House Books*, pp. 487–88 (10 June 1486).

72. In 1482, following several visits of the king and queen, Edward IV granted Norwich a trade fair (NNRO, 16-d, Assembly Book 1, fol. 118; 17-b, Liber Albus, fol. 54v). York received a charter in 1393 that substantially expanded its liberties, in recognition of the hospitality the city had shown Richard II when he moved many of the offices of government to the north (Sellers, *York Memorandum Book* 1:30–33; 2:251–53; and *Calendar of Charter Rolls* 5:333–36). However, Exeter received a sword and cap of maintenance from Henry VII following his 1497 visit to punish western rebels who had supported pretender Perkin Warbeck (DRO, Book 51, fol. 329v; Receivers' Roll, 1496–97; and PRO, E.101/414/16, fols. 1–4).

PART IV

The Political Overtones of
Public Entertainment

CHAPTER 10

The Duke and His Towns
The Power of Ceremonies, Feasts, and Public Amusement in the Duchy of Guelders (East Netherlands) in the Fourteenth and Fifteenth Centuries

Gerard Nijsten

The relation between a ruler and his subjects is often discussed on the basis of political activities and events: diplomacy, decisions, laws, and so on. But the relationship also finds expression in what we broadly term "culture": festivities, ceremonies and rituals, public amusement, and numerous symbolic forms.[1] Here, too, we can recognize a leitmotif made up of political power relations. This chapter will investigate the possibilities of an anthropological-political approach for a medium-sized court, that of the Duchy of Guelders,[2] a court that has hardly been studied so far. The Burgundian, French, and English courts have been studied many times. Their rich court culture is well documented in narrative sources, art objects, and so on. In the smaller centers, fewer sources have survived. As a result, they have appealed less to the historian's imagination; their *Nachleben* is ailing. Yet the smaller courts are interesting because, more than the great centers of the nobility, they offer some sort of "average" of the kind of court culture present in Europe; one reflecting the imitation and emulation of international trade and fashion (Figure 10.1).

Anthropology is the discipline par excellence that deals with culture, and therefore also with festivities and ceremonies. At first sight it may seem odd that historians in their study of the dead (the past) should make use of anthropological fieldwork dealing with the living (the present). The importance of anthropological studies for historians lies not only in models and theories, but also in the language we use to talk about history. As Peter Burke puts it, anthropologists (and sociologists) "have given us a new vocabulary for talking about myth, ritual, symbol, communication; in short about culture.... They show us how to interpret the unfamiliar; how to discover cultural norms through the study of the everyday."[3] As part of the everyday, politics belongs to the realm of culture. To find articulation, politics (and the power to be attained) has to be expressed in symbolic forms. These symbolic forms bring about

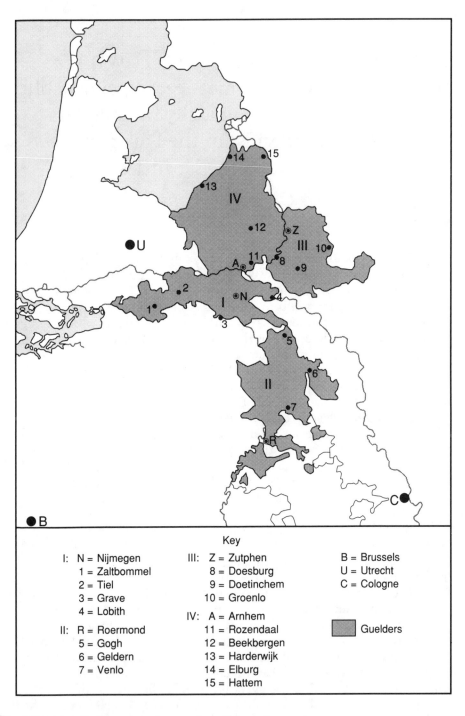

Figure 10.1. Guelders in the fourteenth and fifteenth centuries.

Key

I: N = Nijmegen
1 = Zaltbommel
2 = Tiel
3 = Grave
4 = Lobith

II: R = Roermond
5 = Gogh
6 = Geldern
7 = Venlo

III: Z = Zutphen
8 = Doesburg
9 = Doetinchem
10 = Groenlo

IV: A = Arnhem
11 = Rozendaal
12 = Beekbergen
13 = Harderwijk
14 = Elburg
15 = Hattem

B = Brussels
U = Utrecht
C = Cologne

Guelders

communication between the players of the political game and ultimately shape political reality and the balance of power.[4]

A study of Guelders's political culture in the fourteenth and fifteenth centuries is a challenge, since hardly any narrative sources survive.[5] Guelders lacks a Jean Froissart, a Philippe de Commynes, or an Olivier de la Marche to provide pages of descriptions of clothing, colors, and festivities. Other types of sources, such as the ducal accounts, help to form a picture.[6] From roughly the mid–fourteenth century to 1477 a vast series of accounts containing a wealth of data has survived. The often sober remarks of the clerks who wrote the accounts deal with everything on which money was spent. Most forms of art and culture cost money and are, therefore, represented. The sources, however, are beset with their own kinds of problems. The accounts have a number of lacunae (from some years no account has survived at all).[7] Moreover, the information is often sparse and its meaning unclear. Since account books are obviously not intended to serve as a narrative source for twentieth-century historians, they contain only data that are necessary for financial management. We must frequently read between the lines, both in search of what was considered obvious and was recorded *en passant* and of what was special and was recorded explicitly. If we find such data, however, we are entitled to assume that they are fairly reliable, precisely because of the sources' nature and the casual way in which they were often taken down.[8]

The sources' imperfect nature brings us to the second problem: How can the notions derived from the social sciences help us to interpret the data; how can the divide between the sparsity of the data and interpretation be kept to a minimum? Naturally, caution is a precondition. The historical basis on which the interpretation is to be tested must be strengthened with the support of letters, documents, and wills present in the ducal archives or in archives elsewhere. In addition there are— and this is important for our subject—accounts from the towns. In the case of Guelders the accounts (often unpublished) of towns such as Arnhem, Zutphen, Venlo, Grave, and Geldern have largely survived; in other towns such as Nijmegen, Hattem, and Doesburg they have survived in part. These town accounts offer the same kind of information as the accounts from the ducal court, this time from an urban point of view. Together with the ducal sources they supply the elements for the picture that is to be created.

In studying the relationship between the duke and the towns, we will start from the following assumption: Forms of culture are not only an expression of power relations, they also play a part in determining those relations. Ultimately, the discussion will center on the power of culture. This assumption implies that festivities and rituals achieved goals that went beyond mere entertainment or irrationality. Ritual is the propagation of a message, according to David Kertzer.[9] Could the duke use the festivities and ceremonies to bring about and maintain unity—unity in diversity? Did the ceremonies create solidarity among the inhabitants of the towns, sometimes against their lord, in their attempts to maintain or increase their privileges and independent position? Could festivities and ritualized acts defuse social tensions and threats of conflicts? In order to be able to answer these questions, we must consider the urban social context in which lord and "subjects" met and acted out their meaningful parts. The paper will discuss the annual festivities in the towns, organized and sponsored by the town patriciate, to which the duke or members of his court were invited: festivities, tournaments, and banquets organized by the court in the towns; the celebration of "national events," both by the towns and the court; and dynastic events such as births, marriages, and deaths.

Rituals create relations. They connect individuals to groups, and individuals to the holy. They interconnect members of groups and connect groups to the holy. Ultimately, they bring about contact between the "earthly" and the "heavenly." The rituals that will be discussed in this chapter concern relationships between groups, namely, between the duke and his court on the one hand and the towns on the other. The importance of festivities and rituals for the *internal* coherence of a town or the court will only be mentioned in passing.[10]

The Court's Presence at Town Festivities

The church calendar dictated the rhythm of the year, differentiating between work days and feast days. No festivity lacked a religious dimension, not even the often raucous entertainments at the beginning of the year or the events before and during carnival.[11] Especially in towns, festivities developed that stood the established order on its head. For a few days the town's inhabitants could play a part that they could never have during the year. Children ruled over adults with their pseudo-bishop or king, and groups of masked revelers (*mommen*) were allowed to disturb the town rulers during their meals and to be the center of attention without any repercussions. The reversal created a sanctuary for expressing criticisms against the town rulers in farcical speeches, against the church through the boy bishop, and against the nobility in mock tournaments and the pig chase carried out by the blind.[12] In the numerous rambunctious festivities, the town, or more specifically the town council, could show its many-faceted nature. By loosening the reins, the council strengthened order, because reversal rituals ultimately resulted in a confirmation of order. Shrovetide was not simply a period of merrymaking, a break from everyday routine, but was also a period in which the community could be welded together. Joy unites.

The ducal court took part in the annual "fraternization of fools." In doing so, however, it pursued its own goals, just as the town rulers who invited the duke and his retinue had their own—subsidiary—goals. A town increased its status in the eyes of neighboring towns when it succeeded in making the ruler take part in the town's festivities. By his presence the duke revealed his power and authority. He took part in the meals and dances; he listened sympathetically to reciters and the town's actors; he showed his generosity to all those and to the numerous minstrels and buffoons.

The town and court accounts provide ample evidence of encounters between the court and the towns. We can see a change taking place in their relations from the end of the fourteenth to the end of the fifteenth century. Initially, the noble world of the court was barely oriented toward the towns. Shrovetide was celebrated in the duke's castles, separately from the towns, or elsewhere with other rulers of the duke's acquaintance. In 1383, for instance, the count of Cleves organized a great Shrovetide celebration and invited his "neighbor" from Guelders.[13] Even so, the duke did pay short visits to towns near the castle where he resided, such as Arnhem, which was not far from Rozendaal Castle.[14] When the duke did celebrate carnival in a local town, he did so in the local castle (which was exempt from the town's authority) and largely apart from the town's entertainments. Thus, in 1383 the duke and duchess received their guests (*een geselscap*) at the great castle of Nijmegen rather than in their house in town.[15] It was largely a private affair including noble guests and relatives.

The duke did, however, send personal representatives to the towns, so that doubts about his power would be ruled out. In Venlo, Johan van der Velde, Duke William's bailiff, represented the duke "opten raesenden maendach" (on crazy Monday) in 1394.[16] Later, when the court routinely celebrated in the towns, the custom of representation was retained, for the duke could not be in several places at the same time. William of Egmond, for instance, took part in the Shrovetide celebrations in Arnhem in 1430 on behalf of his brother, and fifteen years later Adolf, who was six years old at the time, represented his father in the same town. The *ambtman* (bailiff) of the land of Cuyck, a ducal official, represented his lord in Grave in 1447 (Figure 10.2).[17]

In the course of the fifteenth century the dividing line between the court and the towns seems to become blurred. At court the custom arose of celebrating Shrovetide together with the subjects, that is, the towns. During the reign of Duke Arnold, the first duke from the house of Egmond, that is from the 1430s onward, the town accounts refer to visits by the duke, the duchess, their children, and their household. Initially, Arnold preferred Arnhem, where he had a court, but later shifted to the small town of Grave with its castle.[18]

Once the duke had decided on one or more days' visit, the town would go out of its way in making gestures of hospitality to him. In 1440, the town council of Arnhem welcomed Duke Arnold, Duchess Cather-

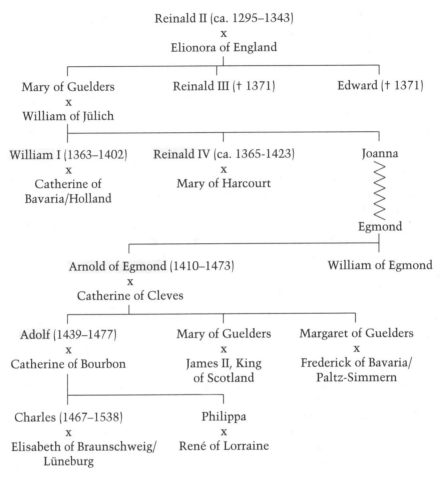

Reinald II (ca. 1295–1343)
x
Elionora of England

Mary of Guelders   Reinald III († 1371)   Edward († 1371)
x
William of Jülich

William I (1363–1402)   Reinald IV (ca. 1365-1423)   Joanna
x   x
Catherine of   Mary of Harcourt
Bavaria/Holland

Egmond

Arnold of Egmond (1410–1473)   William of Egmond
x
Catherine of Cleves

Adolf (1439–1477)   Mary of Guelders   Margaret of Guelders
x   x   x
Catherine of Bourbon   James II, King   Frederick of Bavaria/
of Scotland   Paltz-Simmern

Charles (1467–1538)   Philippa
x   x
Elisabeth of Braunschweig/   René of Lorraine
Lüneburg

Figure 10.2. Dukes of Guelders.

ine, and a large retinue treating them to great quantities of wine. On Shrove Monday the number of guests was even larger. The duke's brother, William of Egmond, his wife, and many other nobles had joined the company. They too were treated to wine by the town, and all the guests were invited to the dance house at night. At the town's expense a great party was organized there. The count of Bentheim's musicians and the minstrels from Kampen assisted the town instrumentalists in providing the music.[19]

During the day the noble lords engaged in fighting games, for tournaments were connected closely to carnival.[20] The town had put the old market square at the nobles' disposal and prepared it for the jousts. The square was swept clean and covered with heather, so that the horses would not hurt their feet. The brook that ran alongside the square was fenced off with a wooden barrier in order to prevent the knights from riding into it in the heat of combat. Wooden palings marked off the jousting area. The town council erected a dais for female guests in front of the school.[21] The location is significant. The market square was the center par excellence of a medieval town. It was the location of great urban festivities and public events, including executions. At the same time the duke's court was situated on the *alden merct* (old market square). His palace, situated at this central point in the town, symbolized his position in the world of the town as well. The tournament as a meeting point of court and town could only take place here, and not in any of the other squares or places in Arnhem. Even though the town organized the festivities, probably considering this to be a duty of honor, the duke most certainly kept an eye on the preparations. On a last inspection, for instance, he ordered that extra manure be taken to the jousting area. The heather that was there already was considered insufficient.[22]

What was true for the Shrovetide celebrations in general was true for tournaments. In the fourteenth century these were strictly a matter for the nobility but shifted to the towns in the fifteenth century. Duke William frequently went to grand tournaments, where he met the "flower of the nobility" of the German Empire: in Cologne (1387), Kreuznach (1390), Sint-Geertruidenberg (1395), Sinzig (1397), and so on.[23] The duke of Guelders himself regularly hosted such events.[24] By order of their lord, heralds went to the various courts that were on friendly terms with the duke to invite the nobles to attend.[25] This emphasis on the German Empire, which was so clearly present during the reign of the dukes from the house of Gulik (Jülich), disappeared under the Egmond dynasty. Duke Arnold did take part in tournaments but increasingly left the organization to the towns. Arnhem, Grave, and, to a lesser extent, Nijmegen took over the initiative. This probably meant that members of the town patriciate could measure their agility against the nobles.

Gradually the monopoly of the nobility over tournaments was broken.[26] Arnhem town accounts reveal an interesting development. Originally it was impossible to imagine a town organizing a tournament without the court's participation, but from the 1460s onward the town council did so. The ducal dynasty's tarnished status played a part in this. But, more important, the custom had developed of organizing a tournament in the town. Fighting games and jousts had become part of the standard Shrovetide repertoire, independent of the court. From now on the patricians were the combatants, with or without the support of friendly nobles. Soon a mock tournament was to be part of the program as well.[27] The development of the town tournament is a clear example of the court's impact on the towns.

Shrovetide offered a whole range of festivities: eating, drinking, dancing, tournaments, playacting, sword dancing, cockfights, and so on.[28] The three days preceding a period of reflection and fasting presented an exuberant spectacle. The duke, his family, or his representatives showed their alliance with the subjects by appearing in splendor before the "people." The duke's power was visible; "people" could admire the luxury, pomp, and circumstance of the ruler and his court. The "people" also played a more active part. By means of masquerades and farcical entertainment they could get closer to their lord than was the case at other times. Groups of men and women, oddly rigged out and disguised (*mommen*), visited the noble guests. Schoolchildren approached the duke and his wife with their boy bishop. Others—young men (*gezellen*) or young women—treated all those who were willing to watch to playacting.[29] All this was not without its reward, of course. The duke showed his generosity by giving the *vrouwen van Arnhem* (women of Arnhem—probably the wives and daughters of members of the patriciate) a contribution for their Shrovetide meal, "in honor of the duke," as the clerk added in the account.[30]

The duke reciprocated by offering a meal to the town councillors and the members of the town patriciate. In 1467, for instance, four inns in Nijmegen were completely filled with Duke Adolf's guests. He had 308 meals served to members of the court and to "den burgeren mytten priesteren" (the citizens, including the clergy).[31]

The amalgamation of court and town was not complete. Both remained separate and to a certain extent enjoyed themselves in isolation. But their embrace gradually became more intimate, as their need for each other's support became mutual. It cannot be coincidental that this development runs parallel to the growing political importance of the towns in the duchy. In the meetings of the estates of the four *kwartieren* (quarters)[32] the towns played an increasingly prominent role. They contributed a large part of the duke's taxes (especially the *beden* [aids]);[33] they provided the majority of the men and provisions in times of war; their citizens were increasingly to be found in the court's chancellery and administration. The political situation was reflected in the places where the duke celebrated his festivities. Arnold of Egmond, the duke who was becoming alienated from the powerful town of Nijmegen from the mid-1440s onward, hardly ever celebrated Shrove Tuesday there, in spite of Nijmegen's legendary castle—once Charlemaghe's *palts* (palace). The towns of Arnhem and Grave, which supported the duke, provided him with a welcome location for observing the festivities. Adolf, Arnold's son and successor, who was getting into a bitter conflict with his father, found in Nijmegen and Venlo loyal allies. He celebrated carnival in either of these towns.[34]

The duke's presence at feast days could also be used as a way of making it clear to a defiant town who its lord was and to whom obedience was due. During carnival in 1455, for instance, Duke Arnold decided to have his court in Nijmegen, even though the relationship between him and the town was strained.[35] In doing so, Arnold undoubtedly wished to stress his authority. His decision must be seen as a warning to the disobedient town of Nijmegen. In view of the situation in the duchy at the time, however, it may be wondered whether the duke's presence was a powerful signal. Nevertheless, the fact that the duke opted for this approach indicates that he recognized its potency.

After Shrove Tuesday the towns observed a calm period in which hardly any public amusement occurred. Easter was the conclusion of the silent "dead" weeks; it was Christ's victory over death, the victory of spring over winter. Easter was the time of the Passion and Resurrection plays, which were performed in towns such as Grave and Venlo.[36] The accounts mention nothing about visits by members of the court. The solemn feast of Easter, like Christmas, was no occasion for a meeting between town and court. Celebrating the feasts and solemn masses separately, the inhabitants of the towns went to their parish churches, while the duke and duchess went to the court chapel of the castle in which they were sojourning. These were not feasts involving exuberant entertainment; rather, devotion was paramount.[37] Court and towns apparently only celebrated merry forms of entertainment together. The May Day festivities and the day of Saint John's Beheading (29 August) found both the duke and duchess in Arnhem. Only rarely did they spend these days elsewhere.[38] Numerous customs from the pre-Christian May Day celebrations had survived. Symbolic of the annual agricultural cycle in which flowers and trees had previously been worshiped, a maypole was planted in the town market.[39] During the day townspeople went out to collect May branches in the forest, to dance, and to make merry. The duchess, her husband, and members of the court often took part. In 1399 Duchess Catherine had ridden "anden Musschenbergh, te meye" (on the Mussenberg—"Sparrows' Mount"—on the occasion of May Day), accompanied by her brother, the bishop of Liège.[40] In the evening, the town treated members of the patriciate, their wives, and noble guests to wine and a banquet. Afterward they went to the dance house, where more than once the duke's or duchess's musicians played for the party. The less privileged danced in the streets around the maypole.[41]

Elsewhere May Day celebrations took place without the duke and his wife being present, but a contribution—financial or otherwise—for the May King's or May Queen's festivities expressed their commitment to these festivities. In 1406 the May King of Geldern and his company received grain for their meal. A number of years earlier, in 1380, the duchess had ordered that the young women (*meghden*) of Goch be given a sum of money for their celebrations.[42]

Lighting Saint John's fires was also a custom dating back to Germanic times.[43] An overlay of Christianity turned it into a supplication for a rich harvest. In many places the feast was celebrated on 24 June, "St.-Jansdag te midzomer" (Saint John's Day in midsummer); in Arnhem, on the other hand, it was celebrated on 29 August, which turned it into a harvest festival. On the evening and night preceding Saint John's Day the townspeople and their guests went in procession through the town, carrying torches and fire-pans, dancing and drinking, accompanied by musicians and militiamen (*schutters*),[44] whose role was to monitor the situation because of the fire risk. The following evening the elite would go for a dance in the dance house. If the celebrants were too numerous, they moved to the nearby school.[45]

An important annual town event was the procession of the Virgin Mary, the day on which "Our Lady was carried" (*[men] Onze Lieve Vrouw droeg*). In each town in the duchy, the great procession took place at its own particular time. On the day of the procession all sections of the town, in hierarchical order, walked the route through the town. The procession was the symbol par excellence of the town's *concordia*. As one body, the town united around Christ's body (the sacrament) and the statue of the Mother of God, in a show of internal unity.[46] Such processions were purely a town matter. The court had nothing to do with them.[47] Only in special cases could the duke's power be seen, as in 1398, when Duke William had taken the small town of Schöneforst (south of Aachen) after months of siege. Since his position was new and fragile, he ordered his local representative, Emmerik of Kutzden, to have eight torches made to be carried in the procession of the Sacrament. The duke's coat of arms was to be depicted on these large candles and on the banners that were to be included. In this way all doubts about the new lord of Schöneforst would be dispelled among the population gathered there.[48] In a similar political show in 1458, Duke Arnold donated a precious cloth under which the Holy Sacrament was carried in Arnhem. Embroidered with silver and gold thread and decorated with depictions of religious scenes,[49] the silken cloth expressed Arnold's tie with the town. He probably hoped to bind the town to him with a gift that would include him in the town's sacred ceremony, for in precisely these years he urgently needed Arnhem's support against the rebellious Nijmegen and his son.

The towns had numerous activities and entertainments that were originally intended for certain sections of the population only but that often turned into manifestations of the town as a whole. Archery contests and the ensuing festivities belonged to this category. With the growth of the urban *libertas*, the need for a town militia had arisen to keep internal peace and to defend against external danger. Moreover, the townspeople were obliged to participate in the *heervaart*, the lord's military service. These circumstances had resulted in the emergence of civic militia.[50] Every town had more than one of these groups.

The duke fully recognized the urban militia's importance by supplying several archery companies with an annual contribution to their contests and the ensuing festivities, either in money or in kind (wine).[51] The tie between archery companies and their lord was expressed even more emphatically in the ruler's presence at the annual "parrot-shooting" (the archery contests in which the champion was entitled to call himself *schutterskoning* [shooters' king] for a year). The duke watched the contest, thereby stressing the importance of the archery companies for both town and himself. His presence also emphasized his military leadership over these potential soldiers. No doubt the event's highlight was when the duke himself participated. In 1404 Duke Reinald competed with members of the Arnhem archery companies, while Arnold (his successor) took part in the contests of 1437 and 1464. Arnold had new targets erected near Rozendaal Castle so that he and members of his court could practice their marksmanship.[52] When Adolf was entrenched in Venlo during the struggle against his father, the *oude schutterij* (old archery company) of Venlo presented him with a *schutterkogel* (shooter's hood) with silver trimmings.[53] In this way the town, which had paid for the silver, expressed its unconditional support for the rebellious son. The old archery company (that is, the oldest company and, therefore, the one with the highest status) thus stressed its position of eminence with respect to other groups in Venlo. If the duke's son were to wear this article of clothing, he would wear the colors of the old archery company; he had joined their ranks, he was one of them.

If the duke could not be present himself, or if he did not wish to take part in the archery contest and the ensuing festivities, his steward could represent him. In Arnhem in 1410 the steward came at the express request of the militiamen themselves: "Ende hadden den rentmeister gebeden in myns gnedigen heren stat mit hen te schieten ende oir geselscap te helpen starken" (and the militiamen had invited the steward to shoot with them in our gracious lord's town [i.e., Arnhem] and to swell their numbers). The meal they had afterward was said to be "na der alder gewoenten in die eer myns gnedigen heren" (according to ancient tradition and in honor of our gracious lord), an honor that cost the duke six guilders.[54]

As with other celebrations and festivities organized by the town councils or groups in which the duke and others took part, these were *merry* events. Eating, drinking, and participating in games of skill emphasized shared values and goals. Apparently, the town elites recognized the unifying effect of such entertainments, as did as their lord, and attempted to use the court for their own ends. Both parties derived power from these convivial shows of unity.

Ceremonies of Welcome in the Towns

Inaugural Entries

Ducal policy was dressed in festivities. The duke's political actions had to be forceful as well as convincing and elegant. Legitimizing sovereignty entailed obtaining recognition for the duke as the personification of order, justice, and the common good. This required the staging of power and majesty in the brief, festive events that served as means of communication from the duke to his subjects. Ceremonies of entry on the assumption of power, on return from travel abroad, and on celebration of political and military victories were among the most important.

The duke's entries into towns in connection with his inauguration as ruler were a valuable means of communicating his new power. During the ceremonious entries the entire urban community could behold their new lord with their own eyes and have direct contact with him. While the duke attempted to "stimulate the loyalty of the inhabitants and demonstrate his princely authority,"[55] the town elites stressed the confirmation of their collective identity—that is as a social body—vis-à-vis their lord. They had to strike a precarious balance between praising the duke on the one hand and impressing him on the other.

Reinald's assumption of power in 1402 and Arnold's in 1423 can be reconstructed reasonably well on the basis of the surviving accounts. When Duke William suddenly died without legitimate offspring in 1402, his brother Reinald was the rightful successor. In the various towns a series of time-consuming and costly rituals began. The new duke rode from one town to the next to be inaugurated at each. On Monday, 27 February, for instance, he arrived with a large retinue in Zutphen,[56] where he spent the next two days banqueting, exchanging gifts, and confirming the town's privileges. In the duke's presence *dat kundighboeck*, the manuscript containing Zutphen's rights, privileges, and statutes, was read out.[57] The ceremonies cost the duke more than 505 guilders, plus the requisite expenses in kind. This was no small sum if one takes into account that dozens of towns had to be visited. A town's size and importance determined the extent of the duke's expenses. The ceremonies in the quarters' capitals were more expensive than those in the smaller towns. The entries into Groenlo (1 March) and Doesburg (2 March), two small towns in the quarter of Zutphen, cost the duke's treasury 212 and 225 guilders, respectively. After Doesburg it was Doetinchem's turn. Here Reinald stressed his role as *pater patriae* through his generosity; he donated 50 guilders for the construction of a church in the town.[58]

The duke's caravan stayed at the small town of Beekbergen (in the Veluwe area) on 3 and 4 March and moved to Tiel on 7 March.[59] In both places the *ridder ende knecht* (the knights and squires) of the area, along with the townspeople, also swore their allegiance to their new lord.

From Tiel, the duke moved to Zaltbommel (8 March). The majority of his retinue, including a number of Englishmen, stayed in Tiel.

After visiting the Tielerwaard and Bommelerwaard (the areas around the towns of Tiel and Zaltbommel), the duke moved to the Overkwartier. The Venlo town accounts mention handsome rewards for the ducal musicians, the keeper of the seal, and the scribes accompanying the duke. The latter were there to draw up the town's charter of privileges, which the duke was to uphold.[60] The music, particularly that of the trumpeters, was added to that of the town bells.[61] Bells not only called people to the spectacle, but also expressed the town's "joy" at the new ruler, who had sworn (or was soon to swear) to respect the town's privileges and to protect the inhabitants against injustice and violence. The sounds, joining with the visual aspects, made the subjects' sensory experience as full as possible.

Arnold's inauguration in 1423, when he was still a minor in the charge of his father and regent John of Egmond, is even better documented in the Guelders sources. The ceremonies lasted for months. From 8 to 11 July the duke and his company stayed in Nijmegen.[62] As of old, the exchange of banquets marked the occasion, with the town council inviting the duke and he entertaining them and the town's clergy. A trumpeter from Delft supported the duke's musicians, and two heralds from Cleves graced the ceremonies. Since negotiations for a marriage between Arnold and Catherine, the daughter of the duke of Cleves and Mary of Burgundy, were at an advanced stage, their presence was obvious to all. A small silver statue made by a local goldsmith, which young Arnold donated when visiting the great church, was to be a lasting memento of the entry.

The new duke and his regent moved on to the towns in the Veluwe area. On 27 July they stayed in Beekbergen, where the *richter* (*iudex*) of the Veluwe was to swear allegiance to Arnold and pay homage to him. Shortly afterward they toured Hattem, Elburg, and Harderwijk. From Rozendaal Castle, near Arnhem, the duke rode to Lobith and sailed from there to Tiel. He spent 13 and 14 August in Tiel and on Assumption Day made his ceremonious entry into Zaltbommel. The *ambtman* of Tielerwaard and Bommelerwaard met the young duke on horseback and accompanied him on the visits. The *ambtman*, on ducal orders, summoned the area's knights to Tiel, "onsen lieven heer dair huldingen te doene" (to do homage to our dear lord there), as the clerk who wrote the accounts recorded.[63]

The procession did not arrive in Zutphen until more than a month later. As was the case elsewhere, the duke was given presents, including wine and a large sturgeon, and Arnold confirmed the town's privileges. After visiting the capital of the quarter, in accordance with the customary sequence, it was the small towns' turn. A delegation from Zutphen accompanied the duke on his tour of the quarter, and two of them took ship with him, en route to Roermond, the capital of the Overkwartier. On 23 September Arnold met a group of horsemen, mobilized by the *ambtman* of Venlo (another of the duke's officials), who escorted him through the gates of Roermond. Three days later, the same horsemen accompanied Arnold to Venlo.[64]

For the *ambtman* of Venlo the inauguration was more than a purely ceremonial occasion. In putting an end to a period of uncertainty, the dangerous power vacuum that arose because of a ruler's death, the subjects' oaths of allegiance and homage established order. The time between Reinald's death and Arnold's assumption of office had been a precarious period for the *ambtman*. He had continually stationed part of his men at strategic places (for example, near the small town of Wachtendonk), awaiting the day "dat mynen gnedigen here gehuldt wairt" (that my gracious lord would be inaugurated).[65] The threat of danger and the wish to avert it are clearly shown in a letter the new duke and his regent sent to all their officials in the Veluwe area. In this letter they called on these officials to ensure that all churches had a public procession carrying "dat heilige sacrament" (the holy sacrament). By this means, Arnold was hoping to implore the blessing of the Almighty, to put an end to the danger (in the person of the duke of Berg, pretender to the duchy of Guelders), and to make every inhabitant aware of their new lord, to whom support and allegiance were due.[66]

On occasion a substitute might be sent for the duke. The *ambtman* of Geldern (the *sluiter* [steward]) records such an event, which took place five months after the entry.[67] On 23 February 1424, the duke's father, John of Egmond, had ridden to Geldern to receive homage for his future daughter-in-law. The marriage contract between Guelders and Cleves had apparently been drawn up by then, and the towns could begin to swear allegiance to Catherine as the future duchess.[68] Delegating representation was not unique. As the son who had dethroned his father Arnold in 1465, Adolf was not immediately accepted as lord of the Overkwartier, which remained loyal to Arnold. When Adolf broke the resistance in 1469, he did not personally visit all the towns in the area for inauguration. In Wachtendonk, he had himself represented by "friends," undoubtedly nobles loyal to him. They were assisted by the bailiff of Geldern.[69] A similar situation occurred in 1473 when Charles the Bold, duke of Burgundy, finally managed to take control of the duchy of Guelders. He did not personally come to all towns in Guelders for the oath of allegiance but rather had some towns pay homage to his ally and representative, the duke of Cleves.[70]

Only a confidently powerful duke could delegate the entry ceremony. In 1471 Arnold attempted to restore his authority by visiting his towns with a particularly large retinue. His herald and numerous musicians — the minstrels from Roermond, Zutphen, and Nijmegen, as well as his own trumpeter — attempted to raise his status with an illusion of power and thus win the support of the confused and divided towns. But only in the Overkwartier did Arnold receive a sincere welcome.[71]

Entries on Return from Travels Abroad

An absence from the dukedom could also unsettle the power structure, so it became customary to have new grand entries to advertise a homecoming and reassert power.

Duke William was a keen traveler and crusader. He journeyed to Prussia seven times to fight against the "heathen,"[72] visited the Holy Land in 1391, and probably fought against the Barbary corsairs off Tunis. Twice a visitor to England, he regularly traveled to various parts of the German Empire. His motives ranged from diplomacy and war to an urge for adventure and devotion.

Following in the footsteps of his father, the duke of Gulik, William went to Prussia in 1388 to spread the faith there by the sword, and above all to gain knightly honor. Before he left, a Flemish *spreker* (speaker) boosted the morale of the duke and the various members of his retinue. Members of the clergy received a small remuneration to pray for the duke's safe return.[73] With all necessities and the required luxuries, including the *steekgetouwe* (jousting gear) for the tournaments that the grand master of the Teutonic Order would hold, the duke left.[74] The "crusade" did not proceed as planned. Arriving in Pomerania, the duke was captured and only regained his freedom in August 1389, after his subjects paid a high ransom. Once released, the duke first rode to Prague, where his brother-in-law, Wenceslas, king of the German Empire and king of Bohemia, had been trying to get him released.[75]

On 27 September the duke returned to his territories, arriving first at Kaster and staying one night in his castle in Gulik. Rather than proceeding to his duchy, he went on a pilgrimage to Aachen, honoring a vow he had made in captivity. His visit, however, was not as a repentant sinner, but as a ruler. His "piper ende trumpener" (pipers and trumpeters) and heralds loudly proclaimed the arrival of a "brave prince." His visit to the town of Charlemagne, and its famous shrine of the Virgin, lasted for one day. Via Cologne he returned to Kaster. After a brief second pilgrimage, this time to the small town of Grevenrade, Duke William at last arrived in his duchy, cleansed of his sins. On October 10, the town of Geldern had the honor of being the first to welcome the duke. As was customary on such occasions, the town council presented him with great quantities of wine.[76] After a short visit to Goch, the duke arrived the next day in Nijmegen.[77] From here Duke William made a number of town visits until New Year's Day 1390. From Zaltbommel William sailed to Dordrecht and Woudrichem, paying a short visit to his father-in-law, Albert of Bavaria, count of Holland. The duke was accompanied on all these visits by a large retinue, including Herald Gelre, famous for his glorification (in verse) of chivalric culture, who must have proclaimed his lord's heroic deeds.[78] Henric den Behemer (Henry the Bohemian), whom the duke had taken with him from Bohemia, bore witness to the duke's journeys and exploits abroad.[79]

No sooner had his subjects become accustomed to their lord's return than William went on a journey once again, this time to England, where King Richard II proposed to honor his valuable ally in the struggle against France with the Order of the Garter. William was the first continental nobleman to be awarded the Garter.[80] Such an honor required a large retinue and great pomp and circumstance. The journey through England, including the visits to London and Windsor, where the duke received the order's insignia during a solemn ceremony, were all recorded extensively in the account books.[81] William's return was equally glorious. After a short visit to the court of Holland in The Hague, he sailed for Zaltbommel, where several delegations, consisting of members of his own court as well as those of the towns, greeted him. All wished to honor their lord and to share in the rejoicing.

Duke Arnold's reign witnessed a shift in emphasis. His journeys were less "chivalrous," more "devout," and, therefore, rather modest. Arnold's pilgrimage to Italy and Palestine (1450–52) is a good example. In part, he undertook this trip to ease political relations within the duchy, which had reached a feverish pitch. With a motto of austerity, he avoided a large retinue with heralds and musicians. Unlike William's crusades to Prussia, his was a pilgrimage to the Holy Sepulchre and to the Holy Father in Rome. In the late autumn of 1450 (21 October) Arnold went first to Saint-Josse-sur-Mer (in Picardy) and from there to Rome. After visiting Rome he traveled to Venice, where he embarked for the voyage to Jaffa. To keep his subjects informed of his well-being, he sent messengers to Guelders, both to the court (where Duchess Catherine, aided by a "Council of Sixteen," was governing on behalf of her husband) and to the towns.[82] The towns in their turn sent messengers to Italy to be informed about their sovereign. When Arnold returned to Venice after his visit to Jerusalem and its environs, Arnhem sent a man to welcome the duke on his return from the Holy Sepulchre ("willecoem te heyten vanden heilighen grave").[83] His absence apparently occasioned some anxiety, for at the first news of his safe return to Venice, the aldermen of Arnhem dined at a local inn.[84]

From a political and tactical point of view Arnold's journey succeeded; his subjects displayed greater loyalty. For the time being, at least, they forgot their internal divisions and grievances against the duke. In the churches prayers were said for his safe homecoming, and the people drank to his swift return to the duchy. Arnold had taken the lead as a pious pilgrim. In contrast to his usual noble pomp, he had suffered hardships so as to kneel humbly by the side of the Holy Sepulchre. He had ventured into "dangerous territory," into a land dominated by infidels (the Muslims). He had left the comfortable "center"; he had gone off to the unknown "periphery." No matter how much Jerusalem may have been the Christian focal point, and therefore the center of the world, in actual fact the city was situated in a dangerous area where one could only rely on God's grace and protection. In other words, this was both a journey from the center to the periphery (in an actual sense) and at the same time a journey from the periphery to the center (in a figurative sense). In the eyes of numerous subjects, the duke's pilgrimage proved him to be the true head of the duchy. The magnificent and exuberant receptions he received, coinciding as they did with the Shrovetide celebrations, bore witness to his popularity.

After an initial greeting at Bois-le-Duc in Brabant, Arnold arrived in Grave on 14 February 1452 (Saint Valentine's Day). The small town on the Meuse hastily prepared for the occasion. The town council presented the duke with a silver cup filled with wine and afterward gave him a banquet at which minstrels performed.[85] The following Friday the duke met his wife, who had ridden with her retinue part of the way to meet and accompany him to her castle at Lobith. They celebrated their reunion with a select group of people.[86]

Arnold's entry into Nijmegen took place on Shrove Sunday, 20 February. Riding from Grave to Nijmegen with more than one hundred horses and numerous members of the knighthood, he met a delegation from the town.[87] Nijmegen, which until recently had been quite rebellious (it was to oppose the duke again soon afterward) received him with full honors. The celebration coincided with the first day of carnival, and thus a festive mood presided. The choice of this particular day must surely have been made on purpose; its effectiveness was too great to be mere coincidence.

On Shrove Tuesday Arnold went to Arnhem. Here too the greetings and celebrations were exuberant. The duke was presented with two beautiful silver jugs ("2 Scoen silveren kannen"), gilded and probably adorned with the town arms. As was the custom, they were filled with *malvesien* (malmsey) and *romenyen* (rumney)—two exclusive wines. Hundreds of guests attended a banquet, which took place in three inns. Local schoolchildren paid their respect to the duke, possibly with their boy bishop, and musicians contributed to the merry atmosphere. The whole town celebrated.[88]

Messengers were sent ahead to inform Zutphen of the time of the duke's visit. Prior to this Zutphen had sent a letter to Grave, intended for the duke, that was probably a first welcome.[89] Arnold proceeded to the Overkwartier during Lent and was received at Venlo and Geldern as elsewhere. In Geldern the duke's retinue was offered dinner and money for drinks, and Arnold himself was presented with a silver jug adorned with a banner on which the town arms were depicted. The jug was, of course, filled with wine. Once more a banquet followed, enlivened by entertainers. For this occasion the duke had brought Hans, the herald of the archbishop of Cologne, as well as his own herald.[90] An anonymous herald had announced the return of the duke in Venlo shortly after New Year's Day, but it took weeks before Arnold visited the town. The celebrations took place around Easter, in accordance with the by now familiar pattern.[91]

Political Meetings and Military Victories

Towns might initiate receptions for their own political ends. Usually these were more modest than solemn entries. A *dagvaart* (a meeting of the duke with representatives of the four quarters, the states) was sometimes seized upon by the town council to make a favorable impression. In 1422, for instance, when Geldern had "onzen genedigen heren toe eren gebeden" (invited our gracious lord in honor of him), the town feasted the assembled knights and the urban deputies in the duke's honor.[92] Even a town uninvolved in the discussions might offer a meal, with the expectation of gaining from its hospitality. During the week after Easter 1446, Duke Arnold had a meeting with the bishop of Utrecht (Rudolf of Diepholt) and the eldest son of the duke of Cleves at his ducal court in Arnhem. As bishop-elect, Rudolf had been an opponent of the duke's, so that the meeting must have been tense. The Arnhem town council considered it a worthwhile precaution to invite the important guests and their retinues (almost two hundred people) to a banquet on this occasion. A few months later the duke rode to Brussels to consult with the duke of Burgundy, and on his return home the town of Arnhem again offered him a meal.[93]

When the duke returned from successful campaigns, towns offered magnificent receptions. In August 1387, during the war against the duchess of Brabant, Duke William had harried the Brabant countryside, pillaging and ravaging villages. Having apparently gained enough "honor" to enter Venlo as conquerors, the town presented him and his most prominent noblemen and citizens (including the burgomaster and aldermen of Roermond) with a meal.[94]

Adolf's victory over Cleves in 1468 was perhaps more "honorable." In the struggle between Arnold and Adolf, the duke of Cleves supported Arnold, his brother-in-law. Declaring himself the enemy of Guelders after Adolf's assumption of power, he encouraged various skirmishes between Cleves and Guelders. These culminated in the battle near Straelen on 23 June (Saint John's Eve).[95] The fighting was fierce, but Adolf's triumph was resounding and the duke of Cleves barely managed to escape. The battle of Straelen considerably strengthened Adolf's position. He had convincingly defeated an enemy and won the support of various towns and noblemen in his duchy that until then had wavered between Arnold and Adolf. Before the engagement Zutphen had held a procession and prayers for a favorable outcome. When the first reports that Guelders was victorious reached Zutphen, it rewarded the messengers handsomely.[96] In Geldern, Midsummer's Day (Saint John's Day, 24 June) was celebrated even more exuberantly than in other years, for "Got van hemelrych, gracy end gnaden, onsen gnedigen heren van Gelre verloent hadde tot Stralen opder lantweren die Cleefschen te keren end tverslaen" (God in Heaven, gracious and merciful, had allowed our gracious lord of Guelders to hold off and defeat the army of Cleves near Straelen).[97] To express his gratitude, Adolf founded a monastery at the battle site and an order of knights. Both the monastery and the order of knights were dedicated to the Virgin Mary, because it was through her intercession that the duke had gained the victory.[98] Although the order could only be conferred on noblemen (initially Adolf's brothers-in-arms), other people were allowed to participate in the anniversary celebrations. On 23 June 1469, Arnhem held a lavish banquet in honor of God and His Mother Mary: "Want doe die irste Jairgetyde was, dat ons ghenedigen here hertoge Adolph van Gelre syn victorie had tot onser vrouwen voir Straelen" (as it was the first anniversary of the victory of gracious duke of Guelders at "Our Lady of the Sand" at Straelen).[99] The schoolchildren had a day off, and the schoolteacher received a quart of wine. The writer of the accounts adds that the banquet was held so as to please the duke. Why? Perhaps it was because Adolf had lost his wife not long before? Whether or not the duke was present at the dinner or ordered an anniversary celebration, the event commemorated was one of state importance. In this way a growing sense of unity was developed—or developed further—that transcended the town, village, or manor. Farmers, townspeople, clergymen, and noblemen had to be imbued with a sense of statehood.

Celebrations of Dynastic Events

Marriages and Ducal Births

The sense of being one state, however rudimentary, was linked to the personality of the duke. Since he personified authority and unity, his presence in the towns was essential. In continuously playing the role of a *ruler*, he had to dress in precious garments and be surrounded by courtiers, dignitaries, clergymen, servants, and entertainers. This ideal of personal lordship meant that personal markers of stages in his life cycle were highly political. Birth, baptism, marriage, and death were "state events," just as much as entries or battles. In their rites of passage the duke or members of his family crossed borders and took their "land and people" with them on their way to a different status.[100] Delegations of the subjects were present as witnesses at these ritualized transitions at court and in the towns of the duchy.

In the fourteenth century the court still held celebrations in connection with weddings or births privately, at the very most sending messengers to the towns to report the happy news. Town councils usually confined themselves to rewarding the messengers. In view of the event's importance, the duke sometimes sent special messengers, as he did in 1394, when Squire Gelijs, a noble courtier, informed the towns of the intended marriage between William, the duke's bastard son, and Johanna of Cuyck.[101] Townsmen were absent at the marriage of another bastard son, John of Guelders, in 1400. The only urban presence was provided by the minstrels from Arnhem, who formed part of the group of entertainers for the noble assemblage.[102]

Towns could show festive participation in private marriages only in welcoming the duke's new wife. While the duchess's entries resembled those of the duke, their political significance was not as great. As a result, they were simpler and perhaps more personal. For instance, during her 1379 entry into Zutphen, Catherine of Bavaria was presented with a number of pikes intended to be eaten at the meal on this occasion. As usual, the town bells were rung here and at Arnhem. The duchess, like her husband at his entry, was embarking on a new phase in life. In her new position she was mistress of the town and the country. The bell ringing marked the rite of passage in a symbolic sense. It was a nonverbal form of communication that was as essential as the welcoming speech or the gifts.[103]

After the turn of the century the towns' role in private ducal ceremony began to change. The marriage between Reinald and Mary of Harcourt, contracted in 1404, took place on 5 May 1405 in Bastogne, outside the duchy.[104] This union sealed the bond between the duke of Guelders and Charles VI, King of France, and had come about through the mediation of the duke of Orleans, the most influential man at the French court.[105] Although the towns had been notified of the intended marriage, they were not represented at its solemnization.[106]

In the summer of 1405, however, the people of Guelders prepared themselves for the French princess's arrival. Venlo was especially generous. In addition to wine, the town council presented the new duchess with a piece of jewelry made of precious metal, worth almost seventy guilders. Prior to this the town had sent a messenger to Roermond to inquire what kind of present the duchess would receive there; Venlo did not wish to be outdone.[107] When Mary made her festive entry into Rozendaal Castle on 16 August, the Deventer musicians added luster to the event. The quadrumvirate who had ruled the duchy during Reinald's absence waited in Arnhem to escort her during the final stretch of her journey.[108]

After this slow start, the towns' involvement in the marriages and entries of members of the ducal family increased. When Edward, Duke Reinald's bastard son, married a daughter of Sir William of Arnhem in

1410, the marriage took place in the town of Arnhem.[109] While the bride and groom, the duke, and most of the guests celebrated at the ducal court, their numbers were too large for everybody to be feasted in the town palace. Local inns had to be used in the celebrations.

When Arnold of Egmond's marriage contract with the young Catherine of Cleves was arranged in 1423, the capitals of the four quarters affixed their seals on the "marriage letter."[110] The duke's marriage had become a matter of town political importance. Since Arnold and Catherine were still minors (Arnold was thirteen years of age, while Catherine was only six), the solemnization was delayed until 1430.[111] In January 1430, accompanied by many noblemen, including the count of Meurs and the lords of Voorst and Berg, Arnold went to the bride's residence in Cleves. Councillors of the various towns (*raetsvrienden*) rode to the castle of Cleves and witnessed the effectuation of the marriage: "daer myn here sijn vrouwe beslyep" (where our lord slept with his wife).[112] The duke performed the rite of passage in the presence of his subjects, for his new status concerned them all.

The next day the company from Guelders left Cleves. The marriage celebrations coincided with carnival and lasted most of February, a combination of rejoicing and exuberance that was planned. A tournament to celebrate the marriage alliance, originally scheduled at Cleves on Shrove Tuesday, did not take place. Instead, Duke Arnold invited his guests to come to a tournament in honor of his new wife at Nijmegen, on Shrove Sunday and Shrove Monday (26 and 27 February). On Tuesday Arnold escorted the company from Cleves on their way home. Ash Wednesday signified the end to both the Shrovetide and the marriage celebrations.

As had been agreed, Catherine stayed with her parents for a year after the wedding. Perhaps her tender age—she was not yet thirteen—played a part in this arrangement. In the course of this year the duke visited Cleves more than once. In the meantime the court of Guelders began preparations for the arrival of the duke's wife. Arnold went on a pilgrimage, most probably to the Holy Blood chapel in Bruges, staying abroad for four weeks (from 26 January until 22 February). Perhaps Arnold, a devout man, wished to prepare himself spiritually for his marriage? His younger brother, nineteen-year-old William, had been asked to collect the bride. On 3 February 1431 he arrived at Lobith Castle with a large retinue. This Guelders castle, situated on the Waal (Rhine), was close to the border with Cleves and therefore an ideal place to meet the bride.[113] Catherine arrived at Lobith escorted by her brother, who was heir to the throne of Cleves, and a large retinue. The following week, carnival was celebrated at Lobith Castle (again the festivities coincided). John of Egmond, regent of the duchy, had come to the castle for this occasion. The young duchess took a conclusive step toward her new position, staying behind with her new relatives when her party returned to Cleves. On the first Thursday of Lent (15 February), Catherine bade farewell to her mother, Mary of Burgundy, and embarked for Rozendaal, arriving at the castle the same evening. The warden of the castle had prepared the rooms for the duchess, decorating them with fresh greenery, undoubtedly as a symbol of hope and anticipation of a bright future. A week later the duke returned to Rozendaal and met his wife for the first time on his own territory. The married couple stayed at the castle until Palm Sunday (25 March), when they moved to Grave. This was the beginning of a more active life.[114]

In Grave the duchess's tour of the Guelders towns commenced. True to tradition, the town presented the duchess with a gilded drinking cup and a meal.[115] On the Tuesday after Easter (13 April) Catherine, accompanied by Arnold, made her entry into Nijmegen. It was Arnhem's turn on 19 April. The Arnhem militia and *statknechten*[116] rode out to meet the married couple and accompanied them to the town. Catherine was presented with a pair of silver jugs, filled with red and white *lotterdranc* (claret), sweetened wine, specially intended for ladies. The banquet that the Arnhem magistrate offered to the duke and his wife in the afternoon was lavish and delicious. The duchess proved herself to be generous and charitable. She saw to it that money was handed out to the poor "omb Gaetzwille" (for the love of God) and donated a sum of money inside the great church, where she attended mass together with her husband, both their retinues, and the townspeople. The Arnhem clergy blessed the young couple.[117] In October, the ducal procession arrived in Venlo. A similar reception followed. It was not until July 1432 that Zutphen could welcome Catherine.[118] She took her time over the tiring trip, as she had become pregnant.

In the autumn of 1431 Catherine, who was fourteen years old at the time, gave birth to her first child, a daughter, who died shortly afterward.[119] More than a year later, on 17 January 1433, the second child was born, once again a girl, Mary, who lived to become queen of Scotland. Messengers were sent to the towns to announce the happy news of her birth, and soon afterward they were sent a second time to announce her baptism. For a short time Grave, the town where this child too was born, was the center of attention. The town council congratulated the father by presenting wine. Since the baptism took place in the town hall, the town was involved in the preparations. Delegations from other towns arrived. Arnhem, for example, had sent Ludeken Kremer to Grave some time before the ceremony to reserve an inn for its dignitaries. During these frosty weeks the court itself was busy organizing the required celebrations. Cooks were summoned to the castle and food supplies arrived by the cartload. Ducal *ambtmannen* and officials received letters in which they were summoned to go to Grave on 2 March. Their presence at the ceremony was desirable to increase the duke's prestige. No less a dignitary than the archbishop of Cologne was invited to baptize little Mary.[120]

The towns' involvement became even greater. When on 24 October 1434 Arnold and Catherine's first son was born at Grave, the town council assembled to determine how to deal effectively with the arrival of the guests. Since an heir to the throne had been born, a "jonge hertoge van Gelre" (young duke of Guelders), as the Venlo town account states jubilantly,[121] a great number of guests were expected. The town of Grave became quite experienced in cooperating with the court. Sadly, Arnold and Catherine's little son William died shortly after being baptized. A second son, born in 1435, died in childbed as well. In Arnhem the duchess finally gave birth to a healthy and "viable" son, Adolf, who was born 12 February 1439.[122]

This time it fell to Arnhem to help organize the celebrations connected with the baptism of the duke's son. Setting aside the grievances it had nursed against Arnold, the town offered him a banquet to congratulate him on his son. This occasion enabled them to distinguish themselves from other towns in Guelders by means of flawless organization. Fixing the date of the baptism brought about feverish activity. Torches were made, the great—or old—church was decorated, the streets and squares were swept clean, and in the church and the dance hall benches were made to seat all the numerous guests. The civic militia took care of security. A group of citizens rehearsed a dance. On 15 March the great day had come. The entire Arnhem council had assembled at the town hall to consider their presence at the celebrations that day. Should the council only send a delegation, or should all members attend the baptism? They decided on the latter option. All councillors wished to take part in the parade that was to accompany Adolf and his parents to the church. The civic militia and the Arnhem clergy were there, as were the members of the court and the Guelders noblemen. The urban authorities had prepared the church ceremonies with great care. A correct placing of the guests and all those present was a matter of the utmost concern. The "people" had to stand at the back, on a platform. Apparently there was such a jostling during the baptismal ceremony that the *ghereemt* (construction) collapsed. The account mentions the expenses this had caused. After the ceremony the distinguished guests and the town council feasted on a lavish banquet in the town hall and ended the day in the dance hall.[123]

Civic Ritual on the Death of Members of the Ducal Dynasty

The death of a duke or a member of his family heralded a period both of mourning and danger, raising worries and fears. Every change in status, every crossing of boundaries—in this case the boundary between life and death—had to be approached with the utmost care. Ritual acts made it possible to imagine a transition so that the uncertainty could be overcome and fears allayed.[124] To allay uncertainty regarding the hereafter, masses, offerings, and gifts to religious institutions were supposed to contribute to the salvation of the deceased. The duke's death affected every inhabitant of the duchy. All had to be made fully aware of this.

The process began with the news of the lord's death. Sometimes this came as a complete surprise, as in the case of Adolf's violent death; at other times people were somewhat prepared. Reinald, for instance, had repeatedly been ill. His failing health had made his subjects fear the worst. Messengers carried the news to towns, noblemen, and monasteries and convents.[125] The ringing of the bells commenced at once, making it clear that an important event had taken place.[126]

The duke's death occasioned a flurry of activity at court, especially with respect to the funeral. But the local administrators also were involved in the period of mourning, which they had to convey to their towns or villages in a suitable fashion. When news of the death of Mary Queen of Scots reached the duchy in 1464, Duke Arnold sent letters to his subordinates. The castellan of Hattem (an *ambtman* residing at the castle of the same name) received two letters. In the first, dated 21 February, the duke announced the death of his daughter, and ordered the official to see to it that the bells were rung in all the churches within his *ambt*. Two hours prior to this someone was to go around "kleppen" (rattling) in each village. In addition the duke wanted masses to be celebrated in every church. In his capacity as ducal representative, the *ambtman* had to attend the funeral ceremonies together with all the "good men" he could muster. On 4 March Arnold sent the second letter, fixing the commemorative service for 13 March. The official from Hattem went to Arnhem on the preceding evening to be present at the official funeral. The duke charged him to "take care of all that was required," assuming that the official knew what was involved in the usual preparations for a funeral service.[127]

The ritual of official mourning was well known in the towns. When Mary's husband had died four years earlier, Duke Arnold had called on the towns "den conynck van Schotlant alsoe eerlicken te averluyden ende te begaen als men kond" (to ring the bells for the king of Scotland in as honest and sincere a way as was possible and to celebrate the funeral solemnly).[128] The towns observed the usual funerary ceremonies, even for a king whom no one had ever seen and, four years later, for a queen who had been born in Grave, to be sure, but whom few in the duchy knew. The duke paid for part of the meals that the town councils had after the ceremony.[129]

The court arranged and paid for the actual funeral. When duchess Catherine had died in Hattem on 11 November 1400, the solemn requiem mass was celebrated in Zutphen and took place before her body was buried at Monnikhuizen monastery (near Arnhem). The court spent hundreds of guilders on the black clothing that the courtiers and local officials wore for the ceremony.[130] A year later, at the first annual mass, the court gave the Geldern poor white bread and herring. Parish and monastery churches had prayers said for the duchess, but the court paid for the costs of the candles and torches that burned during those masses and invited the knighthood and the town magistrates assembled in Geldern for a modest meal.[131]

Not long afterward (16 February 1402), William himself died at Arnhem, and his remains were taken to Monnikhuizen the same day. The wagon and horses that transported the deceased, as well as the escorting servants, were dressed in black.[132] The duke lay in state in the monastery, and afterward he was buried next to his wife. Delegations from the duchy were present at the burial.[133] Until 1404, the grave was only provisionally covered until the large gravestones, which had been manufactured in Bruges, arrived.[134] Meanwhile two annual masses had been celebrated. The ducal steward, the highest financial official, recorded the expenses in Nijmegen, including remuneration to the priests for reading mass, to a woman who had led the women of the town in prayer, and to the man who had called on the inhabitants to donate gifts. In addition, a substantial number of loaves were baked for distribution to the poor.[135] By going to church the subjects underscored their alliance with the dynasty. They kneeled before God, to be sure, but also in remembrance of their lord in Guelders. In this way the deceased and the authority of his dynasty remained alive. The duke's memory was kept alive in monasteries, convents, and churches, where "eternal" lights burned and numerous masses were celebrated.[136]

The funereal and memorial symbolism and rituals strengthened the bond with the ducal dynasty, articulating a shared experience of death and sorrow.[137] The funeral ceremonies created a unity of time and space. Everywhere in the duchy a moment of mourning was observed. Once again the ringing of the bells marked its beginning and summoned the duchy's inhabitants to the hallowed places. The simultaneous nature of the mourning service created a relationship between the local and the territorial level.[138] In Venlo, for instance, a *baer* (bier) was placed in the church during the requiem mass, beside which a number of grieving women seated themselves. The bier's function was to create an illusion among the townspeople that the deceased was in their midst. Was a coffin present, or can we even go one step further and assume that the deceased had been represented with an effigy?[139]

The grave also symbolized the deceased's presence. When Duke Adolf died in Tournai, the town council of Zutphen organized commemorative ceremonies, including candles and the mourning attire, and an imitation grave inside the church. The grave was covered with a black sheet and flanked by shields on which the coat of arms of the deceased duke had been painted. The local painter, Master Rutger, had manufactured these shields and had them attached to the torches.[140]

Traditional numerology surrounded the transition from life to death and the final journey of the deceased. For three whole days the bells were rung at fixed hours (sometimes for an hour and a half on end). On eight consecutive days priests read masses for the deceased in all the duchy churches. In the most important churches twelve clergymen celebrated a requiem mass, and twelve pounds of wax was used for making the candles.[141] The numbers had various meanings.[142] Three was the number of the Trinity, eight symbolized the Resurrection, twelve represented the Apostles (as well as the Jewish tribes and the articles of the Creed). The symbolic power of the numbers gave the event a ritual dimension.

Conclusions

Ceremonies and festivities had a political overtone in towns in which the ducal presence received expression. Not only major occasions such as entries and funerals drew attention to the duke, but also any appearance of his musicians, heralds, and buffoons underscored ducal authority.[143] The town palaces and ducal houses bore witness to their owners' power and riches; the duke and duchess's coats of arms, painted on the stained-glass windows of churches, pointed to the court as well. All these were a means of communication that joined the ducal house with the towns through rituals and festivities.

The entries, tournaments, meals, and so on derived their political power in part from their ritual nature. They were standardized events that were repetitive and dramatic in presentation. A ritual gave the impression that it would last "eternally," reinforcing the idea that the duke's power was independent of the "here and now." The sacralization of power contributed to this idea.[144] By using religious festivities, the duke added a sacral dimension to his authority. During ceremonious entries he invariably proceeded to the local church to pray. In commemoration of military victories he built chapels, as he did in Nifterik after 1388,[145] or founded a monastery or convent. The duke presented town councils with meals in honor of both God and himself. By emphasizing bonds with the supernatural, he became the intermediary between it and his subjects.

The duke's power and authority thrived on political unity. The duke had to bind individuals and groups to himself, as well as establish a relationship between the local and the territorial level. He tried to put the urban elites in his debt by giving them political privileges and positions: gifts, meals, and "honorable" invitations to ducal festivities. The duke likewise took pains to bind other groups, such as archery companies and charities, to himself.

Since political unity was centered around the duke's dynasty, it was of great importance to the duke to heighten his family's prestige. Annual masses for deceased dynasty members kept the memory of the "illustrious family" alive. The funeral services for a Scottish king and queen, for instance, added a royal luster to the ducal dynasty; they indicated that the family moved in the highest circles of European nobility. Local celebrations of "national" events—the duke's return from abroad, entries, marriages, deaths, and the like—perpetuated the idea that the town-dwellers' allegiance should rise above the town to include the dukedom.

Why did the dukes feel the need to consolidate town allegiance to their dynasty? Because the notion of territorial unity with defined boundaries had hardly developed yet, dynastic power over towns could be questioned. Within half a century, two new dynasties came to power in Guelders: the Gulik dynasty in 1371 and the Egmond dynasty in 1423. On both occasions the new dynasty had to "prove" itself to the subjects. The first time this happened in a period of fierce strife between two parties (the Bronckhorsts and the Heekerens). Duke William had to rise above the party that had helped him to come to power (the Bronck-horsts) and become a *pater patriae* as soon as possible. The princely dynasty from which he descended contributed to his success. After his father's death in 1394, William also became duke of Gulik.

Arnold of Egmond came to power under much less favorable circumstances. Although the political conflict had somewhat subsided, the international situation became considerably more threatening. In the south the Burgundians were advancing and, in the east, the duke of Berg beleaguered the young duke. What was more, Arnold was confronted with self-confident states in which the towns made themselves heard more and more clearly. Internally as well as externally, the Egmond duke had to fight hard to establish his authority. Time and again he had to demonstrate his authority in political, military, and cultural spheres. He was forced to spend his scarce monetary resources and much of his time on entries and festivities. Arnold, in particular, was disadvantaged since he descended from a less "illustrious" family and, unlike the Gulik family, had not come to Guelders with a princely title, only *becoming* a prince in 1423.

Considering the frequent occurrence of rituals, symbols, and festivities in Guelders, we may assume that the dukes were convinced of their political efficacy. The letters in which the duke instructed his subjects to celebrate "in a suitable manner" point in this direction, as do the coincidences of entries and weddings with carnival celebrations. If the duke had not realized the importance of his presence at urban festivities, he would not have gone to such great pains to be present or have himself represented there. He could have continued to celebrate privately in his castles with his court.

The immediate question that comes to mind is why the dukes considered it important to co-opt the towns in ducal celebrations. A secondary question is the attitude of the towns. It has been claimed that the political and economic position of the towns in Guelders was rising in the fourteenth and fifteenth centuries, and that their entry into "national" politics was a reflection of their increasing power. In the field of culture, too, the towns were making their mark. When the town councils invited the lord or members of his court, they expressed their prosperity by offering banquets and organizing festivities. In doing so, they set themselves up as a power with which the duke had to reckon. At the same time these activities were a form of diplomacy. The urban elites could discreetly remove imbalances in their relationship with the duke by a display of their wealth and power. Clothing their demands in gestures and elegant display, they could achieve such benefits as ratification of their charters. They represented local interests vis-à-vis territorial interests. In the duke's army the civic militia carried their own emblems (the towns' coats of arms adorned clothing and banners). In the course of the fifteenth century the towns gradually obtained a better hold on the cultural monopoly of the court. More and more it was the towns that initiated the organization of festivities whose importance went beyond that of the towns themselves. At the same time the town councils continued to endorse festivities of their own (the processions of the Virgin Mary, for instance). These were especially suited to strengthening internal solidarity, since they constituted an internal regulatory mechanism for which the court's services were not required.

That the town councils had begun to engage in organizing "national" festivities suggests a new sense of territorial awareness. Perhaps the repetition of the duke's entries over the years gradually awakened the local rulers' understanding that in some cases national interest coincided with town interest. With some reservations, we may observe in the town rulers' cultural initiatives a beginning of the reification of an abstraction such as "political unity." The towns as well as the duke could contribute to a sense of unity.

In some respects the new urban initiatives involving "national unity" forced the dukes to escalate their interactions with the towns in order to retain control. If the duke wished to remain the personification of the "common good," he would have to prove his authority time and again. Duke Arnold was successful in his return from Palestine in 1452 and in his victory over Cleves in 1468. His attempts did not always succeed, however. The ducal carnival celebrations in Nijmegen in 1455, for instance, failed to improve his strained relationship with the disobedient town.

By the fifteenth century a conflict between towns and dukes developed over the ceremonial activities. The duke continued to build a sense of territorial awareness among his subjects, but as soon as the notion started to take shape it became a threat to him. The duke found himself in competition with the towns and the states of Guelders, which also began to represent the "common good." The battlefield where both parties clashed was situated largely on cultural territory.

Political tensions could lead to cultural conflicts, but the sources from Guelders offer few data on cultural articulation of such conflicts.[146] The applicability of insights from the social sciences (anthropology in particular) to the study of a medium-sized court is determined to a large extent by the available sources. The accounts supply "dry" material, terse and factual data. Insights from anthropology can help to bring the facts to life and can also be of help in structuring the fragmentary statements. Nevertheless, the sources determine the limits of what is possible. Although the data from Guelders allow us to make statements about the potency of symbols in the context in which they occur, they block our view of changes in the meaning of a symbol or a symbolic activity, which may have changed in the course of a century.[147] For tracing these kinds of changes, accounts are not a suitable source. A discreet silence is appropriate.

Notes

I want to thank Professor Anton Weiler for his comments on an earlier version of this paper. The original Dutch text was translated by Frank van Meurs and Arnold J. Kreps. The map was drawn by Vincent Boele.

1. The concepts of "ceremony" and "ritual" are confusing. There is no agreement among social scientists about these. A distinction is frequently made between the two; the former is said to be "secular ritual," the latter "religious ritual." I will adhere to R. Trexler's definition: "By ritual I shall mean formal behavior, those verbal and bodily actions of humans that, in specific contexts of space and time, become relatively fixed into those recognizable social and cultural deposits we call behavioral forms" (R. Trexler, *Public Life in Renaissance Florence* [New York, London, Toronto: Academic Press, 1980], p. xxiv). Compare D. Kertzer: "Ritual [is] symbolic behavior that is socially standardized and repetitive" (D. Kertzer, *Ritual, Politics and Power* [New Haven, Conn., and London: Yale University Press, 1988], p. 9). Neither author wishes to distinguish between ritual and ceremony, because this leads to an awkward dichotomy between the religious and the secular.

2. Henceforth, whenever Guelders is mentioned, it will include the county of Zutphen.

3. P. Burke, *Historical Anthropology in Early Modern Italy: Essays on Perception and Communication* (Cambridge: Cambridge University Press, 1987), part 1; P. Burke, "Cultural History: Past, Present and Future," *Theoretische geschiedenis* 13 (1986): 190; and A. Burguière, "L'anthropologie historique," in *La nouvelle histoire,* ed. J. Le Goff (Paris: Editions complexe, 1978), pp. 137–66.

4. See among others S. Orgal, *The Illusion of Power* (Berkley and Los Angeles: University of California Press, 1975); S. Price, *Rituals and Power* (Cambridge: Cambridge University Press, 1984); S. Wilentz, ed., *Rites of Power* (Philadelphia: University of Pennsylvania Press, 1985); and D. Cannadine and S. Price, eds., *Rituals of Royalty* (Cambridge, 1987). Kertzer, *Ritual, Politics and Power,* p. 2, states that "politics is expressed through symbolism."

5. M. Carasso-Kok, *Repertorium van verhalende historische bronnen uit de middeleeuwen* (The Hague: Martinus Nijhoff, 1981); J. Romein, *Geschiedenis van de Noord-*

Nederlandsche Geschiedschrijving in de Middeleeuwen (Haarlem: Theenk Willink, 1932; supplement by H. Bruch, 1956); and W. Jappe Alberts, *Van heerlijkheid tot landsheerlijkheid* (Assen and Amsterdam: Van Gorcum, 1978), esp. chapter on historiography, pp. 240–68.

6. Rijksarchief Gelderland (Gelderland national archives) in Arnhem, Hertogelijk Archief (ducal archives, henceforth RAG HA), inv. no. 210-1766.

7. P. Meij and A. Jenniskens, *Het archief van de graven en hertogen van Gelre, graven van Zutphen* (Arnhem: Rijksarchief Gelderland, 1977); and G. Nijsten, "Hertog en hof in Gelre: Bronnen en perspectieven," *Groniek: Gronings historisch tijdschrift* 93 (1985): 124–43.

8. Compare L. Hunt, ed., *The New Cultural History* (Berkley and Los Angeles: University of California Press, 1989), p. 14. In her introduction, Hunt points out the importance of source criticism (in an introduction to an article by R. Chartier).

9. Kertzer, *Ritual, Politics and Power*, p. 101. Rituals are at the same time "contractual" and "conflictual": Trexler, *Public Life*, pp. xxiv–xxv.

10. For this, see G. Nijsten, "Openbare feesten, toneel en 'volksvermaak' in Arnhem ca 1430 - ca 1500," *Bijdragen en mededelingen Gelre* 79 (1988): 29–47, and "De stad en haar metafoor: Processie, toneel en openbare feesten in Venlo ca 1380–1525," *Volkskundig bulletin* 17, no. 3 (1991): 223–48.

11. That carnival and Shrovetide had older roots, that is, roots in antiquity and Germanic times, is well known. See, for example, J. Heers, *Fêtes de fous et Carnavals* (Paris: Fayard, 1983); and M. Grinberg, "Carnaval et société urbaine XIVe–XVIe siècles: Le royaume dans la ville," *Ethnologie française* 4 (1974): 215–45.

12. Nijsten, "Openbare feesten," 30–33, and "De stad en haar metafoor," pp. 224–25.

13. RAG HA 384, fol. 20v (Rozendaal, 1380) for celebrations in castles; RAG HA 211, fol. 100v (Cleves, 1382–83) for Shrove Tuesday spent with sovereigns of the duke's acquaintance; and RAG HA 223, fol. 68v (The Hague, 1394) for the duchess's visit with her father, the count of Holland.

14. RAG HA 384, fols. 20v–21r (1380); RAG HA 223, fol. 68v (1394); and RAG HA 232, fol. 60v (1399) provide some examples.

15. RAG HA *aanwinsten* (acquisitions) 1953 II.4, fol. 7v (1383). In 1406 they again had their court in Nijmegen, where their guests included the bishop of Liège and the count of Cleves (RAG HA 241, fols. 37v, 38r, 66v [1406]).

16. Venlo town archive (Oud Archief Venlo, henceforth OAV) stadsrekeningen 1394, p. 7.

17. For 1430, see W. Jappe Alberts, ed., *De stadsrekeningen Arnhem* (Arnhem: Gemeentearchief Arnhem, 1985), vol. 5 (1428–32), p. 181; Arnhem town archive (Oud Archief Arnhem, henceforth OAA) 1244, fols. 9v–10r (1445); and Grave town archive (Oud Archief Grave, henceforth OAG) 217, fol. 264r (1447).

18. Arnhem, for example, in the town account of the years 1439, 1440, 1441, 1444, 1446, 1447, 1460, and 1463 (OAA); and Grave, in the town accounts for the years 1453, 1455, 1456, 1458, 1462, and 1464 (OAG).

19. OAA 1244, fols. 42v–43v (1440). For other years in Arnhem, see OAA 1244, fols. 52r–v (1439); OAA 1244, fols. 43r–v (1441); and OAA 1245, fols. 7r–v (1447).

20. Nijsten, "Openbare feesten," p. 39, shows the relationship between tournament and carnival. Tournaments were, of course, organized at other times as well.

21. OAA 1244, fols. 45r, 57r, 59v, 61v–62r (1440).

22. OAA 1244, fol. 61v (1440): "Want onse here des begheerden ynt lesten" (for our lord desired this at the last moment).

23. RAG HA 214, fols. 9v, 11r (Cologne, 1387); RAG HA 220, fols. 33r–v, 34v–35v, 42r–v (Kreuznach, 1390); RAG HA 225, fol. 232r; Algemeen Rijksarchief (Dutch National Archives), The Hague, Archives of the Counts of Holland, the Account of 1395, fol. 44r (Sint-Geertruidenberg, 1395); and RAG HA 227, fols. 8v, 18r, 100r, 101r, 141r (Sinzig, 1397).

24. In 1390 Weyndkerren, the duke's herald, proclaimed the *hof* (court) that was to be held in Cologne (RAG HA 220, fol. 48v), and in 1406 Duke Reinald organized a tournament in Nijmegen (RAG HA 241, fol. 15r).

25. In 1395 a herald from Holland invited the duke of Guelders to a tournament in Holland (Sint-Geertruidenberg), organized by Duke Albert of Bavaria, count of Holland, and William of Gulik—Guelders's father-in-law (RAG HA 225, fol. 232r).

26. In view of an entry in an account from 1437, it is likely, but not certain, that the duke invited delegations from the large towns to the Shrove Tuesday festivities that he organized in Nijmegen (OAA 1244, fol. 48r).

27. OAA 1248, fols. 35v, 46v (from 1464); OAA 1248, fol. 62r (1466); and OAA 1249, fol. 34v (1470). For mock tournaments, probable in 1476 and certain in 1480, see OAA 1249, fol. 7r (1476), and OAA 1250, fol. 19v (1480).

28. Nijsten, "Openbare feesten," passim and "De stad en haar metafoor," passim. The duke was regularly treated by a town council, for example in Grave in 1453 (OAG 218, fol. 31r).

29. For *mommen* (masked people), for instance in Arnhem in 1399, see RAG HA 232, fol. 60v; for the boy bishop (often in the weeks preceding the actual Shrovetide, for example on Holy Innocents' Day) in 1380, see RAG HA 384, fols. 19r, 43r, and RAG HA 226, fol. 243r (1396); for playacting by *gezellen* (companions), for example in 1394 in Arnhem, see RAG HA 224, fol. 102r, or by young women, for example in 1390 in Tiel, see RAG HA 220, fol. 37v.

30. For example, in 1395 (RAG HA 225, fol. 237v). In 1418, RAG HA 252, fol. 101v, states "Na der alder gewoenten yn die ere myns gnedigen heren..." (according to the old custom and in honor of my gracious lord).

31. RAG HA 455, fol. 88r (1467).

32. The *kwartieren* (quarters) of Nijmegen, Roermond, Arnhem, and Zutphen. For the development of the states, see W. Jappe Alberts, *De staten van Gelre en Zutphen tot 1459* (Groningen and Jakarta: Wolters, 1950); and K. Nüsse, *Die Entwicklung der Stände im Herzogtum Geldern nach den Stadtrechnungen von Arnheim* (Cologne: Universität Köln, 1958).

33. R. van Schaïk, *Belasting, bevolking en bezit in Gelre en Zutphen (1350–1550)* (Hilversum: Verloren, 1987).

34. RAG HA 449, fol. 9r (Nijmegen, 1458); RAG HA 454, fol. 198r (1466); and RAG HA 450, fols. 93v–94r (Venlo, e.g. in 1459). See also Nijsten, "De stad en haar metafoor," p. 236.

35. RAG HA 274, fol. 21r (1455).

36. Nijsten, "De stad en haar metafoor," pp. 226–27.

37. The accounts of the court refer to dancing only once: on Christmas Day 1425 John of Egmond, father and regent of Arnold—who was still a minor—went dancing in Arnhem (RAG HA 257, fol. 68v). Occasionally the court organized a tournament at Easter, as in Grave in 1462. However, this was exclusively a matter for the nobility (RAG HA 452, fol. 104r).

38. For May Day in Arnhem in 1410, see RAG HA 248, fol. 61v; and in 1426, see RAG HA 260, fol. 86r. See especially the Arnhem town accounts from the mid-1430s onward, for example OAA 1243, fol. 56v (1435; only the duchess, not her husband); OAA 1244, fol. 11v (1444); and OAA 1248, fol. 7r (1464; accompanied by Alexander, "Prince of Scotland," the second son of James II and Mary of Guelders, who was brought up at his grandfather's court). For May Eve in Nijmegen, 1441, see RAG HA 540, fol. 5r. For Saint John's Beheading in Arnhem, see RAG HA 246, fol. 10r (1407), and the Arnhem town accounts in OAA 1243, fol. 8r (1433); OAA 1246, fol. 30r (1455); and OAA 1248, fol. 37v (1464).

39. J. Heers, *Fêtes, jeux et joutes dans les sociétés d'occident à la fin du moyen âge* (Montreal and Paris: Institut d'études médiévales Montréal, 1971), pp. 52–53.

40. RAG HA 232, fol. 89v (1399). It is not clear whether the Mussenberg was situated

near Arnhem. Perhaps a place outside Nijmegen is meant, situated near the present-day village of Beek.

41. For example, in 1464 (OAA 1248, fol. 7r).

42. RAG HA 384, fol. 21v (1380); and RAG HA 1390, fol. 8r (1406). The gift was for the honor of the ducal dynasty.

43. Heers, *Fêtes, jeux et joutes*, pp. 53–54.

44. In this article, both "militia" and "archery company" will be used for the Dutch *schutterij* or *schuttersgilde*.

45. For dancing in the school, see OAA 1245, fol. 27v (1446).

46. M. James, "Ritual, Drama and Social Body in the Late Medieval English Town," *Past and Present* 98 (1983): 3–30; and Nijsten, "De stad en haar metafoor," pp. 206–7, 229–34.

47. The Duke's task was confined to protecting the road used by the pilgrims and those who took part in the procession (RAG HA 518, fol. 5r [1408]).

48. Algemeen Rijksarchief (National Archives), Brussels, Chambre des comptes 51207, fol. 8r (1398/99).

49. Nijsten, "Openbare feesten," p. 33.

50. M. Carasso-Kok, "Der stede scut: De schuttersgilden in de Hollandse steden tot het einde der zestiende eeuw," in *Schutters in Holland: Kracht en zenuwen van de stad*, ed. M. Carasso-Kok and L. Levy–van Halm (Zwolle and Haarlem: Waanders, 1988), pp. 16–36.

51. For example, RAG HA 384, fol. 22v (Arnhem, 1380); RAG HA 238, fol. 21r (1404); RAG HA 218, fol. 43v (Nijmegen, 1389); RAG HA 224, fol. 110v (1394); RAG HA 238, fol. 26r (Hattem, 1404); RAG HA Varia III (Grave, 1467); and RAG HA 399, fol. 62r (Zutphen, 1468–69).

52. RAG HA 237, fol. 34r (1404); RAG HA 425, fol. 17v (1437); RAG HA 670, fol. 4r (1464); and RAG HA 483, fols. 61r–62v (1439–40).

53. OAV stadsrek. 1459, p. 23.

54. RAG HA 248, fol. 48v (1410).

55. "Loyaliteit van de inwoners [te] stimuleren en het vorstelijk gezag [te] demonstreren..." (H. Soly, "Plechtige intochten in de steden van de Zuidelijke Nederlanden tijdens de overgang van Middeleeuwen naar Nieuwe Tijd: Communicatie, propaganda, spektakel," *Tijdschrift voor Geschiedenis* 97 [1984]: 343).

56. RAG HA 343, fol. 10r; and RAG HA 344, fol. 3r (1402).

57. R. Wartena, ed., *De stadsrekeningen van Zutphen (1364–1445/46)* (Zutphen: Gemeentearchief Zutphen, 1977), p. 130 (1402–3).

58. RAG HA 344, fols. 3r–v (1402).

59. RAG HA 235, fol. 78v (Beekbergen, 1402); and RAG HA 618, fol. 16r (Tiel, 1402).

60. OAV stadsrek. 1402, pp. 8, 11.

61. See, for instance, the Arnhem town accounts for 1402 (W. Jappe Alberts, *Stadsrekeningen van Arnhem*, vol. 3, p. 29).

62. RAG HA 257, fols. 9v, 11r–12r (1423).

63. RAG HA 654, fol. 6r (1423); RAG HA 593, fol. 5v (1423); RAG HA 413, fol. 5r; RAG HA 635, fol. 5r; RAG HA 755, fol. 41r (1423); and RAG HA 593, fol. 6r (1423). The burgomasters of Tiel had been present at the inauguration in Nijmegen.

64. RAG HA 1529, fol. 3v (1423); and OAV stadsrek. 1423, p. 37.

65. RAG HA 1529, fol. 4v (1423).

66. RAG HA 654, fol. 7v (1423).

67. Geldern town archive (Stadt Archiv Geldern, henceforth SAG), abt. A, Band G.2a, fols. 95r, 97r; and RAG HA 1399, fol. 24r (1423). The duke visited the small town of Geldern on 29 September 1425 and Goch the day after. The knighthood of the *ambt* (administrative unit) of Geldern, who had come to the town for the occasion, were treated to a banquet at the town council's expense.

68. RAG HA 1399, fol. 24v (1424). Catherine was also still a minor.

69. RAG HA 1470, fol. 11r (1469). See also Rijksarchief Limburg (Limburg National Archives), Maastricht Scheres d'Olme XV R.4 inv. no. 59, p. 17 (henceforth RAL).

70. OAA 1250, fol. 8v (1473).

71. OAA 1249, fol. 27r (1471); and SAG abt. A, Bd. G.5, fol. 18v (1471). See especially the account of the town of Geldern (SAG abt. A, Bd. G.5, fol. 21r [1471]).

72. W. Paravicini, *Die Preussenreisen des europäischen Adels* (Sigmaringen: Jan Thorbecke Verlag, 1989), pp. 60–66, 245–53.

73. RAG HA 218, fol. 22v, 23v, 25r, 27r (1388).

74. Goldsmiths, painters (including members of the famous Maelwael family of artists), tailors, and the like, were involved in the preparations (RAG HA 218, fols. 51r, 61r, 62v–63r, 67r–v). For the jousting gear, see RAG HA 218, fol. 76v.

75. Wenceslas of Luxemburg (1378–1400) was married to Joan of Bavaria, who was the sister of Catherine (Duke William's wife). Both women were daughters of Albert of Bavaria, count of Holland. For the part played by Wenceslas in William's release in 1388/89, see RAG HA 218, fols. 30r, 32v.

76. RAG HA 219, fol. 1r (1389), 2v, 3v; RAG HA 220, fol. 6r (1389); RAG HA 219, fol. 6r; RAG HA 220, fol. 7v (1389); and SAG abt. A, Bd. G.I, fols. 84r–v (1389).

77. RAG HA 219, fol. 6r (1389).

78. W. van Anrooij, *Spiegel van ridderschap: Heraut Gelre en zijn ereredes* (Amsterdam: Prometheus, 1990); and M. Keen, *Chivalry* (New Haven, Conn., and London: Yale University Press, 1984), passim.

79. RAG HA 220, fol. 31v (1389/90).

80. L. Sloet, "De reis van Willem van Gulik, hertog van Gelre en graaf van Zutfen, naar Londen, in het jaar 1390," *Bijdragen voor vaderlandsche geschiedenis en oudheidkunde* 1, 3rd series (1882): 319–36.

81. RAG HA 219 and 220, passim (1390).

82. RAG HA 274, fol. 10v; RAG HA 446, fols. 66v, 68r, 79r, 81r–v (1451); OAG 217, fol. 15v (1451); Zutphen town archive (Oud Archief Zutphen, henceforth OAZ) 1039, fol. 31r (1451); and OAA 1245, fol. 58r (1451). A priest in Arnold's retinue would later write an account of the journey to the holy places in Palestine. The unpublished manuscript is kept in the Royal Library in The Hague, shelf mark Hs 75 H 36. See G. Nijsten, "Vanden gestant des heiligen landes: Op zoek naar een vijftiende-eeuwse auteur en zijn publiek," in *Die fonteyn der ewiger wijsheit: Opstellen aangeboden aan prof. dr A. G. Weiler*, ed. P. Bange and P. de Kort (Nijmegen: Centrum voor middeleeuwse studies, Katholieke Universiteit Nijmegen, 1989), pp. 82–97.

83. OAA 1245, fol. 55v (1451).

84. OAA 1245, fol. 22v (1451).

85. OAG 218, fols. 23r–24r (1452).

86. RAG HA 446, fol. 91v (1452).

87. RAG HA 274, fol. 19r (1452).

88. OAA 1245, fol. 59r (1452); and OAA 1245, fols. 7r–v, 11r, 24r (1452–53).

89. OAZ 1039, fol. 21v (1452); and OAA 1245, fol. 24r (1452).

90. SAG abt. A, Bd. G.4, fols. 23v–24r (1452).

91. A silver, gilded drinking cup adorned with the Venlo coat of arms was presented to the duke, after which he was invited to a banquet (OAV stadsrek. 1452, pp. 8–13 [Venlo, 1452]).

92. SAG abt. A, Bd. G.2a, fol. 60r (1422).

93. OAA 1245, fol. 7r (1446); and OAA 1245, fols. 9r, 10r (1446–47, 2nd volume).

94. OAV stadsrek. 1387, p. 21.

95. F. Nettesheim, *Geschichte der Stadt und des Amtes Geldern unter Berücksichtigung der Landesgeschichte nach authentischen Quellen* (1863; reprint Kevelaer and Geldern: Butzon und Bercker, 1963), pp. 80–82; and L. Henrichs, *Das alte Geldern: Gesammelte Schriften zur Stadtgeschichte* (Geldern and Kevelaer: Butzon und Bercker, 1971), pp. 206–9.

96. OAZ 1053, fols. 18v, 25r (1468).

97. SAG abt. A, Bd. G.4, fol. 265r (1468).

98. RAG HA 458, fol. 105r (1469); and Schloss-Archiv Haag (Germany) inv. no. 926 (a charter dated 1 April 1469). See also R. Schiffler, *Die Bau- und Kunstdenkmäler des Kreises Kleve: Stadt Straelen* (Berlin, 1987), pp. 114–18; and P. Brimmers, "Onse Lieve Vrouwe int Sandt," in *Geldrische Heimatkalender* (1968), pp. 121–34.

99. OAA 1248, fol. 13v (1469).

100. A. Blok, "Communicatie en berichtgeving in het vroegmoderne Europa," *Tijdschrift voor Geschiedenis* 97 (1984): 336–41; and "Openbare strafvoltrekking als rites de passage," *Tijdschrift voor Geschiedenis* 97 (1984): 470–82. The classic study of the subject is A. van Gennep, *The Rites of Passage* (London: Routledge and Kegan Paul, 1977, translated from the French).

101. OAV stadsrek. 1394, p. 22; and SAG abt. A, Bd. G.Ia, fol. 48r (1394).

102. RAG HA 233, fols. 84r, 85r, 103r (1400).

103. Wartena, ed., *Stadsrekeningen van Zutphen*, p. 15 (1379); Jappe Alberts, *Stadsrekeningen van Arnhem*, vol. 2, p. 27; and RAG HA 384, fols. 18v, 16r (1379). She paid a short visit to the monastery of Monnikhuizen to say a prayer and make an offering along the way (RAG HA 384, fol. 19r [1379]). The entry into Arnhem took place on Holy Innocents' Day, the day on which the boy bishop "resided." As in other entries, he probably paid his respects to Catherine. The town representative, who had presented the duchess with two oxen and a quantity of wine, received a fitting reward. The more elaborate reception for the duchess was at Rozendaal Castle and was hosted by courtiers and noblemen.

104. Is. Nijhoff, *Gedenkwaardigheden uit de geschiedenis van Gelderland* (Arnhem: Gouda Quint, 1847), vol. 3, no. 273; and RAG HA Charterverzameling (collection of charters), no. 1077. An intended marriage to Lucia, the sister of the Duke of Milan, had not taken place.

105. Hauptstaatsarchiv Düsseldorf (henceforth HstD), Jülich Urkunden nos. 553, 561, and 1081.

106. For example, Venlo (OAV stadsrek. 1404, p. 29). Accompanied by friends and noblemen, Reinald rode to Bastogne; all were dressed expensively in red and black. The duke's attire was sumptuous. The court tailors, furriers, and embroiderers had used silk, gold, and silver (RAG HA 238, fol. 89v [1405]). The colors red and black appear to be typical "wedding colors." Compare RAG HA 251, fol. 87v (bastard son William of Wachtendonk's wedding, 1416); and R. van Uytven, "Rood-wit-zwart: Kleurensymboliek en kleursignalen in de middeleeuwen," *Tijdschrift voor geschiedenis* 97 (1984): 447–70. Van Uytven points out that the meaning of the colors was not fixed but varied according to the context in which they occurred.

107. OAV stadsrek. 1405, pp. 23–25.

108. RAG HA 241, fol. 3r; and RAG HA 239, fol. 25v (1405).

109. RAG HA 248, fols. 73r, 74r, 76v; and RAG HA 249, fol. 137r (1410).

110. Nijhoff, *Gedenkwaardigheden uit de geschiedenis van Gelderland*, vol. 4, no. 9; and Wartena, ed., *Stadsrekeningen van Zutphen*, p. 334.

111. F. Gorissen, "Historisch-Heraldische Betrachtungen über ein Stundenbuch der Katharina von Kleve, Herzogin von Geldern," *Bijdragen en mededelingen Gelre* 57 (1958): 206–11. On 23 January 1430 the chapter of Cleves had determined the degree of consanguinity and granted the required dispensation. After this the consummation of the marriage, which probably occurred on Thursday, 26 January, could take place.

112. Jappe Alberts, *Stadsrekeningen van Arnhem*, vol. 5, p. 161 (1430). Compare Gorissen, "Historisch-Heraldische Betrachtungen," pp. 209, 214.

113. A further step in the development in the relations between court and town was made in 1437. The proceedings had by then shifted to the town. The wife of Duke Arnold's brother (William of Egmond) was met by the duke himself, and he accompanied her into Venlo. The wedding itself took place at Brüggen Castle (RAG HA 269, fols. 30v, 45r–v, 48v, 50r; and RAG HA 270, fols. 23r, 23v [1437]).

114. RAG HA 264, fols. 31r–38r; RAG HA 482, fols. 13v–14r; RAG HA 480, fols. 6v–7v (1431); and Gorissen, "Historisch-Heraldische Betrachtungen," pp. 209–11.

115. OAG 217, fol. 134v (1431).

116. The word *statknechten* is ambiguous. It could either refer to soldiers or to servants of the town council.

117. RAG HA 386, fol. 82v (1431); and Jappe Alberts, *Stadsrekeningen van Arnhem*, vol. 5, pp. 238, 243, 253, 264.

118. OAV stadsrek. 1431, pp. 41–42 (Venlo); Jappe Alberts, *Stadsrekeningen van Arnhem*, vol. 5, p. 317; and OAA 1242, fol. 15r (Zutphen, 1432).

119. RAG HA 503, fol. 15f (1431–32); compare Gorissen, "Historisch-Heraldische Betrachtungen," p. 211.

120. OAV stadsrek. 1433, pp. 16–17 (Venlo); OAG 217, fols. 162v, 164v, 165v (Grave, 1433); OAA 1243, fol. 10r, 43r (Arnhem, 1433); RAG HA 266, fol. 83r; RAG HA 420, fol. 7r; RAG HA 1533, fol. 6r; RAG HA 533, fol. 5v; RAG HA 604, fol. 1v; and RAG HA 1492, fol. 1v (1433). It is not known whether the archbishop accepted the invitation.

121. RAG HA 422, fol. 4r (1434); OAG stadsrek. 217, fol. 178r (Grave, 1434); Wartena, ed., *Stadsrekeningen van Zutphen*, p. 467 (Zutphen, 1434); OAV stadsrek., 1434, p. 28 (Venlo); and OAA 1243, fols. 74v, 26v (Arnhem, 1434).

122. In 1436 a second daughter had been born, Margaret. She would later marry Frederick I of Paltz-Simmern.

123. OAA 1244, fols. 6v, 13v, 53ff (1439); and Nijsten, "Openbare feesten," pp. 34–35.

124. One could view a corpse as "dirt" in Mary Douglas's sense, since it evokes fears because it is "a matter out of place" (esp. M. Douglas, *Purity and Danger: An Analysis of the Concept of Pollution and Taboo* [London: Routledge and Kegan Paul, 1966]). A corpse then would require rituals to restore it to its proper place. By thus removing it from the world of the living, purity and balance would be restored. See also Blok, "Openbare strafvoltrekking," p. 472; P. George, "La mémoire des morts," *Le Moyen-Age: Revue d'histoire et de philologie* 95 (1989): 527–35; P. Pégeot, "La noblesse comtoise devant la mort a la fin du moyen age," *Francia* 11 (1983): 303–19; and Ph. Ariès, *Essais sur l'histoire de la mort en occident du moyen âge a nos jours* (Paris: Seuil, 1975).

125. For instance, in 1423 (Wartena, ed., *Stadsrekeningen van Zutphen*, p. 334).

126. OAV stadsrek. 1393, p. 32, describes "overluiden" (ringing of the bells at the death) of the Duke of Gulik.

127. RAG HA 4.22 and 4.23.

128. SAG abt. A, Bd. G.4, fol. 151r (1460).

129. OAZ 1046, fol. 20r (1460); OAG 218, fol. 147r (1464); RAG HA 1595, fol. 6v; RAG HA 1462, fol. 8r; and SAG abt. A, Bd. G.4, fol. 202r (1464). For the duke's payment of a meal, for instance in Geldern, 1460, see SAG abt. A, Bd. G.4, fol. 151r.

130. RAG HA 342, fols. 2v, 3v; RAG HA 1432, fol. 10r; and RAG HA 618, fol. 5r (1400).

131. RAG HA 344, fol. 2v; and RAG HA 1384, fols. 12r, 13r, 25v (1401). Duke William had ordered this in a letter of 28 October 1401, which has been preserved (RAG HA Varia III).

132. RAG HA 235, fols. 189r, 208r, 196v (1402).

133. See, for instance, the Arnhem town account (Jappe Alberts, *Stadsrekeningen van Arnhem*, vol. 3, p. 21).

134. RAG HA 236, fol. 34r (1404).

135. RAG HA 236, fol. 4r (1403). The poor were also given herring on an occasion in 1404 (RAG HA 236, fol. 29v).

136. RAG HA 1534, fol. 19v (1404/5), and HstD Jülich Urkunden 634 (1413) give some examples. The undated *Distribuenda iussu domini* (probably issued by Arnold of Egmond) also contains many examples (RAG HA aanwinsten [acquisitions] Buren 1884, inv. no. 85, pp. 11, 15).

137. RAG HA 281, fol. 7r–v; RAG HA 644, fol. 18v; RAG HA 655, fol. 11r (1460); RAG

HA 1465, fol. 7r (1464); and RAG HA 668, fol. 9v. While James II and Mary of Guelders had been buried in Scotland, the ceremonies in Guelders attempted to represent them in the most tangible way possible. In Arnhem, a "funeral" was attended by Duke Arnold and Alexander, prince of Scotland. Both their retinues were dressed in black, and, as was customary, the local officials had been summoned to Arnhem. On the same day, masses were celebrated elsewhere, too, interrupting the everyday routine.

138. Compare Kertzer, *Ritual, Politics and Power*, p. 21ff.

139. RAG HA 1572, fol. 4r (1464). For the effigy, see H. Bloem, "De optochten en decoraties bij de koninklijke begrafenis van Anna van Bretagne," *Millennium: Tijdschrift voor middeleeuwse studies* 4 (1990): 23–26.

140. OAZ 1060, fol. 28r (1477).

141. For instance, at the death of Catherine of Bourbon in May 1469 (RAG HA 672, bijlage [appendix], blad [leaf] a, c.; OAZ 1054, fol. 28r; and OAA 1248, fol. 32v (the number 3); RAG HA 672, bijlage, blad b, c.; and OAA 1248, fol. 32v (the number 8); RAG HA 672, bijlage a.; and OAA 1248, fol. 32v (the number 12).

142. H. Meyer, *Die Zahlenallegorese im Mittelalter: Methode und Gebrauch* (Munich: Wilhelm Fink, 1975).

143. For instance, the death, funeral, and memorial service of *landrentmeester* (steward) Arnoldus of Goer (died 1460) (RAG HA 405, bijlagen [appendices]; RAG HA 398, fols. 16r, 18v, (1462–63); RAG HA 401, fol. 19r (1469–70).

144. This notion derives from E. Durkheim; see Kertzer, *Ritual, Politics and Power*, chapter 3, esp. pp. 37ff.

145. In 1388 Duke William had defeated a Brabant army at the village of Nifterik on the Meuse. To express his gratitude for the victory, he had a chapel built dedicated to the Virgin Mary.

146. Kertzer, in *Ritual, Politics and Power*, chapters 7 and 8, criticizes Durkheim's thesis of social cohesion (esp. pp. 61ff.). See also Nijsten, "Openbare feesten," passim. One of the few expressions of this is the conflict between Arnold and Adolf in 1459 and 1460. The festivities in Venlo—in Adolf's presence—can be seen as a release of the tensions that had arisen between Venlo and the duke's son, on the one hand, and Arnold and Roermond on the other.

147. A related problem is that of decoding: the problem is to decide whether meaning and symbol coincide. There is no intrinsic link between the two. In contrast to what is true for indices and signs, a symbol can have several meanings (Blok, "Communicatie en berichtgeving," pp. 338–39).

CHAPTER 11

In the Pit of the Burgundian Theater State
Urban Traditions and Princely Ambitions in Ghent, 1360–1420

David Nicholas

The notion of a Burgundian "theater state" has entered the vocabulary of historical clichés that so enrich our understanding.[1] Unfortunately the reigns of Philip the Bold (1384–1404) and John the Fearless (1404–19) do not permit us to conclude that all Burgundian counts of Flanders tried consciously, as part of a deliberate policy, to enhance a sense of loyalty to their regime by creating a "theater state" of symbol, display, and pageantry. First, although all the Burgundian dukes patronized artists, musicians, and men of letters, most of their investments were for private conspicuous consumption, not for public display. Secondly, most of the Burgundians' festivals were not even held in Flanders. The counts much preferred the quieter pleasures of Brabant. Thirdly, although the first two counts seemed to make a conscious effort to link lavish expenditure on festivals to political goals, the period of Count Philip "the Good" (1419–67) presents a more obvious case. Finally, exclusive focus on the Burgundian counts as organizers of ceremonies ignores the sometimes centuries-old traditions of civic ceremony in Flanders. Nearly every Flemish town had its festivals, markets, and religious processions, and many of them had little to do with princely power or subsidy either before or during the Burgundian period.

Ghent was a city of new money and old hatreds, of raw sex rather than courtly love, where the level of violence seems to have been unusually high even by the dismal standards of the time. The feuds among its leading families tore the city apart, making it infamous in Flanders for disorder. Between 1338 and 1385, furthermore, Ghent was usually in rebellion against the counts of Flanders or at the very least was on a war footing. Although Ghent did not revolt openly against the dukes of Burgundy between 1385 and 1451, it was the most particularistic of the Flemish cities. There were frequent riots, some against the counts but others simply against the local rulers. An Anglophile party troubled the peace after 1385. The only issue on which Ghent consistently supported the dukes of Burgundy was in their efforts to reach a peace with England, in order to guarantee the wool supply on which Ghent was so dependent. More than Bruges or Ypres, Ghent resisted the counts' efforts to centralize their domains.[2]

Thus it is not surprising that the Flemish counts, whose presence, as we shall see, was closely tied to the development of civic festivals in Ghent, spent as little time in the city as they could. They seem to have preferred Bruges, although it was hardly better disposed toward them than Ghent and was the scene of major personal embarrassments of the counts in 1382, 1436, and 1482. They had only three significant properties in Ghent in the Burgundian period, fewer than in other Flemish cities. Their great castle, the Gravensteen, which is so prominent a part of the landscape now, was not used as a residence; it was the seat of government for the Ghent bailiwick and the Council of Flanders. At the accession of John the Fearless (1404–19), the Flemings demanded that he live in the county. In response, he had his heir, the count of Charolais, reside continuously in Ghent from 1411.[3] Despite this, the princely family left few traces on the operation of the city administration.[4]

Ghent also displayed a profound particularism among cities of the Low Countries, especially with regard to its traditions of urban festivals and its general hostility to its counts' political ambitions. This essay suggests that Ghent's political posture against the Burgundian counts of Flanders adversely affected the development of festivals. Contrary to the notion of a "Burgundian theater state," Ghent actually witnessed more festivals before 1384 than after, simply because they hinged so much on the prince's presence. Evidence for this thesis comes chiefly from the municipal accounts for the years 1360–1420.[5] Account evidence is obviously restricted to those spectacles for which the city government incurred expenses, but it is the only source that casts significant light on the problem of public display and festivals in Ghent before the late fifteenth century.

Even before the advent of the Burgundians, Ghent was not particularly rich in festivals. Perhaps because it was an inland city, was notoriously dangerous, and had no major shrines, Ghent did not attract many transients. Some of the counts were buried at Saint Peter's Abbey, but Ghent had nothing to compare in scope with the Chapel and Procession of the Holy Blood at Bruges. Ghent was, furthermore, not a center of secular culture. The first Chamber of Rhetoric in Ghent was established in 1448, considerably later than in most other Flemish cities.[6]

Perhaps most important, major festivals in this part of Europe were inspired either by churches or princes, rather than by city governments. Since Flanders had no bishopric until the modern period, one source of festivals was absent. Other than the Corpus Christi Day processions sponsored by individual parishes in the fifteenth century, Ghent had few church processions. Some brotherhoods attached to churches also had processions. Guild members paraded under the banners of their individual organizations in the order prescribed by their position in the hierarchy of "members" that governed the city.[7] Guilds had banquets, but apparently no public displays or processionals were attached to those of Ghent until the late fifteenth century. Admittedly, the absence of evidence of public display may result from the paucity of guild records, but it is hard to believe that if guild or parish festivals were as important a part of the urban scene at Ghent as, for example, in most Italian cities, so few traces would survive in the written record. There are oblique references to "city festivals," but the expenses were so minimal that they generally have not entered the city records.

Ghent's embrace of the typical festivals of chivalry also seems to have been lukewarm. Some evidence suggests that Ghent was the scene of many jousts and tournaments in the early fourteenth century. Tournaments were held in honor of King Philip IV when he entered Ghent as its conqueror in 1301. A chronicler reported that, together with presents to the king and queen, the town government spent some 27,000 *lb. gro.* (pounds groot).[8] The period of open alliance with the English in the 1340s—Edward III proclaimed himself king of France at Ghent in 1340—coincided with significant festivities.[9] Even so, Ghent appears to have been less active in promoting festivals than its neighbors. Juliet Vale has noted that in the fourteenth century the Flemish cities had regular jousting. But Ghent had no equivalent of the Espinette festival at Lille or that of the forester of the White Bear at Bruges.[10] Although Tournai sponsored a joust of the "Thirty-one Kings" from 1331, and most larger Flemish and northern French cities sent delegations, Ghent apparently did not.[11]

Most of Ghent's expenditure on festivals was incurred when the counts of Flanders were in the city, and the counts themselves helped to finance these extravaganzas. When Philip the Bold, duke of Burgundy, married Margaret of Male, the heiress of Flanders, in Saint Peter's Abbey at Ghent on 19 June 1369, he provided musicians, heralds, and jousting equipment and horses. The king of France sent twenty destriers. The duke's banquets and gifts for the count's family, court officials, and Flemish nobles had a total value of over 5,966 francs, roughly 150 percent of the entire expenditure incurred by the city for his wedding.[12] But the city also contributed heavily; the wedding was by far Ghent's most costly and elaborate ceremony during the period.[13] The town had to borrow to finance the enormous expense of 406.57 *lb. gro.*, which the aldermen assigned on the lease of the wine tax.[14] The city record tells us little of the nature of the festivities, but Sir Jean Froissart notes that "there were many great and noble festivals, and many lords, and there was jousting for three days."[15]

The city documents show a pattern that would characterize virtually all Ghent's civic ceremonials during this period: the most onerous municipal expenses were not for materials or entertainments but rather went for presents to the dignitaries. Nearly half was a payment of 200 *lb. gro.*

to the bride's father, Count Louis of Male of Flanders, to help with his expenses. Another 67.07 *lb. gro.* went for cloth and wine to the count and his court. The bishop of Tournai received a substantial amount, and the countess of Artois, at the request of Louis of Male, was exempted by the toll leaseholders for bringing twenty-six vats of wine into the city. Smaller amounts of wine were given to the count of Namur, the "lords from England," and the "good people" of Bruges, Ypres, Lille, and Douai.

The wedding was clearly a Flanders-wide celebration. While Ghent was normally patrolled by 12 sergeants and a guild watch of 17 men,[16] 139 sergeants were hired for 8 *gro.* (grooten) per day during the wedding festivities. The city sergeants received an annual wage of 1 *lb.* 4*s. gro.* (schellingen groot) in this year;[17] if they worked for even as few as two hundred days apiece, this was only about 1.5 *gro.* daily, although it is true that they received uniforms and other gifts in addition to their wages. Guard duty during the wedding festival was clearly well rewarded. The city acquired wax in quantities comparable to what it would buy for the Shrove Tuesday celebrations in the fifteenth century. It also provided special clothing and hoods for the aldermen of both benches and for both bailiffs and their deputies. The sergeants and the two deans received special uniforms. Wine and cloth for the aldermen of Ghent totaled 97 *lb. gro.*, and they had to rent horses at the astronomically high rate of 4.25 *lb. gro.* for three days, which they used while riding out to meet the duke of Burgundy at his entrance and at celebrations at the abbeys of Saint Peter and Saint Bavo. Saint Bavo's had a jousting platform, and the aldermen of Ghent and the "good people" of the other four great cities got wine as they watched. In addition to the 139 sergeants who watched Ghent proper, the city paid 25 men to patrol Saint Bavo's. "Minstrels of the city who accompanied the aldermen playing their trumpets" and who were with them on the grandstand at Saint Bavo's received substantial payments, as did heralds who came to the festival and the "king of the ribalds," the leader of a brigade of menials who were sometimes sent on military expeditions outside the city. Minor expenses were incurred building the grandstand, but since it was prefabricated, the parts were taken down and stored for future use.

In the fifteen years between his marriage and his accession to the countship in 1384, Philip the Bold tried to win over the Flemings. Until war broke out in 1379, he visited Flanders every year except 1373. He spent most of March 1370 in Ghent, and he spent a month there in the summer of 1371, participating in crossbow shooting. He spent a week in the city early in the spring of 1375. He organized tournaments at Ghent, the most famous of which was in the spring of 1376, when the jousts and dancing lasted four days. The guests included the dukes of Lancaster, Brittany, Anjou, and Brabant; Louis of Male; various lords from England and Germany; and Albert of Holland-Hainault. Perhaps characteristically, as soon as the games were over, the dignitaries returned to Bruges for some serious diplomatic maneuvering.[18]

Apart from the marriage of 1369, we shall consider four categories of festivals in Ghent: the tournaments, most of which were held when the count was present; other public celebrations of a secular sort, notably when the magistracy was rotated; church processions and religious holidays and celebrations in the city or in nearby towns; and the participation of the city in the great annual procession in honor of the Virgin at Tournai.

The expenses for a spring joust in 1363 on the Friday Market, the largest square in Ghent proper, are typical.[19] Most of the materials cost was for wood and sand, which the king of the ribalds and his men carted to the market square in nailed wooden containers and guarded for fourteen nights. The tournament lasted three days, Monday through Wednesday (the exact dates are not given), with the actual fighting occurring on Tuesday. On Wednesday the count, several foreign dignitaries, and the city magistrates went to a house that the aldermen had rented for the occasion. The guards received a special payment for circulating armed for three days with the guild deans. A payment of 2 *lb. gro.* was made to "seven kings of the heralds and many other heralds and minstrels who came to the said festival," and the king of the ribalds and his boys got the same amount for recrating the sand, which had been brought from the castellany of Ghent, after the festivities were over.

The costs of the festival are extremely suggestive. Slightly over one-third (36.40 percent) went for materials and transport, while 6.97 percent was spent on guards and 6.56 percent on the minstrels from outside the city. Half (50.17 percent) went for aristocratic display. The bulk of this (41.37 percent) was for presents of wine to foreign dignitaries: the count of Flanders, the duke of Brabant, and Duke Albert of Holland-Hainault. Wine and food for the local dignitaries of Ghent accounted for a mere 5.52 percent, and the rental of the house where the two groups together had their meal was 3.28 percent of the festival cost. As with the festivities surrounding the wedding of 1369, the major drain on the city's finances was for foreign dignitaries rather than the aldermen. In the Tournai procession, as we shall see, the opposite was true.

An archery contest was held on the Friday Market in 1365–66, but it does not appear as a separate rubric in the accounts; rather, it was considered a "daily cost."[20] Although manure was used instead of sand, the costs were comparable for transport and hiring the king of the ribalds and his band. The total cost was about one-third (35.75 percent) of the cost of the joust of 1362–63. The only foreign dignitary in attendance in 1365 was the countess of Flanders, and the separate expense for her was limited to renting a house. The costs for wine are also quite low. Heralds attended, and payments were made to the count's pipers and drummers and to eight archers of Courtrai. The largest single expense for this contest was the cost of the archers.

A festival on the Friday Market and a tournament on the Kouter, a large square on the north end of the abbey village of Saint Peter, just outside the walls of Ghent proper, are mentioned together in the account of 1366–67.[21] The total cost is just over half the outlay for the 1362–63 joust. Of this, 69.27 percent went for wood, iron, carpentry, transport, unloading and spreading sand on the square and guarding it, and blocking off the gates to the Friday Market. The four "kings of the weapons" and seventeen heralds received 8.89 percent of the cost. The rest, 21.81 percent, went for wine and food for the aldermen and their party and renting a house where the magistrates were lodged during the festival; they did not stay at the town hall during tournaments but had more commodious quarters. The price difference with the 1362–63 joust is striking. The savings were almost exactly the amount spent on wine for the foreign dignitaries who came to the earlier festival. Although the aldermen spent more on themselves than in 1362–63, these games were still much cheaper than their predecessor.

In 1369–70 a tournament was held in Ghent itself at a cost of 3.69 *lb. gro.*, or 23.17 percent of the cost of the joust and festival of 1366. Of this, however, the ceremonial cost (wine and food for the aldermen, heralds, and the rental of the house) was 43 percent, rather higher than the earlier ceremony that did not involve foreign dignitaries. A second festivity this year, a joust at Saint Bavo's abbey village, had a total expense of 3.11 *lb. gro.* The aldermen in this case spent 19*s. gro.* (30.98 percent) on themselves. These games were undoubtedly part of the nuptial festivities, but they were apparently the real expenses that the city incurred on the public displays, except for the patrols, for they are not listed in the special account. They were relatively inexpensive, involving the usual costs of grandstands, sand, wood, and heralds in addition to the aldermen's expenses.[22]

Another tournament at Saint Bavo's in 1372–73 cost 5.11 *lb. gro.* This amount was more than the same activity at Saint Bavo's in 1369 but less if one includes the festivities on the Kouter, which are not mentioned here. The aldermen spent 25.74 percent on themselves. Again, most of the expenses except for those used for conspicuous consumption are on wood, sand, and iron rods. The city at this stage was not spending much — most accounts do not mention it at all—on banners and other adornments during festivals. In 1376–77 there was an elaborate festival on the Korenmarkt, costing 13.38 *lb. gro.*, for which the city built thirteen quintains. As was customary with the tournaments, manure was spread on the market and then covered with straw. The king of the ribalds and fifteen of his men got 36.94 percent of the total expenditure for collecting the ordure from the stalls around town and spreading it on the market, a considerably higher figure than for earlier tournaments. The cost of wine and food for the aldermen and the rent of their quarters was only 16.45 percent of the total expense this time. This festival lasted for three days, and the two guild deans and fourteen deputies got 1.5 *lb. gro.* for circulating armed.[23] The count was evidently present for the engagement of 1377, which his records show occurred between 15 and 17 February. His household accounts record payments to Master Jehan de Gand, painter, and several others for commissions for himself, his knights, and squires for jousts at Ghent at that time.[24]

The next year the city account mentions a tournament on the Korenmarkt and "the other festival held there." The two events may have followed each other, for the deans and their guards were paid for doing four days watch this year, against three last year. The distribution of the expenses was comparable to the previous year, with a total of 23.04 *lb. gro.* for the two, of which 75.64 percent was for materials.[25]

The tournaments and contests of the 1360s and 1370s naturally suggest that the local shooters' guilds were active. Those of Ghent would later be very prominent socially,[26] but there is little evidence of it in these accounts. The crossbowmen (the Guild of Saint George) got a supplement of 3 *lb. gro.* for their banquet in 1365, and this item became a regular feature of the accounts. It was raised to 4 *lb. gro.* in 1367–68, and in that year the town government also gave them 3 *lb. gro.* for going to Antwerp to participate in a joust. The next year the shooters went to Vilvoorde, for which the town contributed 2 *lb. gro.*, and received another 4 *lb. gro.* for their banquet. At this time, at least, Ghent seems to have been sponsoring teams at archery contests. In 1369–70, the year of the Burgundian marriage, the shooters still got the subsidy for the banquet, but they evidently did not leave the city. We have seen, however, that a tournament was held at Ghent itself in 1369–70, and all of this evidence suggests that there may have been a competition circuit of sorts in the Low Countries at this time. On August 30, 1369, while with the French army, the duke of Burgundy authorized a payment of forty francs "to the master of the confraternity of the crossbowmen of the city of Ghent, who took to my lord the uniform of the livery of the said crossbowmen of the said confraternity." On September 9, 1371, the duke paid forty *livres tournois* to the "shooters of the city of Ghent for their performance." He also made separate payments to the "trumpets and minstrels of the shooters of Ghent."[27]

But the shooters were soon in some trouble. In 1376–77 they got 4 *lb. gro.* for their banquet but also a subsidy of 3 *lb. gro.* "this time" because of the guild's great debts. Clearly there was not much market for their displays in their hometown. The next reference to the shooters leaving the city for a competition is in 1419, when the archers (the Guild of Saint Sebastian) went to Essen and received a subsidy of 4 *lb. gro.*[28]

Between 1377 and 1386 only fragmentary accounts survive, and they are not very instructive for urban spectacles. The numerous references to jousts and tournaments before the advent of the Burgundian counts in 1384 indicate that Ghent was following a path suggested by the example of other cities in northern Europe and the fabulous festivals of the Italian cities. The chivalric entertainments depended largely on the presence of the counts, however, and they ended abruptly with the outbreak of the Flemish civil war of 1379–85, in which Ghent was the driving force. The rebellion seems to have soured the counts on the city. During a twenty-year rule (1384–1404) in Flanders, Philip the Bold was actually in the county six months, visiting Ghent only three times: on 4 January 1386, when he made his Joyous Entry into the city—which had only ended its rebellion the previous 18 December—and confirmed its privileges; again in the winter of 1389–90; and in March 1398 with his son John.[29]

The Joyous Entry of 1386 involved a public celebration that Froissart described. The ceremony seems similar to that held nearly two years earlier at Bruges, but with the difference that the count placed greater emphasis at Ghent on the city's subjection to him than on his assumption of an ancestral role as protector and counselor.[30] The count and countess came to Ghent after spending three days at Oudenaarde. The magistrates and leading ecclesiastical dignitaries met them outside the town and accompanied them in a solemn procession. They went first to the abbey church of Saint Peter, then to Saint John's in central Ghent, where they took their oath to maintain the city's privileges.

And as soon as the oaths had been given, the trumpets, clarions, and minstrels began to play with all manner of instruments and sound with one voice, which is a pleasing and melodious thing to hear. Then messengers of the city of Ghent led the count and countess to their residence "ten Walle," passing by the great market of Ghent, where there were present the town leaders, men, women, servants of both sexes, and many burghers. And when they saw the count and duchess of Burgundy enter the market, each fell to his knees, crying in a loud voice "Mercy! Have mercy on your poor people and subjects of Ghent."[31]

The municipal officials then entered ten Walle with the count, taking the occasion to present him with Rhine and French wine and two cows for slaughter. The duke reciprocated by giving them a banquet. The citizens took the precaution of returning to the couple the jewels and ornaments that they had pillaged from the establishments of the countess's late father during the uprising. Philip and Margaret left the next day for Sluis and then Bruges, "and more beautiful lighting [presumably a procession of candles or torches] has never been seen than what the Brugeois did when the lord and lady of Burgundy entered their city."[32]

Occasional references to jousting at Ghent continue. In 1392–93 the city gave 1.67 *lb. gro.* to "fellows who jousted and tilted at poles on the Kouter," in courtesy for their costs. They also paid a herald for announcing the festivities, but this was a pittance and suggests that the city government simply thought that it should give a courtesy payment to some entertainers, rather than sponsoring the entertainment themselves. The payments occur under the "presents" rubric of the accounts, not as a separate entry. The magistrates did attend and gave themselves and their guests a payment of 1.52 *lb. gro.* for their costs.[33]

The first clear reference to a municipally sponsored joust in the Ghent records after 1377, however, is to a contest on the Korenmarkt in 1414. It involved a total expense of 21.72 *lb. gro.*, which is comparable to the cost of the jousts of the fourteenth century. The countess of Charolais (the wife of the heir apparent) was present. The materials and collapsing them required 61.93 percent of the outlay. The rental of the countess's house was 2.25 *lb. gro.*, and two houses for the magistrates cost 3 *lb. gro.* The banquet, at which the aldermen, deans, receivers, clerks, messengers, and others feasted for three days, included bread, wine, cheese, and fruit and cost 2.04 *lb. gro.* Red candles enhanced the festive occasion. There was another tournament in 1415–16 but no others through the rest of the reign of John the Fearless.[34]

The city seems to have taken a rather casual attitude at this time toward the goings and comings of its princes, although later tradition made much of these events. Whenever the count or countess entered the city, a delegation of aldermen, deans, clerks, sergeants, and gendarmes rode out to meet them, accompanied by the chief trumpeter. But the total expenditure was minimal; in 1367 the city spent 2.28 *lb. gro.* on such an expedition, but this was unusually high.[35] Even this figure was only slightly higher than it cost to have the Virgin's canopy fringed for the Tournai festival.[36] In 1404–5, at the Joyous Entry of John the Fearless, he was presented with 52 *lb.* 14s. 1d. *gro.* worth of wine. Apart from this, the only mention of his Joyous Entry in the city account is a special payment to the chief trumpeter and twelve associates for trumpeting, piping, and beating drums at the Pedercellepoort and the tower of Saint Nicholas when the count entered the city. Since the magistrates usually sent only eight musicians to Tournai, they seem to have been stretching the city's resources to call out the entire brass, woodwind, and percussion section. At various other times the count had a city escort, including the chief trumpeter and the aldermen. When he arrived, bells were sounded in all six parish churches, and the aldermen's bell was sounded three times "when my lord entered the city and came to the market, where the common folk of the city was." The city spent a substantial sum of 7.43 *lb. gro.* for horse rental for the magistrates, sergeants, and messengers who at various times rode to escort him.[37] Most accounts mention small payments to the trumpeters when the count or countess entered on other occasions. In 1415 when the count entered the city from Biervliet, the city gave an extra donation (in addition to the presents that were usually made to the count's officers, even the most menial) to his trumpeters and pipers.[38]

The death of Countess Margaret in 1405 evidently caused some sense of loss at Ghent, although the lady—despite her Flemish birth—needed a translator for documents written in Flemish and spent most of her time in Lille.[39] Minor expenses were incurred in the parish churches for requiem masses, and the musicians, poets, minstrels, and players got a payment for *not* performing at Shrove Tuesday because of her death.[40] But the celebration itself went on, with the normal watch and expenses for wax and torches. When John the Fearless died in 1419, the city had a memorial ceremony for him that was considerably more complex than his Joyous Entry had been. This service and the Joyous Entry of Philip the Good were inserted together in the city account and cost the city 101.69 *lb. gro.*, or 3.49 percent of the total city income that year. Most of the entry expenses were for wine and cloth for the new count and countess and the bishop of Tournai and presents to the personnel of the count's court. The funeral included special tabards for "thirteen poor men," torches for the funeral, and special payments to the priests. Charitable donations to the religious orders were also made, but the total funeral expenditure was quite restrained. Nearly two-thirds, 64.95 percent, of the total for the Joyous Entry and the funeral went for the wine and cloth presents for the count and countess alone. The public celebration was clearly quite modest by comparison.[41]

Apart from the festivals connected with the counts, we have little information about receptions and secular festivities. In 1372–73 the city received the cardinal of Beauvais in a state visit, but the actual ceremonials seem minimal. The city spent the substantial sum of 24 *lb.* 2s. 8d. *gro.*, but 81.54 percent of this was for cloth sent to him. The rest included horse rental for the aldermen and for the chief trumpeter, "who rode around with the trumpet."[42]

The city occasionally sponsored displays of a minor sort. When the lord of Saint Jans-ten-Steene, north of Ghent, entered the city in 1404, a green banner was hung before the Hoghehuus on the market; the painter Peter van Beerevelt painted three banners with the city coat of arms.[43] There was apparently an annual ceremony at the belfry where the city's privileges were read and confirmed by the prince's bailiff.[44]

The most significant secular municipal celebration that occurred regularly took place when the magistracy was rotated on Assumption Day, 14 and 15 August, but few details of what was done are recorded until later. The account of 1367–68 records festivities lasting four days, but others only mention two-day celebrations. The trumpeters received substantial payments each year for performing and for announcing publicly that the accounts would be presented (not audited!). It is clear that the majority of the population was not involved, but a banquet of gargantuan proportions was billed to the city government by the eight electors—four chosen by the count and four by the outgoing aldermen—who chose the twenty-six new members of the two city councils. The dinner guests normally included the members of the count's council.

The outgoing aldermen incurred separate expenses at their rotation, and in the fourteenth century these were more substantial than those of the electors. This changes abruptly in 1389 with the advent of the Burgundian dukes, and after 1408 the separate expenses of the outgoing aldermen stopped altogether. The expenses of the two groups together were 18.27 percent of the costs of the Tournai festival in 1372–73, but there may have been extra costs this year due to the count's presence in the city. In 1407–8 this expense was 13.09 percent of the entire cost of the Tournai festival. It dropped the next year, probably under pressure from the count, to a single expense for the electors that was 4.71 percent of the cost of the Tournai expedition. But from this time there were also expenses when the deans of the weavers and of the small guilds were rotated, amounting in most years after 1408 to between 50 and 60 percent of the electors' costs. Separate banquets were held during the selection of the two overdeans and when the fifty-three small guilds met to choose their individual deans. The total suggests, although we cannot provide many graphic details, several days of celebration involving a large number of persons, or at the very least the governing groups and the guild masters.[45]

The major business of the town trumpeters and pipers was performing at the Tournai procession, but they also had some other duties for the city, such as night watch from the church tower of Saint Nicholas. The *cnapen,* low-level functionaries, were paid wages for duties that included everything from doing messenger service outside the city to digging ditches.[46] The trumpeters also received a regular payment for services on six occasions each year: when the magistracy was rotated on 14 and 15 August, All Saints' Day, Christmas Day, Whitsuntide, Shrove Tuesday, and Easter.[47]

In addition to the secular celebrations, several religious festivals had considerable significance for Ghent.[48] By 1283–84 at the latest, but probably much earlier, an annual procession to the village of Sint-Lievens-Houtem, east of Ghent, was made on 28 June from Saint Bavo's Abbey, which housed the saint's relics. This became the high point of the liturgical year for Ghent. Although the city sent a delegation regularly in the early fourteenth century, the procession developed a bad reputation because of the participants' disorderly conduct, particularly on the route back with the saint's relics. The authorities disapproved, and in 1346 two aldermen and one captain went to Houtem "to observe the celebration and make sure that there was no trouble." A statute of 1412 prohibited "arguments" and forbade throwing anyone into water or ordure.[49] The late fourteenth-century accounts are silent about this procession, but from 1404 to 1405 the aldermen usually made a small payment to "the little devils (*dievelkins*) who circulated with Saint Lievin," presumably mummers. The language suggests a certain reserve, and the expense (8 *s. gro.*) was not major.[50] Disorder was worst when pilgrims following the saint's relics thronged onto the Friday Market. When Count Charles the Bold had the bad judgment to stage his Joyous Entry into Ghent on 29 June 1467, the day when the pilgrims returned from Sint-Lievens-Houtem, a riot erupted that permanently soured the prince's relations with the city.[51]

Ghent spent some funds to celebrate the Festival of Innocent Children (28 December) and Epiphany (6 January), but the amounts were small and not given annually. In 1392–93 the aldermen, deans, bailiffs, clerks, sergeants, messengers, and "many other persons" were paid 16*s. gro.* for food and wine. The amount was so trivial considering the number of persons that it sounds more like an office party than a public celebration. When it is mentioned next in 1412–13, the expense was only slightly larger, 17*s.* 10*d.*[52]

The most significant celebration of religious origins that was held inside the city was the nocturnal procession of armed guildsmen and the city elite on Shrove Tuesday. Shrove Tuesday celebrations were notoriously riotous elsewhere in Flanders, but little direct evidence of disorder in Ghent appears until the late fifteenth century. What we do know, however, confirms the regional pattern.[53] In 1393 the bailiff warned the Council of Flanders and the sovereign bailiff about the dangers of men circulating armed, which was normally forbidden. But the city statutes have only one regulation about it: on 20 March 1419 all participants were admonished "to offer themselves only to the fellows who carried the torches," and the procession should not be the occasion of undesirable conversations or rumormongering.[54] A sign of the growing problem with Shrove Tuesday comes in 1411–12 accounts, when the city's chief trumpeter received a special payment "for having ridden around with his trumpet to make the streets clean at Shrove Tuesday," presumably summoning the people to clean up the mess. This lasted until 1415–16 and then was discontinued.[55] Given the probable state of the citizenry, this must have been a horribly unpopular job while it lasted, but he only got 12 *gro.* for it. Although the Ghent authorities were suspicious of the festivities, the count himself celebrated the holy day in Ghent in 1430–31 and 1443–44.

The Shrove Tuesday expenses occurred as part of a general rubric for guild guards. It is thus difficult to distinguish precisely Shrove Tuesday costs from more general expenses. Accordingly, I have not included Shrove Tuesday in the general totals for festivals represented in the figures.[56] The amount spent on the festival was insignificant as late as 1360, becoming important only after 1400. Even then 12 *lb. gro.* or less was allotted, or less than half of 1 percent of the city's annual total expenditure. About half the amount was for torches, one-quarter for the night watch of the aldermen and the other dignitaries at the town hall (including wine and food), and the rest was spent on guards, cartage of the torches, and the poets and singers.

Before the 1392 account, only that of 1372–73 suggests a major expenditure for Shrove Tuesday (245 pounds of wax for torches and candles and a procession of the king of the ribalds and twenty-five of his companions carrying the torches).[57] A special night watch was maintained at the town hall on Shrove Tuesday throughout our period, but except during 1372–73, the amounts spent were insignificant. After 1392 the costs of wine and spices at the town hall for the watch undertaken by the aldermen and other dignitaries grew from a low of 1.62 *lb. gro.* in 1392–93 to a high of 4.87 *lb. gro.* in 1419–20, but these totals were a small fraction of the city's expenditure on the Tournai procession and about one-fifth of that for the 1414 joust.

The increased outlay for torches and wax shows the growing importance of the Shrove Tuesday celebrations. The figures are somewhat misleading, for torches can be used for more than one purpose and they can be kept across fiscal years. Nonetheless, while in 1389–90 the city bought 3,200 torches, this grew to 6,000 in 1392–93. Only 2,400 were purchased in 1401–2, but the number fell to less than 12,000 in only three of the remaining sixteen years surveyed. The figures for wax, which was even more likely to be stored than torches, also show some growth. In the two years when torch purchases were down significantly (1407–9), wax purchases grew. Except in 1409–10, however, the city never purchased less than three hundred pounds of wax for illumination between 1389 and 1420, and in 1407–8 the amount exceeded four hundred pounds. The king of the ribalds and twenty of his boys received 9s. 8d. for binding the torches through 1419, then got a raise to 20s. 9d. in 1419–20. The guild deans and their guards also circulated armed and in most years received a small payment in addition to their yearly wages.[58] The trumpeters and pipers got special payments for their services, and a bellringer received a small bonus from 1392. An apparent innovation in the 1401 account mentions "minstrels, singers, poets, and players" who were paid for performing in the aldermanic hall at the night watch on Shrove Tuesday. In 1405 and throughout the rest of our period only "poets and singers" are mentioned, one of the few hints that Ghent aldermen patronized any of the literary arts.[59] Shrove Tuesday was, however, the period of the Ghent free market (the only time during the year when outsiders could sell anywhere in the city), a major component of which was an art market at the city's main meat hall.[60]

To this point the expenses of festivals and celebrations has seemed very minor indeed. The accounts do show, however, that municipal expenditures on festivals were growing between 1360 and 1420. Most of the new growth came as a result of Ghent's participation in the annual

Procession of Our Lady, which was held at Tournai, the episcopal seat for eastern Flanders, where the Virgin's reliquary was carried in solemn procession. Throughout our period, except for the Burgundian wedding in 1369, the city incurred its greatest festival expense on this celebration. Although persons from throughout Flanders attended—indeed, many of the Flemish festivals, both in and outside the major cities, had a countywide or even diocesan character—Ghent was the only city that sent an official delegation. Ghent's major contribution to the festivities was a canopy of fine material—velvet, silks of various types, gold woolens, and, in the fifteenth century, damask—that was used to cover the reliquary in the procession. The canopy was painted with the city's coat of arms, the Flemish lion. A Ghent delegation attended this festival on 14 September every year for which records survive from 1321.[61] The trip to Tournai and back began on 12 September and lasted three days for some visitors, four for others. The participants evidently stayed overnight at Oudenaarde, halfway between the large cities, and the accounts from 1401 onward suggest that the procession was repeated there, evidently on the route back to Ghent. The reliquary then was presumably returned to Tournai, while the various participants and the pipers and trumpeters returned home.[62]

Only for the Tournai procession can Ghent's expenses on festivals and display have conceivably constituted a drain on the city's finances. I have graphed the expenses for all festivals (except the electors' costs, where "festival and spectacle" may be an inappropriate term for what actually transpired), the visit of the cardinal of Beauvais, and Shrove Tuesday, where exact totals cannot be made.

Figure 11.1, shows that before 1385, at the end of Ghent's civil war against most of the rest of Flanders, the total festival expenses generally consumed less than 5 percent of the city's budget. The single exception was the Burgundian wedding festival of 1369, which cost the city 5.22 times the amount of the Tournai procession. When this is added to the costs of the jousting that year, the result was a debt that the city had to assign on the tax farms; the wedding alone was 16.62 percent of the total municipal expenditure that year.[63]

Figures through the 1370s are the more striking in that for only nine of the thirty-three years for which accounts survive are payments recorded for jousting and other festivals on the city squares. Only two of these years, 1414–16, fall in the period after the Burgundians took power, and the amounts spent then per festival were comparable to those of the period before 1377. Only in 1366–67 and 1377–78 (the fiscal years in Ghent extended from August 15 to August 14) was more than one of these extravaganzas held, but even then Ghent's expenditure on festivals did not increase significantly. The conclusion seems inescapable that the jousts were so dangerous, and the Burgundians were so distrustful of Ghent, that they did not encourage such activities except

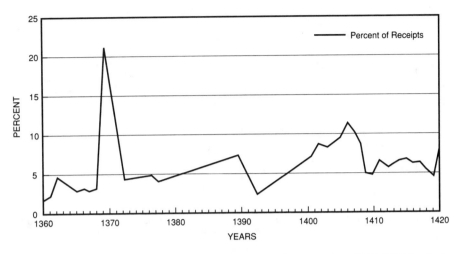

Figure 11.1. Festivals and processions as a percentage of city receipts, 1360–1420 (excluding Shrove Tuesday). (Sources: Municipal Archive of Ghent, Series 400, volumes 9–12; Alfons van Werveke, ed., *Gentse Stads- en Baljuwsrekeningen [1351–1364]* [Brussels: Royal Commission of History, 1970]; and Julius Vuylsteke, ed., *De Rekeningen der stad Gent. Tijdvak van Philips van Artevelde: 1376–1389* [Ghent: A. Hoste, 1893].)

when under their own patronage, as seems to have been a regular practice in the 1370s, but not thereafter, as the princes absented themselves from the city.[64]

Only fragments of the accounts survive between 1377 and 1389. Delegations from Ghent did not visit Tournai for the Virgin's procession during the war. Figures 11.1 and 11.2 show that there was a major rise in expenditure on festivals and processions when the records resume, particularly after 1400, but growing costs of the Tournai festival explain the rise, not the development of more elaborate city festivals. The exceptions were a momentary high in 1404 and 1405, when the change was due less to a significant growth in expenses of the Tournai procession (8.34 percent over two years) than to a decline of 21.62 percent in the total city receipts, and in 1419–20, when the funeral of John the Fearless and the entry of Philip the Good caused a substantial temporary growth.

The rising cost of the Tournai procession did not result from an increasing number of participants. Until 1376–77 the total number of persons for whom horses were rented varied from a low of fifty-four in 1366–67 to a high of sixty-one in 1360–61. Thereafter the expenses of the horses were listed as a lump sum. Eight trumpeters (after 1389 four trumpeters and four pipers) accompanied the procession.[65] The king of the ribalds and his boys, five of them from 1360 to 1362, six or seven between 1368 and 1386, and seven from 1389 to 1420, participated as torchbearers and guards of the city's parade equipment. Although most of the horses were for the aldermen and other high officials of the city

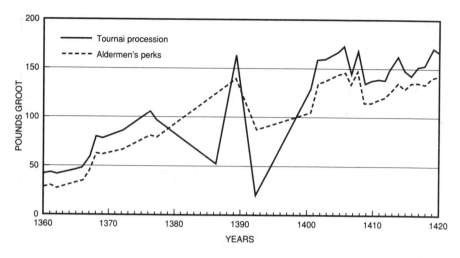

Figure 11.2. Tournai procession, expenses for 1360–1420. (Sources: Municipal Archive of Ghent, Series 400, volumes 9–12; Alfons van Werveke, ed., *Gentse Stads- en Baljuws-rekeningen [1351–1364]* [Brussels: Royal Commission of History, 1970]; and Julius Vuyl-steke, ed., *De Rekeningen der stad Gent. Tijdvak van Philips van Artevelde: 1376–1389* [Ghent: A. Hoste, 1893].)

government, the eight minstrels also rode. The total delegation was about seventy-five persons, varying only slightly between years.

In addition to their compensation for horse rental, the aldermen received cloth for fine uniforms. From 1389 they also received allowances for food and a present (*kermesse*). Figure 11.2 shows that the total expense of the Tournai festival to the city government was driven by these payments, not by the celebration itself or by the number of participants from Ghent. The dignitaries' perquisites amounted to a virtually constant 80 to 85 percent of the total outlay.

The other expenses are, by contrast, remarkably steady over the sixty-year period surveyed. Except for the clearly atypical year 1400–1401, which is distorted by the omission of the normal rubric for food and gifts to the dignitaries, the expenses of the festival, exclusive of the dignitaries' perquisites, were generally between 12.50 *lb. gro.* and 13.00 *lb. gro.* in the 1360s. They rose in the 1370s to between 15.50 *lb. gro.* and 18.10 *lb. gro.*, a change that seems to have been due largely to a rise in the price and grades of cloth used for the canopy. In the fifteenth-century accounts, the difference between total expense and dignitaries' perquisites was between 20 and 30 *lb. gro.* in virtually all years.

Items of expense for Tournai included one or two carts for transport, the cloth for the canopy over the reliquary (usually between 3 and 4 *lb. gro.*), and smaller amounts for pennants to be hung from the trumpeters' and pipers' instruments. A regular expense was incurred for four great torches, weighing between twenty-nine and thirty-three pounds, and substantial amounts for wax candles. The total wax purchased was about three-quarters of the amount bought in most years for the Shrove Tuesday celebrations. After 1392 the Tournai festival expenses become increasingly formulaic, although some innovations are perceptible. In 1392 the pipers were to receive pennants for their instruments and the four great flags were adorned with the city's coats of arms.[66] From 1405 the chief trumpeter got a separate pennant for his instrument as he led the Ghent delegation in the parade. Pennants were placed on the torches from 1414 on; these considerably raised the costs. The pennants must have been very lavish, for they were nearly equal in cost to the canopy for the Virgin by 1415.[67]

The Tournai procession occasioned some patronage to artists. Painters were always hired to adorn the festival banners, and in 1418 they were paid cart rental for taking their own works to the festival.[68] Clearly, more persons went to the procession than were compensated by the city government. A mid-1330s source suggests that at least five hundred people made the trip to Tournai and back.[69] The same few people, however, appeared year after year as painters of heraldic designs and as purveyors of cloth, candles, wax, and the like to the city. Work for the city for the festivals thus cannot have been much stimulus for the arts in Ghent.

The city also incurred expenses for wages. The king of the ribalds and his men received 28 *gro.* for three days in 1360, 32 *gro.* in 1361, rising to 40*d. gro.* by 1389 and 40.75*d. gro.* in 1402; the rate was unchanged after 1402. These amounts, which were for three days' work, are roughly double the daily wage of master artisans in the skilled trades. The work was not steady, but the king and his boys also did other work for the city and received wages not connected with their duties at the festival. The trumpeters and pipers also were not paid much, although they did somewhat better than the king and his band. In 1360 an eight-man team of trumpeters and pipers received 36 *gro.* for three days. This amount had risen to 63 *gro.* by 1377. Between 1401 and 1420, except for payments of 47.25 *gro.* apiece in 1411 and 1412, the musicians received 54 *gro.* for the three-day period. The pipers and trumpeters were obviously considered more skillful and essential to the city's image and prestige than the king and his boys, but it is also clear that they were hardly getting rich. The trumpeters performed on other occasions, but they did not receive a steady or continuous wage. In 1411, when Ghent had to send the militia to France to fight for the duke, the trumpeters got no uniform for Tournai, "because the old servants, minstrels, were then with the Ghent army in France" with the count, and the replacements were evidently inexperienced.[70]

Like the magistrates, the musicians also received cloth for uniforms, but it was of a decidedly less luxurious grade than theirs. I have plotted the uniform costs for the Tournai procession in Figure 11.3. The raw

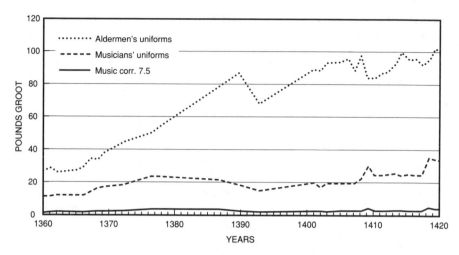

Figure 11.3. Tournai festival, uniform costs. (Sources: Municipal Archive of Ghent, Series 400, volumes 9–12; Alfons van Werveke, ed., *Gentse Stads- en Baljuwsrekeningen [1351–1364]* [Brussels: Royal Commission of History, 1970]; and Julius Vuylsteke, ed., *De Rekeningen der stad Gent. Tijdvak van Philips van Artevelde: 1376–1389* [Ghent: A. Hoste, 1893].)

totals for the musicians' uniforms are somewhat misleading, for the cloth was purchased for only eight people. Although it is not possible after 1377 to determine exactly the number of persons whose uniforms were included in the total for the magistrates, the number of named officials suggests that it did not grow much from the levels of the 1370s. I have assumed that some sixty persons received uniforms under this rubric and have thus multiplied the raw total for the musicians by 7.5 to get a more accurate comparison. Even on this approximately per capita basis, the magistrates were receiving about 2.5 times as much for cloth as were the musicians in the 1360s and 1370s, as the rates of increase were comparable. In 1389—when the change actually came is impossible to say, since only fragments of the accounts for the intervening years survive—the difference was suddenly 4.67, and thereafter usually hovered around 4.0. Only in 1417 was there a substantial increase in the musicians' uniform costs.

The late-medieval price rise explains in part the rapid rise in expenditure on festival cloth, but it is not the whole story. Prices on both the luxury and ordinary grades of Ghent cloth rose noticeably from the 1350s, and especially rapidly in the late 1360s and early 1370s.[71] But Ghent also improved the canopy, employing finer grades and introducing embroidery for the canopy's edge in 1365. Gold cloth was introduced in 1367.[72] The most rapid rise in cloth costs incurred for the Tournai procession, however, occurred between 1369–70 and 1372–73. A comparison of the Tournai expenses for the two accounts shows that the same types and amounts of cloth were used for the canopy—only the colors differed—but the cost rose 41.76 percent.[73] Apart from the perquisites of the magistrates, the major expenditure on the festival was for cloth for the canopy. The cost actually rose more rapidly than the perquisites between 1367 and 1372. Thereafter, the cost increases on all grades of cloth was more gradual.

The tremendous jump in expense at the end of the century, which continued through the rest of the period under investigation, was due once again to the use of finer grades of cloth than in the fourteenth century, but this time the rise affected only the uniforms; the fabric costs for the Virgin's canopy remained at the fourteenth-century levels or even slightly below them. A second cause was the practice of valuing the uniforms of the magistrates in large numbers of *schellingen groot*. They received this sum as a cash compensation if they did not attend the festival, with the schedule varying according to the magistrate's rank. The result was a tremendous increase in outlays. The first recorded example of magistrates receiving money in lieu of their uniforms for Tournai is a 20*s. gro.* payment in 1401 to two aldermen. In 1404–5 the rate of 12*s. gro.* is given for their food and presents. Beginning in 1409–10 this rate was dropped to 8*s. gro.* and remained there for the rest of our period.[74]

Status of the officeholders clearly determined the luxuriousness of different textiles for the outfits. Rates of 1.75 *lb. gro.* for a first alderman and of 1.36 *lb. gro.* for the dean of the weavers are mentioned in 1407, and the dean of the small guilds got 1 *lb. gro.* in 1408. Three aldermen got 30*s.* in 1412. By 1415 the rate was 1.59 *lb. gro.* for an ordinary alderman.[75] These are substantial amounts—a single person could live in Ghent for this amount per year—and it shows the level of wealth of the city's rulers that so few of them took the compensation, probably because they valued the status of the show, which was by far the most important spectacle in which they would engage in an official capacity all year.

These are undoubtedly flagrant cases of self-enrichment that became enshrined as one of the many perquisites of office. The cloth allowance for the Tournai festival came to be considered such an important privilege of the magistrates that, although Ghent ceased to send a delegation to the procession after 1487, the aldermen continued to receive their cloth until 1540, when Charles V ended the practice.[76] Yet we must beware of taking these figures out of a total context. We have seen that most of the expenditure on jousts and tournaments was on presents to the noble dignitaries who came to Ghent for the festivities. A comparison of the magistrates' perquisites for the Tournai festival with donations to the princes suggests that, however undesirable by contemporary, twentieth-century values the conspicuous consumption of the aldermen may have been, they were not especially generous with themselves in the context of the time.[77]

Thus, while there was a substantial increase in expenditure for festivals in Ghent between 1360 and 1420, most of it went for prestige items for the town aldermen and was only tangentially involved with spectacles that would heighten public consciousness of the city and its glory. The major public investment in ceremonies was for a procession that was not even held in Ghent. We have no way of estimating the number of persons who paid their own way to Tournai, but the official delegation was of fewer than one hundred persons. The city undertook some expenses, but no more than it thought it could get away with, at the Joyous Entry of the Burgundian counts. Jousts, which were frequently held before 1379, coincided with the visits of the counts or other dignitaries to Ghent. They became much less frequent after 1385, evidently because the counts, who liked them, tended to avoid the city, sending their relatives and councillors instead. Expenses grew at the annual rotation of the magistracy in August, but the major festival held in Ghent, which was growing in importance and expense throughout our period, was Shrove Tuesday.

While city governments elsewhere made use of festivals to keep the masses happy and solidify the power of the ruling elite, this did not happen at Ghent. During the period under discussion here, the "Three Members" (landowning *poorters,* weavers and their dependent trades, and "small guilds") dominated the magistracy, doing so virtually without challenge after 1385. Only after the power of this oligarchy weakened and participation on the town councils became somewhat less restrictive after 1453[78] do we find more evidence of municipal festivals generated by the city rather than the prince. The "Three Members" apparently felt secure in their control and did not need to use spectacles as a means of social control.

Philip the Bold tried to promote concord with the Flemish cities before 1379 by staging spectacles in them, hoping thereby to make his accession to the countship smoother. The war of 1379–85 ended this phase of the Burgundian counts' relationship with their cities. But festivals again became a major part of their agenda in the 1440s, when Philip the Good made an effort to conciliate Ghent with a series of spectacles, evidently in the hope that the city would agree to accept a permanent tax. Ghent was the scene of a succession of triumphal entries, a state visit including the recently ransomed Duke Charles of Orléans, an archery contest, the rebuilding of the prince's residences in the city, and a meeting of the Order of the Golden Fleece there in 1445.[79] When the tactic failed to anesthetize the city fathers into accepting a tax, Philip provoked a civil war, defeated Ghent in 1453, and imposed a humiliating and financially disastrous peace. At the next princely entry in 1458, Count Philip organized a great festival, replete with tableaux illustrating historic acts of princely grace, that clearly was intended to enhance the citizens' awareness of his generosity in forgiving them their recent and as always ill-starred rebellion.[80] Ghent discovered that, like swords, entries in Burgundian Flanders could be double-edged. Far from seeing the birth of a "theater state," therefore, the Burgundian period actually brought a decline in traditions of urban ceremony at Ghent. It is thus best to conclude that if there were a theater state in Flanders, it was Burgundian or, more accurately, comital, rather than Flemish or urban.

Notes

1. Of the vast literature, see for example the classic work of Johan Huizinga, *The Waning of the Middle Ages: A Study of the Forms of Life, Thought and Art in France and the Netherlands in the XIVth and XVth Centuries* (London: Edward Arnold, 1924); Richard Vaughan, *Philip the Good: The Apogee of Burgundy* (London: Longman, 1970), pp. 127–63; Richard Vaughan, *Valois Burgundy* (Handen, Conn.: Archon Books, 1975), pp. 176–83; and Wim Blockmans and Walter Prevenier, *The Burgundian Netherlands* (Cambridge: Cambridge University Press, 1986), pp. 223–25.

2. An exposition of the internal conflicts of Ghent, their family basis, and its battles with Count Louis of Male and the first two princes of the Burgundian dynasty clearly transcends our topic. See in general Blockmans and Prevenier, *Burgundian Netherlands*; David Nicholas, *Town and Countryside: Social, Economic, and Political Tensions in Fourteenth-Century Flanders* (Bruges: De Tempel, 1971); Nicholas, *The van Arteveldes of Ghent: The Varieties of Vendetta and the Hero in History* (Ithaca, N.Y.: Cornell University Press, 1988); Nicholas, "Crime and Punishment in Fourteenth-Century Ghent," *Revue Belge de Philologie et d'Histoire* 48 (1970): 289–334, 1141–76; Andrée Holsters, "Moord en politiek tijdens de Gentse opstand 1379–1385," *Handelingen der Maatschappij voor Geschiedenis en Oudheidkunde te Gent* 37 (1983): 89–111; Nicholas, "The Marriage and the Meat Hall: Ghent/Eeklo 1373–75," *Medieval Prosopography* 10 (1989): 23–52; Henri Pirenne, *Histoire de Belgique*, vol. 2, 3rd ed. (Brussels: Lamertin, 1922); A. Zoete, *Handelingen van de Leden en van de Staten van Vlaanderen. Regering van Jan zonder Vrees (21 maart 1405–10 september 1419. Excerpten uit de rekeningen van de steden, kasselrijen en vorstelijke ambtenaren* (Brussels, 1985); W. Prevenier, *Handelingen van de Leden en van de Staten van Vlaanderen (1384–1405). Excerpten uit de rekeningen der steden, kasselrijen en vorstelijke ambtenaren* (Brussels: Paleis der Academiën, 1959); W. Prevenier, *De Leden en de Staten van Vlaanderen (1384–1405)* (Brussels: Paleis der Academiën, 1961); W. Prevenier, "Les perturbations dans les relations commerciales anglo-flamandes entre 1379 et 1407: Causes de désaccord et raisons d'une réconciliation," in *Economies et sociétés du Moyen Age: Mélanges Edouard Perroy* (Paris: Publications de la Sorbonne, 1973), pp. 477–97; Marc Haegeman, *De Anglofilie in het graafschap Vlaanderen tussen 1379 en 1435: Politieke en economische aspecten* (Kortrijk: UGA, 1988); and W. P. Blockmans, *De volksvertegenwoordiging in Vlaanderen in de overgang van Middeleeuwen naar Nieuwe Tijden (1384–1506)* (Brussels: Paleis der Academiën, 1978). The comment about sexual standards is based on examples and data in D. Nicholas, *The Domestic Life of a Medieval City: Women, Children, and the Family in Fourteenth-Century Ghent* (Lincoln: University of Nebraska Press, 1985).

3. Marc Boone, *Gent en de Bourgondische hertogen, ca. 1384–ca. 1453: Een sociaalpolitieke studie van een staatsvormingsproces* (Brussels: Paleis der Academiën, 1990), p. 213.

4. Marc Boone, "Het vorstelijk domein te Gent (ca. 1385–ca. 1453): Speelbal tussen vorstelijke centralisatie en stedelijk particularisme?" *Handelingen der Maatschappij voor Geschiedenis en Oudheidkunde te Gent*, n.s. 42 (1988): 70.

5. There are substantial gaps in the accounts. There are only thirty-three usable

accounts, and some of these are not complete but have material that is usable for the problem of city spectacles and festivals. Only one complete account survives between 1377 and 1400, a period of considerable civic turmoil, but between 1400 and 1420 only one year is missing. The accounts are found in two printed editions: Alfons van Werveke, ed., *Gentse Stads- en Baljuwsrekeningen (1351–1364)* (Brussels: Palais der Academiën, 1970); and Julius Vuylsteke, ed., *De Rekeningen der stad Gent: Tijdvak van Philips van Artevelde 1376–1389* (Ghent: Hoste, 1893). For the period 1365–76 an edition is being prepared for the Royal Commission of History by Walter Prevenier and David Nicholas. The manuscript documents are in the Stadsarchief te Gent (Municipal Archive of Ghent), series 400, volumes 9–12 (hereafter SAG, ser. 400, with volume and folio number).

    6. Paul Trio, *De Gentse Broederschappen (1182–1580)* (Ghent: Maatschappij voor Geschiedenis en Oudheidkunde, 1990), pp. 16, 27.

    7. On the Corpus Christi processions, see Boone, *Gent en de Bourgondische hertogen*, pp. 75, 93. Boone gives the most recent and comprehensive account of the rule of the "Three Members," a topic that clearly transcends our subject here.

    8. *Annales Gandenses. Annals of Ghent.* Translated from the Latin with introduction and notes by Hilda Johnstone (London: Nelson, 1951), p. 12. The city account does not survive for this year, so we cannot corroborate this, but the figure is probably an exaggeration. The actual coin was the *groot.* When gro. appears alone, it refers to *groot* or *grooten* (plural). When it appears as *lb. gro.* (equivalent to 240 gro.) or *s. gro.* (equivalent to 12 gro.), these are units of account.

    9. See, for example, N. de Pauw, ed., *Cartulaire historique et généalogique des Artevelde* (Brussels: Commission Royale d'Histoire, 1920), pp. 234–35.

    10. Juliet Vale, *Edward III and Chivalry: Chivalric Society and Its Context, 1270–1350* (Woodbridge, Suffolk: Boydell Press, 1982), p. 25.

    11. Pierre Desportes, *Reims et les Rémois aux XIIIe et XIVe siècles* (Paris: Picard, 1979), p. 291.

    12. Bernard Prost, ed., *Inventaires mobiliers et extraits des comptes des ducs de Bourgogne de la maison de Valois (1363–1477)*, 2 vols. (Paris: Leroux, 1902–4 and 1908–13), 1:175–84, 197, 199, 200; compare Peter Spufford, *Handbook of Medieval Exchange* (London: Royal Historical Society, 1986), pp. 179, 187, 191, 215.

    13. See in general J. J. Vernier, "Philippe le Hardi duc de Bourgogne, son mariage avec Marguerite de Flandre en 1369," *Bulletin du Commission historique du département du Nord* 22 (1900): 89–133.

    14. A special municipal account survives for the celebration. Due to the enormous expenses involved, it was only included in summary form in the main city account of the following year (SAG, ser. 400, 9, fol. 338r–v; SAG, ser. 400, 10, fol. 7r).

    15. *Œuvres de Froissart, publiées avec les variantes des divers manuscrits*, ed. Baron Kervyn de Lettenhove (Brussels: Devaux, 1867–77; reprint Osnabrück: Biblio Verlag, 1967), vol. 7, *Chroniques*, p. 320. I discuss the city's expenses on the jousts later in this chapter.

    16. David Nicholas, "The Governance of Fourteenth-Century Ghent: The Theory and Practice of Public Administration," in *Law, Custom, and the Social Fabric in Medieval Europe: Essays in Honor of Bryce Lyon* (Kalamazoo, Mich.: Medieval Institute Publications, 1990), pp. 254, 256.

    17. SAG, ser. 400, 9, fol. 329v.

    18. *Œuvres de Froissart* 8:373.

    19. Van Werveke, *Rekeningen 1351–1364*, pp. 580–81.

    20. SAG, ser. 400, 9, fols. 247v–248r.

    21. SAG, ser. 400, 9, fol. 269r.

    22. SAG, ser. 400, 10, fols. 17r, 18v.

    23. For the city's expenses on these festivals, see SAG, ser. 400, 10, fol. 53r; and Vuylsteke, *Rekeningen 1376–1389*, p. 34.

    24. Prost, *Inventaires mobiliers* 2:16.

25. Vuylsteke, *Rekeningen 1376–1389*, pp. 103–4.

26. See the summary with relevant literature of Boone, *Gent en de Bourgondische hertogen*, pp. 114–18.

27. Prost, *Inventaires mobiliers* 1:202, 263–64.

28. SAG, ser. 400, 9, fols. 310r, 333v; SAG, ser. 400, 12, fol. 270r; and Vuylsteke, *Rekeningen 1376–1389*, p. 31. In 1408 the count held a three-week shooting festival at Oudenaarde, twenty-five kilometers south of Ghent; although it seems likely that archers from Ghent participated, it cannot be proven, for the municipal accounts make no mention of it (Otto Cartellieri, *The Court of Burgundy* [New York: Barnes and Noble, 1929], p. 120).

29. Richard Vaughan, *Philip the Bold: The Formation of the Burgundian State* (Cambridge, Mass.: Harvard University Press, 1962), pp. 4, 6, 18, 34–38, 76.

30. See chapter 5 by James Murray on the Joyous Entry of 1384 at Bruges.

31. *Œuvres de Froissart* 10:448–51 (quotations from pp. 448–49, 451).

32. Ibid. (quotations from p. 451).

33. SAG, ser. 400, 10, fols. 334v, 343r.

34. SAG, ser. 400, 12, fols. 48v, 134r.

35. SAG, ser. 400, 9, fol. 300v.

36. Marc Boone, *Geld en Macht: De Gentse stadsfinanciën en de Bourgondische staatsvorming (1384–1453)* (Ghent: Maatschappij voor Geschiedenis en Oudheidkunde, 1990), p. 77.

37. SAG, ser. 400, 11, fols. 69v, 85r–v, 87v.

38. SAG, ser. 400, 11, fols. 133r, 155v–156r, 181r; and SAG, ser. 400, 12, fol. 118v.

39. C. A. J. Armstrong, "The Language Question in the Low Countries: The Use of French and Dutch by the Dukes of Burgundy and Their Administration," in *Europe in the Late Middle Ages*, ed. J. R. Hale, J. R. L. Highfield, and B. Smal (London: Faber, 1965), reprinted in C. A. J. Armstrong, *England, France and Burgundy in the Fifteenth Century* (London: Hambledon Press, 1983), p. 197.

40. SAG, ser. 400, 11, fol. 89v.

41. SAG, ser. 400, 12, fols. 273r–274r; see comment by Boone, *Geld en Macht*, p. 67.

42. SAG, ser. 400, 10, fol. 44v. I have perhaps arbitrarily not included this among public festivals in the totals represented on the graphs accompanying this chapter, since apart from the procession into the city, the cardinal's activity seems to have been limited to the banquet with the aldermen.

43. SAG, ser. 400, 11, fol. 86v.

44. SAG, ser. 400, 12, fol. 132r.

45. The information on the electoral festivities is found in SAG, ser. 400, 9, fols. 247v, 267r, 310r, 333v; SAG, ser. 400, 10, fols. 17r, 342v; Vuylsteke, *Rekeningen 1376–1389*, pp. 31, 179, 421; SAG, ser. 400, 11, fols. 35r, 58r, 85r, 112r, 133r, 155v, 181r, 205r, 231r, 303r, 343r; and SAG, ser. 400, 12, fols. 19v, 46r, 131r, 159r, 187r, 216r, 250v, 287v.

46. Van Werveke, *Rekeningen 1351–1364*, p. 467; see more generally Nicholas, "Governance of Fourteenth-Century Ghent," p. 246.

47. Van Werveke, *Rekeningen 1351–1364*, pp. 484, 529, 577; this entry is also found in all municipal accounts of the period under discussion.

48. Others did not. The church of Bourbourg also had a confraternity of Our Lady of Rozebeke. Relief elsewhere in Flanders at the defeat of Philip van Artevelde in November 1382 was so instantaneous that by the summer of 1383 the people of Bourbourg were doing a procession to Westrozebeke, the site of the battle that had cost van Artevelde his life. The Brugeois were joining them by century's end, and the procession became an annual affair on the third Sunday of each July. For reasons that need no elaboration, Ghent did not participate. Jacques Toussaert, *Le sentiment religieux en Flandre à la fin du Moyen Age* (Paris: Plon, 1960), pp. 269–70.

49. Henri Nowé, "Gentse voorgeboden op de Sint Lievinsbedevaart," in *Miscellanea J.*

Gessler 2 (Deurne: Govaerts, 1948): 967–70; and N. de Pauw and J. Vuylsteke, eds., *De Rekeningen der stad Gent: Tijdvak van Jacob van Artevelde, 1336–1349*, 3 vols. (Ghent: Hoste, 1874–85), 2:493.

50. SAG, ser. 400, 11, fols. 71v, 99r, 124v, 145v, and passim.

51. Trio, *Gentse Broederschappen*, p. 36; Boone, *Geld en Macht*, p. 97; Nowé, "Gentse voorgeboden," pp. 967–68; and J. Gessler, "De aloude bedevaart naar Sint-Lievins-Houtem," *Oostvlaamsche Zanten* 161 (1941): 67. For an example before our period of disorder connected to this festival, see *Annales Gandenses*, p. 14. The men of Ghent were carrying the statue of Saint Lievin to Houtem in 1301 and "fell out with countryfolk and others who had collected there for a festival and dedication." We are not told expressly that it was the festival of Saint Lievin, but it seems likely. As a result, the Gentenars sent the militia to Houtem and burned the village.

52. SAG, ser. 400, 10, fol. 343r; and SAG, ser. 400, 11, fols. 181v, 343r. Epiphany was a riotous occasion elsewhere, but the evidence from Ghent is from the sixteenth century (L. Lievevrouw-Coopman, "Dertienavond in het Gentsche," *Oostvlaamsche Zanten* 17 (1942): 149–81.

53. Herman Pleij, *Het gilde van de Blauwe Schuit: Literatuur, volksfeest en burgermoraal in de late Middeleeuwen* (Amsterdam: Meulenhoff, 1979), pp. 48–50.

54. Boone, *Geld en Macht*, pp. 96–97.

55. SAG, ser. 400, 11, fol. 315v; and SAG, ser. 400, 12, fol. 49v.

56. These are percentages of the total expenditure of the city for the years in question. Boone, *Geld en Macht*, Table 14, column F, gives extremely high percentages of "total administrative expenses" for festivals and processions, ranging in most years between 1400 and 1420 from 15.0 to 16.5 percent of the expenditures, reaching a high of 24.22 percent in 1404–5, the year when John the Fearless succeeded Philip the Bold as count. He refers here to total expenses of the city minus payments to the prince and other large categories of administrative expenses such as for public works and military matters and thus arrives at a much higher percentage for festivals than do I.

57. SAG, ser. 400, 10, fol. 54r.

58. The figures for Shrove Tuesday are in SAG, ser. 400, 10, fol. 244v; SAG, ser. 400, 11, fols. 38r–v, 60v, 89v, 114v–115r, 136r–v, 159r–v, 183v–184r, 208r–v, 234r–v, 315r–v, 345r–v; and SAG, ser. 400, 12, fols. 23r–v, 49v–50r, 135r, 162v, 190v–191r, 220r, 254r–v, 291r–v.

59. SAG, ser. 400, 10, fol. 244v; and SAG, ser. 400, 11, fols. 38r–v, 114v, and passim.

60. Els Cornelius, "De Kunstenaar in het laat-middeleeuwse Gent. I. Organisatie en kunstproduktie van de Sint-Lucasgilde in de 15de eeuw," *Handelingen der Maatschappij voor Geschiedenis en Oudheidkunde te Gent*, n.s. 41 (1987): 121.

61. Henri Nowé, "De Gentenaars en de processie van Doornik," *Oostvlaamsche Zanten* 18 (1943): 11–24.

62. SAG, ser. 400, 11, fols. 10r, 25v, and passim.

63. In an article written in 1985 and published in 1990, I calculated the percentage of the city's expenditure on festivals, subtracting the 1369 wedding figure as atypical but noting a drastic jump from an outlay of 1.75 percent in 1369 to 5.17 percent in 1372, the next surviving account (Nicholas, "Governance of Fourteenth-Century Ghent," Table 2, p. 253). The difference is not a larger expenditure, but the fact that the earlier figures place compensation of the town aldermen for their festival uniforms under a separate rubric; from 1372, this item was included with festivals. In the present essay I have corrected the 1360s figures to take account of this.

64. The jousts are recorded in van Werveke, *Rekeningen 1351–1364*, pp. 580–81; Vuylsteke, *Rekeningen 1376–1389*, pp. 34, 103–4; SAG, ser. 400, 9, fols. 247v–248r, 269r; SAG, ser. 400, 10, fols. 18v, 53r; and SAG, ser. 400, 12, fols. 48v, 134r.

65. Other sources show one of the trumpeters doing piping, a fair comment on the sophistication of the musicians and/or their audience. The pipers were called "pipers of the city" in 1418 (Vuylsteke, *Rekeningen 1376–1389*, p. 402; and SAG, ser. 400, 12, fol. 238r).

66. SAG, ser. 400, 10, fol. 335v.

67. SAG, ser. 400, 11, fol. 100v; and SAG, ser. 400, 12, fols. 36r, 119v.

68. SAG, ser. 400, 12, fol. 238v.

69. Nowé, "Processie van Doornik," p. 14, after De Pauw, *Cartulaire des Artevelde,* pp. 107–8.

70. SAG, ser. 400, 11, fol. 302v.

71. John H. Munro, "Mint Outputs, Money, and Prices in Late-Medieval England and the Low Countries," *Trierer Historische Forschungen* 7 (1984): 102–3, 118, 121.

72. SAG, ser. 400, 9, fol. 241v, compared with van Werveke, *Rekeningen 1351–1364,* p. 654.

73. SAG, ser. 400, 10, fols. 10v, 46v.

74. SAG, ser. 400, 11, fols. 26r, 73r, 196v.

75. SAG, ser. 400, 11, fols. 147r, 172r, 333v; and SAG, ser. 400, 12, fol. 119v.

76. Nowé, "Processie van Doornik," p. 24.

77. For example, wine worth 23 *lb.* 17*s.* 10*d. gro.* was given to the duchess of Burgundy and the countess of Nevers when they entered the city in 1388. The delegation of aldermen to Tournai had travel expenses of 29 *lb.* 12*s.* 1*d. gro.* that year. In 1389 the city presented the count with wine and wax worth 36 *lb.* 16*s.* 7*d. gro.* when he entered the city (there is no mention of a celebration). By comparison, the cost of the Tournai festival apart from the perquisites of the magistrates was 22 *lb.* 9*s.* 9.5*d. gro.* (Vuylsteke, *Rekeningen 1376–1389,* pp. 370, 373, 400, 418).

78. Boone, *Geld en Macht,* pp. 85–100, 216–17; and Boone, *Gent en de Bourgondische hertogen,* pp. 40–48; W. P. Blockmans, "Mutaties van het politiek personeel in de steden Gent en Brugge tijdens een periode van regimewisselingen: het laatste kwart van de 15e eeuw," in *Bronnen voor de Geschiedenis van de Instellingen in België: Handelingen van het Colloquium te Brussel. 15–18.IV.1975* (Brussels: Algemeen Rijksarchief, 1977), pp. 92–103; and W. P. Blockmans, "Het wisselingsproces van de Gentse schepenen tijdens de 15e eeuw," *Handelingen der Maatschappij voor Geschiedenis en Oudheidkunde te Gent,* n. s. 41 (1987): 75–96.

79. Walter Prevenier and Marc Boone, "The 'City-State' Dream," in *Ghent: In Defence of a Rebellious City: History, Art, Culture,* ed. Johan Decavele (Ghent: Marcatorfonds, 1989), p. 100.

80. Hugo Soly, "Plechtige intochten in de steden van de Zuidelijke Nederlanden tijdens de overgang van de Middeleeuwen naar Nieuwe Tijd: Communicatie, propaganda, spektakel," *Tijdschrift voor Geschiedenis* 97 (1984): 343–44.

CHAPTER 12

Elite and Popular Culture in Late Fifteenth-Century Castilian Festivals

The Case of Jaén

Teofilo F. Ruiz

During the Christmas season of 1463, two hundred knights, "the best and better appointed of those belonging to the household" of Don Miguel Lucas de Iranzo, constable of Castile, pleased their master and the people of Jaén by joining in festive displays. One hundred of the knights donned false beards and Moorish garbs, pretending to be Muslim knights. The other hundred retained their clothes and arms, emblems of their place in the martial and Christian world of the Granada frontier. Richly dressed, the hundred feigned Moorish noblemen entered Jaén in a ceremonial procession. Leading the way, under a lush cloth canopy held high by four *alfaquíes* (Muslim doctors of law), a knight, playing the role of Muhammad, rode on a lavishly adorned mule, carrying in his hands the Koran and other books of Islamic doctrine and law. Another of Miguel Lucas's men followed him playing the role of the king of Morocco, and after him the aforementioned one hundred men.

Once settled within specially prepared lodgings, two knights rode to the constable's quarters. There, after kissing Miguel Lucas's hands, they delivered to him a red (*bermeja*) letter. The missive, which included much praise for the constable, the "killer of Moors," plaintively told of how Muhammad had forsaken his own people, allowing for their defeat while the god of the Christians granted them victories against the Nasrid of Granada. The letter concluded with a challenge to a joust, a trial of arms, in which, if defeated, the feigned Muslims promised to repudiate their faith.

On the square of Santa María, within the walls of Jaén, the hundred knights with false beards and Moorish dress broke lances (*cañas*) against their Christian counterparts for more than three hours. After the mock combat, which of course ended with a Christian victory, the king of Morocco approached the constable and, acknowledging his defeat and the superiority of the Christians, abjured the Muslim faith. Muhammad and the Koran were hurled, first to the ground and then into a fountain where a theatrical baptism was enacted. Having become Christians, Muhammad, the king of Morocco, and the Moors approached the constable and kissed his hand in a gesture of obeisance. After the playacting ended, the entire group, over two hundred strong, proceeded to the constable's palace for a collation of fruits and wine.[1]

The festivities of 26 December 1463 were followed by the constable's generous distribution of gifts to the people of Jaén, by formal banquets for the cathedral chapter and clergy of the city, and by colorful mummers' dances and *tableaux vivants* in the streets of Jaén. On 6 January, the day of the Epiphany, this culminated in a great celebration that intertwined courtly elements with carnivalesque ribaldry and debasing of the constable's enemies. After a great deal of eating, dancing, and singing throughout the day, the streets were lit with numerous torches and lanterns. A large crowd gathered in the plaza facing the constable's house to witness the festivities. Down the street of the Magdalene, the main thoroughfare of the city, eight drummers and ten or twelve trumpeters walked toward the plaza. Following them, twelve knights (a symbolic representation of the twelve apostles) rode on beautiful and well-appointed horses. They wore masks and crowns and carried lances. Behind them, riding on a small nag, came a *loco* (a madman, a fool), who was known in Jaén as the *maestre de Santiago* (the master of the Military Order of Santiago and a sworn enemy of the constable). Approximately thirty footmen, carrying torches, formed the next line in the procession and behind them, on a "beautiful and graceful horse," rode the constable, Don Miguel Lucas de Iranzo. The chronicler describes his appearance in detail. He was dressed in blue damask with silver and gold adornments and wore rich furs. His face was covered with a mask, a crown adorned his head, and in his hands he carried the sword of justice. Ten or twelve men closed the ranks, discharging their muskets into the air.

In the main square, the constable and his men engaged in a lively running of the ring (*sortija*); this was followed by a lavish banquet for the knights of Jaén. The evening concluded with a theatrical event. Three men, dressed as the Magi, followed a star (held suspended above the street) through the city. The star led them to the house of the constable where, waiting for their worship, rested a statue of the baby Jesus. The constable and his wife led more dances, and more feasting closed the night and this particular cycle of festivities.[2]

Introduction

In this short account and in numerous similar descriptions found in the *Hechos del condestable,* we gain an entry into the rich and complex world of public and private festivals in late medieval Castile. This particular cycle of festivities, as well as other calendrical and noncalendrical ludic events, are reminders of how those above represented their power to those below, and how, within the civic space of Jaén, elaborate social dramas and well-staged political theater were continually enacted and reenacted to further the interests of those who ruled.[3] As Steven Mullaney has argued, paraphrasing Foucault, "Ritual and spectacle are not spontaneous; they are staged events, orchestrated manifestations of power, studied representatives of authority and community. In early modern society power was inseparable from such public manifestations."[4] In Jaén these festivals, one must add, were paid from general taxes collected in the city and, above all, in the city's hinterland. Some of the expenses were also covered by booty gained in the war against Granada. As such, these festivities, while seeking to bind the population of Jaén in obedience to the constable, served as well as a source of popular irritation and hostility against the constable.

The focus of Mullaney's study was Renaissance England and the place of the stage in the Elizabethan political and cultural world, and few would argue today against the historical significance of festivals and rituals in the political and communal life of medieval and early modern Europe. But the question is not whether festivals functioned as representations of power and/or forms of resistance to constituted power; rather, the question remains how and why this was so.[5] For medievalists, they are familiar manifestations of the ways in which power was articulated before 1500. The simplest reading of the opening description of the *burlas moriscas* (Moorish tricks) and of the feast of the Epiphany in Jaén in 1463 resonates with memories of early modern masques. But there is a wide gulf separating the elaborate courtly masques written by Ben Jonson and staged by Inigo Jones in Jacobean England from the performances of Don Miguel Lucas de Iranzo and his knights in the streets of Jaén.[6]

The main difference was that Castilian festival performances, in this specific case the feasts paid for and managed by the constable in Jaén, blurred the distinctions between the private and the public and between high and low culture. This they did by integrating into public ritual and civic festivals elements of courtly and popular culture. Popular culture (however we may wish to define this term) and its quintessential manifestations—carnival, ribaldry, debasing, and travesty—were not, as Bakhtin has argued, a form of resistance to the established order in late medieval Castile or in Jaén of the 1460s. In the examples below, the constable and his court used travesty, carnival, and the linking of courtly and popular motifs as instruments of power for the purpose of maintaining their precarious grip over the city and kingdom of Jaén.

In the following pages, I will explore the political context of civic festivals in Jaén, focusing on how these highly ritualized and symbolic feasts cut across the boundaries between public and private, urban and rural, high and low.

The Constable of Castile, Jaén, and
the Realm of Castile in the 1460s

The *Hechos del condestable*, attributed to Pedro de Escavias, *alcaide* of Andujar and loyal follower of Don Miguel Lucas de Iranzo, is our guide to the life of the constable and his activities in Jaén. One of the most important sources for the history of Castile in the second half of the fifteenth century, the *Hechos del condestable* begins in 1458 with the investiture of Miguel Lucas as constable of Castile and concludes, somewhat abruptly, in 1471, less than two years before the assassination of the protagonist in the cathedral of Jaén. A highly laudatory and partisan defense of the constable's life and deeds, the *Hechos del condestable* contains numerous descriptions of festivals, ceremonial entries, and other ludic events that celebrated the liturgical calendar, important moments in Miguel Lucas's life or those of his family and friends. These careful accounts of feasts, by what must have been an eyewitness, are interrupted from time to time by lyrical descriptions of the constable's martial deeds on the Granada frontier, by a thorough review of his administrative reforms in Jaén, and by a narrative of his struggle against enemies within the city and in the realm.

The lavish descriptions of festivals, however, constitute most of the chronicle. This section of the *Hechos del condestable,* despite its liberal use of documentary sources and textual references, served, as de Mata Carriazo has shown, merely as a backdrop for the depiction of Don Miguel Lucas de Iranzo on a heroic scale.[7] This was accomplished, first and foremost, by exhaustive examples of the constable's largesse, courtliness, and piety, as demonstrated by his sponsorship and faithful celebrations of liturgical and secular festivities. His unwavering loyalty to his king, Enrique IV (1454–74), and his struggle against the Moors added to the glorified view of the constable. The chronicler thus wove the personal life of Don Miguel Lucas de Iranzo into the troubled tapestry of Jaén's civic life and the upheavals plaguing the realm.

The Constable of Castile and Jaén in the 1460s

Royal and aristocratic festivals and ludic performances enjoyed a long tradition in Castile, with its deeply ingrained mixture of popular and courtly themes.[8] Outside the context of the constable's life, of the peculiar history of Jaén, and of Castile in this period, these festivals are not always intelligible. We must begin, therefore, by placing them in the appropriate historical setting.

Of humble origins, the son of a poor *labrador* (farmer), as his enemies were wont to remind contemporaries, Don Miguel Lucas's rise to power and eventual demise can be told in a few words. Born in Belmonte, a village under the lordship of the marquis of Villena, Miguel entered the service of the Infante Enrique, the future Enrique IV, through the intercession of Villena. At court he soon became a favorite of the Infante and was lavishly rewarded for his service with a patent of nobility in 1445, and with important monetary grants and dignities. A *doncel* (the prince's page) in 1452, Don Miguel Lucas was awarded an annual income of 20,000 *maravadíes* (*mrs.*) that year from the sales tax of Baeza; his income was further augmented the next year by a gift of 112,000 *mrs.* per annum from the rents of Agreda and Molina. An even more important step was his marriage, arranged by the Infante, to Teresa de Torres, the sole heir to the rich and noble Don Carlos de Torres. Further grants, his naming as *corregidor* of Baeza, his knighting with golden spurs in 1455 (after Enrique became king in 1454), and his appointment to the profitable position of *canciller mayor* of the realm gave Miguel Lucas de Iranzo a prominent place in the court and the kingdom.[9]

Enrique IV's animosity toward the high nobility (the influential magnates or *ricos hombres* family groups) was expressed in his choice of favorites and officials. They were, on the whole, new men or *conversos*, outsiders to the networks of patronage and power, who owed their promotion solely to the king. But Miguel Lucas's success, culminating in his being named constable of Castile on 25 March 1458, was short-lived indeed. His hold on the king and his newly gained power antagonized influential rivals, chiefly Juan Pacheco, the marquis of Villena. Enrique IV himself, inconstant and wary of those wielding too much power, had already found someone else upon whom to bestow his favors. Miguel Lucas's imprisonment shortly after his investiture marked the ascendancy of Beltrán de la Cueva and the effective removal of Miguel Lucas from the main stage of Castilian politics. Escaping to the kingdom of Aragón, the constable reached a compromise with the king and his enemies. As long as he abandoned the court and any pretension of playing a role in the affairs of the realm, he could keep his position and income. In the king's name, he was also given the rule of any city he chose. He chose Jaén on the Granada frontier.[10]

As bizarre as these developments appear, they formed part of the confused world of fifteenth-century Castile. Throughout most of the reign of Juan II (1406–54), the realm suffered violent conflicts. Factions of the high nobility, led by the Infantes of Aragón, Don Enrique and Don Juan, waged war on the crown. The Infantes were cousins to the king of Castile, brothers of the king of Aragón and the queen of Castile, and the richest landholders in the realm. Don Enrique was master of Santiago; Don Juan was king of Navarre and, after 1458, king of the Crown of Aragón as well. Thwarting their efforts and protecting his weak king stood the enigmatic and capable Don Alvaro de Luna (d. 1453), constable of Castile.[11]

This protracted struggle for control of royal revenues and political power worsened after the ascent of Enrique IV. A much maligned king, his cautious policies in the war against Granada and their eventual failure, as well as his lavish and irresponsible grants to favorites and friends, did not check the rapacious ambitions of the high nobility. This combination of royal incompetence and noble selfishness hurled the kingdom into bitter civil war. For all practical purposes, after 1461, Castile was divided into quasi-independent fiefdoms. Royal income and lands were alienated as kingly authority waned. In 1464 the conflict came to a head. That year a league of nobles sought to overthrow Enrique IV, their efforts culminating in the theatrical and ritualized trial and decrowning of an effigy of the king, the so-called farce of Ávila, outside the walls of Ávila on 5 June 1465.[12]

For almost another decade Castile suffered the convulsions of civil war, disputed successions, and magnate violence; the anarchy ended only with Isabella's ascent to the throne in 1474. It is against this background of almost total anarchy that the constable rode into Jaén in 1461, his own hold on the constable's sword, on the city, and on his annual income greatly imperiled by the king's misfortunes. Jaén had to be held at all costs. To his honor, although the opportunities for betrayal were many indeed, Don Miguel Lucas never wavered in his loyalty to his king.

Jaén in the Mid–Fifteenth Century

An engraving of sixteenth-century Jaén, commissioned by Philip II and undertaken by Anton van den Wyngaerde, shows a strong walled city with little or no urban development outside its contours. The cathedral and other important landmarks in van den Wyngaerde's engraving date from the early modern period, long after Miguel Lucas's death in 1473 and long after the conquest of Granada in 1492. If we remove them from the drawing, we are left with a fortress city, a military enclave on a troublesome frontier.[13] In the eleventh century, still under Muslim rule, the city had been a strong place and the center of an extensive, albeit sparsely populated, hinterland. After the collapse of the Cordoba caliphate and the successive invasions of Almoravids and Almohads, the region had an uncertain life as one of the so-called kingdoms of *taífas*.[14]

Conquered in 1246 by Ferdinand III, the city and its territory, the kingdom of Jaén, faced an uncertain future as the farther outpost of Christian advance on the Granada frontier. It was a role that Jaén played for more than two centuries. The late thirteenth and the early fourteenth centuries brought periods of famine, pestilence, and demographic decline. In the next century, its population sparse—probably around eight thousand inhabitants in 1407—Jaén suffered frequent invasions by Nasrid armies that inflicted "great damages" on the entire region, damages "so intense" as to lead almost to its depopulation.[15]

In the fifteenth century, the city supported a modest textile industry, with some significant production of silk cloth, but the economic mainstay of the region was agriculture—the typical diversified rural landscape combining cereal-growing lands, vineyards, olive trees, and the specialized cultivation of cochineal for cloth dyeing. Although the *Hechos del condestable* barely mentions Jews and *conversos*, the city population included a significant number of both. They were engaged in a variety of economic activities: farming, crafts, commercial enterprises, as well as a small amount of moneylending and tax collecting. Don Miguel Lucas de Iranzo was often accused of favoring the *conversos* and lost his life, in 1473, during a popular anti-*converso* uprising instigated by the constable's enemies.[16] The task at hand in 1463 was a formidable one. The constable had to establish his rule over the city and the region, reform Jaén's militia and government, then in total disarray, and, more important, meet the challenge of Nasrid Granada.

Civic Festivals and Political Power

Throughout most of his tenure at Jaén, the constable faced the fierce opposition of the bishop. Exiled in Baeza, he sought to undermine Miguel Lucas's authority and, in one instance, even attempted to storm the city. Noble factions within the city and in the realm at large presented similar threats. None of these threats, however, was as menacing as that of Miguel Lucas's most deadly enemy, the marquis de Villena, master of Santiago. Villena sought to undermine the constable and his position in Jaén and to gain control of the war effort against Granada and its profits. At the same time, the constable had to balance carefully the volatile social tensions between the popular classes and the *conversos*. Finally, there was the ever-present threat of Muslim raids and the psychological and political need of maintaining a militant stance against Islam. Great profits were to be gained in frontier warfare, but, more significant, the very *raison d'être* of the constable, as well as the justification for his incessant demands for income, was that he was to carry on the struggle against Christ's enemies.[17]

For the sake of brevity one can offer this tentative typology—by no means exhaustive—of some of the themes, or better yet, of the goals of those festivals sponsored by the constable. They are as follows:

A. The blending of urban and rural spaces: Jaén as a stage for social and political drama.
B. The mixing of sacred and secular motifs as the means of enhancing the prestige of the constable.
C. The linking of the private and the public, of high and low culture for hegemonic purposes.

The City and Its Countryside

We must visualize Jaén, the entire city, in the 1460s as a theater. Its squares and streets, what we describe today as public spaces, served, in fact, as stages for the representation of liturgical, secular, and social dramas.

On the Sunday before Ash Wednesday (in 1863), four Moorish knights, in the service of the king of Granada, came to Jaén on a diplomatic mission to the constable. In their honor, but also as a salutary lesson, they were to be guests of and witnesses (with "fear and wonderment," the chronicler tells us) to a "ferocious" joust in which Don Miguel Lucas's men and the knights of Jaén broke many lances. Later that evening, the constable rode a "good and well-furnished" mare, with his wife, the countess, riding behind him on the horse's croup. Both were dressed in gold. Preceded by twelve drummers and many men playing trumpets, clarinets (*chirimías*), and tambourines, a large procession of Jaén's notables and officials accompanied the Moors as they meandered "through all the streets of the city," the night lit with lanterns and torches. In the squares and open spaces along the way, mummers danced, and *tableaux vivants* and skits were presented.[18]

Wherever we turn in the chronicle, references to theatrical representations to honor distinguished guests or to celebrate religious festivities or events in the life of the constable appear. The plays, *entremeses*, and *tableaux*—the *Hechos del condestable* includes one of the earliest mentions of the play of *Los tres reyes magos*—were alternatively performed indoors, at the constable's lodgings, or in church,[19] but more often than not, playacting involved the entire urban population, including the constable, his family, and his household, with the city of Jaén as a stage. In the opening description, we already witnessed Miguel Lucas's men playing the roles of Muhammad, the king of Morocco, and Moorish knights, and the constable playing himself as a victorious warrior, receiving the obeisance of his enemies. This was followed by the public enactment of the journey of the Magi through the streets of the city, with the adoration of the Christ Child in the constable's chambers as a fitting finale. Miguel Lucas, participant and spectator, served as the link between the "artificial" theatrical representation and the "reality" of civic life.[20]

In the chronicle, the constable and his wife are continually in the public eye; their clothing is described with meticulous care, so much so that we have an inventory of what Don Miguel Lucas wore for more than a week after his wedding.[21] Each color, fabric, and fur articulated very specific messages about the hierarchical nature of society and about the constable's power.[22] In almost every feast, whether intimate gatherings of the mighty or festivals for the entire population of the city, the constable and his wife, the constable's family, and his household retainers led the dance. We must visualize the theatrical impact of such per-formances in the context of the life of the late medieval city.

On the eve of Ash Wednesday, the last day of Carnival, 1464, the con-stable ordered a game of the ring *(sortija)* to be set in front of his lodg-ings. The square was lit by a large bonfire. In public view, seated on a high stage covered with rich French tapestries, the constable, his wife, and guests dined under the gaze of the people of Jaén. Once their meal was finished, they repaired to the high tower in the constable's palace to view the running of the ring. The constable's *ballestero de maza* (his mace-bearer) entered the square to run the ring, but, keeping to the spir-it of the feast, fools and buffoons also attempted to capture the prize. Once the courtly game concluded, the constable and his company descended to the public square to see mummers dance, and, after that, Miguel Lucas, his wife, and other important members of his family and court danced in the public square.[23]

Later we will have an opportunity to see other examples of the role of the constable and his immediate family as the main protagonists in Jaén's social drama, but the city also played a continuous and lasting role as the locus for these representations. Undoubtedly, at the onset of the early modern period, Castilian cities in general and Jaén in particular functioned as stages for the display of the rulers' power, piety, and for-tune. Urban centers also served as settings for the playing out—albeit under the secure control of those above—of multivocal cultural motifs. This constant parading of the pageantry and power of the monarchy and high nobility stands in sharp contrast with sixteenth-century Habsburg rulers of Spain, who defined their rule not in terms of public displays but of secrecy, privacy, and silence.[24]

Castilian urban festivals and, above all, those of Jaén served as ways of linking the city with its hinterland. Because of the peculiarities of the Reconquest, the demographic weakness of the realm, and the nature of frontier life, cities such as Jaén ruled over a vast and sparsely populated countryside. Jurisdiction over distant rural villages and towns was always precarious and prone to conflict.[25] This was doubly so in the case of Jaén, which faced challenges to its lordship within its territory from the municipal councils of Baeza and Ubeda and from magnates in the region. Thus, almost every festival, whether calendrical or not, involved a transposing of urban order and life into the surrounding country-side. Ceremonial entries into the city—royal, ecclesiastical, or noble—always required the bringing out of urban symbols of power or those of the constable's to the adjoining countryside, to that liminal place (usu-ally half a league, or a bit less than two miles) outside the city gates.

In 1464 Enrique IV, already facing the open rebellion of some noble factions, came to Jaén. The constable, riding a white horse with a scarlet damask banner in his hand and followed by a large contingent of men-at-arms, met the king at Alcalá la Real to escort him into the city. Half a

league from Jaén, the canons of the cathedral chapter and municipal officials led a ceremonial procession. Five hundred knights with false beards
(disguised as Moors), thirty others dressed as Moorish women playing
tambourines and bells, four thousand children riding wicker horses,
another thousand children armed with wicker crossbows, and "many
other men and women," the entire city, brought the king in ceremony
into the city. This was both in imitation of Roman triumphal entries
and of the liturgical precedent of Jesus' entry into Jerusalem on Palm
Sunday, but at the same time it brought the symbols of the city to an
area outside its defensive perimeter.[26]

Festivals, as I have noted elsewhere and in this paper, served as a link,
as a language between city and country. They drew the rural population
of the kingdom into the city and acquainted them, through symbols,
colors, and play, with the very nature of hierarchical power. Ludic celebrations imposed an urban order on the countryside and brought, as did
most of the constable's celebrations, "all the population of Jaén" into
the fields and meadows outside the city for festive banquets, bearbaiting,
and the running of bulls. This was no binary opposition between city
and country, but rather a dialogue dominated and played out by urban
interests.[27]

Sacred and Secular

The author of the *Hechos del condestable* carefully weaves together secular and sacred motifs to enhance the prestige of Don Miguel Lucas de
Iranzo. The intertwining of martial references with descriptions of the
constable's piety served very explicit political purposes, for the constable was engaged in an open conflict with the bishop for control of the
city and its resources. The chronicler tells us that in 1463 when the
bishop's men entered the city, seeking to occupy its strong places, the
constable refused to interrupt the mass to face the danger, demonstrat-
ing by his actions his true religiosity and the bishop's hypocrisy.

Every festival the constable sponsored began with a private or public
banquet for the canons, whom Miguel Lucas sought to sway to his cause.
The *Hechos del condestable* makes the point repeatedly, showing his
respect and goodwill for the clergy. Drawing from historical, courtly,
and liturgical precedents, the chronicler presents the reader with the
image of the perfect ruler, the perfect knight, the perfect Christian. After
the rich and fantastic description of the nuptials of Don Miguel Lucas
and the countess in 1461, the *Hechos del condestable* praised the Christian and chivalrous behavior of its main protagonist: "For a year, everyone said, they had shared a bed night and day like husband and wife, but
he [the constable] never *wished* to consummate the marriage until receiving the Church's blessing." How different Don Miguel Lucas is, the
chronicle added, from the lascivious and unchivalrous men of the age.[28]

During the 1462 cycle of Christmas festivals, a woman with a child in her arms—a representation of the Virgin Mary and the Child—entered the constable's lodgings. There, she was received with great honor and seated *between* the constable's wife and his mother. Disguised as the Magi, Don Miguel Lucas and two of his pages, wearing crowns, masks, and holding offering cups in their hands, entered the room and presented their gifts to the Virgin to the accompaniment of trumpets and drums. This representation and appropriation of sacral images—the constable as one of the Three Kings, his mother and his wife sitting on both sides of the Virgin and the Child—was followed by festive dances. The chronicler concludes the description with a revealing aside: "And this feast the constable celebrated and solemnized every year as it is told [here], one because of [his] devotion [piety] and because on such days [the Day of the Epiphany] the king [Enrique IV], our lord, was born, on whose service he did and wished for much."[29]

Service and piety are brought together as a reflective reminder. The author, stepping outside his narrative, provides his contemporaries and posterity with a worthy example of piety and loyalty. In 1462, after a successful raid on Granada, about which the chronicler waxes enthusiastic in his description of Don Miguel Lucas's bravery and victory against overwhelming numerical odds, the constable returned to Jaén with numerous captive Moorish men, women, and children, and a rich booty of jewels, cattle, and other goods. He was received into the city with "great happiness ... as Rome used to welcome its emperors when they returned from their conquests." And such was the fame of his martial deeds that the king ordered a romance to be composed in his honor.[30]

But the good judgment and administrative skills of the constable, illustrated by many examples throughout the *Hechos*, are not always sufficient to ward off treachery and envy. When in 1468 one of the *regidores* (crown-appointed city council members) of Jaén, Fernand Mexías, and others conspired to murder the constable and to attack and pillage the houses of the *conversos*, a "miracle by God," the chronicler relates, altered Mexías's vision and thwarted his plans. Instead, he and his accomplices fell easily into Miguel Lucas's hands. What was to be expected? For the author of the *Hechos*, it was indeed a sign of the times, of the "malice of the age," that the constable receive such rewards for his efforts. If he were a Roman emperor, the Roman people would have erected statues, written histories, and treated him with the "solemnity and reverence" he so well deserved.[31]

In late medieval Castile, where the *defensores* (the knights) are the keystone, the foundation of the well-ordered tripartite society,[32] Don Miguel Lucas de Iranzo—courageous knight, worthy of comparison with the Roman emperors because of his leadership, pious and dutiful Christian—is represented as the culmination of courtly, classical, and Christian ideals. This is, of course, almost a topos in late medieval literature, and Jorge Manrique's extraordinary "Ode on the Death of His Father" weaves the same motifs into the praise of Don Rodrigo de Manrique. But Manrique's poem was a panegyric bestowed upon the dead, while the *Hechos del condestable* was neither a funeral poem nor a mirror of princes. Its author, Pedro de Escavias, if de Mata Carriazo is correct, was an important participant and witness to the events described, and he appears prominently in the chronicle as a faithful ally of Miguel Lucas de Iranzo. The narrative is contemporaneous with the constable's deeds, victories, and reverses; but amid the chronicler's dogged attempts at accumulating documents, accounts of eyewitnesses, and other evidence that would grant "veracity" to his account, an underlying but explicit theme plays throughout. It tells us of the constable's secular and divine right to power, of the duty of the citizens of Jaén to obey and be thankful to their master, of how much the king owed Miguel Lucas—as he certainly did—for his loyalty and courtly valor.[33]

The Uses of Carnival: Life Cycles, Private and Public, High and Low

In the Middle Ages, distinctions between the private and the public, between elite and popular culture, are often nothing more than the artificial semantic constructs of later scholarship and are seldom reflected in historical reality. My point here, following Gurevich, is that the boundaries between these categories were at times nonexistent or very blurred.[34] I will argue that there is, in fact, a discernable and easy-to-document flow from private to public, from courtly to popular, and vice versa, and that this movement to and fro, a process described by Le Goff as "internal acculturation," was not, as Bakhtin and others have argued, a form of resistance, at least not in Jaén.[35] Rather, the linking of these two aspects of culture, "high" and "low," "private" and "public," in the feasts of the constable represented a conscious effort to appropriate and utilize the language, the festive forms, the very culture of those below for hegemonic purposes. Admiring Gramsci but not really being a Gramscian, I will argue that this borrowing was done to facilitate ruling, to foster that religion of power and obedience that lay at the roots of the nascent nation-state. The late Middle Ages suffered from what Weber called the "disenchantment of the world" or from that widespread fear described by Delumeau, which accompanied the breakdown of medieval society and the birth of capitalism. In this period, the exercise of power, whether royal or, as was the case in Jaén, noble, could only be effective when manifested in forms, theatrical or otherwise, that cut across class and culture, that bound together the different orders of society and the distinct temporal and spacial spheres of urban and rural life.

After so many anecdotal examples and a discussion already too long, we must still refer anew to the present debate on whether there is such a thing as popular culture. Is culture imposed on the popular classes, or is there a reciprocal influence, as Bakhtin argued?[36] Whenever we look at the relations between ruling elites and the oppressed, the carnival stands as a conflicting border, one in which the "world is turned upside down" and representations of power are debased. In some cases, these metaphorical acts of resistance can be translated into direct and violent actions against the existing structures of power. Such was indeed the case at Romans in the sixteenth century.[37] There is no question that carnivalesque images were and are subversive, but the issue—one that probably can never be resolved satisfactorily—is the question of the nature of that resistance. Was it resistance at all?

Medieval culture, as Gurevich and others have pointed out, was an "impossible combination of opposites."[38] The festive performances of the Castilian monarchy or, in this case, those of Don Miguel Lucas de Iranzo, served as the locus for the meeting of these opposites. Ceremonial entries, tournaments, *pas d'armes*, and other courtly pageantry reaffirmed the existing hierarchies of power, the values of high culture— what James Scott, in a lively paper to the Davis Center, described as the public transcript, or in Bakhtinian terms, "the official culture." At the same time, these same manifestations of culture and power were played out against a background of colors, mostly red and white, to which both high and low were responsive.[39] Moreover, the festivals of those who ruled included popular carnivalesque aspects, which, through ribaldry and travesty, debased and decrowned the very values of those in power. How and why was this possible?

The Integration of High and Low Culture

From classical times to the present, those who rule have allowed and even encouraged public festive events as yet another means of control. This is of course a commonplace. The well-known images of bread and circus, Machiavelli's biting remarks on the political uses of religion and liturgical festivals, the ludic displays of our own times, whether football or television evangelists, are reminders of the ways in which those who rule provide for distractions, for making the exercise of naked power more "acceptable." The other side of this argument is that the "private transcript," the feasts of fools, carnival, and other popular festivals were and remain the means to expand the boundaries of resistance, to turn, at least from time to time, the established order upside down. In Lawrence Stone's words, "Is it sand in the machine [slowing it down, destroying it] or just harmless noise?"

I argue instead that popular elements in the feasts of late medieval Castile and, in particular, those of the constable in Jaén did not represent the spirit of the "folk," expressing itself in direct opposition to official culture. This was no private transcript, attempting to subvert hegemonic relations between the powerful and the weak. If at all, these popular motifs were employed by the powerful for their own internal struggles or to preserve their privileges. Popular carnival, divorced from elite culture, may have existed in Castile, but the sources for the period are mostly silent as to their nature and intent.[40] What these extant sources do show are festive events that combined courtly and popular themes. They were staged and managed by the elite for their own political ends.

We may wish to look at these festivals from yet a slightly different perspective. Festivals, as Roger Chartier has pointed out, are artifacts and, thus, culturally neutral. Each group or class in society brings into them its own vision, its own system of value, and takes out of them what each is able to grasp. Popular culture cannot be recaptured in its original form. In the pages of the *Hechos del condestable* and in other chronicles of the period, the festivals come to us through the mediation of the learned and the semilearned and are thus altered. The appropriation of the culture of those below, of its symbolic forms, occurs at two levels. First, it is claimed and transformed by the texts that are our windows into the past. Second, popular motifs are integrated into the rituals of the feast as a way of including and binding the people into obedience to the powerful.

Many of the symbols displayed in ceremonial entries or in courtly tournaments could have been understood only by those sharing in the culture. The language of these messages required a level of abstraction and a knowledge of literary traditions to which few, except the elite, had access in Castile. Some of the elements found in the festive events described above, specifically jousts and ceremonial entries, belonged almost exclusively to the realm of high culture. On the other hand, there were other festivities or even celebrations within the festive cycle that appealed to a broader audience. At this level, there was no need to explain to the people what the colors, symbols, and gestures meant. They were readily understood without a need for explication. In fifteenth-century Jaén, the feasts of Don Miguel Lucas de Iranzo juxtaposed well-known courtly themes with carnivalesque aspects, and this combination of high and low culture, of the theatrical and fantastic reenactments of literary models, of carnival and ribaldry, appealed to everybody. This mixing of two levels of culture allowed for play, but it also served as a powerful means for instructing those below as to their social status, place, and duties to the constable.

It is difficult to provide convincing evidence for these assertions. We do not possess that unimpeachable source showing the conscious blending of high and low culture for political ends. While there was an obvious link between the symbols and colors of the constable's feasts and his struggle against his enemies in Jaén and the Muslim power in Granada, the use, as the *Hechos del condestable* described in excruciating detail, of certain colors, mummery, public dances, and other carnivalesque elements by the ruling groups for the purpose of co-opting and taming the people, is far more difficult to prove. What sort of evidence can one marshal to support such a hypothesis? How did Castile compare with other medieval realms in the West?

I am not arguing here that these developments were limited to Castile. Popular motifs were present in festivities elsewhere. Red and white were also the colors of the papacy, of English kings and queens (the French royal color was blue). My point, rather, is one of degree: that in Castile as a whole and in Jaén in particular, the crown and the high nobility integrated elements of popular culture into their rituals and festivities far more than elsewhere, and that they did so with a great deal of success. First, as I have already argued elsewhere, the Castilian monarchy was peculiar, precisely because of its popular, secular, and martial nature. From the mid–twelfth century on, with few exceptions, the kings of Castile rejected the sacral trappings of royalty and marked their ascent to power through ceremonies of distinctly popular and secular flavor. Castile, therefore, had a well-established tradition of blending elements of high and low culture.[41] Second, if I am correct as to the nature of festivals in late medieval Castile and the way in which they expressed the relations of power between rulers and the ruled, then the results benefited the elite. There are, of course, other explanations for the docility of the Castilian masses. Among them, one can mention the impact of the Reconquest in directing violence against the Moors; the peculiar nature of the Castilian rural economy, with its lack of servile bonds; and the noble and military ethos governing Castilian social relations, but these factors cannot be discussed here in detail. The fact remains, however, that Castile was one of the few European kingdoms in which there was no Jacquerie, no general peasant uprising, no Ciompi. The late Middle Ages were fraught with social conflicts, but popular anger and frustration were either diffused in local conflicts or channeled against Jews and *conversos*. If, from time to time, one of the mighty lost his life, as when Miguel Lucas was murdered in Jaén, it was because the common people served as pawns for the ambitions of noble factions, and because the constable became identified with the *conversos*.[42] Despite oppressive conditions, the Castilian masses were relatively acquiescent to relentless royal and noble violence against the poor: the image of the rich as wolves, the people as lambs, emerges as a topos in the literature of the period.[43]

Life Cycles, Festivals, and the City

Important stages in the life cycles of the constable, his family, and allies were occasions for elaborate festivals. Whether celebrating the births of Miguel Lucas's children, the feast of his patron saint, his wedding or the weddings of relatives and friends, or mourning the death of the constable's brother, these feasts followed a well-established pattern. They began somewhere in the private spaces, the inner chambers, of the constable's lodgings and were then transferred to the streets of Jaén, drawing the entire population of the city into festive or plaintive moods, as befitted the moment. They concluded with a return to interior spaces and the exclusion of the common people from more intimate and courtly aspects of the celebrations. These patterns of inclusion and exclusion, the progression to and from private and public spheres, were paralleled by a similar flow: the interweaving of courtly and popular culture. Courtly pageantry—jousts and reenactments of chivalrous romances—often marked spatial transitions from private to public. The inclusion of the populace signaled an increase in the use of mummers, ribaldry, and travesty. The end of the feast, indicated by the return to the constable's lodgings and the exclusion of the masses, meant a return to more courtly forms of entertainment.[44] In the constable's celebrations of important events in his own life, in those *rites de passage* (both personal and civic), we find many examples. A few will suffice here.

Weddings

The nuptials of Miguel Lucas and of his relatives and friends reported in the *Hechos* show the same blending of courtly and popular, moving spatially and thematically from private to public, from the close circle around the constable to the inclusion of the whole population of Jaén. His wedding to Doña Teresa de Torres in 1461 attracted visitors from all over the realm and from Jaén's hinterland, "more people than when they flock to the city on the feast of the Virgin in August to see the relics of the Veronica." The chronicle describes how the constable and his wife-to-be were dressed—in scarlet, black, and gold—and how the ceremonial procession took them through the streets of Jaén, from the privacy of their lodgings to the public religious ceremony in the cathedral. The music of trumpets, drums, and other musical instruments and the unpredictable behavior of fools and buffoons served as counterpoint to, and inversion of, the martial splendor of the knights riding in the retinue and the symbols of justice and power carried aloft by the mace-bearers. Minstrels played and sang sweet courtly tunes.

The lavish wedding was followed by a nuptial banquet held in the more restrictive private space. In a richly appointed room, the constable and his wife sat on a stage, surrounded by the great and served by noble knights and high officials. Outside, food was distributed to all: laity and clergy, citizen and alien, rich and poor. And the feasts, the *Hechos del condestable* tells us, lasted for twenty-three days.

Dances by the constable and his wife in the inner chambers of their palace, runnings of bulls in the square outside their lodgings, playacting by members of Miguel Lucas's household, jousts, and more theatrical skits culminated with a representation that included a huge wooden serpent or dragon hurling children and flames through its mouth. Further performances by fools and buffoons, more jousts and *pas d'armes*, running of bulls, distribution of gifts, and so on, carried the celebrations into mid-February, by which time the poor citizens of Jaén must have been thoroughly disgusted with such excesses.[45]

Births and Baptisms

The birth of Don Miguel Lucas's son on Monday, 11 April 1468, in the midst of growing anarchy, marked a swift transition in the narrative. After a somber account of a failed plot against the constable's life, the chronicler moves on to a detailed description of the feasts accompanying the birth of the first male heir. He begins by noting the jubilation of all the people of Jaén, "great and small." Early in the morning, in a clearly hierarchical order (by rank and sex), the high municipal officials, noblewomen and maids, merchants and artisans, peasants and their women abandoned their labors and poured into the constable's house at the sound of trumpets, tambourines, and bells. A singing and dancing mob crowded the streets around the palace. Borne by two of his knights, the constable was paraded in triumph through the throng and taken to a nearby monastery, where for one hour he talked to the cloistered nuns and solicited their prayers.

After a private meal attended by the important people of the city, a great joust was held in the square of Santa María in the afternoon. That evening, city officials of the parishes (*collaciones*) organized and paid for public banquets and festivals in front of their respective local churches. Lit by great bonfires, dancing, singing, eating, and drinking took place throughout the city. The following day, Tuesday, 12 April, tables were set in the cemeteries of the city at the constable's expense, and all the parishioners were invited to yet another banquet. Once sated, the crowd marched back to the constable's palace with such clamor "that the world seemed to be falling down." Riding on a mule to the sounds of barking hounds and the blowing of hunting horns, the *regidor* Fernando de Berrio and the officials of the parish of the Magdalen led a live wolf back and forth across the city. That evening mummers, dances, banquets, and short theatrical skits were performed and held throughout the city.

Six days later, on 18 April, the baptism took place in the cathedral. Elaborate descriptions of the clothes and tapestries adorning the newborn and the church, of the silk canopy covering the ceremonial bed, of the hierarchical procession to and from the cathedral serve as reminders of the courtly character of the feast and of the symbolic and historical importance of the birth of the constable's son. After the baptism, Miguel Lucas, accompanied by all the people present, walked to an open square outside Jaén. From a high place, clothed with silk and rich French cloth, he witnessed the running of six bulls and an additional distribution of food. The night ended with a private banquet for the mighty and mummery, skits, and other entertainment for the masses.[46]

Funerals

Among the several funerals reported in the *Hechos del condestable,* the one marking the death of Don Alonso de Iranzo, archdeacon of the cathedral of Toledo and brother of the constable, in early August 1464 was the most remarkable. Although the funeral and official period of mourning did not include such popular forms of entertainment as mummery, travesty, and other carnivalesque ribaldry, in every other aspect they were almost inverted mirror images of the celebrations described above. There is the same flow of action: from the immediate circle of the constable's household to the wider confines of the city and its hinterland, the same patterns of inclusion and exclusion, which served to define the boundaries between those above and those below.

Once the news was received of the death of the archdeacon, the constable withdrew to his chambers for nine days into almost complete solitude. At the end of this period, the constable, his family and retinue, all dressed in black and with great show of tears, sat on *the same stage* from which he presided over festivals to hear vespers. The people of Jaén, and those who had come to the city for the Feast of the Virgin, flocked to pay condolences to Miguel Lucas de Iranzo. They approached the stage in hierarchical order, municipal officials and canons first. Some days afterward, a whole cycle of funeral masses, with all the important people of Jaén in attendance, began. For ten pages in the printed edition of the chronicle, the author describes in excruciating detail the staging of the funeral, the number of candles, the rich tapestries and rugs laid in the church, the decorations in black wool and silver, as well as the huge amounts of money spent in the liturgy. There, as was the case in the funeral of the constable's daughter six years later, the entire city was drawn into public mourning, showing, by their tears and clothes, their solidarity with and love of their ruler.[47]

Carnival

Every feast sponsored by the constable—whether the celebrating of the Christmas cycle, Easter, events in his life, or elaborate banquets to the chapter—included mummers, performances by fools and buffoons, bearbaiting, running of bulls, and ritual debasing of the constable's enemies. Closing the reception of the four Moorish knights to Jaén in 1463, a description of which opened this chapter, on the last of *Carnestolendas* (the last day of carnival, the *mardi gras*), the constable, his wife, family, and

313

court sat on a public stage to witness the running of the ring. Pero Gómez de Ocaña, the constable's mace-bearer, captured the ring thrice, only to be rewarded by a flurry of blows (from cotton maces) ordered by the *loco*, the master of Santiago. This was followed by such an excessive distribution of food (chickens, partridges, and kids) that the people gathered in the square began hitting each other with the chickens ("la gente se davan unos a otros con ello"). Mummers, dressed in white, red, and black, danced "genteelly" for a long while, until they were replaced in the square by the constable and his wife dancing with "grace" for the entertainment of the people of Jaén. The carnival ended with a fierce battle, engaging one hundred and fifty men armed with dried pumpkins.[48]

The return of the constable to Jaén in 1461, after a visit to the monastery of Guadalupe, coincided with Easter week. On Easter Monday, the constable sponsored, supervised, and participated in a bizarre egg battle in which, according to the chronicle, between nine thousand and ten thousand eggs were spent. A public banquet in the outskirts of the city for the entire population, bearbaiting, and a joust concluded the day.[49]

The carnival celebration of 1464 included the same order of events: running of the ring, mummery, dancing by the constable and his wife, and a mock joust by the gardeners of Jaén, armed, once again, with dried pumpkins. Once Lent was over, the Easter and May Day celebrations featured another egg battle (four thousand eggs), another elaborate joust with pumpkins by the gardeners (*ortelanos*), public banquets outside the walls, mummers, bearbaiting, and public dancing by the constable and his wife.[50]

Conclusion

These examples, evoking the land of Cockaigne, subverting of established order, and playing out courtly and carnivalesque motifs, point to the use of festivals as important tools for ruling. In the celebrations held at Jaén in the 1460s, the constable and his wife, his relatives and retinue were not reluctant observers but active participants. In fact, financed by taxes and tribute collected in Jaén and its hinterland, the festivals were the creation of the constable or someone in his service—otherwise how to explain the frequent debasing of Miguel Lucas's enemy, the master of Santiago?

Travesties, ribaldry, and the setting of the world upside down had been appropriated and employed as a way to release the despair and anger of those below. If sometimes, as in Jaén, those below rose up in arms and wreaked havoc upon the city, it was because the ruling elite of Jaén was divided, and the populace once again served as instruments, as battering rams in the internecine wars of the powerful. The will and need to resist is real. All of us engage and have engaged in many veiled and not-so-veiled forms of it every day of our lives: at home, at work, in the world at large. But, resistance from below is ultimately just noise in the machine, almost always deflected by the ways in which those above continuously appropriate and transform popular unrest and culture for their own benefit. Such was the case in Jaén in the 1460s; such is the case today.

Notes

I would like to thank Professor Jacques Le Goff for his many suggestions and bibliographical leads, and also Scarlett Freund and Charles M. Radding, who read and commented on an early draft. I also would like to thank Natalie Zemon Davis for her comments and suggestions. As she pointed out, my article on festivals in 1428 addressed horizontal conflict between factions of the elite, while this article focuses on vertical relations between those above and those below. What has not been answered in these pages is the way in which these festivals were used for dealing with horizontal conflicts in Jaén. This is very much work still pending. For these omissions, opinions, and mistakes, however, I am solely responsible.

1. The description of these events is found in Juan de Mata Carriazo, ed., *Hechos del condestable Don Miguel Lucas de Iranzo: Crónica del siglo XV* (Madrid: Espasa-Calpe, 1940), pp. 98–100. In a companion piece to this chapter, "Festivités, couleurs, et symboles du pouvoir en Castille au XVe siècle: Les célébrations de mai 1428," *Annales: Economies, Sociétés, Civilisations* 3 (May–June 1991): 521–46, I have already discussed the use of festivals for political purposes. Focusing on a cycle of royal festivals held in Valladolid (1428), I show the use of colors and ludic performances in late medieval Castilian society and provide a broad interpretative context for my discussion here of festivals in Jaén.

2. De Mata Carriazo, ed., *Hechos del condestable*, pp. 98–100.

3. On ceremonial displays elsewhere, see Johan Huizinga, *The Waning of the Middle Ages* (New York: Doubleday Anchor Books, 1954), pp. 67–106, passim. The idea of social dramas is borrowed from Victor Turner, *From Ritual to Theatre: The Human Seriousness of Play* (New York: Performing Arts Publications, 1982), pp. 13ff.

4. Steven Mullaney, *The Place of the Stage: License, Play, and Power in Renaissance England* (Chicago: University of Chicago Press, 1988), p. 23.

5. On these issues, see the suggestive Mikhail Bakhtin, *Rabelais and His World* (Bloomington: Indiana University Press, 1984), pp. 196–302; Roger Chartier, *Cultural History: Between Practices and Representations* (Ithaca, N.Y.: Cornell University Press, 1988), pp. 1–16, 83–91, 115–26, passim; and Sean Wilentz, ed., *Rites of Power: Symbolism, Ritual and Politics since the Middle Ages* (Philadelphia: University of Pennsylvania Press, 1985), pp. 13–38, 41–64, passim.

6. For Jacobean masques, see Stephen Orgel, *The Illusion of Power: Political Theater in the English Renaissance* (Berkeley: University of California Press, 1975), pp. 65ff.

7. De Mata Carriazo, ed., *Hechos del condestable*, p. liii.

8. See my "Festivités, couleurs, et symboles du pouvoir," pp. 521–46. Also see T. F. Ruiz, "Unsacred Monarchy: The Kings of Castile in the Later Middle Ages," in *Rites of Power*, ed. Wilentz, pp. 127–32.

9. Luis Suárez Fernández, *Nobleza y monarquía: Puntos de vista sobre la historia castellana del siglo XV* (Valladolid: Universidad de Valladolid Press, 1975), p. 184 n. 13; Enrique Toral Peñaranda, *Jaén y el condestable Miguel Lucas de Iranzo* (Jaén: Instituto de estudios Giennenses, 1982), pp. 10–22; and de Mata Carriazo, ed., *Hechos del condestable*, pp. xxxviiiff.

10. Toral Peñaranda, *Jaén y el condestable*, pp. 21–25; de Mata Carriazo, ed., *Hechos del condestable*, pp. 23–32; and Suárez Fernández, *Nobleza y monarquía*, pp. 186–92. On the figure of Enrique IV (Henry IV), see *Crónica de Enrique IV*, in *Crónicas de los reyes de Castilla*, ed. Cayetano Rosell, vol. 3, Biblioteca de autores españoles, 66 (Madrid: Bibliote-

ca de autores españoles, 1953), pp. 220–22; and William D. Phillips, Jr., *Enrique IV and the Crisis of the Fifteenth Century Castile, 1425–1480* (Cambridge, Mass: Medieval Academy of America, 1978), pp. 45–79.

11. For the reign of Juan II, the role of Alvaro de Luna, and the political upheaval of his reign, see Joseph O'Callaghan, *A History of Medieval Spain* (Ithaca N.Y.: Cornell University Press, 1975), pp. 549–66; Nicholas Round, *The Greatest Man Uncrowned: A Study of the Fall of Don Alvaro de Luna* (London: Tamesis Books, 1987); *Crónica del rey don Juan II*, in *Crónicas de los reyes de Castilla*, vol. 3; and Suárez Fernández, *Nobleza y monarquía*, pp. 119–79.

12. On the reign of Enrique IV, see Suárez Fernández, *Nobleza y monarquía*, pp. 181–222. For the farce of Avila see Angus MacKay, "Ritual and Propaganda in Fifteenth Century Castile," *Past & Present* 107 (1985): 3–43.

13. See Richard L. Kagan, ed., *Spanish Cities of the Golden Age: The Views of Anton van den Wyngaerde* (Berkeley: University of California Press 1987), pp. 264–65.

14. F. Javier Aguirre Sádaba and María del Carmen Jiménez Mata, *Introducción al Jaén islámico (Estudio geográfico-histórico)* (Jaén: Instituto de estudios Giennenses, 1979), pp. 201–48.

15. José Rodríguez Molina, *El reino de Jaén en la baja edad media: Aspectos demográficos y económicos* (Granada: Universidad de Granada Press, 1978), pp. 43, 138–40; and José María Pardo Crespo, *Evolución e historia de la ciudad de Jaén* (Jaén: Instituto de estudios Giennenses, 1978), pp. 54–56.

16. For the social and economic history of Jaén in this period, see Rodríguez Molina, *El reino de Jaén*, pp. 159ff., 180–208; for the *conversos* see Luis Coronas Tejada, *Conversos and the Inquisition in Jaén* (Jerusalem: Magnes Press of Hebrew University, 1988), pp. 11–18.

17. For the role of war in Castilian society see James F. Powers, *A Society Organized for War: The Iberian Municipal Militias in the Central Middle Ages, 1000–1284* (Berkeley: University of California Press, 1988), pp. 162–87; and Ruiz, "Unsacred Monarchy," pp. 127–32.

18. De Mata Carriazo, ed., *Hechos del condestable*, pp. 110–11.

19. Ibid., pp. liii, 40.

20. On the questions of the *merveilleux* in the West, see Jacques Le Goff, *L'imaginaire médiéval* (Paris: Gallimard, 1985), pp. 17–39.

21. De Mata Carriazo, ed., *Hechos del condestable*, pp. 41–57.

22. Ruiz, "Festivités, couleurs, et symboles du pouvoir," pp. 536–39.

23. De Mata Carriazo, ed., *Hechos del condestable*, p. 163.

24. For the manner in which this display of power was internalized in the theater in sixteenth-century England, see Leonard Tennenhouse, *Power on Display: The Politics of Shakespeare's Genres* (New York: Methuen, 1986), pp. 72–101.

25. On the administration of the *alfoz* or jurisdiction of the municipal council in fifteenth-century Castile, see Juan Antonio Bonachía, *El señorío de Burgos durante la baja edad media, 1255–1508* (Valladolid: Universidad de Valladolid Press, 1988), pp. 111–262; on the organization of the space after the reconquest of al-Andalús see José Angel García de Cortazar et al., *Organización social del espacio en la España medieval: La corona de Castilla en los siglos VIII a XV* (Barcelona: Ariel, 1985), pp. 163–236.

26. De Mata Carriazo, ed., *Hechos del condestable*, pp. 189–96.

27. Ruiz, "Festivités, couleurs, et symboles du pouvoir," pp. 533–36.

28. De Mata Carriazo, ed., *Hechos del condestable*, p. 48.

29. Ibid., pp. 71–72.

30. Ibid., p. 89. For other romances composed in honor of the constable, see ibid., pp. 328–29, and for other reflective asides see p. 69: "What charity, what liberality and honesty ... it should be compared to divine benevolence." For frontier ballads and romances, see Angus MacKay, *Spain in the Middle Ages: From Frontier to Empire, 1000–1500* (London: Macmillan, 1977), pp. 197–205. For the importance of the military triumph in the lit-

erature of the period, see Alonso de Palencia, *Tratado de la perfección del triunfo militar*, in *Dos tratados de Alfonso de Palencia* (Madrid: Durán, 1876), pp. 105–63, passim.

31. De Mata Carriazo, ed., *Hechos del condestable*, pp. 122, 375.

32. Ibid., p. 203: "E que así como el estado de los oradores era de muy grande escelencia, por atañer a lo espiritual, así el estado de los labradores era muy nescesario, para sustentamiento del mundo e dar mantenimiento a los que en él biuen. Pero que sin el estado de los defensores, que era la orden de la cavalleria, no se podrían, en ninguna manera los otros dos estados sostener."

33. See Jorge Manrique's poem, in a ghastly translation by Longfellow, in Eleanor Turnbull, ed., *Ten Centuries of Spanish Poetry* (Baltimore: Johns Hopkins University Press, 1955), pp. 23–77. See also a formidable discussion of the idea of fame in Spain in the late Middle Ages in María Rosa Lida de Malkiel, *La idea de la fama en la edad media castellana* (Mexico: Fondo de cultura económica, 1952).

34. For this whole discussion, see Aron Gurevich, *Medieval Popular Culture: Problems of Belief and Perception* (Cambridge: Cambridge University Press, 1988), pp. xiii–xx, 176–210. See also editorial preface by Peter Burke, pp. vii–x. Also Gurevich, *Les catégories de la culture médiévale*, trans. Helene Courtin and Nina Godneff (Paris: Gallimard, 1983), pp. 5–32. Throughout the formulation of this chapter, I have benefited by the comments of Jacques Le Goff and his many suggestions for reading and approach. See Jacques Le Goff, *Time, Work, and Culture in the Middle Ages* (Chicago: Chicago University Press, 1980), pp. 225–36, passim.

35. Bakhtin's arguments were far more complex. In Gurevich's summary, "Bakhtin describes the mutual influence—the confrontation—of official and unofficial culture as an ambivalence, a duality, in which the oppositions are dialectically connected, mutually changing places, and retaining their polarity" (Gurevich, *Medieval Popular Culture*, p. 180).

36. See note 34, above, for references to Gurevich. See also Carlo Ginzburg, *The Cheese and the Worms: The Cosmos of a Sixteenth-Century Miller* (New York: Penguin Books, 1982), pp. xiv–xvi.

37. See Emmanuel Le Roy Ladurie, *Le Carnival de Romans: De la Chandeleur au mercredi des Cendres, 1579–1580* (Paris: Gallimard, 1979); and Chartier, *Cultural History*, pp. 115–26.

38. Gurevich, *Les catégories de la culture médiévale*, p. 12.

39. I have not discussed the colors and fabrics of the festivals of the constable in Jaén nor the symbolic meaning of red, white, and black. For a full discussion of these topics, see my "Festivités, couleurs, et symboles du pouvoir."

40. The best treatment of the carnival in Spain is found in Julio Caro Baroja, *El carnaval: Estudio histórico-cultural* (Madrid: Taurus, 1965), pp. 101–50, passim. The earliest text of the battle between the carnivalesque spirit and religion is found in Juan Ruiz, *El libro de buen amor*, which is discussed by Caro Baroja, "Análisis," in *El carnaval*. The battle between carnality and Lent ends with the victory of Lent, but the expression of Don Carnal's carnival spirit is confined mostly to hyperbolic descriptions of food and eating. For carnivals and popular feasts elsewhere and their opposition to official culture, see Jacques Heers, *Fêtes des fous et carnavals* (Paris: Fayard, 1983), pp. 9–30, 105–304.

41. Ruiz, "Unsacred Monarchy," pp. 127–33.

42. See Michael Mullett, *Popular Culture and Popular Protest in Late Medieval and Early Modern Europe* (New York: Croom Helm, 1987), pp. 1–27; Julio Valdeón Baruque, *Los conflictos sociales en el reino de Castilla en los siglos XIV y XV* (Madrid: Siglo XXI de España editores S. A., 1975), pp. 140–210; Angus MacKay, "Popular Movements and Pogroms in Fifteenth-Century Castile," *Past and Present* 55 (1972): 33–67; and P. Wolff, "The 1391 Pogrom in Spain: Social Crisis or Not?" *Past and Present* 50 (1971): 4–18. The death of Miguel Lucas de Iranzo is described in Diego de Varela, *Memorial de diversas hazañas*, in *Crónicas de los reyes de Castilla*, vol. 3, Biblioteca de autores españoles 70 (Madrid, 1953), pp. 78–79.

43. See Julio Rodríguez Puértolas, *Poesía de protesta en la edad media castellana: His-*

toria y antología (Madrid: Gredos, 1968), pp. 26–51, 207–15; and Julio Rodríguez Puértolas, ed., *Poesía crítica y satírica del siglo XV* (Madrid: Castalia, 1981), pp. 7–29.

44. I do not mean at all that either courtly or popular culture were distinct entities; on the contrary, each included elements of the other.

45. For weddings described in the chronicle, see de Mata Carriazo, ed., *Hechos del condestable*, pp. 41–61, 305–8, 350–52.

46. Ibid., pp. 376–80. The celebration for the birth and baptism of his daughter and other similar events are described in pp. 257–63.

47. Ibid., pp. 234–51, 312–13, 385–86, 413–15.

48. Ibid., pp. 111–12.

49. Ibid., pp. 63–65.

50. Ibid., pp. 163ff.

Contributors

Lorraine Attreed is associate professor of history at the College of the Holy Cross in Worcester, Massachusetts. She has edited *The York House Books, 1461–1490,* a study of English urban politics, and is the author of numerous articles on urban and legal and constitutional development, the English Crown, and the social history of the later Middle Ages. She is completing *The King's Towns,* which studies the relations between English provincial towns and the medieval royal government between 1400 and 1540.

Brigitte Bedos-Rezak, *archiviste-paléographe,* a graduate of the Sorbonne and of the Ecole nationale des chartes, is associate professor in the Department of History at the University of Maryland (College Park). She is the author of *La châtellenie de Montmorency des origines à 1380: Aspects féodaux, sociaux, et èconomiques* and *Anne de Montmorency, seigneur de la Renaissance.* Her studies of the implications of medieval seal usage and iconography have been collected for a forthcoming volume entitled *Form and Order in Medieval France: Essays in Social and Quantitative Sigillography.*

Elizabeth A. R. Brown is professor of history emerita of the City University of New York (Brooklyn College and the Graduate School). She has also taught at Harvard University and has served as Directeur d'etudes at the Ecole des Hautes en Sciences Sociales and as senior clinical lecturer in the department of psychiatry at Downstate Medical School. *The Monarchy of Capetian France and Royal Ceremonial* and *Politics and Institutions in Capetian France,* two volumes of her essays, appeared in 1991. She has also published *The Oxford Collection of the Drawings of Roger de Gaignières and the Royal Tombs of Saint-Denis; "Franks, Burgundians, and Aquitanians" and the Royal Coronation Ceremony in France;* and *Customary Aids and Royal Finances in Capetian France: The Marriage Aid of Philip the Fair. Jean du Tillet and the French Wars of Religion: Five Treatises, 1562–1569* will appear in 1993.

Lawrence McBride Bryant is the author of *The King and the City in the Parisian Royal Entry Ceremony: Politics, Art, and Ritual in the Renaissance* as well as many articles on ceremonies and politics in early modern Europe. He teaches at California State University, Chico, and has been an Andrew W. Mellon Faculty Fellow at Harvard University, a visiting member of the Institute for Advanced Study, and a fellow at the Folger Shakespearean Library.

Maureen Flynn is assistant professor of history at Hobart and William Smith Colleges in Geneva, New York. She is the author of *Sacred Charity: Confraternities and Social Welfare in Spain, 1400–1700,* along with several articles dealing with popular culture and spirituality in early modern Spain. She is currently working on a book manuscript entitled *The Cult of Suffering in Renaissance Spain.*

Barbara A. Hanawalt is professor of medieval history and director of the Center for Medieval Studies at the University of Minnesota. Her publications include *Crime and Conflict in English Communities, 1300– 1348, The Ties That Bound: Peasant Families in Medieval England,* and *Growing Up in Medieval London: The Experience of Childhood in History* (forthcoming). She has also edited several collections of essays including *Women and Work in Preindustrial Europe* and *Chaucer's England: Literature in Historical Context* (Minnesota, 1992).

Bram Kempers is professor of the sociology of art at the University of Amsterdam and the author of *Painting, Power and Patronage: The Rise of the Professional Artist in Renaissance Italy.*

Sheila Lindenbaum is associate professor of English at Indiana University in Bloomington, where she also teaches in the medieval studies program. She has published articles on medieval drama and spectacle and is the editor of the Westminster volume in the Records of Early English Drama series. Her recent work has focused on London as a cultural field, and her essay in this collection is part of a book in progress called *Ceremonial Practice in Late Medieval London.*

Benjamin R. McRee teaches medieval and early modern history at Franklin and Marshall College in Lancaster, Pennsylvania. His published work has examined urban and religious life in late medieval England, focusing on the roles played by religious guilds in the politics and social structures of urban settlements. He is currently working on a book-length study of the Guild of Saint George in Norwich from the fourteenth through the sixteenth centuries.

James M. Murray is associate professor of history at the University of Cincinnati. He is currently at work on an extended study of the society and economy of Bruges in the fourteenth century.

David Nicholas is professor and head of the Department of History at Clemson University. A specialist on medieval Flanders and more generally on the urban history of medieval western Europe, Nicholas is the author of *Medieval Flanders; The Evolution of the Medieval World: Society, Government and Thought in Europe, 312–1500; The van Arteveldes of Ghent: The Varieties of Vendetta and the Hero in History; The Metamorphosis of a Medieval City: Women, Children, and the Family in Fourteenth-Century Ghent; Town and Countryside: Social, Economic, and Political Tensions in Fourteenth-Century Flanders;* and major articles in the *American Historical Review*; the *Journal of Medieval History*; *Annales, Economies, Sociétés, Civilisations*; *Past and Present*; *Revue Belge de Philologie et d'Histoire*; and *Bulletin de la Commission Royale d'Histoire.*

Gerard Nijsten studied medieval history at the University of Nijmegen, the Netherlands, and currently teaches at the Hogeschool Holland, Diemen, the Netherlands. He has published several articles on late medieval court and popular culture in the Netherlands. His book on the court of Guelders in the fourteenth and fifteenth centuries (*Het Hof van Gelre: Cultuur ten Tijde van de Hertogen uit het Gulikse en Egmondse Huis, 1371–1477*) appeared in 1992.

Nancy Freeman Regalado is professor of French at New York University. Her publications include *Poetic Patterns in Rutebeuf: A Study in Non-Courtly Poetic Modes of the Thirteenth Century* and *Contexts: Styles and Values in Art and Literature of Medieval France.* She has received fellowships from the National Endowment for the Humanities and the Guggenheim Foundation for the book she is completing with Elizabeth A. R. Brown on contemporary accounts of the royal and Parisian Pentecost celebration in 1313.

Kathryn L. Reyerson is professor of history and former director of the Center for Medieval Studies at the University of Minnesota. Her publications include *Business, Banking and Finance in Medieval Montpellier* and many articles on topics such as commercial fraud, religious asylum, and adolescent apprenticeship. She is the coeditor of *The Medieval Castle: Romance and Reality* (Minnesota, 1984) and *The Medieval Mediterranean: Cross-Cultural Contacts* (Minnesota, 1988).

Teofilo F. Ruiz is professor of history at Brooklyn College and of Spanish literature at City University of New York Graduate Center. He is the author of *Sociedad y poder real* and coauthor of *Burgos en la Edad Media.* His *Crisis and Continuity: Rural and Urban Structures in Late Medieval Castile* is forthcoming.

Index

Index

ships, 69
Shrovetide xiv, 146, 238–41, 251, 282
Siena: Cathedral, 89–125; chapels, 113;
  chronicle of, 92; early thirteenth
  century, 95; icons, x, xiii; inspiration,
  106; inventories, 112, 114, 115; layout,
  93; *palio*, xii, 112; political parties, 90
Silene, 199
sin, 162
singing, 95, 297
Sint-Geertruidenberg, 241
Sinzig, 241
Skevington, John, 180
skits, 303
social order, xvi, 34, 190–91
Solomon, 222
Soly, Hugo, 141
space, xviii, 39, 175, 298
Spanish Holy Office, 161
spectacle: apparel symbolism, 16; the body
  politic, 21; celebrants ix; color
  symbolism, 16; communitas, 7, 56;
  costume symbolism, 19; decentering of
  structure, 8, 24; expense, 217; forms of
  representation, 3, 10, 25; gamelike, 6;
  humanism, 3, 4, 12; idea of community,
  24; image of kingship, 5; impact, xiv;
  interaction, 216; Lancastrian, 6;
  metahistorical nature of, 10;
  motivation, ix, xii, xiii, xvii, 211;
  notion of "proto-event," 9; as objects of
  study, 3, 8; origins of, 9; periodization,
  xvii; propagation of political conceits,
  xiii, xv, 17, 22; reiterated form of, 6;
  religious, xvii; role and practice of
  community, 5; spectators, 163;
  symbolism, 13; value dramatization, 56
Spiegel, Gabrielle M., 8
Spinelli, Lodovico, 171
Steen, 143
Stratford-on-Avon, 191
Suffolk, 196, 198; Duke of, 196
supplication, 162
sword, 21, 22, 197, 249
symbolism, xvi, 34, 39, 223, 309;
  collective, 153; forms, 235, religious,
  217

tabernacle, 107, 115, 118; of Wisdom
  pageant, 22
tableaux, ix, xvi, 56, 67, 71, 180; Biblical,
  70; from Biblical and popular tales, 67;
  not full dramas, 69; on platforms, 69;
  vivants, 10, 67, 297, 303

taifas, 301
Tartars, 72
taxes, 160, 242
Te Deum, 22
Templars, 58
Tents, 62
theater, 25, 163, 271
theologians, 156, 159
Three Estates, 21, 306
Tiel, 246, 247
Tielerwaard, 247
Tizio, Sigismondo, 92
Toledo, Inquisition of, 156
Tomè, Luca di, 120
Tommaso Montauri, Paolo di, 98
Tonghio, Francesco del, 94
Tonghio, Nanni del Maestro Francesco del,
  116
Toppes, Robert, 198
torches, 62
Tournai, 273
tournaments, xiii, 62, 146, 240, 276–77;
  children's, 67. *See also* chivalry
town hall, 39
town writings: administrative documents,
  36; archives, 39, 42; categories, 36;
  control, 39; copies, 40; deeds, 35;
  spectacle, 42; symbolism, 44
trade, 235
Trinity Sunday, 71, 72
triptych, 99
Troyes, Treaty of, 13
trumpeters, 198, 247, 281, 283, 287
Truth, figure of, 22, 24
Tudenham, Thomas, 198
Tudor, Henry, 219; rose, 223
Tunis, 249
Turner, Victor, 7
Tzimisces, John, Emperor, 106

Ubeda, 304
uniforms. *See* livery
university, 24, 64
urban society: documentary practices, 34;
  elite, participation of, 70; franchise, 36;
  identity, 34; revival, 34; social network,
  37

Valois, 13, 14, 15, 18, 25
Valois, Catherine of, 13
Valois, Charles of, 66
Velde, Johan van der, 239
Venice, 106
Venlo, 237, 239, 245